From Culture to Ethnicity to Conflict

From Culture to Ethnicity to Conflict

An Anthropological Perspective on International Ethnic Conflict

JACK DAVID ELLER

Ann Arbor

THE UNIVERSITY OF MICHIGAN PRESS

Published in the United States of America by
The University of Michigan Press
Manufactured in the United States of America
⊗ Printed on acid-free paper

2002 2001 2000 4 3 2

A CIP catalog record for this book is available from the British Library.

Library of Congress Cataloging-in-Publication Data

Eller, Jack David, 1959–
From culture to ethnicity to conflict : an anthropological perspective on international ethnic conflict / Jack David Eller.
p. cm.
Includes bibliographical references and index.
ISBN 0-472-10961-8 (cloth : alk. paper)
ISBN 0-472-08538-7 (pbk. : alk. paper)
1. Ethnic relations. 2. Ethnicity. 3. Nationalism. 4. Culture conflict. I. Title.
GN496 .E55 1998
305.8—ddc21 98-25516
CIP

For Anita, who *always* believed in me

Contents

Maps

Preface

This book arose from my vain search for one like it to adopt for use in my classes. For several years I have taught a course on cultural diversity and ethnic conflict from within the discipline of anthropology. While there are many fine books on ethnicity and ethnic conflict, most of them either analyze one area or conflict in great detail or survey the entire conceptual field of ethnic conflict with brief illustrations from an assortment of regions; alternatively, collections of essays offer the kind of variety I sought but usually treat only one or more aspects of each area or conflict. What I wanted was a series of short but in-depth case studies of major ethnic conflicts that presented not only the cultural "facts" of each case but also an investigation of how those facts have been constructed, interpreted, and manipulated in the service of group competition and conflict.

Such is the book that I have tried to create. It is a daunting and perhaps impossibly ambitious undertaking. I cannot claim—probably no one human being can claim—to be an expert in every area discussed in this book. Where I can claim some modest expertise as an anthropologist and student of ethnicity and ethnic conflict is in the analysis of culture, and therefore the conflicts that follow from it, as a product of both tradition and of contemporary circumstances and interests. For the details of the cases I have relied on the experts in each field, to whom I am greatly indebted. Therefore, it will be noticed that my sources consist of primary, secondary, and in some cases even tertiary material. I believe, nonetheless, that, by bringing these resources together and by cross-checking them, a valuable service has been provided.

This book does not attempt to be definitive or exhaustive in regard to the cases presented. It does not aim to recount the details of the actual conflicts at all; in fact, it usually deals rather briefly if at all with the given conflict itself. For information such as that, there are other places to turn.

Rather, what I have tried to do here, as the title suggests, is to show the process by which "culture" or "tradition"—remembered, interpreted, or invented—is transformed into ethnicity, that is, into an ethnic identity and argument, and then that ethnicity is transformed into conflict. It should be readily appreciated that not all culture is ethnicity and that not all ethnicity is conflict and that the transformation from one to another is not simple, direct, or automatic.

It is a truism that knowledge, in the social sciences and everywhere else, is perspectival, "paradigmatic," negotiable, even defeasible, but one never encounters this fact so starkly as when one attempts to assemble divergent sources and reports in a single space and time (something that anthropology discovered in its attempts to attain a "synoptic" view of a culture from the various informants in any given ethnographic experience). Subjects as complex—and as emotionally charged—as ethnicity and ethnic conflict present a special challenge, because there are many diverging opinions, interpretations, and interests. This is one reason why I have not tried in this volume to arrive at the "truth" about each case (the other is that I do not believe that a single truth exists). Where there is difference of opinion, polemic, partisanship, or blatant abuse of the facts, I have included this as important data rather than screening it out as "noise." In this cause I have included not only scholarly but also journalistic as well as blatantly partisan sources; however, while extreme or deviant interpretations may not characterize the main or whole situation in any case, they do represent a part of the spectrum of thought on the subject and have often been particularly motivational in the events that flow from it.

A particular problem with a work of such international scope is the variety of languages in which one must work. For one thing, it is incumbent upon us to use vernacular terminology to discuss things for which there is no equivalent in English; thus, the reader will swim through Sri Lankan caste terms, Rwandan clientage terms, and Kurdish organization names. As writer, I had a special problem settling on spellings for many of these words—for example, Kurdish town names. Again, there is little agreement in many instances on correct transliterations, spellings sometimes even differing within the same source, so I have made a choice on some occasions, often with expert guidance, to follow one particular conventional spelling for each problematic item. I hope I will be forgiven by the reader who finds or is perhaps committed to some other rendering.

There are many who deserve thanks in the realization of this project. I owe a great debt to the many scholars, reporters, and activists whose work contributed to the book. Many anonymous reviewers offered invaluable advice, which has hopefully made this a better and more accurate piece of work. Special thanks go to Richard Handler and Susan Whitlock, two of the gentlest mentors a scholar could hope to encounter. Much logistical support was provided by Teikyo Loretto Heights University in the preparation of the manuscript, and the library staff (particularly Larry Rouch and Eiko Rattenbury) gave me great assistance in research. Ultimately, of course, I am most indebted to and humbled by the millions of people whose lives and struggles are chronicled in these pages. In the end, however, the conclusions—and errors—in this book are mine alone.

Introduction

"The conflicts of the future are more likely to be between people rather than states over issues related to culture, ethnicity or religion," according to Mahbun ul Haq, Special United Nations Development Program advisor (qtd. in Wright 1994, 159). If he is correct, then for many parts of the world the future is already here. Our televisions, our magazines and scholarly journals, our minds, are full of images of seemingly vicious, irrational, intractable, ancient conflict. It seems that, at a time when we expected the world to become safer and saner, it is increasingly dangerous and crazy. But is this true? And, even if it is, is our understanding of the sources of these persistent problems accurate?

Two things seem to be happening simultaneously and probably not coincidentally. Violent conflict between countries—or, to be precise, between "states"—has become less common in recent decades. Open conflict between smaller "nonstate" groups or against small nonstate groups by state governments has increased, however, in frequency and ferocity. According to one source, at least eighty times since World War II such conflict has escalated into war, and over two hundred such groups have organized themselves at one time or another "to defend or promote their collective interests against governments or other groups" (Gurr and Harff 1994, 6). Not inconsequentially, a majority—though by no means all—of these problems have surfaced in non-Western postcolonial states in Asia, the Middle East, and Africa.

It was not supposed to be this way. The end of the earth-threatening superpower standoff was to usher in an era of political tranquillity and economic rationality, a Pax Americana and a triumph of capitalism and liberalism. And economic development and political rationalization were to render obsolete other forms of sociality and identity and especially old grievances. Instead, we are surprised and alarmed as a society and a species to see such "primitive" behavior reappearing in such a modern and enlightened age.

This book takes an anthropological look at this phenomenon we call ethnic conflict, exploring several specific instances of communal violence from various parts of the world. It also considers the surprise of the public and of scholars at the outbreak (or upsurge? or return?) of such conflict. Anthropology is one of a number of social sciences that approach the subject of ethnicity and ethnic conflict; other frequent treatments are historical or political. Anthropology embraces these latter approaches, but it adds some critical specialized perspectives: (1) it is holistic, incorporating historical, political, economic, and other data into a complete description of social phenomena; (2) it takes culture as its central focus and brings well-tuned concepts to the task; (3) even as it takes culture seriously, it does not take it for granted but questions or "deconstructs" cultural concepts and claims, whether advanced by ethnic participants or academic colleagues, to expose interests, power relations, structural interconnections, and factional interpretations; and (4) it gathers and analyzes data, as far as possible, from an emic point of view, wary of the imposition of foreign distinctions and definitions.

A question we might want to ask is why so many citizens and scholars alike are caught off-guard by the apparent prevalence, virulence, and persistence of contemporary ethnic conflict. One of the most obvious reasons is that most believed until very recently that ethnicity and ethnic identities, thought of as primitive, particularistic notions of self and group, were declining or destined to decline in the "integrative revolution" that is the modern age; other higher-level forms of solidarity, national or class, would inevitably replace them. But the recent rise of ethnicity and culture as political issues and the spread of ethnicity-related conflict has shattered this belief. Another reason is the assumption of national homogeneity, to which Americans may be especially prone. Our ideal of assimilation and the melting pot leads us to assume that all individuals really are alike in our society and that all societies are like ours; both of these assumptions are challenged by the recent emergence of multiculturalism and ethnic/racial strife at home and of open ethnic conflict abroad. Most states in the world today are in fact plural, many in an extreme and dangerous way, aggregating groups with no common identity or with real mutual animosity. Taking state names and identities as the names and identities of populations or peoples is a great and often false leap of thought.

Two other reasons why we failed to anticipate current ethnic conflict are a lack of historical perspective and terminological confusion. Many people, scholars among them, do not know enough about ethnic or national activity before the last decade or two and so see today's events as somehow new or unprecedented; however, ethnic mobilization and conflict can certainly be observed a century or more ago, when many of Europe's "nations" were first created out of larger, increasingly moribund multinational empires. And, if we take a certain attitude toward events, we would find "ethnic" behavior and "ethnic" conflict in the more distant and even ancient past in cases that we are not accustomed to thinking of as ethnic—for example, Chinese resistance to Mongol invaders, Jewish resistance to the Roman Empire, and so on. Finally, as noted earlier, there is a cacophony of related yet different terms that are often either taken as synonymous or, although semantically distinguished, used carelessly, such as *ethnic group, society, nation, people, state,* and others.

The anthropological study of ethnic conflict, while aiding in an understanding of such conflict itself (who the members of the group are, how they have come to be in conflict, what they are fighting about currently) also reflects light back on some of our own concepts and theories. Ethnicity and ethnic conflict compel us to think again about the idea of culture, its components and characteristics, its relation to the individual, and its construction. They also lead us to think again about a perennial anthropological problem—the unit of analysis: what group precisely should we be investigating? Where are its boundaries? What characteristics distinguish it from other groups and members from nonmembers? And what are the relations between groups; are they really in the end distinct? In the final analysis are our "groups" real, or are they a fabrication of the mind of the analyst or of some ethnic innovator? Anthropologists have noted before that some groups have porous boundaries, some potential groups lack a current sense of groupness, and some groups do not exist at all as groups except in our descriptive models.

We must be careful to make distinctions within the very concepts of ethnicity and ethnic conflict, for all instances of these phenomena are not alike. All have something to do, we would agree, with culture or history or kinship or destiny, but what precisely this "something" is remains uncertain or, better yet, empirically specific to each instance. And, last, we must attend to what we might call the field of conflict as specific to each instance. This field of conflict consists of such features as the particular aspects of culture that are foremost for the groups (religion, language, history, etc.); the other social phenomena that are conjoined with them (class, race, etc.); the level of solidarity or consensus within the group (are there, e.g., rival factions and leaders, or are there means for keeping group cohesion and mobilization high, i.e., some organizational forms for ethnicity?); the relationship between the group and state organization (wholly contained within a state territory, divided across state territories, in control of a state territory, dispersed throughout many state territories, etc.); and the stake of international interest in the situation and the willingness of the international community to take part in it.

The topic of ethnicity and ethnic conflict is a dauntingly complex one. By some accounts there are as many as five thousand distinguishable ethnic groups in the world today or seven to eight thousand "linguistic, ethnic, or religious minorities" in plural societies. Moynihan (1993) has called the current state of ethnicity and ethnic conflict "pandaemonium," not without justification and not only in one sense. What follows, then, is a conceptual and empirical analysis of this pandemonium, an attempt to establish the relation between ethnicity and ethnic conflict and culture and history. The point will be made that there is no simple or automatic correspondence between culture or cultural difference and ethnicity or ethnic identity and that there is also no simple or automatic correspondence between ethnicity or ethnic identity and ethnic conflict.

The first two chapters present a conceptual and theoretical framework within which to understand the cases included here as well as any others. Chapter 1 discusses the terminology of ethnicity and culture, pointing out where distinctions that already exist are sometimes overlooked or where new distinctions need to be made; in particular, it problematizes the relationship between culture or tradition and ethnicity and ethnic conflict. Chapter 2 surveys anthropology's and related social sciences' struggles with and contributions to the description and elucidation of ethnicity. While anthropologys focus has not always been ethnicity, many of the issues of cultural traits and boundaries and of tradition and identity have proven to be central to the phenomenon, and the changing nature of societies and cultures have forced the field to evolve as well.

The five case studies that follow were selected for their global sweep—no more than one from any geographic region—and their political importance but also for the diverse issues each raises. Sri Lanka serves as an unusually clear episode of the construction and manipulation of history in the cause of contemporary competition and conflict and illustrates the escalation of that conflict in recent decades. The case of the Kurds shows how a group's culture and history, while making them in a sense an ethnic group, may also hinder their realization of consciousness and mobilization as such; it also highlights the role of outside, international forces in "internal" ethnicity. Rwanda and Burundi provide a laboratory not only to see how "traditional" identities have been turned into ethnic ones but also to compare two states with seemingly similar ethnic compositions. Bosnia, perhaps the most familiar case in the book, makes the point that groups may base their claims and conflicts on a combination of memories, myths, and maps and that even group names and identities are open for debate and negotiation. Finally, Quebec, while not violent during most of its history, offers a local example of the vicissitudes of identity and of the centrality of one cultural "marker" or another in the construction and defense of that identity. Particularly, it reminds us that state identities, even in supposed stable and peaceful states, are not nearly as solid as we might like to believe.

The ultimate conclusion of the book is that ethnicity is no mere reflection or reflex of culture, especially of traditional culture, but a complex reworking, remembering, sometimes reinvention, and always employment of culture in the light and service of present and even future considerations. Further, culture may as easily hinder as facilitate ethnic mobilization. Ethnicity and the conflict that ensues from it is not purely instrumental or practical, but both are shaped by the conjunction of culture or history as remembered and of present challenges and conditions and future goals and visions. It is perhaps the most fertile opportunity at the present time to consider the construction of culture and identity and the relation between cultural resources and social action.

Chapter 1

Ethnicity, Culture, and "the Past"

It is understandably difficult to determine in general—and even in a concrete individual case—what influence specific ethnic factors . . . have on the formation of a group. . . . Any cultural trait, no matter how superficial, can serve as a starting point for the familiar tendency to monopolistic closure.

—Max Weber

In the late twentieth century "ethnicity" and "ethnic conflict" captivate the world's attention like perhaps no other social phenomenon on earth. Even relatively peaceful societies like the United States are not immune to it, although it only infrequently erupts into open conflict and violence and then only briefly. But, in fact, despite its ubiquity—or perhaps because of it—ethnicity and ethnic conflict are not particularly well understood, either by the public or by many scholars. This is due to both terminological confusion and to inadequate knowledge of the details and background of specific cases. Ethnicity and ethnic conflict are particularly fertile subjects for conflation of categories, mystification of facts, and general demagoguery, in no small part because the issues, as in the United States, are so emotionally charged. This chapter is dedicated to clarifying some of these confusions and to presenting some of the details and background information crucial to understanding these momentous social forces.

Some of the most perplexing problems arise from the vagueness of the term and phenomenon called *ethnicity* and from its indefinite and ever-expanding domain. One of the central arguments of this chapter will be that ethnicity is in fact not a single unified social phenomenon but a congeries, a "family," of related but analytically distinct phenomena. The foundations of ethnicity, the "markers" of ethnicity, the history of ethnicity, the aims and goals of ethnicity—these things vary from case to case. For instance, in one circumstance religion may be the decisive distinction between two ethnic groups (say, in Northern Ireland), while in another language or history or race or any number of other qualities may serve the same function. Even within one case of ethnicity or conflict the referents or the emphasis on referents of the groups concerned may shift over time. Further, not all culturally distinct groups are ethnic groups precisely, and (in an odd paradox) not all ethnic groups are culturally distinct groups; the relation of ethnicity to "culture" is less than perfect. Not all ethnic groups are ancient and organic social entities; some can make the claim, while others are noticeably recent. Finally, not all ethnic groups are in conflict, not all conflicts are equal in intensity, and not all conflicts seek the same ends.

This very elusiveness of ethnicity is largely responsible for its expandability, which is largely responsible for its utility in the modern world. When is a group an ethnic group? There are no hard or fast rules or standards by which to judge. The answer, of course, as unsatisfying as it is, is that social collectivity, of any nature and antiquity, can don the mantle of ethnicity—one of the most elastic of social concepts—and stake a successful claim to identity and rights *as a group* and can achieve the status of ethnic group. The point is this: it does not matter if any particular group is really an ethnic group or what a real ethnic group is; instead, ethnicity has become so central to social discourse—and social competition—that its salience and effectiveness have become attractive to all sorts of collectivities.

Ethnicity and Ethnic Groups

Ethnicity is, at first glance, the process or phenomenon that underlies or gives rise to ethnic groups. DeVos defines it as the "subjective symbolic or emblematic use of any aspect of culture [by a group], in order to differentiate themselves from other groups" (1975, 16). For Burgess it is "the character, quality, or condition of ethnic group membership, based on an identity with and/or a consciousness of group belonging that is differentiated from others by symbolic 'markers' (including cultural, biological, or territorial), and is rooted in bonds to a shared past and perceived ethnic interests" (1978, 270). These and other definitions repeatedly raise points about symbolism, meaning, and identity and about cohesion, solidarity, and belonging. In terms of the former I am talking about a social and psychological process whereby individuals come to identify and affiliate with a group and some aspect(s) of its culture; ethnicity is then what emerges when a person, as affiliated, completes the statement: "I am a ____ because I share ____ with my group." Ethnicity is consciousness of difference and the subjective salience of that difference. It is also mobilization around difference—a camaraderie with or preference for socially similar others. It is in this sense a "familial" kind of relationship, with emotional characteristics—a bond, a tie, a sentiment, an attachment. It is even regularly likened to kinship, as a kind of kinship writ large. Horowitz writes that, based on the primacy of birth and shared origin, "ethnicity and kinship are alike. . . . The language of ethnicity is the language of kinship" (1985, 57). He also quotes Michael Fischer as saying that "ethnicity may be the maximal case of societally organized intimacy and kinship experience" (60). Pierre van den Berghe, as is well-known, goes even further in asserting that "ethnic and racial sentiments are extensions of kinship sentiments" (1987, 18), developing this observation into a biological or ethological theory of ethnicity.

This much being said, there is much diversity within the phenomenon of ethnicity. One of the first things that ethnographers of ethnicity discover is that the strength and significance of ethnicity vary between individuals and groups as well as over time for any particular individual or group. Some ostensibly ethnic groups (say, some indigenous people or urban minorities) with authentic shared origins and culture have little ethnic feeling, and other groups with much less in common have strong feelings. Not only that, but a group may have vibrant, even militant, ethnicity at one moment in time and much less so at a later moment, or vice versa. And, of course, in any particular group some individuals have powerful ethnic sentiments, while others do not, and some individuals with powerful sentiments engage in ethnic-based confrontation and violence, while others do not.

Ethnicity is, thus, subjective, even while it is based on, refers to, or invokes "objective" or shared cultural or historical markers. The first of several issues I might raise, following DeVos's earlier definition, is which part of culture is used by a particular group and why. No ethnic group treats all aspects of its culture or history as markers of its identity; it would be awkward if not impossible to do so, and besides, for any group, some elements of its culture will be *the same as* those of another group, thus defeating the purpose of distinguishing it from the other group. Any part, no matter how small, of a group's trait list can make a perfectly adequate ethnic marker. What is more, for any one group, the parts of culture that it chooses and uses may vary over time, from religion at one stage to language in another to class or what have you.

As a subjective phenomenon, as a "consciousness," a second issue is that having distinct social/cultural characteristics is not sufficient to make ethnicity—and not having them is not sufficient necessarily to prevent it. A group that is distinct in some way may not be aware of or mobilized around that distinction and may not *use* it for any social or political purpose (again, all groups are distinct in some ways: senior citizens are distinct, but most people do not ordinarily think of them as ethnic). For example, the difference between *ethnicity* and *ancestry* has been highlighted by some students of ethnicity. Ancestry is a more or less objective fact (although not one that all of us readily know), and, if asked to give one's ancestry, most Americans can and will list one or more societies that enter into one's family history. Yet, if asked one's ethnicity or ethnic identity, these facts often recede into the background: individuals tend to choose *one* (even if two or more lines of ancestry obtain) or to ignore them all and choose *American* or some other generic term.

By the same token a group may overlook differences in the pursuit or definition of its ethnicity—in fact, ethnicity generally demands the overlooking of internal differentiations. *Hispanic* as an ethnicity embraces a remarkable amount of cultural, historical, and economic diversity. Mexican-Americans, Cuban-Americans, Puerto Rican–Americans, and all of the other "Hispanic"Americans are distinguished by a tremendous variation of society and culture and of economic class in the United States; the only thing that unifies them is language (or linguistic descent) and the general part of the world from which they, or their ancestors, hail. The same can be said of *Asian-American,* an even more diffuse term, since the groups so encompassed do not even share language. In fact, many Hispanic Americans and Asian Americans have not affiliated with those ethnic identities and still conceive of themselves in more particularistic, local terms; they have not (yet?) developed the self-concept and group concept implicit in the label.

To a certain extent ethnicities are labels, often labels created for administrative purposes. Labels can be made and unmade and remade. In Canada the ethnicity of *French-Canadian* has lately been quietly replaced with *Quebecois,* which carries a territorial connotation. Labels, however, also have consequences. The shift from *French-Canadian* to *Quebecois* changes the membership of the group created by the label (e.g., are francophone Canadians living outside Quebec "Quebecois"?). The shift from *black* to *African-American* in the United States does not change the membership much but does change the marker of ethnicity, from skin color to ancestral origin in the broadest sense. And, since any trait, large or small, can be a marker and the basis of a label and an ethnicity, it is possible to see today a move to create new labels and ethnicities such as *mixed race*. If, in the end, individuals with a particular trait achieve consciousness and organization on the basis of that trait, then it is an ethnicity, even if it was not one yesterday.

Accordingly, if a group is not conscious of or organized in terms of its characteristics, then there is no ethnicity, no matter how distinct it may be. Many indigenous peoples, radically distinct from any other groups, did not and do not have "ethnic consciousness." As I will explain, ethnicity and mobilization as an ethnic group require a certain consciousness of difference, a certain objectification of culture and cultural difference, and a certain "distance"—cognitive if not temporal—from culture, a certain reflexive relation with one's own culture. People who live their culture unproblematically tend not to be ethnic in the proper sense of the word.

In other words, ethnicity is not and cannot be an objective phenomenon. There is, first and foremost, no one-to-one correspondence between culture and ethnicity. Cultural differences alone do not ethnicity make; culture, or cultural difference, becomes ethnicity if and when a group takes it up and uses it in certain specific and modern ways. Naturally, too, ethnicity does not always or necessarily make for conflict; certain kinds of ethnicity in certain situations with certain catalyzing events make conflict out of ethnicity. Thus, small differences in culture may make for large and contentious differences in ethnicity, while large differences in culture may lead to small or no ethnic differences or conflicts. If scholars want to understand ethnicity, they will not succeed by merely listing the empirical cultural traits of groups (which in itself is not as simple as it sounds) or describing their empirical, or "true," history.

In concluding this section, it is well to remember that not all instances of ethnicity will be the same. In terms of cultural marker, intergroup relations, and intragroup subjectivity there is in actuality not one ethnicity but many. Yinger (1994, 4) for one offers a schematization of this variety, finding eight types of ethnicity depending on three variables that are only indirectly related to objective cultural characteristics: self-perception (or avowal) of ethnicity, other perception (or ascription by other) of ethnicity, and participation in ethnicity. The eight resulting types become: (1) full, if self-perception, other perception, and participation are all present; (2) unrecognized, if self is absent but other and participation are present; (3) private, if self and participation are present but other is absent; (4) hidden, if participation is present but self and other are absent; (5) symbolic, if self and other are present but participation is absent; (6) stereotyped, if other is present but self and participation are absent; (7) imagined, if self is present but other and participation are absent; and (8) nonethnic, if all three are absent. This complexity is, I believe, not only important but also salutary for ethnic studies.

Ethnic Group

It goes without saying that ethnicity is not the only way to affiliate, organize, or categorize human beings. Neither is ethnicity the only source of conflict in the world, even between cultural groups, loosely construed. For example, the ongoing problems in Algeria would hardly, under normal circumstances, be considered ethnic in nature. Religious, political, economic, ideological, gender, and other kinds of groups can have the same quantity of cohesion, salience, and even animosity and conflict as ethnic groups, and it is very inadvisable to confuse the disparate types. What, then, is an ethnic group? It is one of the types of human social collectivity, named identity—groups based on some shared quality of social behavior, thought, or feeling. One of the main problems for social scientists is the specification of its difference from or relation to other social collectivities such as "nation," "people," "society," "tribe," "minority," "race," or "class." Students of ethnic phenomena offer various definitions and characterizations; some even suggest differentiations or substitutions within the term itself. A discussion of terminology like the one that follows may seem sheer pedantry, but it actually serves two critical functions: to clean up conceptual sloppiness that interferes with description and comparison and to articulate issues of "unit of analysis" that are increasingly important in anthropology and other social sciences.

In, if not the first, then the classic definition of *ethnic group,* Weber describes it as one of "those human groups that entertain a subjective belief in their common descent because of similarities of physical type or of customs or both, or because of memories of colonization and migration; conversely, it does not matter whether or not an objective blood relationship exists" (1968, 389). R. A. Schermerhorn has defined *ethnic group* as "a collectivity within a larger society having real or putative common ancestry, memories of a shared historical past, and a cultural focus on one or more symbolic elements defined as the epitome of their peoplehood. . . . A necessary component is some consciousness of kind among members of the group" (1970, 12). Abner Cohen calls it "an informal interest group whose members are distinct from members of other groups in that they share a measure of . . . 'compulsory institutions' like kinship and religion, and can communicate among themselves relatively easily. [In] strife between such ethnic groups . . . people stress their identity and exclusiveness" (1969, 4). Yinger defines *ethnic group* as "a segment of a larger society whose members are thought, by themselves or others, to have a common origin and to share important segments of a common culture and who, in addition, participate in shared activities in which the common origin and culture are significant ingredients" (1994, 3). For Anthony Smith an ethnic group is "a type of cultural collectivity, one that emphasizes the role of myths of descent and historical memories, and that is recognized by one or more cultural differences like religion, customs, language, or institutions" (1991, 20).

As different as these definitions are, there are clearly certain commonalities between them. Most basically, they return always to *difference,* however conceived or however employed—to a difference between groups that is apparent and important to the members of the groups. The crucial domain of difference is *culture,* or, more precisely, some part of a shared culture; some theorists also allow that physical or "racial" traits may figure into ethnic groups, but this is not always the case, and even when it is those traits, in the modern phenomenon of ethnic group, are inscribed with cultural significance. This culture may be real, however, or it may be putative or subjective without compromising the power and salience of the group's identity; specifically, the culture (often taken as "tradition") exists as *memory* of the true, or "original," condition of the group—whatever its actual condition in the present. *Origin* and *descent* are frequent idioms in positing this group identity, and, even more critically, an ideology of continuity with that past, that traditional culture, or that blood or kinship line is regularly maintained. It is unimportant whether these views are true or demonstrable. Ultimately, the group is based more on its consciousness, or "awareness," of difference and shared traits and past than on the objective quality of those traits.

Further, the various definitions emphasize the *relational quality* of ethnic groups; an ethnic group is a "culturally distinct" segment of a larger social whole. It is impossible, or better yet nonsensical, to think of an ethnic group in isolation from other groups or "at home" in a culturally homogeneous society or state (e.g., Japanese are not an ethnic group in Japan). Arguably, then, groups that are not part of a larger social whole cannot be ethnic in the strict sense of the word; fortunately for us, there are few if any such groups in the world today (although in the past some indigenous societies probably qualified, but not all of them). In fact, Barth (1969) helped shift the attention away from the "contents"—that is, the list of traits—of ethnic groups to their "boundaries" and relations. His and other studies have actually shown that the contents of a group may change, and the membership of the group may change through assimilation and such processes, while the boundary of the group—its name, its relative status, etc.—remains. Finally, they conceive of ethnic groups as moving, as *movements,* in the sense of "doing something about" their culture or social situation, having some goal; an ethnic group at rest, without an agenda, is almost a contradiction in terms. Ethnic groups thus differ according to the nature and direction of their movement; as an illustration, Gurr and Harff (1994) note four types of "politically active ethnic groups" (which begs the question of whether there are other politically *inactive* types), including ethnonationalists, indigenous peoples, communal contenders, and ethnoclasses. Each type differs in such characteristics as size, geographic distribution, relation to other ethnic groups and to government, relations to the economy and class system, and political aims. Eriksen (1993) also identifies four types: urban ethnic minorities, indigenous peoples, protonations (or ethnonationalists), and ethnic groups in plural societies.

Clearly, then, ethnic groups are multifarious things, with a problematic relation not only to one another but also to the culture and origin, or "descent," that they brandish. Conventionally, however, much of this subtlety is lost, and ethnic groups are conceived as conceptually uniform from one to another, continuous with their own culture and history (*ancient, fixed, primordial,* and other such words), coterminous with their culture (*bounded, discrete,* and so on), and fundamentally different from other types of groups. These are some of the fallacies that I aim to dispel. First, "it would be misleading to state simply that ethnic groups are identical with cultural groups" (Eriksen 1993, 36), for all the reasons raised previously. This flies in the face not only of popular wisdom but also of the founding principle of anthropology—that discrete culture-bearing units, true to their original cultural state (i.e., traditional), with specific names and occupying specifiable territories, exist for our inspection and analysis. These units were deemed *societies* or, even worse, *tribes* and were the unit of analysis of choice in early anthropology. What anthropology began to discover and to admit, especially after Edmund Leach's seminal ethnography, is that the cultural world is not quite so neat: groups exist with vague and permeable boundaries, social "identity" is flexible and negotiable, and even the most "primitive" and "isolated" of tribes can be in contact with other societies, not least European/colonial society.

In fact, continuity and discreteness are ideologies of ethnic groups and not necessarily veritable qualities of such groups. To go even further, it might be argued that the *ideology* of cultural continuity and discreteness is the essential distinguishing characteristic of ethnic groups and their permutations, as opposed to other human collectivities. A century of observation has taught us that, while some ethnic groups may indeed be ancient, others are brand new, and not only the groups but also the cultures or traditions, or "heritages," to which they refer can be of recent vintage. It is not, as I have stated, important that the memory of the "past" be true, only that it be strong and convincing. Greeley goes so far as to say, "that if there are no differences supposedly rooted in common origin by which people can distinguish themselves from others, they will create such differences" (1971, 42). We will discuss the role in subsequent pages of *ethnic entrepreneurs, cultural enthusiasts,* and *elites* in just such a creative process.

Part of the mystification of ethnic groups and ethnicity is that they exist apart from any instrumental ends or interests. The group would still be a group independent of such crass considerations as economics and politics because the group is premised on more ancient, more noble, more authentic grounds that those. While this may be true for some ethnic groups, it is ideological for all of them, and even the old authentic groups would not be ethnic groups without the politicization and "economization" (to coin an awkward phrase) of their cultures. The question remains this: why should groups be ethnic groups instead of some other kind? And why should ethnic organization—the discourse of ethnicity—be so common and effective today? The answer, proposes Bell (1975), is that the ethnic group as a species of collectivity "can combine symbolic and instrumental purposes," can merge "an interest with an affective tie." Immanuel Wallerstein goes even further to assert: "Behind the ethnic 'reality' lies a class conflict" (qtd. in Aronson 1976, 15). This facility to clothe practical interests and competitions in the garb of antiquity, authenticity, and kinship—not to say that it is a lie, only a translation—makes ethnicity and ethnic groups uniquely attractive, uniquely real, and uniquely irresistible to their opponents: the ethnic ideology is a "discourse of and for value dissensus and disengagement from an inclusive sociopolitical arena [which] says in effect that we do not agree on the ultimate values (or goals or ends) of the system, and we want to be left alone (perhaps with enough resources) to pursue 'our' own ends, whatever you may be doing" (Aronson 1976, 14–15).

As such, it is the radical appropriation and application of "otherness" to the practical domain, potentially denying any cultural common ground between groups—"to each group its culture and values"—and taking the practical competition or conflict out of the realm of the practical, where no other group can question or refute you. This is why Geertz (1963) and his contributors found ethnic or "primordial" claims so extremely corrosive to political integration, since those claims base legitimation on an alternate system of values and truths that is unimpeachable from any other system. In this way ethnic groups are products of a politicized version of cultural relativism.

Ethnic Group, Nation, and State

Ethnic group, nation, and state compose a constellation of related yet discrete phenomena that are all-too-often confused or conflated. *Ethnic group* and nation are often used synonymously, and *nation* and *state* are often used synonymously, which is not only empirically wrong but leads to the logical conclusion that ethnic group is synonymous with state, which is absurd. In fact, not all ethnic groups are nations, but some are; not all ethnic groups or nations have or want states, but some do. Terminological sloppiness leads to muddled thinking and mental and political mistakes.

State is the simplest of these terms to grasp, since the political entities that are the principal legitimate actors on the world stage are states; when one looks at a map, what one sees is states, not ethnic groups, not nations, and not any other form of political or social collectivity. Although Americans use the word *state* to refer to the constituent parts of our polity (i.e., Texas, California, New York, and the other forty-seven units), in proper political terminology those are not states; rather, the United States is a state, a sovereign centralized political entity with a government empowered over a territory to make laws, collect taxes (including coining money), and maintain an army. State and statehood are an objective, if contested and contestable, reality (consider Taiwan in 1997 as an example of both qualities: Taiwan exists as a sovereign polity on world maps, yet the People's Republic of China at least contests its right to be recognized and to exist, i.e., its reality as an independent state). States, even when they are real, are not "natural" or "given" but are generally products of a historical and political (often a military or colonial) process, made and broken and remade as groups and/or individual leaders vie for control over territory; again, as natural as the current United States seems, a glance at maps from 1776, from 1848, and from today shows the gradual construction of the state, a lesson it would be well not to forget. There are various kinds of states, of course, ordinarily distinguished by how they distribute political power through the population (e.g., monarchy, constitutional monarchy, republic, etc., and many permutations thereof—totalitarian, democratic, fascist, communist, and so on), but to an extent the lineaments of all these forms are basically the same, since the state is a fairly recent and generalized political form. At any rate, clearly most ethnic groups lack the powers and prerogatives of state as well as the level of organization and sovereignty.

Nation is a more diffuse term, if only because, unlike *state,* it is not a clearly demarcated, officially recognized, and objective unit. Smith defines *nation* as "a named human population sharing a historic territory, common myths and historical memories, a mass, public culture, a common economy and common legal rights and duties for all members" (1991, 40). This definition is similar to his definition of *ethnic group,* except for the references to mass culture, economy, and law; in a sense (but not a definitive sense) a nation is a fully mobilized or institutionalized ethnic group, but this is to say a lot in a few words. Further, by this definition, and by other considerations, nation is not only different from ethnic group but also from state, and it is not only a different phenomenon from the other two but a different level of reality. Let us use African Americans as a case in point. As a group, they are typically construed as a race. They clearly are not, or do not have, a state. Are they a nation? The difficulty of this question should be immanent. In the United States they do not occupy a distinct territory, and it is debatable whether they share a common economy and political culture (especially one discrete from "white" or general U.S. society); they do share, in the widest sense, a "historic" territory in the form of Africa but originate from a plethora of societies (and nations?) within that geographic field.

The best answer to our question is that they are a nation *if* they can acquire the characteristics—and, even more, the *consciousness*—of nationhood. In a way the move in name from *black* to *African-American* is a move toward nationhood, toward emphasizing historical/territorial qualities over physical/race ones. In other words, nationhood is an achieved status, at least to a degree. Certainly, the peoples of Africa, or even the peoples in most single African states, do not conceive of themselves as one nation but as many; they may, in any one state or across the whole continent, someday come to see themselves as a common nation (as was the dream of pan-Africanists like Kwame Nkrumah) but not yet. Then, if African Americans do not "come from" a single nation, can they be a single nation in the United States? This raises the point that nationhood is not only achieved but *subjective;* it is a "state of mind" (if you can pardon the pun, which is, on second thought, a suggestive one), a will, and a consciousness. It is, as Anderson (1983) phrases it, an *imagination,* not in the sense of falseness but of psychological creativity. In other words, if the "group" embraces a common myth and memory (whether or not it is true in the perfectly objective sense) and begins to act on the basis of shared rights, norms, and interests, then it becomes, it *is,* a nation. Furthermore, as much as the "nationhood" of the nation may be imagined or constructed, the specific markers and elements of its nationhood—its history, its culture, or any part thereof, like symbols, rituals, and so forth—may be imagined, interpreted, or even "invented" as well. This is why it is possible to find within any nation or protonation competing factions and leaders with competing visions of what the nation is, or should be, and competing evidence and interpretations to back up the claims. The nation that evolves is the product of the will-to-nationhood that prevails, an (often personal) imagination that becomes the nation's imagination.

Being thus not only a construction but a subjective and psychological one at that, it is possible to distinguish between different types of nations. Connor (1994, 44), for example, lists three types of nations and two types of related collectivities. *Nations proper* are "the largest human grouping characterized by a myth of common ancestry." *Prenational* or *potential nations* are groups that will or may become nations in the future but which currently lack a "national consciousness," their "meaningful identity [being] still limited to locale, clan, tribe, and the like." In fact, living and identifying at the level of locale, clan, or even tribe they might also be considered "pre-ethnic," although Connor himself does not say this. *Offshoot nations* are larger segments of a nation that have been "geographically separated from the parent group for a period of time sufficient for it to develop a strong sense of separate consciousness"; he illustrates with the examples of Afrikaners and Quebecois. The remaining two groups he calls *diasporas* and *immigrant societies,* the latter being people whose primary affiliation is not to their ancestral nation but to their new society (the ideal in the American "melting pot" philosophy). Thus, nations as a class of social phenomena are as diverse as ethnic groups, and the particular status of a nation or nation fragment will affect its behavior.

The relations between nation and state are numerous but can be distilled into two major categories: states that are coterminous with nations and states that are not. The coterminous state-and-nation is the well-known "nation-state," the model and aspiration of Western nations/states for two centuries and maybe longer—and more recently of most non-Western nations/states. The hesitation here over Western nations and Western states results from the question of whether it was the will of the nation (i.e., the "people") or of the state (i.e., the ruler) to organize polity and identity on the nation-state principle. Plenty of historians point to the fact that rulers of already-existing states (say, Napoleonic France) forged the states' population into a nation through intensified institutionalization, language standardization, acculturation, and military conscription. At any rate, while the nation-state has been the dominant social model for Europe and lately for the whole world, few states actually qualify, even on the relatively generous criterion that 90 percent of the population consist of a single nation. Perhaps Japan, Iceland, and Norway truly constitute nation-states, but even these instances come under doubt as indigenous populations are considered and immigration and internationalization take effect.

All other states would be multinational by definition. The obvious questions are: (1) how many nations occupy the state? (2) are the nations fully contained by the state, or do they spill across state boundaries? and (3) what relations exist between the constituent nations? Perhaps the oldest and most important multinational state form is empire, which is dominated by the military and/or economic power of one of the nations (e.g., the Roman Empire, the Mongol Empire, or the British Empire); in such a state most enclosed nations continue to reside in their homeland, while the power of the imperial nation expands to engulf them. Imperial or colonial arguments and analogies have become an important part of the discourse of ethnicity and nationalism even in places that are not associated with classical imperialism, such as Quebec.

Empire, then, is one type of what Connor calls *multihomeland, multinational states,* which contain two or more (and maybe many more) nations more or less in their discrete and "native" home territories; these states may be heavily dominated by one nation (as in the former Soviet Union or present-day Russia) or be composed of relative equals (as in Belgium or the former Czechoslovakia). Such states would differ from *unihomeland multinational states,* in which one nation claims the entire territory as its homeland and disputes the rights of other nations to own or even occupy it, as the case may be; Connor offers Malaysia, Sri Lanka, Fiji (in which the "homeowning" nation is actually the minority), and Germany as examples. *Nonhomeland multinational states,* significantly, contain two or more nations, none of whose members can claim to be in their national homeland, as is the case in many Caribbean states. A subtype of such states is *immigrant states,* like the United States, in which virtually all the population (excepting some Native Americans) live away from their national or ancestral land while the state is not ethnically defined. Finally, *mestizo states,* unique to Latin America, are set apart for their populations "in which those of joint European-Amerindian ancestry are dominant."

It should, therefore, be clear that not all states are nations and that not all nations are or have states. States encompassing two or three nations in their entirety will, then, differ considerably from states encompassing a dozen or fifty or a hundred nations. States in which one nation constitutes a majority will also differ from states where no nation predominates or all nations are fairly equal in size and power. And states that circumscribe nations in their entirety will differ from states that contain only a portion of a nation, whose people are spread across a multistate area (e.g., the Kurds); such nations might reasonably be called *multistate nations,* and it will be immediately apparent that they face challenges unlike those of nations fully contained in a single state, even if the latter faces explicit discrimination and persecution in their state.

What, then, is the connection between ethnic group and nation? It is as complex and variable as that between nation and state: some ethnic groups are nations; some are not. Conceivably, some nations are ethnic groups; some are not. For instance, if the United States is to be considered a nation in any way, it must be as a nonethnic or multiethnic one. An even better example is the "Arab nation" or the "Islamic nation," two forms of nationhood or ideologies of nation that formulate transstate identity but on a basis other than ethnicity and which, to be precise, reject ethnicity or cultural/national divisions within the broadly conceived nation. Furthermore, I proposed earlier that a nation is a mobilized and institutionalized ethnic group, but this is not completely accurate or sufficient. First, as just argued, not all nations are or start out as ethnic groups, although they may come to be draped in the ethnic rubric and discourse (e.g., Islamic or Arab nationhood might and has at times come to be construed and defended as an ethnic identity—or attacked on that same basis, as in the case of Bosnia). Second, the mobilization and institutionalization of an ethnic group and its culture is no insignificant feat and effects a qualitative change in the group and its culture, creating a new kind of culture and cultural politics and a new perspective on culture that some anthropologists have likened to a "culture cult." Ethnic groups that achieve (some would say awaken to) nation status—and even more so, those that take the next step into nation*alism*—are substantially altered by the fact. Their aims and aspirations, their identity, and even their very culture are changed by the shift in dimension from ethnicity to nationhood—and not in the simple sense of waking up to a preexisting identity and cause. In fact, most ethnic groups that have not attained nation consciousness exist below the threshold of world attention; most of the "ethnic conflicts" that fill our televisions and newspapers, and which fill this volume, are therefore more than ethnic but "ethnonational" or even national in nature. At this stage in history such conflicts, rather than conflicts between states, are the most common and seem the most likely to spread and intensify. The nation, in the modern sense of the word, is thus intermediate, in terms of identity and of political organization, between the micro-organization of the family, clan, tribe, etc., and the macro-organization of the such collectivities as, for instance, as the Islamic *umma* or Christendom.

Ethnicity and Nationalism

Having distinguished ethnic group and nation as two types of collectivity, sometimes empirically overlapping but not conceptually identical, it should be evident that we will also distinguish the forces or processes that underlie or motivate them, namely ethnicity and nationalism. Specifically, nationalism, although often built upon a foundation of ethnicity and using or applying to an ethnic group, is a different species of social force. When ethnicity is implicated in nationalism, or when it evolves into nationalism, it is thereby essentially changed: an ethnic group may or may not be nationalistic, but, when it is, it is significantly different from a nonnationalistic ethnic group in terms both of its relation to its own culture and of its political aims.

Nationalism, writes Alter, is "both an ideology and a political movement which holds the nation and the sovereign nation-state to be crucial indwelling values, and which manages to mobilize the political will of a people or a large section of a population"; "[it] exists primarily whenever individuals feel they belong primarily to the nation, and whenever affective attachment and loyalty to that nation override all other attachments and loyalties" (1994, 21). Minogue calls it "the belief that each nation has both the right and the duty to constitute itself as a state" but goes on to explain that in this sense it "is not a belief but rather a force supposed to move people to both action and belief" (1985, 551–52). In the same volume Smooha maintains that nationalism "is the claim of ethnic groups to self-determination. When an ethnic group achieves sovereignty in a certain state, it will become a nation" (1985, 268). Smith characterizes it as "a *form of culture*—an ideology, a language, mythology, symbolism, and consciousness" with four goals: (1) turning a passive ethnic category or group into an active ethnopolitical community, a "subject of history"; (2) organizing the community's culture and creating a standard, official, and "high" culture if one is absent; (3) forming the community into a "culturally homogeneous 'organic' nation"; and (4) obtaining a home territory or even a state for the nation (1991, 126).

It is readily apparent that nationalism comes in association with four other terms that we have previously discussed—*nation, state, ethnic group,* and *culture.* In conventional thought nationalism represents and mobilizes a nation—a nation that already exists and is ripe and ready for political action. Yet, if the *ism* in *nationalism* is taken seriously, it is a belief in a nation or in the idea of nation—that a nation is an important, arguably the most important, social collectivity and, even more fundamentally, that the nation is a real, perhaps natural, collectivity. The nation is thereby more genuine from this perspective than the state (which is secondary to and derivative of the nation, the political institution of the nation in the best of occasions, the nation-state), especially in the case of multinational states. Yet it is not necessary, or even perhaps ordinary, that the nation precedes nationalism; rather, the belief in a nation, the belief in nations—that nations exist, are good, and have rights—may hypothetically come before the actual existence of nationhood, the "knowledge" or "will" or "consciousness" of being a nation and sharing a national identity among the people, who may still be experiencing their lives through identities, ideologies, and collectivities both smaller than and larger than the nation, such as the family, the clan, the region, the religious community, or the state or empire. Some nations, of course, do have long histories of nationhood (i.e., of being conscious that they are a nation and acting accordingly on the interests of the nation), but others do not; recall Connor's category of prenational groups and potential nations. Thus, while it is seductive to think of nationalism as emerging from and representing real, concrete, perhaps ancient nations, in many actual cases "the nation . . . must be seen as a creation of nationalism" (Smith 1991, 92). In other words, the belief that nations are real, important, and necessary can lead a people, or more accurately leaders of a people, to interpret and construct their identity and their experience as a national one.

This phenomenon, the construction of nations out of other preceding kinds of social collectivities, could be called "nation building." Nation building has been a topic of interest to anthropologists for thirty years or more; by the early 1960s investigators had noted the incidence and significance of "the making and breaking of nations," as Deutsch (1969; also Deutsch and Foltz 1963) has put it. *Nation building* is an ambiguous term, however, which is interesting for both of its possible meanings. Usually, in the kind of terminological confusion I have chronicled here, what researchers discuss in studies of nation building would more accurately be called state building: Geertz's famous essay "The Integrative Revolution," for instance, actually analyzes the "reduction of primordial [ethnic] sentiments to civil order," and the cases he provides are of states, not nations: Indonesia, Malaysia, Burma, India, Lebanon, Morocco, and Nigeria. The nation that is being built in these cases is "the whole society encompassed by the new civil state." Such state building—the creation of statewide civil and political institutions, often across great cultural divisions—is in itself a fascinating and serious subject of study but should not be confused with nation building (although the two can be related). After all, building the Roman and British imperial states would not be quite the same as building the Roman or British nations.

That being said, one of the regular and fundamental aspects of state building is precisely nation building—not only creating the legal-political apparatus of state (police, military, political parties, tax system, etc.) but also creating a sense of nationhood among all the people within the territory of the state. The task is, as Geertz indicates, to amalgamate different and independent groups (which may already conceive of themselves as nations on the smaller scale) into a single large unit whose horizon is not local but statewide—to erase ethnic or national differences and to establish a single unified state-nation. This new nation manifests the increasingly inclusive identity that scholars such as Bell and many others saw or foresaw. As numerous students of nations and nationalism have argued, this process of nation building was a particularly strong element in modern (i.e., since the eighteenth century and especially in the nineteenth century)

Europe, whereby the nations and national states of Europe—the French, the English, the Italians, the Germans, etc.—were first constituted. In the reduction of sovereignty and loyalty away from the state in the person of the ruler and toward the people inhabiting the state's territory, the people had to be constituted as a self-conscious and homogeneous group and as a group with cultural and political rights. Differences in language, law, and custom had to be flattened out or assimilated or merely overlooked into some model of national culture and identity. As Smith notes, it is just as important, ideologically, that a nation be internally undifferentiated as that it be sharply differentiated from other nations. By many accounts this is a recent accomplishment in Europe, if it is not still an unfinished project (which one feels when one considers, e.g., the political culture of Italy). In many new states the project has only just begun.

Of course, this nation building is today not what we usually think of as nationalism. Rather, contemporary nationalism connotes particularism, not homogenization; separation, not inclusion. In a sense this result is the fulfillment of the prophecy, for nationalism as an ideology does not specify which groups are nations, what level of collectivity may deserve the distinction of nation (a state society like Spain? an ethnic nation like the Basques? a dispersed minority like the African Americans? a pan-state category Arabs or Muslims?), or which aspects of national commonality will provide the criteria for national recognition. Groups formerly submerged in states (and therefore undergoing the previous kind of nationalization) or from which scholarly attention may have wandered because of our interest in state-level nationalism have launched their claims to nationhood based on "the right to one's own culture" implicit in all nationalism. They can and do say, with more or less justification, that their culture was ignored or threatened by state nationalism and that only *real* nationalism—that is, the nationalism of real nations, which often means ethnic or cultural nationalism—can correct the situation. Hence, the nineteenth and early twentieth centuries were an age of separatist/ethnic/cultural nationalism, frequently leading to new national states in Europe, often out of the larger dynastic empires of the time—for instance, Greece (1821), Belgium (1830), Germany and Italy (1871), Romania and Serbia (1878), Norway (1905), Bulgaria (1908), Albania (1912), Finland (1917), and Czechoslovakia, Estonia, Hungary, Latvia, Lithuania, Poland, and Yugoslavia (1918, as a result of World War I). Under the ideology of "self-determination" nationalist movements representing segments of larger populations, states, and empires could and did press for nation and state status.

Now, not all nationalism necessarily seeks or results in a national state, and not all nationalist movements represent real, concrete, already-existing nations. Some nationalism sets more modest goals, such as national recognition of a region or province and perhaps a certain amount of devolution of power to the regional or provincial level; arguably, early Tamil demands in Sri Lanka and recurrent Kurdish demands in their various host states take this form. On the other hand, as recent events have reminded us, Yugoslavian nationalism—"Yugoslavism," the nationalism of which resulted in the formation of the state of that name—did not refer to a homogeneous, self-conscious nation but, rather, attempted to emphasize (and awaken in people of various nations) the kinship and shared identity between a set of related nations; the same can be said of Czechoslovakian, Hungarian, or many other nationalisms. There is theoretically no lower limit to the size of a group that may call itself, and demand recognition as, a nation; there is also no cultural or political "litmus test" that can establish or deny a group's claims to nationhood, no objective standard or definition to apply. That nationalist movements do stake their claims in terms of culture is no great advance in clarity, but it does present an opportunity for anthropologists to bring their concepts and methods to bear on the phenomenon.

Nationalism may merely seek recognition, respect, and justice for a nation—its people and their culture; the raison d'être for a nation, writes Smith, is the enjoyment and cultivation of "its unique (or allegedly unique) culture values." The relation between nationalism and culture is, however, a problematic one and in fact relativizes once again the entire question of who precisely is the nation. Which aspects of culture are central to the nation: language or religion or homeland or history and so on? The elevation of one or another of these to the status of a national symbol and marker changes the contours of the group that might be claimed a nation. Serbs and Croats speak essentially one language but have distinct religions and histories; are they therefore one nation or two? If a group loses or changes part of its culture, is it thereby less of a nation or a different nation? If so, the Irish, the Ukrainians, and most Native American groups might cease to be nations. Connor finds, however, that national identity "may survive substantial alterations in language, religion, economic status, or any other tangible manifestation of its culture" (1994, 44). In fact, the mere memory of having had a distinct culture in the past may be sufficient to create and maintain a sense of nationhood.

Beyond this issue, once again as at the state-/nation-building level, at a more local, ethnic level the nationalist movement may create or find the nation. Individuals may have, for any number of reasons, never thought of themselves as members of this or that nation, and nationalism may have to provide the cohesion to make of them a nation; Smith writes that to convert "the masses" into a nation "it is first necessary to 'vernacularize' them and thereby bestow a unique identity and destiny upon them" (1991, 140), give them something to rally around or show them that what they possess already should be rallied around. Thus, just as culture is problematic from the standpoint of nationalism, so is the group or nation. I said previously that the nation is an organized and mobilized ethnic group, but we must qualify this assertion with Smith's observation that nationalism can be related to ethnic groups in three different ways: as a revitalization or protection of a "well-formed, ancient but 'decayed' *ethnie,"* as an effort of a segment of the community, especially the elite, to motivate a passive or unorganized group, or as a movement in search of a constituency, which "may actually 'invent' an *ethnie* where none existed" (1984, 288).

But, as Smith notes initially, nationalism is not just about culture but about high culture. Without sounding ethnocentric, a high culture is one that is literate, aesthetic, and politically astute. Now, many groups that would qualify as nations or protonations, which most certainly have a culture, lack a high culture, or more precisely a well- and widely distributed high culture. Such high culture as exists may be limited to the academics, the intelligentsia, the political leadership, often urban, often Western educated. The task of nationalism, of mobilizing or assembling the nation, involves in such instances at least the "vernacularization" of the restricted high culture, its digestion and presentation to a mass audience. At most it may involve the creative elevation or invention of a high culture if none exists: in an interesting paradox based on the powerful claims of culture, nationalist leaders (or would-be leaders) may rummage through, for example, peasant cultures for symbols, behaviors, tales, myths, and the like that can be appropriated, packaged, and "sold" as a national culture and then re-vernacularized, often to the same people from whom it was lifted. Yet, in the process of collection, assembly, interpretation, and vernacularization, what is produced is not the same culture as the "peasant" or "rural" or traditional culture that was ostensibly "discovered."

Marriott (1963) studies how ethnonationalism is related to preexisting high cultures (what he calls "great traditions" or "civilizations") in many new states seeking a kind of national identity and culture. Where dominant great traditions exist, either indigenous to the area or borrowed long ago, nationalism will select from but simplify this culture for popular consumption; India and Pakistan are examples that he cites. Where more than one high culture exists but none is dominant, a cultural struggle will accompany the vernacularization process, as in Sri Lanka and Indonesia. Finally, where no internationally recognized and esteemed high culture exists or is deeply rooted (he uses new African states as an example), such a culture must be borrowed or invented, then struggled over and vernacularized. It is not only high culture but any culture that can be used as a tool and weapon in ethnic or national struggle.

Eriksen presents one example of this invention of culture in the case of Norway. He reports that in prenationalist Norway (as late as the mid-nineteenth century) a distinct and widespread national culture was missing. The main written language, for example, was Danish, not Norwegian. Yet ethnic or nationalist leaders, principally the urban and middle class, desirous to demonstrate that there was a distinct and ancient Norwegian nation, went in search of "authentic Norwegian culture" in the rural and peasant sectors of the country. They brought back "folk costumes, painted floral patterns (*rosemaling*), traditional music, and peasant food," which were elevated to the status of national symbols; high culture creators such as the composer Grieg and the author Bjornson incorporated these "folk" elements into their works; furthermore, Norwegian dialects were reformulated into a "new literary language" called New Norwegian. Never mind that the claim to authentic Norwegian culture was dubious on two counts, that these cultural traits were not the heritage of all or even most people in the nation and that many of the traits (e.g., the floral patterns and many of the folktales and costumes) were not indigenous or unique to the nation at all but were diffused from other parts of the world or invented outright by the nationalists themselves. The newly elevated symbols were offered as "evidence" that "Norwegian culture was distinctive, that Norwegians were 'a people' and that they therefore ought to have their own state" (1993, 102–3), but essentially what transpired is that a national culture was invented and with it a *nation.* Nevertheless, to a greater or lesser extent it worked: Norway became an independent state (ostensibly a nation-state) in 1905, and the new king (interestingly, from a Danish family) took a dynastic name, Haaken VII, to claim continuity with Norway's ancient political past.

This practice of legitimating new states and mobilizing (or consolidating or inventing) nations through invocations of some distant past that is at best of questionable relation to the present people and polity is commonplace in the world of postcolonial states in Africa and Asia. One has only to think of the Gold Coast becoming Ghana or Rhodesia becoming Zimbabwe to see the process in action. The phenomenon is by no means restricted, however, to non-Western and postcolonial societies but can be and has been identified in Western societies as well (e.g., Hitler's Germany has been mentioned as a case of manipulating symbols of traditional culture and history, from folk music to the dead emperor's remains; the same can also be currently or recently observed in the former Yugoslavia). Questions of authenticity, uniqueness, continuity, and even relevance of the old in relation to the new are secondary to the function of the claims and symbols in the nation-building process.

Ethnicity as Past, Present, and Future

The popular perception of ethnic groups and nations—a perception that has been raised to the status of theory by some researchers—is that they have long, continuous, often glorious histories of cultural distinctness (and often conflict) that confer to them the rights of "a people." This may be true in some cases, but it is by no means true in all. Even so, virtually all ethnic groups, and virtually all scholarly conceptions of ethnic groups, make some reference to the past. Smith gives six attributes of ethnic groups, two of which are past related—"a myth of common ancestry" and "shared historical memories"—and Yinger, as quoted earlier, sees a notion of "common origin" as characteristic of such groups. This opinion is nearly universal and quite generally valid, yet what does it really mean? What is the relation between an ethnic group—and especially ethnic conflict—and the past?

Like most terms in anthropology and other social sciences, *past* has a large and diverse semantic field, and its connections to the field of ethnicity and ethnic conflict are numerous. It is possible to identify four such connections, which are quite different though related: the past as tradition or the cultural past, the past as history (i.e., a record of key events that formed or galvanized the group), the past as myth, and the past as "resource" for the present. Most, if not all, ethnic groups incorporate some alloy of all of these factors, sometimes in such a way that the distinctions between them are disguised or mystified in consequential ways.

Past as Tradition or Cultural Past

As cultural past or tradition, the ethnic group defines "what we really are" in terms of "what we were." This is an interesting yet ubiquitous and powerful phenomenon, a little foreign to Americans, with our limited historical memory and our orientation toward the future, but not altogether unknown in our own society. Yet for many people in many parts of the world the past is a strong presence. Thus, the language the group has "always" spoken, the religion it has always followed or that it converted to at some ancient time, the customs, the clothes, the stories and music, the values and morals—these things are effective identifiers and legitimizers of the group. An ethnic group without a memory of its cultural past and without some continuity with that past into present behavior or identity or ideology is, by definition, virtually unthinkable. We might mention at this point the role that anthropology has played in this process, both as a practice of collecting and preserving what might have been lost in the past without it *and* as a perspective and discourse that validates and to an extent reifies the past, or tradition, as something important, real, and available; anthropology cannot take all of the credit, even among the various fields of scholarship (history, linguistics, and philology, among others, have played major parts, too), and certainly both scholars and lay members were aware of and concerned with their past and traditions before anthropology came along; still, anthropology has been a powerful engine for research into and conceptions of tradition that, it would be wise to remember, have had ramifications well beyond the academy.

This does not mean, however, that the past (traditional culture) was what culture is today nor that it was as they remember it in retrospect. Memory is porous and productive, and the past is elusive, especially but not exclusively when the past was a preliterate period. The porosity of memory allows elements to slip out *and to slip in,* rendering the firmest memories contestable. Ethnography is replete with accounts of the traditional conditions of various cultures that are questionable at best, absurd at worst: Rose (1992), for example, reports stories from Australian Aboriginals that place Captain Cook in the Central Desert—a highly unlikely event at best. Beyond that, tradition and culture are not synonymous, as any number of anthropologists have argued; as hungry as anthropology has been traditionally (for we have our own traditions as well) for the past or real culture of a society, it has not been totally credulous and naive about that thing. "Tradition is the past of a culture, as that past is thought to have continuity, a presence, and a future" (Nash 1989, 14).

Even by Malinowski's time, over fifty or more years ago (and probably earlier in some places), what was available to anthropologists was not "tradition lived"—that is, society living in unchanged manner from their distant past—but "tradition remembered." He himself saw and appreciated the significance of this phenomenon (which may have been crucial to the functionalist rejection of history) when he asserted that even the "authorities" of societies, like the old men, give us information about tradition that is "always affected by sentiment, by retrospective regrets, and longings." Even so, he does not dismiss this information; he merely asks us to be circumspect about it. From the point of view of the student who not only aims to piece together the past but to establish its relation to and salience for the present, "retrospective vision, however erroneous, is more important than the myth unknown or forgotten by old informants" (1961, 31). For the purposes of the study of ethnicity often all that is available is the retrospective vision, and its veracity is considerably less critical than its effect.

When a group itself begins to think of its culture as tradition rather than as an almost unconscious "way of life," a conceptual shift occurs within that group: the culture is frozen in time, an ideology of authenticity is produced, and a "new self-awareness, through a kind of 'spontaneous' hermeneutics" is established (Guidieri and Pellizi 1988, 26). Culture becomes an object, maybe a tool, maybe even a commodity. In the most extreme cases the tradition may even be a fabrication, an invention, either from bits and pieces of the past, from disparate local cultures and traditions, or from a stipulation of contemporary culture or social situation as representative of the past.

Past as History

At least as important as the cultural/traditional past is the historical past, the record or memory of actual (or supposedly actual) events that happened to the group; often where the former is lacking, the latter will suffice to give a group identity and solidarity. The historical ethnic past could be thought of in at least three phases—ancient (formative) past, colonial past, and recent political past. Most of the ethnic groups and nations drawing our attention today and involved in the most public conflicts can claim a history of centuries or millennia; the Jews, the Irish, the Sinhalese, are but a few examples. In that ancient time a kind of ethnogenesis occurred, due to the invention or adoption of a religion, the development of a civilization or state, a great national struggle, or some such course of events. This ancient history, interestingly, may be a past of glory and honor or of humiliation and dishonor, or a combination of both, since either can function as a means to define and motivate a group. Particularly common is the reference to a great historical military defeat (Catholic Ireland's Battle of the Boyne, Serbia's Battle of Kosovo) and the desire for revenge and group redemption that the memory evokes even today, centuries later. The defeat of Israel and destruction of the temple were a cause of significant spontaneous hermeneutics and historical exegesis, and for them, as for many groups, the memory of a lost homeland—lost literally or symbolically—may be the central organizational experience for contemporary ethnicity.

Groups will, in fact, go to great lengths to "discover" and systematize a past in which they were either prior to, superior to, or dominant over rival groups or in which they were damaged or shamed by those groups; both are equally calls to action. Groups in the process of nation building will often emphasize the compilation of a national history as a national priority; Sri Lanka's rival groups have done so. Similarly, Russian nationalists, awakened by Peter the Great's contact with and adoption of Western European cultures, discovered an ancient past for the nation in the document known as the *Book of Vlas,* allegedly a chronicle of the earliest rulers of Russia some three thousand years ago. The book claims glorious (interestingly, Aryan) ancestry for the Russian people—the frequency of claims to "Aryan" ancestry and identity in the realm of ethnicity and nationalism being truly astonishing—and priority among the peoples and cultures of Europe. Perhaps most important, it establishes a European and not an Asiatic heritage for Russia, which was an important issue of the day. The orders to compile and copy the records and documents came from Peter himself, suggesting their significance to the nation-building endeavor. It is worth noting in passing that, as in the case of Norway, Russian nationalists also looked to the village and peasant culture for the "authentic" artifacts, values, and symbols of the nation.

Consequentially, anthropological studies can be implicated in this nationalistic historical struggle in a number of ways. Ethnography can be appropriated as an authentic (or problematic) record of culture, and for many groups, like some Native American groups, it is the only written record of a now-defunct culture (as a result of the well-known "salvage" anthropology). Linguistic anthropology can serve as a means to establish antiquity for a language groups or to link it to some glorious language or language family (again, often the Aryan or Indo-European family). Physical anthropology has been appealed to on more than a few occasions to establish racial links and superiorities, and the anthropology of the past per se, archaeology, is particularly valuable to ethnic/national interests. Even in the early 1960s it could be observed that governments were increasingly investing in archaeological research to confirm or invent historical bases for their nationhood or statehood, like the excavation of Great Zimbabwe that led to the reactivation of the name by a modern African state. In Sri Lanka history in general and archaeology in particular have been contentious fields for politics and culture, so much so that the government would only sponsor research on Buddhist (Sinhalese) sites, and ethnic extremists have been known to attack and damage sites that support the claims of their rivals.

After the ancient past the most critical historical age for many groups is the period of European colonialism. A variety of fundamental social and cultural changes to non-Western traditional societies followed from colonialism, not the least of which was prolonged contact with a radically foreign culture. The very fact of conquest, occupation, and an end to (relative) cultural isolation, let alone the contents of the intruding culture, could initiate a sort of cultural reflection, a "spontaneous hermeneutics," on culture, identity, and difference. Certain specific activities and policies of colonial powers, however, had distinct and profound consequences for subsequent ethnicity, nationalism, and conflict. For one, colonial political boundaries were drawn, as is well-known, with little or no regard for sociocultural boundaries; of course, in this pre-anthropological time little was known, and little was cared, about local sociocultural boundaries, and it has been argued that those boundaries were in actuality so vague and porous (if they were "physical" or territorial at all)—groups being much more mixed and permeable than we often allow and often not territorially structured—that any political borders would have done some injustice.

Yet this is precisely the point: the importation of the notion of bounded territorial units (states) and of bounded and usually territorial social units (societies) had a dramatic effect on many parts of the world. In some cases groups that had previously had little contact with one another or which had a history of hostility were thrust into the same colony, while other groups with more or less ethnic or national consciousness were divided across two or more colonies. Thus, "plural" societies were created in a way that may not have existed before. Certainly, plural societies, after a fashion, existed in precolonial times; Colin Turnbull's (1983) study of the

Mbuti "pygmies" and the "Negroes" describes another such society, within which the two groups are so intertwined that it is difficult to place specific boundaries, territorially or culturally, on them. In many places, however, even groups in geographic proximity (e.g., hill people and valley people) may have lived rather autonomously. Only the arrival of colonialism, and with it the effort toward uniform law and administration, brought them into real and sustained social proximity.

Again often for administrative purposes, but also out of genuine conviction, groups were taken to be real, exclusive, and well bounded—that is, to be self-contained societies. Further, they were often taken to be ahistorical, culturally static or stable—that is, primitive or traditional societies. At the very least groups that were not utterly socially discrete were treated as so, administratively and anthropologically, as in the Burma that Edmund Leach finds. In Leach's (1954) famous study of highlands Burma not only were political/administrative boundaries introduced that enveloped a variety of groups, but the perception or expectation that the groups within the colony were discrete, bounded societies—compact, isolated, and distinguishable by such traits as language—led the administrators to demarcate internal boundaries and assign "societal" names and identities on that basis. In other cases groups that were not societies or cultures at all but some other type of collectivity, such as a class or a caste or a dominant or royal lineage, were construed as separate societies or tribes or nations or ethnic groups. One example is Rwanda and Burundi, where the two main groups, Hutu and Tutsi, have been variously characterized as tribes, classes, and castes and in which, by a kind of ethnogenesis the royal line, the *ganwa,* was converted into something approximating a separate ethnic group. Similarly, in Sri Lanka, caste distinctions cause heterogeneity within ethnic groups yet demonstrate how, even in traditional (precolonial) society, a process of incorporation could transform ethnic groups into castes and vice versa.

In many instances racial categories were superimposed upon existing social differences, reifying those differences while often suggesting a closer racial relationship of one group than the other to the white colonizers. The very idea of race was (and to an extent is) a European or Western preoccupation, not endemic to all societies or civilizations—not only as a method to classify peoples but also to explain behavioral differences in terms of physical differences. Like the notion of society, race too was supposedly a real, discrete, bounded phenomenon with a discernible set of traits, this time physical rather than cultural, yet the two concepts worked hand in hand, since a set of cultural traits could ideally be attributed to the group identified by its set of physical traits. Race was often linked to or established on the basis of cultural characteristics, most particularly language or territory: the thinking was "every language group a race, and every race a language group" and "every territorial group a race, and every race a territorial group." *Race* was often even something of a synonym for *society* or *nation,* as in the *British race* or the *French race.* Accordingly, in Rwanda and Burundi the Hutu and Tutsi were construed by administrators as two races, with distinct physical attributes; in Sri Lanka the Sinhalese, with much less physical justification, have employed the race concept. Not only that, but by definition (at least by Western definition) races—unlike societies—are hierarchically related. Race labels communicate the message not only that "we are different from you" but that "we are better than you." In fact, they can encode the even stronger message that "we are more like some third group than you are." Thus, when the Sinhalese claim to be Aryans, they are claiming superiority over the Tamils and racial affiliation with white/Western societies. In Rwanda and Burundi, again, the ascription of Tutsi as a race, as a "noble race," as a "Hamitic (biblical) race," draws the association between them and their former European colonizers.

Having established discrete administrative units, ostensibly on the basis of preexistent social or racial distinctions, colonialists also sought rulers or representatives from the local groups, with various cultural consequences. Some groups, such as Australian Aboriginals or some Plains societies of Native Americans, had no "leaders" or political integration of the sort adequate to Western administration. Groups that did have leaders often suffered the co-optation of those leaders by the colonial government, shifting the balance of power in the group in ways that may have been inconceivable before; Newbury (1988), for instance, describes the intensification of control and exploitation by Rwandan (basically Tutsi) officeholders (chiefs and patrons) after colonialism began. And, where no leadership, or no desirable leadership, existed colonialists, were just as likely to create one—to invent offices and/or install favored individuals in offices. The social and political implications are obvious: new organizational forms and powers were created that later became the subject of ethnic/nationalistic pride, nostalgia, or bitterness (and sometimes the subject of anthropological investigation under the false impression that they were features of traditional society), and, even more important, intragroup rivalries and competitions were initiated or exacerbated that resonate to this day.

Often, this imposition of foreign power had one or both of two other effects. One effect was the elevation of a particular group in the area or colony over others in terms of favor or success vis-à-vis the colonialists; for example, Sikhs in the Punjab were favored over other Indian groups by the British, Tutsis were preferred as leaders and officeholders by the Belgians in Rwanda and Burundi, and Tamils took better advantage of Western education and achieved disproportionate success in Sri Lanka. The results were again animosity and rivalry between these advantaged minorities and the other groups in the society. The other effect was the actual creation of a new advantaged class, an elite class availing itself of the opportunities that education, economy, and politics (e.g., the civil service) presented; interestingly, this elite class, which figures prominently in almost every instance of ethnicity, nationalism, and ethnic conflict—as the sort of "vanguard" movement of the group—often starts out as interethnic or "nonethnic," in the sense that it includes members of many or all ethnic groups and eschews an ethnic ideology in favor of a modernizing, often West-leaning, liberal, and nation-building philosophy. It is often this group that takes the reigns of power upon independence from colonialism as the best prepared to manage a modern Western-style democracy.

Yet, paradoxically, efforts toward some degree of democracy—either in the late stages of colonialism or with independence—have often if not usually has the effect of intensifying group competition and identification; under the practice of "communal representation," which was viewed in some colonies at some times as the best way to represent all the people and to balance the interests of the constituent groups, group differences were reified, institutionalized, and politicized in unprecedented ways to ensure groups a share of power *as groups.* Postindependence democracy continued the group rivalry but removed the foreign obstacles to competition and conflict; the potential for friction, even conflict and war, is immanent when numbers and population count toward power. Groups—ethnic, nationalist, class, caste, race, or what have you—are voting blocks or potential voting blocks, and mobilizing voters on the basis of ethnicity or identity, while natural in a certain sense, is also a powerful enticement to candidates and would-be leaders. Groups have even been inclined to dispute or falsify population figures or to block a census count (as in Lebanon) that might prejudice their numerical representation in the polity and therefore threaten to rearrange communal power relations.

One last area to discuss in regard to colonialism and ethnicity is cultural and economic "development." For instance, the introduction of European education had the effect of training a new set of indigenous elites, as mentioned earlier, often with an explosive mix of Western political ideology (democracy, self-determination, even communism, plus notions of race and society) and practical organizational/administrative skill as well as traditional cultural or ethnic identity. It is good to remember that this elite group's acquaintance with or allegiance to traditional society cannot be presumed, since they may have been more or less completely removed from it in their socialization. Even so, modernized elite leaders may recognize their common cause with, or turn to, traditional authorities, constituencies, or values in their political quest, as did Bandaranaike in Sri Lanka. Beyond the political domain economic factors—arguably the raison d'être of colonialism—cannot be ignored in the genesis and development of ethnicity and conflict. For example, colonial labor regularly brought members of differing groups into sustained contact. Colonial economies had an ambiguous effect on traditional elites and social orders, sometimes strengthening them, sometimes undermining or displacing them. It also created new niches in the economy, like the "middleman" role, in which one group often predominated over others in the provision of some service (throughout history Jewish and Chinese minorities have been especially common and successful "middleman minorities," often to the resentment of their local majorities) and new cleavages, like class stratification and rural/urban distinctions. The "proletarianization" of a large portion of the population is a critical effect, which brought to life an organized and interest-sharing group that was not necessarily bound to find succor in ethnic identities over "class" identities but often did so nevertheless (much to the consternation of Marxist analysts). And migration of labor (internal and intercolonial, voluntary or forced) shifted ethnic relations and even in many cases created ethnic relations, as in Malaysia, where Indian and Chinese groups arrived in numbers, and parts of East Africa like Uganda and Kenya, where certain groups had never been present before. In Sri Lanka the importation of Indian Tamils to the central highland plantations had both effects: it not only upset the balance between Sri Lankan Tamils and Sinhalese, but it created, because of the migrants' isolation from other Tamils on the island, a new third constituency integrated imperfectly at best with its cultural cousins.

Of course, European colonialism, or any colonialism, is not the only "foreign" contributor to ethnic group formation and ethnic conflict; Western states get more than their share of blame for all the world's troubles today. In recent world history Russian imperialism and Ottoman imperialism also played key roles in ethnogenesis and the instigation of ethnic conflict. Besides these important centers of cultural aggregation and contestation, other groups and conflicts have materialized or may yet materialize from other (say, Chinese) or more local (say, Thai or Burman) cultural domination. And, further back in time, Roman, Persian, Abassid, and other imperialisms, one could argue, gave rise to group consciousness or even nationalist movement—perhaps not identical to those of today but similar in ways—with consequences in their time and occasionally in our time as well; consider the group consciousness and historical "hermeneutics" of the Jews as a result of foreign (Babylonian, Persian, Roman) conquest and hegemony over two thousand years ago. It would not be too much of a stretch to regard the Zealots and Maccabees as nationalists.

A final area of the historical past of central significance to contemporary ethnicity and conflict is the recent political past, especially since World War I. In some ways this period is an extension and completion of the colonial period, and in some ways it is a profound break. The early twentieth century saw the collapse or dismemberment of several European empires, notably the Austrian and Ottoman, and the establishment of new states on the Wilsonian principle of "self-determination." This ideology was already current in the late nineteenth century and can be seen in action in nationalist struggles in the Balkans, in Eastern Europe, and elsewhere. The ideas was ostensibly something like *national* self-determination—that is, that groups that could prove their credentials as nations were entitled to states—but the states that were devised were in many cases not nation-states and often no less artificial than the states, imperial or otherwise, that they replaced (e.g., Yugoslavia or Czechoslovakia or the various states of the Middle East, including postwar Turkey). Notwithstanding the (not unreasonable) claims that, for example, Yugoslavs really were one people or nation or the efforts to create or instill a single national consciousness and to minimize or suppress particularistic identities, the failure of this new state and others like it in Europe and elsewhere bespeaks the fault in the original plan.

Further, where empire ended national self-determination did not always follow, especially outside Europe; the Sykes-Picot Agreement and the postwar fate of the Middle East is one glaring example. Like so many ideals, self-determination was applied selectively, especially against the enemies of its proponents, again the Austrians and the Ottoman Turks. There was never any serious suggestion, at least by the victorious European powers, that their own empires be dismantled in the name of national self-determination; there was arguably some rumbling to this effect from the new communist state, the USSR, and even some movement in that direction in the sense of letting subject nations secede from the union, but that practice was ended and reversed within a decade or two under Stalin. National self-determination was apparently not intended to apply, for instance, to Ireland as far as the British were concerned, let alone such regions as India and Africa. In fact, in many places new imperial territories were taken after the war (as in Rwanda and Burundi) or new client states were set up (as in Iraq and Syria). These states especially had more to do with the interests and global politics of Europeans than with the aspirations and identities of the local people. Kurdish claims to nationhood and to a state on that basis, for instance, while at first entertained, were ultimately dismissed on the basis of other factors, including the viability of the state of Iraq and the growing power and nationalism of Turkey.

Nevertheless, an ideal unleashed cannot be fully restrained, and the creed of self-determination could become a battlecry, first, to gain independence from empires (e.g., India and many African states) and, second, to secede or attempt to secede from the resultant states (e.g., Bangladesh, Biafra, Punjab, the West Bank, Croatia and Slovenia, Kurdistan, Chechnya, ad infinitum). And once these "new states" gained their independence their social and political policies often paved the way for further segmental or communal conflict—or even gave birth to previously—undifferentiated segments of ethnic groups. Questions of governance, of political representation, of cultural institutionalization, of economic development, of educational and occupational opportunity—questions that were either unaskable under colonialism or were summarily answered by colonialists—all of these aggravated group sensitivities and often mobilized groups to political consciousness and action. Even well-meaning attempts to redress group disadvantages through communal representation, confederation, or targeted development often only served to institutionalize group differences and create more grievances. Lebanon is an outstanding case of failed communalism, and a recent article in the popular press described how India's caste-oriented "affirmative action" programs are having negative social repercussions; there is undoubtedly some relevance in this experience for the American debate over group-based political programs. And it goes without saying that not all attempts to "level out" cultural differences were well meaning (e.g., Russification efforts in the Soviet Union, institutionalization of Sinhalese language and Buddhism in Sri Lanka, etc.).

In the final analysis one of the biggest problems in the application of the principle of self-determination is that, as I have argued, nations are not objective or absolute things. Which groups qualify as nations? And, even if they are nations, are they in a position to or are they prepared to take possession of a state? In Sri Lanka our first inclination is to conceive of two nations on the island, one Sinhalese, one Tamil. Yet things are not so simple. In an earlier period the Sinhalese group actually presented a case for the consideration of Sinhalese as two distinct, local "interest groups," or ethnic groups, each entitled to its own representation. At the same time, the Tamils are far from a unified nation, divided by regional and caste differences. The Kurds are another case in which nationhood is debatable. There are certain characteristics that Kurds share as a nation—or, better yet, that typify the Kurdish nation, since not all members possess them—but other aspects of culture divide them. Kurdish tribalism and provincialism, as well as religious schisms, have prevented the rise of a unified national consciousness and unified national action. Many other groups suffer from the same problem—a desire, perhaps even an objective quality, upon which to establish nationhood but not the necessary will or consciousness. On the other hand, once the genie of nationalism is released, there is no saying where it will stop. A group that found or thought itself a unified ethnic group or nation at one moment may suddenly find itself riven by sectarian or communal strife as subgroups attempt to apply the self-determination principle to themselves. The simplest example would be post-colonial India, which was immediately torn in two between Hindus and Muslims and continues to struggle with local particularism, especially in regards to the Sikhs and the people of the Punjab. In other words, a nation being a subjective and constructed thing, any number of interpretations and constructions are possible.

Thus, although the new states uniformly inherited cultural and ethnic problems from their colonial period, their own actions since then must be considered in a full account of contemporary ethnic conflict. The very decision to retain colonial boundaries was riddled with ethnic consequences. Attempts to establish official languages or religions, refusals to allow the fulfillment of self-determination in the form of ethnic/national separatism, ethnic-based political parties, discriminatory social and political practices, and often the outright use of force against groups by the new state (often dominated by one ethnic group) all revived or preserved old differences and animosities or created new ones.

Past as Myth

At any rate, a third sense in which history and the past are relevant to ethnicity and ethnic conflict is myth. Naturally, I mean this not in the sense of "lie" or even necessarily of "religious story" but in the anthropological sense of "remote and unprovable history" and "charter for the group's existence and culture in the present." Many of the definitions and characterizations of ethnic groups refer to common history or to common descent or kinship, *real or supposed,* and it is this supposed aspect to which I refer. Smith, for example, calls up the "myth of common ancestry" by which "members are thought, by themselves or others, to have a common origin." Gurr and Harff show that the myths of ethnicity may contain any number of kinds of stories: "of origin; of migration and liberation; of descent; of an heroic age; of communal decline, conquest, and exile; and of rebirth, with a summons to action" (1994, 12–13).

The interesting consequence of the past-as-myth aspect of ethnic history is that it is not particularly important whether or not the history (or the memory of history) is objectively true or correct so long as it functions "to maintain group cohesiveness, sustain and enhance identity, and to establish social networks and communicative patterns" (Patterson 1975, 305). This is the essence of mythology from an anthropological perspective—and a significant difference between this perspective and that of the discipline of history, as Eriksen eloquently notes:

> While many historians try to find out what *really* happened . . . most anthropologists would rather concentrate on showing the ways in which historical accounts are used as tools in the *contemporary* creation of identities and in politics. Anthropologists would stress that history is not a product of the past but a response to requirements of the present. (1993, 72)

Many books on specific ethnic groups or conflicts emphasize history and attempt or purport to give the true history of the situation as if an accurate, objective reporting of events gives us a complete understanding of those groups and conflicts. My position, however, in accordance with anthropology, is that objective history, if it is possible at all, is not as important as subjective history—subjective, that is, as remembered by the groups in conflict.

Myths, like other memories, are not in simple and immediate correspondence with the truth or the "facts." Rather, ethnic past-as-myth is a complex and empirically (i.e., case-by-case) specific amalgamation of *remembering, forgetting, interpreting,* and *inventing.* Some events must have transpired to provide the grist for the mythical mill, but not all parts of these events are necessarily preserved in present-day ethnic memory. Further, some events or aspects of events may be systematically denied or forgotten; for example, Serbs may remember that Bosnian Muslims were Christians in the past, before Ottoman conquest, but forget or deny that the Bosnians' conversion was real and serious; or Jews may remember that they had a homeland and state in Palestine twenty-five hundred years ago but forget or deny that they lost it subsequently and that the land has been occupied by other groups since then. Beyond this, whatever is remembered of the past is interpreted, infused with meaning, and this meaning may not have been part of the experience of events at the time of their occurrence. Such memory is usually, if not always, nostalgia in the purest sense, seen through the lens of "sentiment, retrospective regrets, and longings." This memory, or the meaning of the memory, may vary in the present in significant ways—*because of* the present and the interests, circumstances, feelings, and dreams of the present. For instance, different groups may interpret the same event in vastly different ways. Or, more important, a group may change its interpretation in the light of more recent or even contemporary developments and events, "finding" new injustices or calls to action in the past that were unnoticed or unemphasized before. Finally, groups may manufacture (out of the disparate pieces and scraps of history and culture or out of thin air) and disseminate a past that is partly or wholly fallacious but which is thereby no less powerful or effective.

Past as Resource

"The ethnic 'past' is always a subjective reconstruction" (Roosens 1989, 17). As such, it represents a very special anthropological class of the past, which has been called the "usable past," the "respectable past," or the "suitable past." What, then, is this past used or suited for? The answer is our fourth and final aspect of the ethnic past. As a resource, this past has two functions, one of which I have just discussed. The first function is to give individuals some cultural or historical symbols, or markers, to identify with and to rally around; this is the "charter" function, especially related to the mythical character of the past, which gives the group its very existence as a group. It is the function that says, "We/you are a group because of this event, or trait, etc."; it is the creative, ethnogenetic function. The second function provides the crucial link between past and present and *future*—that is, to give the group terms to *understand* the social present and to *make claims on it.* Ethnic groups find themselves, basically by definition, in culturally plural situations, and generally in culturally disadvantageous ones, often as minorities in a state not of their own, often as lower classes in a stratification system, often without a homeland or with a divided homeland. And, at least since the 1800s, one way to stake a claim or find a social voice has been by using culture and history, by invoking group or national uniqueness along with ideals such as social justice or self-determination.

This phenomenon within ethnicity has been acknowledged by most researchers, who point out the instrumental or interest aspect of ethnic groups. Ethnic groups use their culture and history (some one, some the other) as "instruments of struggle as well as communication," "to make demands in the political arena," "as a resource in political, economic, and cultural struggles," as "a useful weapon in peaceful settings"—and also not-so-peaceful settings. Ethnic groups, in this sense, "can thus be considered pressure groups with a noble face" (Roosens 1989, 14). The interests they aim to advance may include cultural recognition and respect; equality of opportunity in jobs, housing, law, and politics; land; local autonomy in institutions like education and cultural promotion; and, in some cases, political sovereignty (i.e., statehood). The pressure they bring to bear, and the "noble face" of that pressure, is their integrity as a group, their antiquity, their cultural uniqueness; it is increasingly difficult for a society that calls itself liberal and democratic (and even for many that do not, considering the international reaction) to impeach or resist this pressure. One has only to note the recent American reaction to the Russian intervention in Chechnya or our own American impassioned debate over multiculturalism and related issues (immigration, affirmative action, bilingual education) to see the efficacy of this creed of ethnicity.

Ethnicity, ethnic groups, and ethnic conflict, then, for all their reference to the past—historical and cultural—only make sense in the context of their contemporary circumstances, challenges, and interests. Groups "manipulate and even re-create or invent the old in order to attain the new" (Roosens 1989, 156), where culture or history offer some competitive advantage; hence, some groups that arguably could advance a claim of ethnicity fail to do so because there is no advantage to it. This also sheds light on the notion of nation building or nation awakening: groups with distinct cultures and histories may not be conscious of their ethnicity or nationality—and thus may not *exist as* ethnic groups or nations—until some external catalyst causes them to become conscious and to come into existence.

It would be a mistake to consider this process of ethnogenesis to be completely spontaneous or populist. Rather, numerous researchers and practical activists, at least since the time of Lenin, have stressed the role of leadership in group mobilization and the role of an elite. This elite (which for Lenin would be a class elite, but which can just as easily be an cultural elite) plays three critical parts in the institutionalization and mobilization of the group: (1) most obviously, it leads the group in actions premised on and in the interest of the group's culture, history, and identity; (2) more subtly, it acts as an agent of group consciousness, of group awakening, alerting the group to some (real or supposed) threat and diffusing or advocating a certain memory of culture, history, and circumstances; and (3) in the extreme it functions as interpreter, discoverer, or even inventor of the culture, history, or identity with which the group is to identify and in the interests of which it is to act. In any of these parts the elites are authors of the group's identity and actions.

Scholars of ethnicity and ethnic conflict have variously named and characterized these elites. Smith refers generally to "intelligentsia," which consists of such elements as the bourgeoisie, the lower aristocracy, and the workers. Kasfir (1979) uses the colorful term *local cultural enthusiasts and political entrepreneurs* to remind us not only that it often takes a team of energetic students of culture to collect and popularize the group's culture but that these parties are often not disinterested agents but have their own career/political agendas, including creating their own constituencies. Paul Brass (1985) describes several different types of elites, in various relations to one another, including religious elites, native aristocracies, and alien conquerors. These group leaders, or would-be leaders, are typically characterized by high levels of education and political consciousness, often urban backgrounds, and even a certain loss of contact with the very culture that they claim to represent. Alba, for one, analyzing white American ethnicity, finds that, contrary to the expectations of many theorists, education actually increases the likelihood of "identifying ethnically" and that ethnic identity is typically not a grassroots development but tends to be associated with "the cosmopolitanism that goes along with higher levels of education" (1990, 58). This is at once reasonable and ironic, for early practical nationalists like Herder and Mazzini also stressed the importance of education to achieve ethnic/national consciousness, yet the "cosmopolitan" ways that made their own awakening possible were among the very conditions they most vehemently rejected. Finally, as Sowell posits, cultural continuity for the elites personally may not only be unnecessary but may be a positive hindrance, for "those who have lost a culture have often been its most strident apostles. . . . Genuine continuity of cultural identity is seldom as strident or as dramatic as artificial revivals" (1994, 28–29). Pellizi (1988), too, notes the importance of distance, or "exile"—physically, historically, or personally—from culture or past in the creation of ethnic identities. No segment of an ethnic group tends to be more conscious of and vociferous about tradition, yet (almost by definition) more alienated from it, than the elites.

This raises a more general issue in regard to the impact of modernization and contemporary sociocultural circumstances on ethnicity and ethnic conflict. One of the major misconceptions that exists in regard to ethnicity is that it is some kind of "survival" from a more primitive and traditional cultural period. It is even often characterized as "primordial." Yet mounting evidence suggests that ethnicity, the groups it engenders, the conflicts it raises, even the cultures and histories upon it is founded, are not always or usually a mere continuation of the past. Ethnicity is, if not essentially then at least often, a product of modern and modernizing conditions. Bell (1975), for instance, cites a number of modern factors that exacerbate or create ethnicity and conflict, including the evolution of the postindustrial society, the decline of traditional authority systems (even if that tradition is fairly recent) like the state or religion, decolonization, the market economy, the politicization of society, and the attempt to impose more inclusive social identities on peoples (one aspect of the nation-building project). Glazer and Moynihan in the same volume mention social stratification, the rise of the welfare state, the ideological inconsistency between egalitarianism and differential achievement, social heterogeneity of states, and the new possibilities of international communication as contributing factors. Parsons, finally, emphasizes how immigration, assimilation, and pluralism in America have transformed the groups that we call ethnic groups; following David Schneider, he calls such groups "desocialized" and "primarily cultural-symbolic groups" rather than true societies or social groups. In sum, Bell writes, "Ethnicity is one response, in many instances of hitherto disadvantaged groups, to the breakup of order, and historically fused social and cultural, political and economic structures, and represents an effort by these groups to use a cultural mode for economic and political advancement" (1975, 172).

As such, the actions of the elites are consequential for the "collective becoming" of the group. As scholars, antiquarians, and cultural enthusiasts they study, collect, and organize for distribution the elements of culture and history that will become the basis of the group's identity and consciousness; as artists, journalists, and other purveyors of culture—including the clergy—they provide a network of communication and symbolization that can reach the unmobilized and "unawakened" masses and convert them into a self-conscious group. Both of these aspects were present in the brief description of Norwegian nationalism. Finally, as political activists or revolutionaries they can provide the organizational principle and the militancy that move the group to specific action—or lead a cadre of other elites who act in the interest of or in the name of the people (interest and name being not at all necessarily the same thing). The elites are thus instrumental in the *definition* of the group, its identity, its critical features, its boundaries, its direction and future. The elites—being educated, urban, sometimes wealthy, often respected or influential—have the resources to conduct research, to found cultural associations, to write books or circulate newspapers and pamphlets, to fill radio and television time, to organize demonstrations, or, more ominously, to acquire weapons and plan campaigns and assaults. These institutions and practices are what I would call the "circuitry," or "infrastructure," of ethnicity and nationalism; without them no such group can achieve or maintain cohesion and solidarity for long or mount a successful movement, peaceful or violent, in the group's cause.

An additional but underestimated issue in regard to the elites is the special interests of the elites themselves and the competition between elites. It is important to remember two facts about many ethnic (or any other kind of) groups: they do not exist as self-conscious actors until they are mobilized or awakened by leaders, and they ordinarily contain various subgroups (classes, regional groups, sects, kinship groups, etc.) with a range of opinions on any political, economic, or cultural topic. The most basic area of disagreement is often over exactly *who is a member* of the group, where the boundaries of the group should be drawn. The answer to this question depends on the definition of the group: which cultural or historical phenomena are held up as markers of the group and how those phenomena are given meaning. As an example, a debate within Sikhism concerns whether individuals who do not adopt the Khalsa discipline are really and fully Sikhs; in other words, should Sikhism have a "loose" or a "strict" construction? Fascinatingly, Hinduism can and sometimes does contest the claim that Sikhism is a separate identity at all; rather, Hindu polemicists can argue that Sikhism is a sect within Hinduism and therefore that Sikhs are Hindus. Similarly, some Turks maintain that Kurds are not a distinct ethnic group or nation but merely a local group of "mountain Turks," and Serbs and Croats sometimes claim that Bosnian Muslims are "nothing but" Islamicized Serbs or Croats. The claims to groupness, to being a real and distinct group at all, are entirely and often easily negotiable or defeasible.

At any rate, within the internally differentiated ethnic group, elites may exist or arise in and represent or draw support from one or more of the internal constituencies. For example, traditional religious elites may represent part of the group, aristocratic elites another part, and bourgeois or proletarian elites still other parts; elites of different local or kinship groups, as among the Kurds, may inspire and mobilize their traditional followers but not any other part of the nation. It is of critical importance to appreciate that what it perceived as, and what is perhaps being advanced as, the "will of the nation," may in fact be the will of a segment or faction of the nation or merely the will of the elite leadership. Further, each of these elites may have a different notion of what the group should be and what the group should do. They are rival elites, with perspectives and interests of their own—to see their own particular version of ethnic history, culture, or identity prevail and "to become the sole political representative of the community" (Brass 1985, 50). Each of the rival elites allegedly sees this as good for the group (giving it maximal cohesion and unity), but it is also good for the elites themselves (giving them maximal power and influence, if not wealth and prestige). Many people criticize ethnic leaders as sheer opportunists and demagogues, and doubtless there are some of these, both internationally and domestically. But it will do us no good to dismiss them on that basis if they are influential and important to all or some of the mobilized group.

The fact of elite rivalry is ignored only at our own intellectual and political peril. The danger is that most people, as scholars or citizens, may mistake ethnic groups for monolithic blocs with a single identity, agenda, and leadership. For instance, one would misunderstand and misjudge the situations in Sri Lanka or Northern Ireland or Israel/Palestine if one were to assume that the ethnic groups involved speak with one voice and act in one interest. Within the Tamil group of Sri Lanka there have been any number of leaders and organizations, often in contradiction or outright confrontation with one another. To use a more familiar and internationally destabilizing example, while we all know the Palestine Liberation Organization (PLO) and Yasir Arafat as representative and leader of the Palestinian people, it would be an error, as is becoming increasingly obvious, to believe that it and he speak for and control the entire group; rival groups, like Hamas and Hezbollah, with different interpretations and definitions of Palestinian nationality and destiny, compete openly and often violently with the "official" party of the group. It is unfortunate but true that it is simply wrongheaded to expect that any agreement with the PLO or the Tamil Tigers is going to bind the entire ethnic group or to hold these parties responsible for what other factions and cliques within the ethnic group do. Overestimating the power and authority of a prominent but by no means exclusive ethnic elite can lead to bad scholarship and bad policymaking, and to serious disappointments. The world is much more complicated than that.

Conclusion

Thus, it can be seen that in many ways an ethnic group is not entirely—maybe not even essentially—a backward-looking social collectivity. Neither is it necessarily an objective, organic, or unitary one. Rather, it is very much a product of the present. It is the product of the past only insofar as it is the *presence of the past* in and under the operation of circumstances new and unique to the present. It is individuals and groups in the present who are remembering and thinking about their culture and history; this memory, this thought, will naturally be filtered through the lenses of the present: present social experience, present opportunity, present discourse, present interest. Ethnic groups are not just interest groups, but on the political stage they are interest groups too or even primarily—groups pursuing an interest using culture or history as their claim and their weapon. Any thorough anthropological study of ethnic groups and ethnic conflicts must include historical and cultural accounts but must also "see through" them into the circumstances, ideologies, and interests that inform them.

Contemporary external social conditions are, of course, not a sufficient condition for ethnicity, ethnic group formation, or ethnic conflict; as I have hopefully demonstrated, no single empirical factor is a sufficient or necessary condition. No doubt many groups or protogroups or potential groups or nongroups could be found in similar circumstances without ethnic organization (but perhaps with some other type of social organization) or without any organization at all. Culture—that is, the list of cultural and historical traits of a group, or the list of traits that it remembers or emphasizes—also cannot be ignored but cannot be idolized; as I have said, any amount of cultural difference is enough to build an ethnic group on, but no amount is enough to ensure that an ethnic group is built on it. Ethnicity is, ultimately, a construction, like all other forms of social and cultural life; within the range of action that history and tradition provide, there is considerable room for human inventiveness and the play of the passions and desires of the present.

In the end a simple tallying of the cultural distinctions between groups or a faithful and objective recounting of their histories will not get us closer to their ethnicity. Nor will it get us to the heart of our main concern: the conflict between the groups. Rather, it is critical to understand how groups marshal, interpret, and use their cultures and histories—or their memories or perceptions of their cultures and histories—to define themselves and press their claims, in confrontational and eventually violent ways in the cases discussed in this book. Yet, when it comes to the ethnic conflicts, my position is that such groups are not fighting *about* culture—about which culture is right or about converting others to their culture—but fighting *with* culture. Culture, despite what the claimants say, is not what is really at stake; rather, culture, a justification or code for authentic and alternative groupness, is the basis of entitlement of the group to certain other stakes and rights, which will be specific to each instance.

Chapter 2

Anthropology, Ethnicity, and the Representation of Culture

The choice of a point of view is the initial act of any culture.
—José Ortega y Gassett

No concept as important or pervasive as "ethnicity" and its constellation of related terms (*ethnic, ethnic group, ethnic conflict*) appears suddenly out of nowhere. Scholars and citizens, long before anthropology itself was born, were aware of, writing about, and occasionally acting on the basis of critical social differences and corporate cultural identity phenomena. Often the language of this discussion and action was quite different from our contemporary analytical and descriptive vocabulary—for example, *ethnic* is a relatively recent word in its modern usage—but other words like *nation* and *race* have been in use for centuries, sometimes approximating the semantic range that *ethnic* occupies today; when the range was different, this revealed significant departures in the conceptualization of group processes, which we need to examine. In this chapter I will review the development of theories and interpretations of culture as related to ethnicity, focusing on the anthropological contributions. A number of central ideas and findings have come before or outside of anthropology, and anthropology's main preoccupation has traditionally not been with ethnic groups, but the relation between anthropology and ethnicity is an interesting and important one in several ways.

The discourse of ethnicity and much of ethnic conflict, the discourse of culture and "difference," is the discourse with which anthropology is most closely associated, and it is in some cases consciously drawn from anthropological description and theory. The study of ethnicity and the qualities of ethnic groups, and evolving sociopolitical conditions in which ethnicity and ethnic conflict operate, reflects back upon the concepts and theories of anthropology and have led to significant rethinking of the methods, terminology, and theories of the discipline, especially in regards to what exactly a society is, what its relation to culture is, and how we should present or represent it ethnographically.

Herder and European Romantic Nationalism

Before there were scholars of ethnicity or nationalism there were ethnic or national phenomena, or, better yet, practical ethnic or nationalist activists and organizers; then, as today, "the significance of the ethnic factor in many societies has been forced upon us more by events than by research" (Yinger 1994, 331). Probably every society in history has been aware of difference, even if it has not always been relativistic and tolerant of difference; terms like *heathen, barbarian, savage,* and *ethnic* in its original sense bear witness to that fact. One of the first and most influential scholar-activists of what we could call "ethnic consciousness" today, however, is the German nationalist philosopher Johann Herder (1744–1803).

Germany in the seventeenth and eighteenth centuries was, of course, more an idea than a fact, politically divided into an assortment of petty states with a weak overarching imperial system. It was also, like many other European societies of the time, under the sway of a cultural cosmopolitanism drawn in spirit and in substance largely from Enlightenment France. As in Russia under Peter the Great, for example, the courts of German states were heavily influenced by French culture in language, literature, art, dress, and manners; it has been said that Frederick the Great's court (r. 1740–86) was more French than German.

The masses of German people, villagers and peasants, were far removed from this cosmopolitanism and the lingering Latinism of European "high culture," toiling away relatively unselfconsciously in their provincial (in the best sense of the word, "local") German culture*s;* their horizon and their identity did not extend much beyond the village, as we find in many rural populations even today. They were, thereby, largely "unaware" of their shared "Germanness," even while they lived their culture daily. Already by the 1600s, however, there were voices of warning and rumblings of activity form learned Germans, expressing concern for German culture and rejecting foreign culture and language. To "awaken an interest in the German language, in German customs, and in German literature" patriotic societies like Fruchtbringende Gesellschaft were established in

1617, and a series of five hundred *Moralische Wochenschrifte* were published in the 1700s. Justus Moser (1720–94) criticized and ridiculed the adoption of French customs and invoked the memory of glorious German power and art. But it was Herder who gave systematic voice to many of these feelings and whose voice can be heard in so much of the later and present-day ethnic and nationalist discourse.

Herder believes that humanity as a species is on a mission of higher development and achievement but that the agent of this development is not the species as a whole nor the individual but an intermediate level, the group. In fact, the essential group is not just any type but a particular type, the *national group,* or *nationality.* This is because each national group, he argues, is an "organic unit," a "national organism" with its own unique and natural qualities and genius, its own special culture and language, its own national soul. Herder uses such terms as *Nationalgeist, Seele des Volks, Geist der Nation,* and *Geist des Volks* to capture this national peculiarity that is, to him, "inexpressible." Being that the "natural and the national were synonymous in Herder's mind" (Ergang 1931, 95), he perceives it as the ineffable yet rightful unit of mankind: "Every nationality is one people, having its own national culture as well as its language" (qtd. in Ergang 1931, 88).

In this view individuals are considerably less valuable, being basically instantiations of the national spirit, cells in the national body. Being a natural unit, "the group becomes a single being, an individuality, a personality," in which *culture* is the national personality, the group mind. The bearers of this culture and, even more so, the authors or creators of this culture, the "individual prophets, writers, artists or poets are but the means employed by the national soul to give expression to a national religion, a national language, or a national literature" (Ergang 1931, 87). Being natural and distinct, national culture and the nation should be cultivated, unfettered by artificial rules and undisturbed by other foreign influences; to do otherwise would be to upset nature's plan and to interfere with the natural processes of human development.

The influence of Herder on later German philosophers like Fichte and Hegel should be obvious. No less important is his influence on German culture and in fact, and in a way simultaneously, on German ethnology—that is, the ethnology of Germany—and indirectly on anthropology. To develop and cultivate a nation's culture the nation must know that culture accurately and authentically, and it is for this reason that Herder emphasizes the crucial role of research in areas of archaeology, anthropology, mythology, and philology. The implication here, however, is that the nation and its national culture are anything but organic and spontaneous, as they must be sought, assembled, protected, and advanced; those who would seem to possess national identity and national culture most completely, the peasants, are the least aware and concerned about it, and the rest (urban types, the bourgeoisie, the courts) do not "naturally" possess it in any serious way.

Socialism and Nationalism: Marx and Lenin

It needs no repeating that Marx and Lenin were not nationalists but *internationalists* and not particularly concerned with national distinctions but with class distinctions. Marx says as much at the outset of his "Manifesto of the Communist Party," originally published in 1848: "The history of all hitherto existing societies is the history of class struggles." While acknowledging national differences (although no anthropologist and without a rich and detailed knowledge of non-European societies), he sees these differences as diminished and diminishing, and he prefers it that way.

"The working men have no country," Marx asserts. By this statement he seems to mean two different things. First, capitalism and bourgeois society have already erased many of the distinctions between nations by creating a homogenized and abstract capitalist culture in which all capitalist nations partake and by reducing the folk of the various nations to the generic status of proletariat (the "working men"); workers in all capitalist nations have more in common *as workers,* he argues, than they have dividing them as members of disparate national cultures. "National differences and antagonisms between peoples are daily more and more vanishing" (1972, 350). Second, the working class is, in his view, already a nation in itself, an international/transborder nation of proletarians but one without a polity of their own—without any political system that *they* dominate and without (so far) the consciousness of their proletarian nationhood. In fact, Marx's desire is to bring them to consciousness, to cause them to rise up and demand recognition; to do so, to acquire "political supremacy," the working class "must constitute itself *the* nation" and discover that "it is . . . itself national"; then the "supremacy of the proletariat will cause [national differences and antagonisms] to vanish still faster" (350). It is in this sense that Communists, he maintains, want to "abolish countries and nationality."

Marx does not speak much about national or cultural issues, but an instructive view into his attitudes toward these issues is possible from a reading of "On the Jewish Question." In this essay he considers the Jewish demands for emancipation in contemporary Germany. But a Christian state, he posits, cannot emancipate the Jews, because the Christian, like the Jew, clings to a religious identity, which must put them in opposition. "How is an opposition resolved? By making it impossible. And how is *religious* opposition made impossible? By abolishing *religion*" (26). In other words, religious identity is "illusory" identity, religious nationality is "illusory" nationality, which gives groups the sense that they must and can separate. Marx proposes not a freedom *of* religion, however, but a freedom *from* religion, by which groups formerly differentiated and opposed by religion come to recognize their "actual nationality" and, more fundamentally, their shared humanness. Religions are "nothing more than *stages in the development of the human mind,*" and breaking through to this realization will expose the human life—the secular, *scientific* life—underneath. The freedom to be "Jew and citizen, Protestant and citizen, religious man and citizen" is, for Marx, *political emancipation,* which is important but incomplete: it is the "reduction" of man into an individual and at the same time an abstract moral participant in politics. The final complete emancipation comes when he becomes, in one of the early Marx's more frequent phrases, a species-being, recognizing his commonality with all humans and his individual powers as social powers.

This shows that Marx sees little value in cultural/national differences in general but, rather, views these particularisms as obfuscating of human unity and in fact often as actual ploys by the bourgeoisie to divide the working class against itself or to advance its (the bourgeoisie's) own interests. Certainly, his political activities and positions at the time indicated as much: he supported nationalist movements, as in Poland, Italy, Ireland, Germany, and Hungary, only insofar as they seemed to him revolutionary against feudalism or capitalism. But, when such movements seemed to serve ruling-class or bourgeois interests, he ignored or opposed them. The revolts of the Czechs and southern Slavs in 1848 he criticized as proving, by their failure, "that Bohemia cannot henceforth exist except as an integral part of Germany" (qtd. in Chambre 1963, 203).

As a Marxian activist, it was Lenin who actually brought Communist praxis to the world. He was, of course, an internationalist like Marx, not a nationalist like Herder, but both his praxis and the theory that underpins it have implications and historical consequences for ethnicity and ethnic conflict, as we are seeing in the world today. For our present purposes the most influential aspects of Lenin's work will be his notion of "revolutionary leaders," his theory of imperialism, and his thoughts on "rights to secession" of national minorities.

Like Marx, Lenin wanted and expected the workers to struggle with the bourgeoisie and the government and to win that struggle, bringing revolutionary socialism to some countries and eventually to the entire world. Unlike Marx, however, he did not expect this development to be a spontaneous movement of the masses, who had not the time, the perspective, or the organizational skill to accomplish it on their own. Rather, he saw the need for a "vanguard party," an organization of "professional revolutionaries"—what we might call an elite—with the requisite ability and theoretical orientation to manage such a movement. In fact, he specifically warns against the dangers of broad mass support of the movement, which makes it more vulnerable to "demagogues." Only the revolutionary elite have the consciousness to keep the revolution on track *for* the masses.

In his theory Lenin updates Marx by describing a late stage of capitalism that had developed only after Marx's time—that is, the stage of imperialism. Earlier capitalism, Lenin writes, was characterized by free capitalist competition, the export of goods, and the acquisition of colonies as "economic territory"; already by the turn of the century, however, he identifies a new phase of capitalism, characterized by monopoly, the export of capital, and the completion of the colonial partition of the world. The international (and revolutionary) consequences of this new stage are the inevitability of war as the only means to repartition colonial-capitalist holdings, all territory being already occupied, and the increasingly acute oppression that this more systematic world capitalism imposes on the occupied colonial peoples. Imperialism is, thus, the new and greatest enemy of the world's working and peasant classes (an extension of Marx's old proletariat concept) and is a fertile ground for Communist revolution.

Imperialism has ramifications, however, beyond the economic. Lenin suggests that it not only increases national oppression but also, as a result, national resistance. He draws a line between oppression and resistance through the "awakening of national consciousness" (1939, 121). In other words, because of imperialism and world capitalism, groups that may have lacked national consciousness—or may have lacked nationality at all—may be transformed into a self-conscious, modern, and organized group and movement; the clear implication is that national consciousness may be a product of modernizing and "capitalizing" processes. The farthest manifestation of this modernized national (we might say ethnic) consciousness and movement is the pursuit of the national state (we might say nation-state) "as a means to economic and cultural freedom" (1939, 12). As an aside, this quotation from Lenin marks the national state as the goal that once was the highest in Europe, suggesting that it no longer is; there is an irony that European-based world capitalism would inspire a desire in oppressed peoples for a social organization that has already been surpassed or abandoned by the Europeans themselves (in favor, no doubt, of an interlocking multinational cartel of finance capital). Lenin, finally, astutely observes that colonialism is not the only international relationship of subordination and dependence, recognizing those countries that are politically independent but still economically and hence diplomatically dependent, a frequent complain of more modern analyses of world capitalism and neocolonialism.

So the world workers' revolution comes; what should be the position of the new people's regime toward national self-determination, that mantra of the late nineteenth and early twentieth centuries? Lenin substitutes the term *national self-determination* with the *right of free secession,* which he grants to smaller nations of the Russian empire—necessarily, as a critic of the old czarist Russian system. He promises immediate recognition of Finland, the Ukraine, Armenia, "and any other nationality oppressed by tsarism" (1932, 94). National secession, however, is hardly his preferred outcome, as the subsequent actions of his own and Stalin's regimes clearly testify. Lenin seeks free unification, revolutionary-proletarian unity of the socialist state, former colonies, and other groups of like mind. He perceives the "abyss of bitterness and distrust" toward Great Russians on the part of the captive nations of the old empire and desires to overcome these negative feelings through real action. Still, world socialism calls for "the brotherhood of *workers* of all nationalities, and not the brotherhood of nations" (1932, 94), illustrating once again that for Marxists class interest and identity are believed and expected to outweigh other types of social identity and solidarity. The subsequent imposition of this ideology on the peoples of the Soviet Union fills most of the history of that state and is, of course, one of the outstanding aspects of many present-day ethnic struggles, such as those in Armenia and Azerbaijan, in Chechnya, and in the Baltic states, where the "breakup" of the Soviet Union arguably began.

The Foundations of a Social Science of Ethnicity: Early Ethnology, Boas, and Weber

At virtually the same moment that Marx was doing his major theoretical and practical work, the discipline of anthropology was being born—that is, at a time of nationalist movements, economic and cultural unrest, philosophical romanticism, and growing European imperialism. The impact of this context for anthropology's birth cannot and has not been ignored. First of all, the relationship between early anthropology and the German philosophers and ethnologists is a critical one for defining the concepts and the interests of the new field; German notions of *Kultur* and especially *Kulturkreis* are central in importance. *Kultur,* as *Culture* with a capital *C,* is seen as one great world phenomenon, unfolding, developing, progressing in Hegelian fashion; in this way all of the particular cultures of the world can be placed on the continuum of "Culture." Hence, one of the prime concerns of early ethnologists (not just in Germany but in England and the United States as well) was to discover the "first" or most primitive forms of culture and the subsequent order of "stages" of culture; all of the ancestors of anthropology, from Bachofen and Bastian to Tylor and McLennan, and many of their contemporary social scientists, like Durkheim, can be seen as participants in this investigation. The belief that there was such a thing as "primitive society" and that it was discoverable through this new scientific approach was a first principle in their work.

The idea of *Kulturkreis,* or "culture circle," is equally significant. The German ethnologist Graebner and others interested in cultural history and evolution used this term to refer to clusters of cultural traits that existed at various places at various times. The original culture circles were the goal of such study, and all of the world's cultures were to be classified in terms of their relation—their proximity or distance, geographically, temporally, and culturally—to the fundamental circles. The distribution of cultural traits thus became a central preoccupation of ethnology, along with the history of their diffusion. E. B. Tylor himself suggests that the geographical distribution and the diffusion of cultural traits must be studied in the same manner in which the botanist and the zoologist study plant and animal species and their diffusion. It might even be argued that ethnology began as a kind of naturalist science, each culture or society viewed as a "species" distinguishable by a list of characteristics.

Two other elements play a major role in the definition of the scope and methods of anthropology in regard to the concepts of culture and social organization. One of these is the "legalistic" roots of early anthropological inquiry; as Kuper (1988) has shown, many of the mid-nineteenth-century ethnologists were lawyers by profession, so that their questions were basically legal questions (e.g., what were primitive property rights? what were primitive family institutions, and how did they relate to political organization?), and their methods were basically legal methods (essentially the case study method). The second of these elements is the "museum" tradition, which saw culture as a constellation of traits and artifacts (a trait inventory) and society as a territorial/spatial intersection of groups and traits.

The birth of anthropology as we know it awaited a final factor—the experience of real live "primitive" peoples, or "fieldwork." This experience became available through, primarily, British colonialism and American contact with its indigenous people. In a way, then, Franz Boas, perhaps the first professional modern anthropologist, is a personification of the emergence of the discipline: a German, originally a natural scientist, conducting fieldwork in North America, he both followed previous intellectual trends and set new ones. Furthermore, especially for our purposes, he saw anthropology as a vital contributor to, and himself wrote about, important issues of the day such as racism and nationalism.

As Boas reminds us, anthropology is always concerned with the group more than the individual, who always "develops and acts as a member of a racial or a social group" (1928, 23). The mention of race and social group in the same sentence is interesting and problematic, but Boas is at least somewhat aware of this fact. He successfully and repeatedly deconstructs race as a concept. He debunks race by arguing that (1) a race is not an objective or demonstrable descent group; (2) there is as much physical variation within a race as between races; (3) there are no "clear-cut geographical and biological lines between the races" (29); and (4) there is no correlation between race on the one hand and either mental or cultural characteristics on the other. This is a valuable lesson that has yet to be learned by all citizens and certainly by all ethnic members and activists.

Boas, however, is somewhat less circumspect in his analysis of social groups, though he does at times anticipate later refinements of anthropological thought. Boas uses terms like *primitive society* and *tribe* fairly freely and asserts that every tribe is a closed society while it is in "continuous strife" from natural conditions and social dangers. Even so, at the same time, in a not altogether intellectually compatible way, he recognizes that primitive societies are not actually socially and culturally isolated, that even "the simplest groups" have been affected and changed by contact with one another. Every culture, then, is, in his view, constructed as much by external factors and influences as by internal ones. He also understands that, while social and racial phenomena are two discrete levels of reality and analysis, the two may overlap—"social divisions [may] follow racial lines" (74)—and, when they do, the racial differences may be important for creating, preserving, and exacerbating social differences and intergroup conflict.

Boas also writes about nationalism in an instructive way, although his use of language is not the same as current usage and his ideas are flawed in some places. For example, he distinguishes between *nation* and *nationality,* using *nation* basically the way we would use *state* today and *nationality* basically as we would use *nation;* a nationality for him is "a group of people alike in speech, culture, and in most cases representing no fundamental racial contrasts" (78). Yet, although nationalities are usually racially homogeneous, he grants "only the slightest relation" between nationality and race; in fact, he finds most racial antipathies "fictitious" and actually derived from other sources than race, and in the final analysis he finds both terms "vague." Nor is there any necessary equation between nations and nationalities. A nationality may inhabit two or more nations (he gives Italy before unification as an example), or two or more nationalities may inhabit the same nation (he gives Czechoslovakia and Poland as examples).

What exactly constitutes a nation, then? This is problematic: objective characteristics like descent or unity of language are not sufficient to make a solidary, identity-sharing group. Instead, it is something more subjective, more psychological or emotional—"the community of emotional life that arises from our everyday habits, . . . thoughts, feelings, and actions" (89). Where that community feeling is lacking, even individuals who share descent and language may not share identity and may actually be in conflict. But where nation boundaries and nationality boundaries are not coterminous, social frictions may arise, eventually taking the form of nationalist movements. Boas distinguishes, interestingly, between two kinds of nationalism: the nationalism of nations and the nationalism of nationalities. Predictably, the nationalism of nations (what we might call "patriotism" today) attempts to unify the people of the nation regardless of the differences of constituent nationalities; it is integrative at the "state" or civil level. The nationalism of nationalities strives to unify the people of the nationality regardless of nation (political) boundaries and is, therefore, disintegrative of actually existing political organization and either separatist or "alternatively integrative" in the sense of positing a new political organization. Boas essentially applauds the efforts of nations and nationalities to integrate at a more appropriate and, in the end, higher level, expressing "full sympathy" with their desire to dismantle "the artificial barriers of small political units" (91). He does not, however, approve of nationalism in the sense of separatism and particularism, that is, of creating smaller and less-inclusive social groupings. Here he belies a prejudice and an expectation that many do not share and which history (so far) has not supported. For him inclusiveness, ever higher levels of social integration, ultimately a "federation of nations," is not only desirable but inevitable. He sees such an inexorable march toward integration in history (notwithstanding moments of revolution and devolution) that he is absolutely confident that this direction "will govern our history in the future" until its ultimate "consummation" (98).

Regardless of Boas's rather dubious claims about the future of groups and states, we can see that he is early and immediately concerned with what we would call ethnic matters, especially the problematic relationship between descent, culture, and group identity. At roughly the same time another founding figure of social science, Max Weber, also spoke of ethnic groups, nations, and nationalism in modern terms; chapter 5 of *Economy and Society* is in fact entitled "Ethnic Groups." Interestingly, Weber begins where Boas begins, with a discussion of race, and he concurs with Boas that race identity and race animosity are not entirely "natural" phenomena. Race (defined as "common inherited and inheritable traits that actually derive from common descent") does not give rise to an identity or a group until it is recognized *subjectively* as common and salient and until it is employed as "the basis of joint (mostly political) action" (1968, 385). Yet actual descent relations are neither a necessary nor a sufficient condition for identity and group formation; he retells the familiar example that persons of mixed black and white ancestry, although the white component may predominate phenotypically, may still be classified, may still identify, and may still behave and associate as black.

From this understanding of descent Weber goes on to offer his famous definition of ethnic groups, quoted earlier. Most important, he stresses that ethnic groups are founded upon a subjective feeling, whether or not any objective kinship relationship exists. And, if we turn to the "custom" or cultural aspect of ethnic groups, things are no less problematic. In actuality group/identity differences are not linked in any regular way to major cultural differences: “Any cultural trait, no matter how superficial, can serve as a starting point” for the formation and closure of groups and group boundaries, even if many other cultural traits are held in common (388). He even lists a few trivial characteristics such as hairstyle, clothes, and food that can mark groups and their members as different. His point is that the nature or degree of objective difference is not as significant as the emotional salience and extent of group consciousness engendered.

This complex relationship between culture and group has several implications. First, a sharp distinction between groups is not necessarily a result of sharp cultural differences; group boundaries may grow from relatively small differences while substantial similarities also exist. Conversely, differences may and to an extent must be ignored within a group, disguising the fact that there is cultural variation within ethnic groups; even differences in language and religion do not necessarily disqualify a collectivity of individuals from experiencing common ethnicity. Second, because of this malleable connection, ethnicity—a sense of likeness and familial association—may survive long after the demise of the initial cultural differences, or even of the original group itself, which undergirded the ethnic identity in the first place. Such may be the case for peoples who migrate or emigrate and return to their group after separation from the home population or even after the disappearance of the home population. This phenomenon also suggests an explanation for why ethnic identity may persist well past the point of substantial assimilation of a group into the culture of some other group. Third, and perhaps most consequentially, the cultural differences upon which ethnic groups are based are often themselves a product, Weber argues, of “the diverse economic and political conditions of various social groups” (392). In other words, he suggests that ethnicity is not always a cause of social differences but also on occasion an effect of such differences.

All in all, it is not surprising that Weber finds it difficult to specify the ingredients and results of ethnicity. He notes, as we have seen, the diversity of social phenomena that fall under the rubric *ethnic* and the ambiguity of our terms and concepts for describing these phenomena, such as *society, tribe,* and *people.* One term, however, that draws his attention, as it did Boas's, is *nation.* For Weber this term has three particular connotations: symbolic/emotive, subjective, and political. He states plainly that the nation is not an economic unit as such and that its identity is not a “practical" or economic one; rather, it is based on "sentiments of prestige" attaching to a group and its history and/or culture. It belongs "in the sphere of values." Like his conception of *ethnic group,* however, his nation is not a simple objective artifact of cultural differences. In fact, a nation cannot be identified or comprehended simply as a set of empirical cultural traits. Surely, he allows, language and religion—and, for that matter, biological descent—are important to nations. But a nation is not the same as a language community; there are distinct and divisive nations that speak the same language, like the Ulster Protestants and Catholics or (generally speaking) the Serbs and the Croats, while there are nations that speak more than one language. Even descent is not an automatic condition of shared or distinguished nationality: again, Serbs and Croats, or Great Russians and Ukrainians, or many others, are closely related yet nationally distinct.

So far this analysis may resemble his discussion of ethnic groups, but there is one critical difference: the "specific objective of its social action," which is to produce or procure for itself a state (395). A nation is a group that sees itself as entitled to rule itself; it is an essentially political phenomenon. Therefore, not all ethnic groups are nations, not all ethnicity is nationalism, and not all nations or nationalisms are ethnic (think, e.g., of "Islamic nationalism" or "pan-Arabism"). He records a spectrum of national consciousness and mobilization ranging "from emphatic affirmation to emphatic negation" and even "nationally 'unawakened' peoples" who are unaware of or indifferent to their shared distinctions as compared with other groups. National identity is thus a fluid and emergent phenomenon; groups that were unaware may become aware, and collectivities and categories that were not groups may become groups. He even goes so far as to mention some specific processes by which national identity may emerge and solidify; the role of "intellectuals" and of techniques of cultural production and dissemination such as books, journals, and newspapers is highlighted, as will be evidenced in the chapters to follow. Finally, Weber concludes that, like its cousin the ethnic group, the nation is in fact not a single phenomenon but a set of diverse phenomena known by a single name. In any given nation economics, social stratification, history, religion, language, and even race may play a part in the organization of identity, in various combinations and strengths. The one thing that all nations have in common is a political will, the will to a political community and political institutions that preserve and advance the community and its identifying characteristics.

Anthropology on Diversity, Change, and Conflict: Malinowski, Evans-Pritchard, and Gluckman

"While social anthropologists consider that their subject embraces all human cultures and societies, including our own, they have . . . for the most part given their attention to those of primitive peoples" (Evans-Pritchard 1951, 4). Methodologically and conceptually, the field has been associated with an attitude that treats these objects of study as fundamentally different from our own or from "modern societies" in general, as static, isolated, clearly bounded, and traditional; additionally, the criticism has been advanced that it ignored the political context and conditions within which, and often for which, it conducted its work. It was considered by early professional anthropologists "to be an advantage to able to study those societies which are structurally so simple, and culturally so homogeneous, that they can be directly observed as wholes, before attempting to study complex civilized societies where this is not possible" (8–9). Thus, a fallacy of pure, objective, disinterested science discrete, simple, homogeneous whole societies was promoted.

Both of these positions are simplistic, however, and overlook anthropologists' own awareness of the subtlety and complexity of cultural phenomena and of the political settings within which they operate. Even "functionalists" like Malinowski readily admitted the realities of cultural diversity, change, and contact; in a way they were bound to make such admissions based on their ahistorical perspective, which de-emphasized the past and tradition, at least the kind of speculative history and traditionalism often practiced before their time. As Malinowski himself writes, the anthropologist as a scientist "has to study what is, and not what might have been" (1961, 3). What is, he asserts, is not the "'uncontaminated' Native" nor the "well-defined, circumscribed entity" called "a society" or "a culture" of anthropological (and popular) imagination but a tumultuous social landscape in which each member and each society is part of a large, interconnected, constantly changing whole that includes not only neighboring "natives" but Western societies and their agents and institutions as well. Therefore, even fifty years ago or more he could maintain that "the scientific anthropologist must be the anthropologist of the changing Native. Why? Because what exists nowadays is not a primitive culture in isolation but one in contact and process of change" (6).

Various kinds of cultural change were of interest to Malinowski, but the one that concerns us here is nationalism, which he refers to as one of the "new and unexpected forces and factors" on the contemporary cultural scene. But two opinions are manifest in his investigation of non-Western (largely African) nationalism: that this nationalism is not a purely "native phenomenon" and that it is not a purely traditional phenomenon. First, Malinowski perceives the role of Western culture, particularly but not exclusively in the form of colonialism and colonial administration, in the evolution or development of native nationalism. In cultural change, whether nationalism or some other type, there are generally "two cultures to deal with instead of one," and the second (Western) culture is experienced through forces such as the politics of administration, the "modernization" or "capitalization" of the economy and the introduction of wage labor, and missionization and religious conversion. New cultural changes and movements are a product of both cultural sources, but they are not a simple combination of the two old sources; rather, they are "entirely new products" born of the impact and hybridization of the two cultures, and the resultant phenomena have "no antecedents in Europe or in African tribalism." The nature, quality, and direction of a development such as native nationalism "is determined by factors and circumstances which cannot be assessed by the study of either culture alone. . . . The clash and interplay of the two cultures produce new things" (25).

Thus, nationalism, or we might add ethnicity, is certainly not a simple continuation of traditional culture into the modern political world. It is, rather, an emergent and original social phenomenon in itself. Even if it takes the form of revivalism or irredentism or millenialism or what have you—even if it refers to or invokes tradition or culture or history—it is not tradition but some new treatment of and perspective on tradition. Such nationalism or ethnicity is precisely "retrospective" in the sense that it is *not* tradition but a memory of or a look behind at a culture and custom that once was—or maybe never was. The former tribalism and the contemporary nationalism are anything but identical for Malinowski: tribalism is unselfconscious, while the new nationalism is sophisticated and self-conscious, reaching for "elements of the old culture . . . with a secondary, almost ethnographic interest in racial history, customary law, and the artistic and intellectual achievements of their race" (158). The old tribalism, according to Malinowski fifty years ago, is already dead, and what is afoot at present is not a memory but an invention.

Accordingly, the objective establishment by anthropological means of the "true culture" or the "true past" of a society, a kind of salvage anthropology, is in the end less important, not only in itself but for understanding contemporary activities, than the study of what is going on presently and how that culture and past is being employed and deployed in the present. In true functionalist fashion he argues that what anthropologists are often eager to collect (i.e., what the "old men of the tribe" have to tell us about the past, the "authentic" culture, etc.) is less than useless as science, as a scientific investigation of the past, since it is memory, "affected by sentiment, by retrospective regrets, and longings," or what Crapanzano calls "desire." Yet in a particularly insightful moment Malinowski suggests that this is not only all right but important—important for understanding not the past but the *present*—since, for the modern anthropologist studying cultural change, "what really matters is not the objectively true past, scientifically reconstructed and all-important to the antiquarian, but the psychological reality of today" (29). Therefore, he allows us to see that native nationalism, even in its early manifestations, is not "traditional culture at work" but "traditional culture remembered" and that the "retrospective vision" upon which it is based is subjective and, ultimately, creative.

Fortes and Evans-Pritchard, almost simultaneously, provide an analysis of traditional African societies, with politics specifically in mind but reverberating throughout the cultures. They find, for example, that supposedly homogeneous African societies actually exhibit a striking amount of heterogeneity; in the introduction they state that groups such as the Zulu, Ngwato, Bemba, Banyankole, and Kede "appear to be an amalgam of different peoples, each aware of its unique origin and history, and all except the Zulu and Bamba are still to-day [*sic*] culturally heterogeneous" (1940, 9). The contributions that make up the book support this general contention, adding that the groups themselves and the territories they occupy are often fairly recent developments. The Zulu, for one, were only constituted as a nation when the defeated peoples of the great leader Shaka were organized into a single political-cultural complex; within the nation "old tribal loyalties and oppositions are still at work and faction fights frequently occur" (Gluckman 1940, 51). Schapera describes how the Ngwato "tribe" is a congeries of people, with about 20 percent actually belonging to the "nuclear community" of Ngwato (and even they were aggregated only in the eighteenth century after a schism from the Kwena group) and the rest coming from diverse populations "who became subject to the Ngwato chiefs at various times through conquest in war, voluntary submission, flight from an invading enemy, or secession from some other tribe" (1940, 57). Richards reports that many of the traditional societies of

Africa have occupied their territory for less than two hundred years and many for as little as fifty to one hundred years.

Finally, Gluckman (1956) argues that not only is diversity within traditional societies ordinary and tolerable but that conflict is also ordinary and may even be integrative. Societies, even small traditional societies, are "always elaborately divided . . . by customary allegiances" that cross-cut and sometimes contradict and come into conflict with one another. The central point of his book is to show "how men quarrel in terms of certain of their customary allegiances, but are restrained from violence through other conflicting allegiances which are also enjoined on them by custom" (1956, 2). Thus, it becomes possible to think of internally diverse and segmented, while still integrated, societies; at the same time, it becomes clear that societies may not be as integrated as ethnic or national ideology and action stipulate or require. As we will see, the Kurds in particular are as plagued by their traditional culture and organization as they are served by it when it comes to national identity and mobilization, and even in more successful instances of "ethnic integration" traditional distinctions and rivalries within the group persist and often lead to important ideological or behavioral differences. Finally, the crucial lesson for us in regard to modern ethnicity and ethnic conflict is lying in Gluckman's analysis of the cross-cutting allegiances that "tend to inhibit the development of open quarreling and worse": in the totalizing, and thus totally segregating, ideology that is contemporary ethnicity, some or all of these cross-cutting and therefore unifying institutions or customs are lost or denied. The totalization of culture and of the claims based on culture let slip the restraints that bind groups in civil, if hostile, relations and create conditions for uninhibited and total confrontation and conflict.

Seminal Field Studies for Ethnicity: Furnivall and Leach

The great early ethnographers—Malinowski, Evans-Pritchard, Mead, and others—tended to give us images of discrete peoples living in traditional cultures in general isolation from other groups and from outside influences, especially Western influence (even when, as we have seen, their own commentary contradicted this image). Colonialism, certainly, made much of this anthropological investigation possible and important, and anthropology has an undeniable debt to colonialism for defining some of the interests, problems, and methods it came to depend upon. In fact, many anthropologists were in direct or indirect service of colonial administrations, and often colonialism and the changes it wreaks on traditional societies appeared at the forefront of the literature.

One of the more interesting and significant such works is Furnivall's *Colonial Policy and Practice* (1956), which is noteworthy for its acknowledgment of the inextricable link between traditional-societies-as-found and colonial and other outside factors and for the elaboration of the concept of "plural society." The book is a study of colonial Burma and Netherlands India (or Java) and was written deliberately and self-consciously as a guide to colonial administration, comparing the virtues of the two colonial systems; this fact is itself rather unique. Apart from the extensive discussions of economic performance and administrative history, the book offers two consequential insights: that the societies are heterogeneous and that nationalism in the two societies is a result of colonialism.

Colonial Burma, for example, is not one society but many; Burmese (or Burmans, as a national or ethnic category) are one of numerous peoples (which he calls "races") in the territory including Shan, Mon, Karen, Kachin, etc. And this diversity refers only to the indigenous population. "Burmese society" as a modern social system also contains other important groups, the exclusion of which from analysis would illicitly simplify or even falsify the picture; these other groups include Indians, Chinese, and of course Europeans. Rangoon, he notes, in the early twentieth century was second only to New York City as a site of arrival of immigrant workers. Not only was this society heterogeneous, but it was also "enclaved," with Indians, Chinese, Europeans, and "Burmese" all filling different niches in the social system (with the Chinese and Indians monopolizing the "middleman" positions of finance and trade between Europeans and the general population). These groups formed what we would only call today ethnic groups and differed considerably in their interests; these differences resulted in communal violence in 1924 and 1931. Not inconsequentially, Furnivall argues that, as fellow foreigners and profiteers, Europeans and their interests are more "at one" with the Chinese and Indians, from the wealthiest middlemen down to the poorest coolie, than with the "indigenous" people.

He makes similar observations in regard to Netherlands India and provides a plethora of details that need not concern us now. Two other elements in his book, however, deserve our attention. One is nationalism and its evolution in the colonial setting. In Burma he sees this at its earliest with religion, on the part of Buddhist monks who organized religious revivalist movements and institutions such as the Young Men's Buddhist Association (something we will see again in my discussion of Sri Lanka); nationalism at this stage took the form of interest in the culture and past of Burma—or *one* of the cultures and pasts of Burma, as it was and remains a multicultural society; this fact must not be overlooked when we consider the invocation or construction of a nation's culture. By 1921, however, he reports that nationalism had passed from religious to political expression, and the new General Council of Buddhist Associations set its goal as home rule or even complete separation from England; one advantage of the new articulation of nationalism was a welcome to the non-Buddhist segments of the population. Still, it was hampered by a set of factors, not the least of which was the very heterogeneity of the polity. The divergent interests of the constituent communities, coupled with the low mobilization of the masses, made concerted action difficult. There was, in effect, no "Burmese nation" from which a movement could arise and for which it could speak. The consequences of impending self-government are profound as well. In a first step a Burma Government was established under the British Parliament in 1937 but showed a number of weaknesses. For one, the legislature had authority only over Burmese people and not other areas traditionally and administratively associated with Burma, such Karenni, the Kachin Hills, or the Shan states. For another, the legislative seats were allotted on two different principles, territory and community; just under a third (40 out of 132) of the seats in the House of Representatives were reserved for communal or other special interests, 37 of those 40 for Karens, Indians, Chinese, and naturally Europeans. Thus, in an odd yet predictable way representative government actually did not help integrate the society but, rather, set the stage for the activation, aggravation, and escalation of "sectional friction" (487). Placing groups in a position to compete for political power *as groups,* and in a position in which some groups are guaranteed minorities and no group has a secure majority—or, more generally, where *numbers* matter—threatened to elevate cultural and economic differences into political and nationalistic ones, with the outcome for the world that we are currently witnessing.

The other element in Furnivall's analysis, and by far the more enduring one, is his concept of the plural society. This term has become a fixture in the discourse on ethnicity and nationalism, often as a positive value and typically as a descriptive term, but in fact it is not routinely used with quite the meaning that he attaches to it. *Plural society* for Furnivall has two domains of meaning, political and economic. Politically, a plural society "comprises separate racial sections" (or, again, we might prefer *ethnic* over *racial,* although in the case of Burma the differences are more than just cultural); there is a mix of different groups, each with its own culture, language, religion, etc., but more crucial than their copresence is their social segregation: "they mix but do not combine" (304). They live side by side as citizens of the same polity but do not form a society in any significant way; they constitute a sort of caste system without the religious integration of the real thing. This is why he rejects the characterization of the United States and Canada as plural societies: they have "plural features" (i.e., a diversity of cultures and races sharing political and economic space), but they also have at least some measure or ideology of integration and equality.

Politically, a plural society is also characterized by the atomization and incompleteness of social life. The sections of society—e.g. Indian, Chinese, European, Burmese—are not real groups but mere "aggregates of individuals," pursuing individual interests rather than communal ones. Each section, he writes, "is a crowd and not a community" (307). Part of this feature is based on the transience of membership in the group: Europeans were usually temporary residents in the society, and even the non-European immigrant laborers often kept some intention of returning home and often did so. Besides this individualism, a general cultural impoverishment was entailed for the native population. Traditional values, structures, and relations (including religious, village, and kinship relations) suffered or collapsed, often leaving little in their place except foreign alternatives or sheer economic relations. In such a society, he asserts, "men are decivilized" (310).

Here, then, is Furnivall's second domain of meaning for the term *plural society.* It is ultimately a purely economic arrangement. In what he calls "the process of the survival of the cheapest," economic forces function "to eliminate all non-economic values," leaving only economic interests and relations with no other common social interests or causes (299). There is, therefore, no social standard that can curb the pursuit of profit and no social bond that links individuals, whether from different groups or the same group, other than the utilitarian bond of efficiency and productivity. This, of course, accounts largely for the political characteristics of plural societies: *Homo economicus,* unfettered by a shared culture or identity, chases private profit, disintegrating community (if it ever existed) and eroding values. This may seem a strong statement, but it is Furnivall's essential position.

An even more important early ethnography for the purpose of elucidating ethnicity and the relation between ethnic groups and culture also took its field in Burma, although it was not explicitly a study of ethnicity at all; in fact, although the term *ethnic* appears in the book, it is not a prominent feature of the argument. The book, rather, has certain anthropological goals and is the first serious and successful challenge to the standard approach of anthropology toward "society" and "social boundaries" up to that time. The book to which I refer is, of course, Leach's *Political Systems of Highland Burma* (1954). Encountering an extremely diverse and tangled cultural situation in the area of fieldwork, the Kachin Hills Area, he finds that it is impossible to maintain simple and consistent distinctions or boundaries between the "social groups."

The two main social categories in the region are Shan and Kachin. Shan are Buddhist, wet rice cultivators, and organized into hierarchical "castes" with a hereditary nobility. Kachin, on the other hand, are an assortment of "hill peoples" with significant differences in language, territory, and politics from one another. Here begins Leach's problem, however. First, there is no systematic relation between the linguistic, the territorial, and the political aspects of Kachin groups; it is difficult to determine where one group ends and the next begins or even whether they are "different groups" at all. Second, transfer of population, individually and collectively, is possible between Kachin and Shan categories; Shan society has been assimilating Kachins for at least a century (and probably much longer), such that "nearly all low class Shans are probably either of slave or commoner Kachin origin" (222). And the overall oscillation between *gumsa* and *gumlao* political structure that he finds within Kachin societies is also a result of association with and imitation of Shan politics: Kachin (*gumsa*) chiefs take Shan princes as their role models and attempt to emulate their powers and prerogatives.

From these observations Leach asks the question that naturally occurs to us today but which he was perhaps the first to perceive: When can we say that two groups are "two different societies" or merely "two segments of the same society"? The failure to tackle or even recognize this problem anthropologically up to this point, he argues, is in the very anthropological concepts of "society" and "culture"; in such complex and enmeshed social contexts as highlands Burma, "ordinary ethnographic conventions . . . are hopelessly inappropriate" (281). In fact, he maintains that the differentiation of Shan and Kachin as distinct societies was an invention of British colonial administration in Burma, which imported Western notions of discrete social units and even more so of race. The entire population was classified, for administrative purposes, by race—race, he finds, "being a synonym for language. . . . The Kachins were deemed to be a 'race,' therefore they must possess a special language" (43). Further, the British tried to draw clear territorial boundaries between the Shan and Kachin societies. Where language/dialect and territory coincided, especially if some order of kinship relation could be established for the "enclosed" group, a tribe was inferred.

Leach's answer to this situation is to reconceive the units of analysis in anthropology and the reasons for cultural variation. Tribe is, at least in many cases, an "academic fiction": "the ethnographer has often only managed to discern the existence of 'a tribe' because he took it as axiomatic that this kind of cultural entity must exist" (291). Rather, he suggests a unit of analysis appropriate to the ethnographic context, which in the present case would be the entire Kachin Hills Area, with its many cultures, languages, and named collectivities; such collectivities would not be considered "social isolates" but as elements in a larger and more inclusive social system. Second, the collectivities that compose the system, and indeed the system itself, should be seen to have *no* stability through time: individuals flow from one political system to another, entire villages or groups undergo structural transformation from one political system to another (his famous *gumsa-gumlao* discussion), and the very form of the overarching system may change as time proceeds. The traditional anthropological notion of equilibrium in society is rejected by Leach.

Finally, he proposes an interpretation for the system of variability exposed in this case. Cultural differences (and he refers especially to language differences) are a ritual system, and using a particular language or presenting a particular cultural characteristic is a ritual act, that is, a communicative act. Why should populations of similar culture maintain differences in language? His answer is that language, as a ritual/communicative act, expresses something about the social relationship between the speakers or language communities: to speak the same language is to express social solidarity, and to speak separate languages is to express social distance or even animosity. In other words, language and other cultural differences are perpetuated and employed to promote collective identity and prestige and to differentiate between collectivities. Here he refers to one of the thornier problems in anthropology—varying versions of the same story, myth, or other cultural account offered by various members of society. Leach, in this new interpretation, sees no contradiction or "informant error" in the differing versions but, rather, a significant commentary on the relations between the tellers, as individuals or members of a collectivity; myth, history, genealogy, are all ritual acts, the rival versions of which are neither more nor less true but are actually a metacommunication about the identities and interests of the sources of the information. Such reports should not be taken as "factual" or "historical" but as "fictional" and "ritual"—and, ultimately, political.

In the end Leach leads us to a more sophisticated appreciation of the meaning of cultural differences and of cultural boundaries, and, although he is not presenting a recognizable (or intentional) ethnic study, his insights have value and consequences for anthropology's and potentially any social science's treatment of ethnic groups and ethnicity. Cultural categories and cultural identity, he concludes, are not really objective, tangible things but subjective, symbolic things; the identity or boundary of a social collectivity "is not necessarily ascertainable in the realm of empirical facts; it is a question, in part at any rate, of the attitudes and ideas of particular individuals at a particular time" (288). In reconceiving culture and society as so open, fluid, even *invented,* the relationship between the two becomes for us analysts and ethnographers much more problematic, various, and unique to each case.

Study and Theory of Ethnicity: Glazer and Moynihan versus Geertz

The year 1963 was an important one for two developing schools of thought on ethnicity with the publication of *Beyond the Melting Pot* (Glazer and Moynihan 1963) and *Old Societies and New States* (Geertz 1963). The two books differ in significant ways: the former deals with American ethnic groups, the latter with international ethnicity; the former is written by nonanthropologists, the latter by anthropologists; the former is a pioneer work in the school of "circumstantialism," the latter in the school of "primordialism." The subtitle of each book shows its empirical focus: the former subtitle is "The Negroes, Puerto Ricans, Jews, Italians, and Irish of New York City," and the latter one is "The Quest for Modernity in Asia and Africa."

Glazer and Moynihan view ethnicity in American society as a product of the mass immigration of the 1800s and early 1900s but not as a survival of old social forms; instead, they interpret ethnicity as a new social form born out of the conditions in which immigrants found themselves in the

United States. The shape of this ethnicity and the groups that it spawned, and even the very fact of ethnicity and ethnic groups in the United States, were not obvious, natural, or inevitable; analysts could not have predicted about any particular group, they argue, "from its first arrival what it might become or, indeed, whom it might contain. The group is not a purely biological phenomenon" (16). The most provocative thing these authors have to say is that "ethnic groups in New York are also interest groups" (17). They acknowledge that "family and fellowfeeling bind the ethnic group" but contend that this is not the full story, since individuals "actually can be anything"; kinship/biological relations and cultural commonality do not by themselves dictate who will experience what ethnic identity or what the subsequent ethnic group will do about it in American society. Instead, they see two other dimensions that give shape and content to the ethnic phenomenon: "'rational' economic interests" and "concrete ties of organization" (17–18). Ethnic groups are formed and mobilized by specific social conditions and for specific social purposes. These conditions may include minority status, discrimination, stratification, segregation, and others; the purposes may include equality, inclusion, social justice, economic opportunity, cultural preservation, and so forth. As we now know, these purposes can also include "entitlements," control of the mechanisms of the state, and even in some cases separatism and the creation of an ethnic or national state.

In other words (and this is anticipating later developments just a bit) they would argue that we cannot completely understand ethnicity and ethnic conflict by looking at the group in isolation or at the cultural content of the group. Rather, we must add to this analysis the relation of the group to its context, to the things outside it, especially the dominant society and its categories, structures, and stratifications. The ethnic group and its behavior are not a priori facts but social products of collectivities, cultures, and circumstances.

Geertz's book is famous for suggesting exactly the opposite, although this reputation may be slightly exaggerated. A number of authors contribute to this volume, but by far the most influential chapter is the one written by Geertz himself, "The Integrative Revolution: Primordial Sentiments and Civil Politics in the New States." The book grows out of and contributes to the increasing awareness among anthropologists of the cultural consequences and problems of the "new states" formed as a result of decolonization; while this topic is compelling enough in itself, it also has implications for the typical "objects" of the discipline, the traditional, small-scale social isolate called a society or culture. With the new nation building, the so-called integrative revolution, these social units are no longer isolated and self-contained but become part of larger, more inclusive social systems. Anthropology's method and concepts would have to adjust accordingly as the objects of study themselves changed, or perhaps even disappeared, bringing on what we will examine as the "crisis" in anthropology.

Geertz, following Edward Shils, sees the problem of the new states as stemming from the primordial diversity of the enclosed societies within the states, which resist or at least complicate the creation of a statewide society or "civil order." In a word, "the new states are abnormally susceptible to serious disaffection based on primordial attachments" (1973, 259). He goes on to explain his notion of primordial and "primordial attachment" in one of the most oft-quoted passages in all of ethnic studies, which I quote in full yet again, because ethnicity theory continues to draw inspiration, positive or negative, from its many facets.

> By primordial attachment is meant one that stem from the "givens"—or, more precisely, as culture is inevitably involved in such matters, the assumed "givens"—of social existence: immediate contiguity and kin connection mainly, but beyond them the givenness that stems from being born into a particular religious community, speaking a particular language, or even a dialect of a language, and following particular social practices. These congruities of blood, speech, custom, and so on, are seen to have an ineffable, and at times overpowering, coerciveness in and of themselves. One is bound to one's kinsmen, one's neighbor, one's fellow believer, ipso facto; as the result not merely of personal affection, practical necessity, common interest, or incurred obligation. but at least in great part by virtue of some unaccountable absolute import attributed to the very tie itself. The general strength of such primordial bonds, and the types of them that are important, differ from person to person, from society to society, and from time to time. But for virtually every person, in every society, at almost all times, some attachments seem to flow more from a sense of natural—some would say spiritual—affinity than from social interaction. (1973, 259–60)

Geertz grants that two or more of these primordial elements (blood ties, race, language, region, religion, and custom) "are usually involved concurrently, sometimes at cross-purposes with one another." The political problem, as he sees it, is that this primordial particularism—"tribalism, parochialism, communalism, and so on"—threatens civil order and state integration in a more aggressive and insatiable way than other forms of social identity or discontent. "Economic or class or intellectual disaffection threatens revolution," but primordial disaffection threatens the boundaries, if not the very existence of the state; it rejects the whole idea and fact of the state and its disembodied civil order outright. For this reason primordial sentiments have "a more ominous and deeply threatening quality than most of the other . . . problems the new states face" (261).

Geertz's argument has often been taken, and criticized, as a manifesto of primordialism, the school of theory that holds ethnicity to be natural, irrational, and retrograde—and therefore pernicious. Yet, if we back up a page from his famous passage, we see that he does not take ethnic attachments completely for granted. The people that compose the new states, he submits, have two different yet interdependent motivations: to be noticed, to have their "identity be publicly acknowledged as having import" (ostensibly a primordial motive) and a second, practical motive, to have economic and social progress, "a rising standard of living, more effective political order," and to be an actor of substance on the stage of world affairs (258). Furthermore, Geertz's description of primordial sentiments may refer, and may even have been intended to refer, more to the "member's" perspective than to the analyst's. The cases he pursues next deepen this impression, for he illustrates how primordial identities vary in context, significance, and effect in various national settings. Toward the end of the essay he finally asserts that, although the modern state "permits the maintenance of a profound rooted 'consciousness of kind' . . . it also simplifies and concentrates group antagonisms, raises the spectre of separation by superimposing a comprehensive political significance upon these antagonisms, and . . . merely modernizes particularistic or ethnic claims" (307–8). Primordial phenomena, then, are not purely primordial but fundamentally alterable (and regularly empirically altered) by modern circumstances.

Geertz allows as much in his oft-quoted, and much-abused, passage. The "givens" are qualified as "assumed givens," and even those assumed givens vary in strength and salience in his account. The cause of this variance is unspecified, but the fact that it "differs from person to person, from society to society, and from time to time" as much as proves that some other factors are at work in each instance. Not all individuals who share a primordial attribute attach equal weight to it; mere contiguity or some objective social characteristic does not ensure any measure of attachment or identity. Not all societies place equal emphasis on primordial attributes. Finally, any individual or society may experience shifts in the intensity and focus of primordial attachments at various times in their life or history. Thus, while the attributes may be primordial in the sense of "already existing" (although they may not be, as we will see), they are not thereby inevitable, automatic, and invariant, as later primordial theory sometimes intimates; nothing at all is suggested by Geertz in terms of the "time-depth" of such attributes; they may be primordial today but have originated only yesterday.

Ethnic Boundaries: Barth

A critical turning point in the debate over ethnic groups, primordial or traditional cultures, and external (intergroup) relations came with the publication of another anthropological work, *Ethnic Groups and Boundaries* (1969). The book consists of a series of cases preceded by an introduction by Barth, which is by far the most important part of the volume. In the introduction he goes immediately to the heart of anthropology's involvement not only with ethnicity but with society in general; in essence he takes up the gauntlet thrown down by Leach to think anew about the units of analysis of anthropology. Traditionally, he says, anthropology has conceived of societies as discrete and cultural variation as "discontinuous"; that is, there are "aggregates of people," living in "geographical and social isolation," distinguished from other such groups by differences in culture. In this view there is a one-to-one correspondence between society and culture: the classification of individuals or local population segments to a particular society, or "an ethnic group must depend on their exhibiting the particular traits of the culture." In a word: "Differences between groups become differences in trait inventories" (12). This should sound familiar, as in the *Kulturkreis* approach, and it should sound wrong in the light of Leach's ethnography.

In place of this conventional perspective Barth and his contributors, like Leach before them, find that cultural variation and social/ethnic boundaries are not coterminous: groups with qualitative cultural differences are often subsumed under the same social/ethnic label and identity by outsiders or even by members, while groups with no major cultural differences are often distinguished into two or more social/ethnic categories. Consequently, "although ethnic categories take cultural differences into account, we can assume no simple one-to-one correspondence between ethnic units and cultural similarities and differences" (14). Failing to find any sure understanding of ethnicity through a description of the content of a culture, Barth directs our attention instead to the relations *between* groups and the ways culture is used to generate and preserve those relations.

The two central notions of this approach are ethnic boundary and social interaction. Ethnic groups are categories or categorial distinctions, socially bounded groups as determined by the social conditions in which two or more groups live and interact (even if that interaction takes the form of *no interaction,* as in total communal segregation). Ethnic groups are thus understood "as a form of social organization," a particular species of social categorization that "classifies a person in terms of his basic, most general identity, presumptively determined by his origin and background" (13). One of the curious and problematic things that he and his colleagues, and many other anthropologists, have noticed, however, is that social identity is not entirely ascribed, that people can in fact change their identity and their social/ethnic affiliation in many cases (although not always or in any way); in the book under discussion Haaland discusses how Fur farmers in Africa can become Baggara pastoralists, Knutsson how Arsi pastoralists may lose their Arsi social status, and Barth himself how Pathans may become Baluchs. What is interesting to Barth and the rest is that, although personnel may flow from one category or group to another, the boundaries of the categories or groups persist. In fact, in this view the continuity of ethnic groups depends neither on biological nor cultural continuity; individuals may come and go, and cultural traits may come and go. On the contrary, the "continuity of ethnic groups . . . depends on the maintenance of a boundary. The cultural features that signal the boundary may change, and the cultural characteristics of the members may likewise be transformed, indeed, even the organizational form of the group may change, yet the fact of continuing dichotomization between member and outsiders" can remain (14).

Simply stated, it is "the ethnic boundary that defines the group, not the cultural stuff that it encloses" (15). But what, then, is the function of this boundary process? For Barth and his fellow ethnographers the function is the *structuring of interaction.* Ethnic categories "provide an organizational vessel" within which people can ascribe characteristics to individuals and *judge* the performance of individuals by categorial standards. Each ethnic category is a specific field of meaning and value, consisting of mutually exclusive rules and roles and criteria of evaluation; ethnic identities, therefore, "function as categories of inclusion/exclusion and of interaction." If a person avows one ethnic identity or another, or is ascribed one by other people, his or her behavior is judged by the standards of that category; shifting category is shifting performance and the criteria by which he or she asks and expects to be judged. Public behavior, as in the cases presented by Erdheim (Lapps and Norwegians) and Haaland (Fur and Baggara), cannot be evaluated by any singly standard but "must be interpreted with reference to the available ethnic alternatives": as Haaland states, a Fur who claims Baggara status may on occasion "be regarded by other Baggara as inferior, but this means that they are inferior as Baggara, not that they are an inferior ethnic group" (1969, 71). Judged by Baggara performance criteria, that is, they do not measure up individually; they are "less successful" or "less skilled" performers of the Baggara role.

One of the really beneficial advantages of the ethnic boundary approach over the ethnic culture approach is the possibility, or even more so the necessity, to consider how ethnic distinctions emerge. Barth proposes that there is no obvious or a priori way in which ethnic groups are formed or in which culture is deployed in the formation; indeed, only circumstances will determine which cultural traits "are used . . . as signals and emblems of difference," which "are ignored," and which "are played down or denied" (1969, 14). Any number of elements—"tribe, caste, language group, region or state," to which we might add religion, history, race, custom, and others to round out Geertz's list of "primordial" attributes—are perfectly adequate and useful as ethnic "diacritica." For empirical reasons, however, some achieve prominence and others do not, and presumably, "under radically different circumstances, the critical factors in the definition and maintenance of ethnic boundaries would be different" (Haaland 1969, 35–36). Additional consequences to mention in this diminution of the role of cultural difference in ethnic identities would be that the loss of difference between groups, assimilation in the purest sense, would not necessarily lead to a reduction in the personal salience or the "organizational relevance" of ethnic identity (which will be observed in the case of Quebec in a later chapter) and that a great knowledge of culture, in particular of the history of culture—of culture in the past, of tradition—would not necessarily lead us to a greater knowledge or understanding of the ethnic group. Culture, history, and groups are not simply identical but exist in a much more interesting and complicated relationship to one another.

The Theoretical Debate Continues

Not all researchers subscribe to this position, of course. We have, then, by the late 1960s and early 1970s two developing and opposing schools of thought on the nature and source of ethnicity and ethnic groups. One takes its primary inspiration from Shils and Geertz, although it can be traced to the romantic nationalism of the nineteenth century with which we opened this chapter and to conventional views of the prevalence and ferocity of some ethnic conflict today; it is known as primordialism. The other draws on a long tradition of thought, from Marxism to Glazer and Moynihan to Barth, as well as from the ongoing field studies of ethnic behavior and ethnic change; it is known by various names, such as circumstantialism or instrumentalism.

Primordialism grows out of Shils's and Geertz's notions of primordial ties, attachments, or sentiments. Shils in particular is credited with introducing the term *primordial* in his influential article "Primordial, Personal, Sacred, and Civil Ties" (1957). The context of his argument is the observation, very much in line with Gluckman's views on social integration and conflict, that modern societies (Shils has nothing to say here about traditional societies) are imperfectly or incompletely integrated by the "civil" or "ideal" beliefs, values, and allegiances that pretend to solidify them. Rather, a wide array of different kinds of loyalties and relationships of more "local" quality bind individuals to one another and indirectly, thereby, to the institutions and structures of society (society resembling the "octopus" or "cluster of clusters" to which Geertz likens it). His definitional reference to primordial ties applies to attachments to such others as family members that are "not merely to the other family member as a person, but as a possessor of certain especially 'significant relational' qualities, which can only be described as primordial. The attachment to another member of one's kinship group is not just a function of interaction. . . . It is because a certain ineffable significance is attributed to the tie of blood" (142). On the following page he mentions the "coerciveness" of primordial qualities. Geertz, as we can see, took up much of the language and imagery of Shils.

From these roots some theorists, emphasizing the apparent antiquity, intractability, and irrationality of much of ethnic phenomena, come to see ethnicity as a primordial phenomenon, a singular form of sociality or solidarity, based on emotional connection to long-standing, objective, and fixed social characteristics. As I have argued elsewhere, primordialism attributes three features to ethnicity: apriority, ineffability, and affectivity (Eller and Coughlan 1993). Apriority, the sense that ethnic characteristics and identities are a priori and before experience or social interaction, suggests that ethnicity is just there, ascribed or founded upon ascribed characteristics that individuals are born into and cannot deny; they are, in Geertz's words, the givens of social life. Ethnic identity, thus, is a natural or even spiritual aspect of the human experience; it is not learned from social experience, but, rather, social experience is defined and determined by it. It is in fact prior to social experience. It is in this sense, they assert, like kinship: you are born a member of a family, and you identify and attach yourself as such simply because you are. Ineffability means that primordial ethnic givens are inexpressible, inexplicable, overpowering and coercive in their social force and follows logically from the apriority of ethnicity; primordial traits are socially binding "in and of themselves . . . by virtue of some unaccountable absolute import attributed to the very tie itself" (Geertz 1973, 259). Affectivity directs us to the essentially emotional nature of ethnicity (with constant reference to ties, bonds, attachments, and sentiments) that makes it irrational or at least nonrational, persistent, and strident.

Centrally, ethnicity differs from other forms of social organization and identity according to primordialism by its relative disengagement from interest, especially economic interest. This is why ethnicity may persist even when economic interests may not be best served by it (in other words, the pursuit of economic self-reliance or even a small independent national state that may be economically unviable), when economic differences no longer distinguish groups (in other words, when most of the economic gap between groups has closed, as we see again in Quebec and other locations), or when there is a real price to pay—economically, politically, or in terms of loss of life—for ethnicity, in the form of discrimination, persecution, war, or genocide. Advocates of a primordial reading return to this irrationality as the major defense of the theory: "we need the primordial approach for a *complete* explanation [of ethnicity's] most extreme, strident, irrational aspects," maintains Scott (1990, 157), for without primordialism "the complexity, resilience, and even irrationality of ethnic bonds are likely to be underestimated" (Stack 1986, 8). Perhaps the most articulate and insistent espousal of the theory (though a highly controversial and criticized one) comes from van den Berghe, who attributes ethnicity to biological/evolutionary processes, dubbing it a form of the "biology of nepotism," serving to preserve and perpetuate the group and its characteristics.

Ethnicity and race identities and sentiments, then, "are to be understood as an extended and attenuated form of kin selection" (1978, 403), giving both of these social organizational types the strongest possible natural bases and the strongest possible distinction from more artificial and interest-based organization.

The dangers of a primordial approach are many. First, there is the chance that it will abort analysis altogether, positing that ethnicity is natural and ineffable, and that's that. Second, it tends, seeing ethnicity as ascribed, to freeze both the culture and the boundaries of ethnic groups, since (1) if the groups are very ancient, they must have existed in precisely their present form for a long period; and (2) if ties or sentiments attach to a group or a culture then these latter must be static. Third, based on the notion that ethnicity is an ancient form of society and identity extending into the present, it leads to two different and mutually exclusive conclusions: either, as anachronisms or "survivals" of an earlier and more primitive time, they must and will give way to more modern, rational, and integrative forms (such as the class or state), or, as time-honored, -tested, and -selected social forces they are inexpungeable, and they and the conflicts they engender will be with us for a very long time to come.

Seeing all of these positions as untenable and ultimately empirically unfounded, circumstantialism offers a different picture of ethnicity. In this second theory ethnicity is not an utterly unique form of social identity and organization *causa sui;* it is, rather, essentially and ultimately associated with two other mundane forces: social conditions and interests. The essence of an ethnic group and ethnic conflict, if *essence* is the correct word, is therefore not within the group and its culture but outside it or between it and its social environment, including other ethnic groups.

If Barth is the bible of circumstantialism, then Glazer and Moynihan's second book, *Ethnicity: Theory and Experience* (1975), is the handbook. In it some of the most powerful scholars of ethnicity and social theory in general build a case for the circumstantialist approach. In their introduction Glazer and Moynihan themselves stake the claim, somewhat cautiously, for ethnicity as circumstantial and interest related. Why is this particular type of cultural/historical membership especially important for group identity and mobilization today? Why is it more important for some groups than for others? Why are some instantiations of it "peaceful and others filled with conflict"? The key to such diversity lies outside the group itself and its cultural peculiarity. In fact, Parsons cites David Schneider's notion of the "desocialization" of ethnic groups, or what we might prefer to call their deculturalization, that is, that their cultural peculiarity has often become diluted to the point where they are not cultural distinct, yet their power and appeal as mobilizing points, as boundaried categories of action, may be nonetheless. The point is that cultural distinctions, although a critical element in the "language of ethnicity," are not even a necessary condition of ethnicity.

Second, and consequently, the essence and "function" of an ethnic group is often not culture but, rather, interest. What is important, in other words, about ethnicity today is that it is increasingly, as we argued previously, *used* for some purpose that is not entirely cultural. In other times, intergroup conflict existed as it does today, but often this conflict was about "culture, language, religion, *as such*" (1975, 8), about the right to practice a culture or religion or speak a language, etc.; consider such conflicts as the revolts of the Jews against the Romans in the ancient period. Other conflicts were "political" or "dynastic" in nature and were basically unrelated to culture, although the two groups at odds were often of different cultures, religions, languages, or what have you; this is perhaps the best way to perceive the struggle (which was far from a constant thing) between the ancient "Sinhalese" and "Tamil" kingdoms of Sri Lanka. Today, however, culture and cultural rights (in many societies, anyway) are relatively secure. Instead, groups raise or invoke their culture in "an emphasis on the interests broadly defined of the member of the group" (8), such as getting jobs or seats in university, or housing, or other practical ends. Ethnicity has become an effective way to pursue group interests—more effective, certainly, than class because class has little motivational appeal, has little authority (the claim of being an old, proud, distinct cultural group carries more weight), and implies a hierarchy of an unflattering sort (classes are stratified vertically by definition, with the dissatisfied class usually underneath, while ethnic groups are stratified horizontally, ideally and ideologically, claiming equal validity and status with their opposites, oppressors, or enemies). It can be more effective than "individual rights," too, because of the strength of numbers, the invocation of an alternative set of traditions and values that gives the actions a greater moral authority (so that the interethnic struggle is "not merely against the norms of some other group, but in favor of the already established norms of its own"[15]), and the power of cultural "intimidation," which forces any detractor from their cause to face the charge of discrimination, racism, or worse.

Finally, the most convincing argument they raise is that many ethnic movements, ethnic groups, or even ethnic cultures are not old at all but that "many of the groups that have engaged in 'primordial' conflict are themselves recent historical creations" (19). Horowitz, for example, here and in his own subsequent book (1985), argues that, while ethnicity is about ascriptive identities, these identities are "highly contextual." He outlines a constellation of processes by which ethnic groups expand and contract, change, and speciate or become extinct, concluding that it is "somewhat inappropriate" to call groups that "are products" of such social processes by the name primordial. Glazer and Moynihan also see ethnic groups not as static and essentialist things but as "forms of social life that are capable of renewing and transforming themselves." Cultural/ethnic characteristics may be primary (in the sense of most important in the discourse of ethnicity) or prior (in the sense of predating any particular individual), but this does not mean that they are primordial (in the sense of having always existed in their current form).

These insights and concurrent field research have largely redirected the study of ethnicity away from the catalogue of cultural traits that may distinguish an ethnic group and toward the processes by which ethnic groups, identities, and even cultures themselves are constructed. Bell (1975), for instance, discusses a series of extra-ethnic or supra-ethnic social trends or forces that tend to exacerbate ethnicity, such as the development of more inclusive identities, the emergence of a "postindustrial society," the rise of an "external proletariat" of dependent developing states, and shifts in ideology and values, particularly the redefinition of the values of "equality" as meaning equality of result rather than equality of opportunity. In other, and critical, words ethnicity is in a manner not at all primitive but positively modern—an effect of modernization and the influences of modern political and economic forces on culture. Kasfir, for example, investigates how new ethnic groups emerged under colonial rule, especially in urban settings rather than rural or traditional ones, where we might expect primordial or traditional allegiances and collectivities to be strongest; in fact, he identifies specific "agents" of ethnicity, what he calls "local cultural enthusiasts and political entrepreneurs" (1979, 370), who are often directly responsible for the construction of social groups or even of the cultural traits that come to define and excite such groups. These ethnic entrepreneurs, some examples of which we will encounter in subsequent chapters, more or less self-consciously give shape and voice to ethnic consciousnesses and mobilizations that may or may not have any real and compelling root in traditional society or culture; sometimes, as politicians or would-be political leaders, they create around themselves the cultural constituency that is the ethnic group that we and the world see. Among others Olzak and Nagel, separately and together (e.g., Olzak 1983; Nagel 1993; Nagel and Olzak 1986), repeatedly stress the roles of circumstances like urbanization, decolonization, the labor market, and state politics in ethnic organization and mobilization, while Hoben and Hefner find that ethnicity is "renewed, modified, and remade in each generation" even if it does in some way refer back to social givens or primordialities (1990, 18).

Traditions, Old and New: The Construction of Culture

These and other studies have come to emphasize creativity and adaptability over tradition and the "survival" of primordial factors. Ethnogenesis as a process has been identified, for example by Roosens, and *invention* has become a key term in the literature, as evidenced by the spate of publications with the word or some rough synonym in their titles; *tradition, culture, primitive society,* even *anthropology* itself have all come under the deconstructing gaze of recent theory and been exposed to the same "constructionist" or "circumstantialist" critique. Hobsbawm and Ranger present data to show that many phenomena that we call traditional are in actuality relatively new, that behaviors or symbols "which appear or claim to be old are often quite recent in origin and sometimes invented" (1983, 1). Such "invented traditions" refer to the past and avow a continuity with the past, but this continuity is "largely factitious," serving an ideological function as "a legitimator of action and cement of group cohesion." Consequentially, they find the process of inventing tradition particularly pertinent to the modern world and the state, where the "rapid transformation of society weakens or destroys the social pattern for which 'old' traditions have been designed" (4), and especially to the social phenomena of nation and nationalism, which are as often as not attempts to create new collectivities and new identities but which do, and must, "claim to be the opposite of novel . . . and the opposite of constructed." The invocation of the past, the establishment of a link to the past, gives nations and nationalism (and ethnicity and ethnic groups, too) what they need most—an *apparent* continuity and naturalness or primordiality. In fact, they assert, as others have, that tradition of this sort is evidence of a distinct and decisive *break* with the past, a new self-consciousness, reflexivity, and problematicization of culture and identity that would be odd, if not impossible, in the traditional setting to which invented traditions refer: after all, "when the old ways are alive, traditions need be neither revived nor invented" (8)—nor, we might add, thought about very much. When culture is truly given, it is also generally automatically and unselfconsciously "taken" as well.

Anderson, in an influential book, goes even further to consider nations as "imagined communities." In the most frequently cited passage of his book he explains the meaning of this imagination, which is sometimes misconstrued to suggest a fabricated or artificial nation but which is actually, in his view, a mental or psychological characteristic of the members of the group, who "will never know most of their fellow-members, meet them, or even hear of them, yet in the minds of each lives the image of their communion" (1983, 15). It is the power to believe, to know, that you are in a group although this collectivity may not be a group in the full sociological sense, as founded upon real and regular personal knowledge and interaction. The particular crucial features of this image of nation are its limitations (that is, finite and bounded, therefore one among other nations, with an "in-group" and an "out-group"), its sovereignty, and its community (that, although there are social differences and inequalities—vertical differences—within the nation, the nation shares a "deep, horizontal comradeship"). Much of Anderson's subsequent discussion analyzes how the development and diffusion of printing and vernacular print languages created "unified fields of exchange and communications" giving rise simultaneously to a culture, an audience for that culture, and the mental image of that audience as a community to its far-flung members. No doubt this is so, for we will find in the case studies that follow that the introduction (where it was a late phenomenon) or growth of literacy and publishing figures prominently in most, if not all, of the instances: newspapers and cultural journals are major loci of ethnic discourse and therefore of ethnic integration and mobilization. In print but not only in print, for also in other mass media like radio and television, as well as in political activity (the formation of parties, the giving of speeches, the casting of votes, etc.) and many other practical behaviors, a disparate group can come to recognize or believe in commonalities with one another, whether or not those commonalities are old or even real. Having acknowledged the power of the imagination in ethnicity and national identity, we cannot underestimate its power: imagination can create where reality leaves only hints or blanks, and it can overlook as much as it grasps.

This long path of discovery and turn of thought in regard to groups, identities, and cultures has had its impact on the discipline of anthropology specifically. The fact can be seen in Barth's (1969) volume and Leach's (1954) monograph, if not earlier; Boas and Malinowski were already struggling against ossified conceptions of culture and society. Of course, it would be an exaggeration to credit ethnicity and ethnic conflict with the full responsibility for paradigmatic shifts in anthropology, partly because other factors were operative concurrently (like decolonization or modernization or Christianization of many traditional societies, which challenged the conception of static, closed societies and which overturned or even reversed the terms of "otherness" for anthropology) and partly because the movements within the field preceded the high tide of ethnicity as a research problem. At any rate, reinventing anthropology, which might mean retooling it for a new world of social phenomena or even abandoning it in the face of the dissolution of its subject matter, became a project and a book title (Hymes 1972).

As mentioned, such a project of "rethinking" anthropology became necessary both because of the changes in the objects of anthropological investigation (ostensibly, primitive or traditional societies) and because of epistemological concerns within anthropology itself. The changes in anthropology's units of study and analysis include but are not limited to phenomena that we might call ethnic in the broadest sense, like (1) the emergence of new social groups; (2) "supertribalization" or the formation of larger social units through amalgamation or absorption of smaller ones; (3) culture-based social movements, cultural revivals, etc.; (4) state-building processes and cultural resistance to these processes, including nationalist and separatist movements and ethnic wars; (5) "tribally" organized resistance to development projects such as the Kayapo anti-dam activities in Brazil; and (6) "nativization" or rejection of postcolonial Western culture and/or the reclamation of (sometimes defunct) traditional cultural features. Other "nonethnic" changes that also caught our attention were native Christianity, indigenous rights (especially land rights) movements, the entry of "tribal peoples" into professional and political positions, and advances in their education that gave them access to anthropological products, among others. Altogether, these factors raised the unavoidable issue of intersociety contact and extrasociety connections, rendering the concept of isolated and static societies utterly obsolete. They helped precipitate an epistemological crisis in anthropology: who exactly is the other? How can we describe the other in ethnographic terms? How can our methodologies cope with the interconnected complexity of the emerging social order? In the end, is knowledge of other cultures possible, and, if so, what responsibilities and guilts do we bear as members (and representatives) of dominant, formerly colonial societies?

These are the kinds of questions that have influenced the reinvention, or the talk of reinvention, of anthropology. Specifically, in Hymes's volume three issues of importance to us and to ethnicity arise. The first of these revolves around the concepts of culture and tradition; the difference between "the cultural as traditional" and "the cultural as emergent" is recognized, in fact is traced back at least to Durkheim and Tonnies and Sapir. If, then, the objects of study are changing, then the study must also change: anthropology should, Hymes states, redefine itself from the study of primitive or small-scale societies to "the study of the emergence of cultural forms in concrete settings and in relation to a world society" (1972, 35). The second issue concerns the role of anthropology in particular and of Western society in general in the political—that is exploitative—relations between "our" society and "the others." Willis defines anthropology as, to a large extent, "the social science that studies dominated colored peoples—and their ancestors—living outside the boundaries of modern white society" (1972, 123). He goes on to say, and is not alone in saying, that this fact has inevitable consequences for what we want to know, what we believe, and what we do with our knowledge. For instance, he argues that anthropology has been anything but a pure scientific endeavor but has been "used for the benefit of white societies" to aid colonial administration and to answer (purportedly) questions about European cultural history by "equating contemporary colored peoples with white ancestors." Even the concepts and theories of anthropology he sees as having political ramifications: ideas of primitive society, of isolated society, of functionalism, of ethnographic voice work to "absolve white people of their crimes" against colored societies, to "facilitate the imperial policy of divide and rule," and to "preclude the discovery of sociocultural links wider than tribal allegiances" (143). Whether or not they see this as a conspiracy or as an unintended outcome of well-meaning, if ethnocentric, beliefs, commitments, and prejudices, Diamond agrees that anthropology and other "are both, if not equally, objects of contemporary, imperial civilization" (1972, 401), and Nader (1972) in a frequently cited chapter proposes the study of the colonizers to be as fit a subject of inquiry as the study of the colonized. Whatever the belief or the reason, anthropology's horizon needed to expand to include the society beyond the societies we conventionally analyzed.

The third issue from Hymes's book is the specifically epistemological one—whether our ethnographic descriptions are objective accounts of other cultures. In an essay not included in the edition but quoted in it, Zaretsky criticizes the positivist ethnographic tradition "that the truth is there and that it is objectively discoverable, if only we experts look hard enough; if only we find the right models" (qtd. in Berreman 1972, 93). Scholte takes a clear stand in asserting that anthropology "is never only scientific" and that, "as cultural products and processes" themselves, its concepts, methods, and "knowledge" are bounded by the culture and interests of anthropologists, making the discipline an appropriate object of investigation to itself. This challenge has been taken up recently.

Wagner, for example, not long after Hymes, considers how anthropology actually invents culture, in two senses, as the general idea of culture and as the particular individual social units or cultures to be described. What this invention consists of, for Wagner, is the assumption and then the construction of "a concrete entity, a 'thing' that has rules, 'works' in a certain way, and can be learned" (1975, 8); that is, as the anthropologist tries to account for, understand, and represent the behavior of others, he or she creates a cultural "object" out of the data and experience. Anthropology, in this interpretation, is "the study of man 'as if' there were culture" (10). "The study of culture is in fact *our* culture" (16). He even likens anthropology to a culture cult.

In itself this is an interesting and probably valuable insight, but he also perceives the implications for what we might call ethnicity or ethnic groups. Having allowed this kind of creativity to anthropologists, he says, we cannot deny the same kind and import of creativity to the culture itself and its members. He goes so far as to suggest that invention *is* culture. The implication of this perspective is that all people—anthropologists and natives, "modern" or traditional—are creatively assembling and advancing their behavior, the reasons for their behavior, and the circumstances (or interpretations of circumstances) of their behavior continuously; especially under conditions of social ambiguity or novelty, which provide a kind of culture shock, people control and make sense of their experience "through all kinds of imagined and constructed 'rules,' traditions, and facts" (35).

Wagner does not, however, privilege invention over stability on continuity, or what he calls convention. Convention "defines the perspective of the actor," giving the terms and resources with and within which people interpret and invent; invention is not purely free and unconstrained but is, rather, guided by already-existing structures and meanings. This follows Firth, who distinguishes between structure and organization, the former serving as the convention or resource for the latter, which may or may not obey and reproduce the former in the action of specific actors in specific situations as well as such social constructionists as Berger and Luckmann. It also, interestingly, anticipates Bourdieu in saying that this invention of culture is a reciprocal or dialectical process of "an invention that constantly re-creates its orientation, and an orientation that continually facilitates its own reinvention" (Wagner 1975, 52). The similarity to Bourdieu's "structured structures, predisposed to function as structuring structures" (1977, 71), is unmistakable, as is the similarity between Wagner's observation that the product of invention is "taken *very seriously,* so that it is not invention at all, but reality" (71) and Bourdieu's concept of *habitus* as "history turned into nature . . . the forgetting of history which history itself produces by incorporating the objective structures it produces in the second nature of habitus" (78–79).

Kuper picks up one thread of this argument to show that a particular kind of culture, or a particular conception of culture, is invented—that is, primitive culture. He demonstrates, through a consideration of the early history of anthropology, how the idea of primitive society was "a fantasy which had been constructed by speculative lawyers in the late nineteenth century" such as Bachofen, Maine, McLennan, and Morgan (1988, 8). The interests of these men were comparative and evolutionary—comparative law and the origins and evolution of various social institutions as an attempt to discover the prehistory of Western society. The significance for anthropology, beyond setting a research agenda for over one hundred years, can be found in the terms and concepts of the discipline and even in the methodology: the case study method, Kuper argues, was introduced from legal practice. For the study of ethnicity and ethnic conflict, however, the key implication is that the "idea of primitive society fed the common belief that societies were based either on blood or on soil, and that these principles of descent and territoriality may be equated with race and citizenship, the contrasting components of every imperialism and every nationalism" (9). Yet, even as he says this, he perceives that anthropology is changing—perhaps, again, reinventing itself. "It is no longer about the primitive, and no longer particularly or necessarily about 'the Other'" (243).

In fact, the object of anthropological inquiry is often these days anthropology itself. There is a discernible line from the insistence that anthropology is also a cultural activity, not a purely or simply scientific or positivistic one, through the suggestion that anthropology has a culture (which is a kind of culture cult), the "knowledge" or "data" of which "must be tempered by the kind of interpretation . . . that will bring the fascinating and mutual invention of anthropologist and 'native' alike into awareness" (1975, 85). This line culminates for the present discussion in the so-called new ethnography and various kinds of "dialogical anthropology"—attempts to represent not only the culture under study but the actual processes, jerky, difficult, problematic, idiosyncratic, incomplete, as they may be, under which it comes into being. These issues are brought together in the influential volume *Writing Culture: The Poetics and Politics of Ethnography* prepared by Clifford and Marcus (1986).

The echoes of all of the concerns we have encountered here can be heard in Clifford's introduction. He asserts that ethnography, the central activity of knowing and describing culture in anthropology, "is always caught up in the invention, not the representation, of culture" (2). Our knowledge of other cultures is not entirely scientific, or "objective," because it is partial and perspectival, constructed in the encounter between anthropologist and member, and conditioned by all sorts of anthropological customs and conventions; in fact, such knowledge could not be scientific or objective, since cultures "are not scientific 'objects' . . . [but] are produced historically, and are actively contested" (18). In particular, the notion of anthropological literature is taken very seriously, alluding to all of the literary devices and tropes that ethnographers employ to represent the knowledge or experience they gain in the field and to present that knowledge and experience, from narrative voice to scene-setting techniques to the dissolution of the investigator into the objective account of the culture. In this and other ways ethnographic literature "can properly be fictions in the sense of 'something made or fashioned.'" Description is implicated with representation (choices about how to make the culture-as-learned-by-the-ethnographer at once clear, convincing, compelling, and relevant) as well as interpretation and, in the end, "invention" by both researcher and informant; the informant invents answers to specific questions, and the researcher invents a coherent monograph and therefore culture out of the answers. Thus, Clifford identifies what he calls the *cultural poesis* that is located in the "specific exclusions, conventions, and discursive practices" of ethnography.

Hopefully, the consequences of the invention, and especially the *poetic* and *political* invention, of culture for an understanding of ethnicity are obvious. Fischer, in analyzing ethnic biographies, explicitly states that ethnicity, like all other facets of culture, "is something reinvented and reinterpreted in each generation by each individual" (1986, 196), even if it may seem natural, incomprehensible, or individual him- or herself. As an invention, it can never be mere or pure tradition but is a contemporary product of "a process of inter-reference between two or more cultural traditions," particularly the ethnic culture and the modern plural culture in which it is currently situated and for which it is currently prepared. Therefore, as we have seen repeatedly, ethnicity may evoke a past to which it is connected—and it may even actually be connected to that past—but the real point of ethnicity, Fischer writes, is to create new values, a new vision of meaning and "the good," "an ethic workable for the future."

Conclusion: Anthropology, Culture, and Desire

According to Crapanzano, the anthropologist is a messenger yet one who is in search of his message. This message we "find" in the society we study. Yet we are not mere and objective messengers: when one of us finds a message (the culture or may even more so the "meaning" of the culture), "he appropriates it, translates it, and makes it 'relevant' to those to whom he delivers it" (1992, 3). In a certain sense, as we have seen, anthropology creates or styles its message and meaning out of its encounter with particular people and social situations—in the sense of representing the encounter in an ethnographic manner (the sense to which Clifford and Marcus refer) and in the sense of importing the very notion of culture and society to the encounter in the first place (the sense to which Wagner refers). The anthropologist does not, in the end, merely discover a society or culture nor "translate" cultural "texts" "the way the translator does. He must first produce them" (Crapanzano 1992, 43).

The production of cultures (as ethnographies) and interpretations based upon them is an artifact of the "culture of anthropology" and the specific qualities of the ethnographic encounter. This encounter has been characterized as dialogical, in the sense that the anthropologist-ethnographer, though often invisible in the final represented version of the culture, is very much a participant in the interactions that give rise to and serve as his "data," or evidence, of the culture. Yet, even as the anthropologist-ethnographer is in a way "hidden" in the account of culture, so Crapanzano unearths other "interlocutors" who are also critically implicated and involved in the encounter: "Dialogues, I suggest, are never dyadic" (6).

This paradox becomes more intelligible when he explains the nature of the side dialogues, which he calls "shadow dialogues," impinging on the main and ostensibly only dialogue, the one between anthropologist and informant. Two types of shadow dialogue are the one that takes place during and in conjunction with the ethnographic dialogue, in the form of "shifters, hedges, and other meta-discursive locutions" (asides, soliloquies, conventionalizations, self-corrections, etc.) and the one that happens after the primary dialogue is finished, potentially even when the anthropologist has returned home from the field, which he calls the "interpretive" one.

There are two points and one implication to be drawn from this consideration. The first point is that anthropology is not and probably cannot be a purely objective, positivistic observation and analysis of culture; anthropology has a vantage point, a point of view (to remind ourselves of the opening quotation to this chapter) and a culture of its own, one that populates its world with "objects" like cultures, societies, and the constituent parts thereof, like institutions, rules, rituals, and so on. Anthropology has tended to find these creatures because it expects to and needs to find them. The second point, and one that flows from the first, is that anthropology is not and probably cannot be a purely dispassionate, disinterested interlocutor in the search for and conveyance of culture. Crapanzano points to two crucial forces that must be considered in the play of culture: desire and power. Much has been said recently in anthropology and the other social sciences about the issue of power and the privileged position of the outsider-analyst vis-à-vis "the Other" in terms of power; some of this we have explored. Less has been said about the force of desire in anthropological or other social scientific encounters and accounts, but in the human world surely this is a force to be reckoned with. As a messenger, the anthropologist "is caught between two desires. The message giver wants the messenger to convey his message and the message receiver (despite himself) wants to receive the message he desires. Each attempts to seduce the messenger" (3). While this is true, it is not the whole story, for the messenger also has desires, professional, political, cultural, and personal. These desires easily, if not naturally, transform into agendas, lenses, and categories with which experience will conform. Given the anthropologist's power in the encounter, his desires—and therefore views, versions, and interpretations—may dominate over those of either the message giver or the message receiver.

The implication of these observations in simply this: if, upon reflection, we can identify and attribute these facets and forces to the anthropological "version" of culture, we can hardly deny them to the "native's" or "member's" version. In other words, as members go about "doing" their culture, they are also *creating* their culture, out of the same "complex play of desire and power" that is heightened and focused in the ethnographic encounter. This is especially so in the realm of ethnicity, the social objectification and political activation of some part of culture or history ("ethnohistory") in some social circumstances for some social end. Culture and history exist as a kind of passive and plastic data that individuals, groups, and protogroups and would-be groups can interpret, consciously or unconsciously, and even manipulate in the service of their desire and power. Desire—to be a group, to be a superior group, to right perceived wrongs, to establish a culture-based society or polity, or what have you—can color the "facts," or "truths," of culture so thoroughly that the desire becomes the truth; in a more sinister manner, if an individual, party, or group desires to achieve power or status by way of culture, by invoking culture and calling upon others to heed the call, it is all too easily done. In this case, and even in the lesser cases, the messenger—here, the "ethnic messenger," the one or ones with the message that there *is* an ethnic group out there, the central characteristics, values, and perspectives of which are thus and so—desires to convey his message and convince others (his or her "coethnics") that the message is true and salient; in the process the messenger takes on a second role, as message giver, although he or she may mystify this role by claiming merely to find or discover or recognize or represent a true culture out there. At the same time, message receiver, the "group-out-there," which may or may not have been waiting for a message, has its desires, which may or may not coincide with those of the messenger—or be made to coincide, through an activation of power and desire.

In a sense, then, the ethnic messenger or leader (or "ethnic entrepreneur") not only carries a cultural truth but creates one, especially when the ethnic group is not fully "self-aware" or "awake" until the leader and his truth appear. This is why we so often find competing leaders with competing messages about what the group is, which part of its culture or history is most critical to its identity and future, and what it should do next. Ethnic members, like anthropologists, are free to look for their message, to let their desire lead them toward certain messages, and to act upon the message that compels or serves them; different members will necessarily find and convey different messages from the same culture and history, and the ethnicity that ultimately emerges can only be understood as a consequence of "the complex play of desire and power" between the competing versions and their competing carriers.

In conclusion, in this chapter we have followed the development of the concept of culture and with it the concepts of ethnicity and ethnic group in social theory from natural and primordial, almost physical and spiritual, phenomena to problematic and variably bounded ones to, ultimately, constructed, political, poetic, and future-oriented ones. We have seen that this development has been driven principally by changes in the phenomenon itself—the rise of new groups, the demise of old groups, the shift of cultural foci of existing groups, and the emergence of political significance for ethnicity. Anthropology, as the discipline originally conceived to study primitive societies or tribes, has necessarily been intimately involved in this process and has itself been altered as a result.

Anthropology, although it has often tended to imagine its objects as isolated and discrete social units and has often further tried to focus on such units where they do exist, has never been unaware of connections, relations, and integrations of such units into multigroup systems. The scope, pervasiveness, and power of such social systems has today become undeniable, which challenges us to call upon all of our resources and insights of a century of study and to renew our concepts and methods. Shifts in terminology are as significant as anything, as in the long-standing reluctance to use the word *primitive* to describe living societies. The growing substitution of *ethnic group* for *tribe* also questions assumptions of archaicness, discreteness, and isolation (as well as internal integration and uniformity) and emphasizes context, interrelationship with other groups in a wider social system, and a construction of group identity as a function of that context and interrelationship.

Finally, before we turn to the investigation of particular instances of ethnicity and ethnic conflict, let us note that anthropology, as the social science of culture, problematized culture in a valuable way for us to apply to cases of ethnicity. Simply put, ethnicity is not identical to cultural distinctness, and ethnic groups are not necessarily distinct cultural groups. Since Weber at least, and certainly through Leach and Barth and most contemporary theorists, it has been clear that we cannot get at ethnicity merely by way of cultural content, of a list of cultural traits on which ethnic groups differ point by point. Groups in any common social system will share some traits and vary on others, and the ethnic lines do not always fall where the cultural lines do—and neither lines are permanent. In fact, as we discovered at the end of this chapter, an objective list of cultural traits does not even exist in a certain sense but is constructed, invented, in social interaction, whether this interaction is the fieldwork encounter, the colonial encounter, or the contemporary ethnic members' experience in his or her plural society. While ethnicity and ethnic conflict are not mere or pure cultural opportunism, and invention (of groups or even of traits) is not completely without restraint, failure to recognize the contextual, circumstantial, fictive, and political qualities of ethnicity render it and its resultant manifestations much more opaque, irrational, and absolute than they really are.

Chapter 3

Sri Lanka: The Politics of History

It cannot be repeated too often that the present tragic situation is the product of specific historical circumstances, and not, as one often hears in Sri Lanka and in the international press, the end product of a 2,500-year-old struggle between ancient enemies.

—Angelo Vidal d'Almeida Ribeiro

In 1983 decades of ethnic grievance exploded into the worst ethnic violence yet in Sri Lanka. Estimates of the death toll vary from a low of 350 (the official government figure) to almost 2,000 according to reports from the minority and main target group of the violence; in the capital of Colombo alone, between 100,000 and 300,000 people fled in search of refuge. All told, well over 30,000 have been killed in Sri Lanka since 1974 and a half-million made refugees, and the violence has been occurring off and on since before that time, with the first modern post-independence incidents coming in 1956, then again in 1958.

This chapter will investigate the ethnic conflict in Sri Lanka over the last half-century or so, attempting to discover its roots and causes in history and culture, especially the hermeneutics of history and culture, and in present socioeconomic conditions. We will see, as the opening quotation portends, that this conflict has not been a continuous or ancient sequence but has resulted from particular and recent action, decisions, and interpretations that have selectively exacerbated certain potential differences between cultural groups while overlooking or even denying other differences or, for that matter, certain levels of similarity. In fact, there may be no place on earth where the "use" of culture and history is more conspicuous, where present claims and past grievances are couched in terms of ancient battles and kingdoms and of cultural revival and survival—where history, mythology, archaeology, are all political tools and weapons. We will also see that the cultural picture in Sri Lanka (as in Leach's Burma) is much more complicated than a mere bi-ethnic face-off and that other groups, and groups within these groups, contoured along other cultural or political or economic lines, exist and help to move and shape the overall and dominant national conflict.

The Groups

Sri Lanka is a state of some 18.3 million people as of 1995 and was known as Ceylon until 1972. The largest and most consequential division in Sri Lankan society is that between the majority Sinhalese, who make up some 74 percent of the population, and the minority Tamils, who account for around 18 percent. The Sinhalese speak their own language, known by the same name, and are predominantly Theravada Buddhists; the Tamils also speak an eponymous language and are characteristically Hindus. There are, however, three critical facts about Sri Lankan ethnicity that cannot be ignored. The first is that these are not the only two groups of considerable size in the state. There is also a substantial number of Muslims, sometimes further distinguished into "Ceylon Moors" (Muslims who have inhabited Sri Lanka for generations, although their original home area is in dispute) and Malays, totaling around 7.5 percent. They are disproportionately represented in certain areas, composing up to one-third of the population of Batticaloa and one-fourth of Puttalam, Trincomalee, and Mannar. Furthermore, the relation between Muslims on the one hand and Sinhalese and Tamils on the other has been varying and fairly important. Most Muslims speak Tamil, yet they do not identify as—or necessarily with—Tamils, therefore both Sinhalese and Tamil political organizations have competed for their support, and as a community they have shown an openness to and tendency to work with the Sinhalese leadership. Even so, Muslim relations with Sinhalese or Tamils are not always amicable: in perhaps the first episode of communal violence in Ceylon, Sinhalese Buddhists and Muslims came to blows in 1907 at the city of Gampola and again islandwide in 1915. In addition to Muslims it is well to remember that there are several other groups or subgroups. In addition, about 0.5 percent of the population is European and "Burghers," a term for descendants of mixed European–Sri Lankan marriages.

The second critical ethnic fact is that the two main groups, while they are to an extent localized into identifiable areas of the island, are also intermingled in significant ways. The Sinhalese dominate in the central, south-

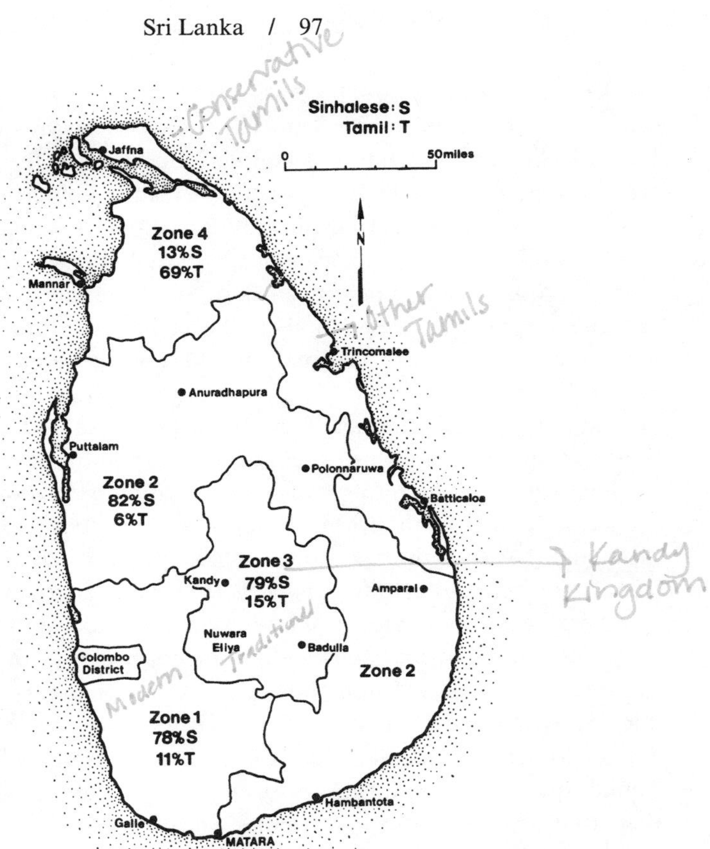

Sri Lankan ethnic distribution by zones. (Reprinted from *Sri Lanka: Ethnic Fratricide and the Dismantling of Democracy,* by S. J. Tambiah [Chicago: University of Chicago Press, 1986], p. 10. Copyright © 1986 by The University of Chicago.)

ern, and western portions of the island, while the Tamils are concentrated in the north and east, especially in the Jaffna Peninsula to the far north. Nevertheless, the Tamils today widely consider the North and East Provinces of modern Sri Lanka to be specifically, and historically, Tamil homelands. Yet, while Tamils predominate in their two provinces, they still share them: over the two provinces Tamils are 69 percent of the population and Sinhalese 13 percent, but the Jaffna area is more purely Tamil, while the east coast is much more heterogeneous. In fact, ethnic Tamils are not even the majority in the East Province, which is almost half-Muslim; this is a further complication, since the vast majority of Muslims in Sri

Lanka speak Tamil although they are not considered and do not generally seek to be considered "ethnic Tamils." In the eastern district of Trincomalee, too, Sinhalese presently constitute 33 percent of the population, up from a mere 4 percent in 1900. As can be readily appreciated, these realities render Tamil territorial claims to the east problematic. Finally, not all of the Tamils live in the north and east. Some 47 percent live outside these zones, and therefore 50 percent or more of all Tamils live in areas where they are a minority. A large number inhabit modern pluralistic centers like Colombo and, for historical reasons, the uplands central region of the island.

The third and final critical fact about Sri Lankan ethnicity is that the major ethnic groupings are themselves not homogeneous but are shot through with various forms and amounts of internal diversity. This heterogeneity comes in the form of religious, linguistic, regional, and caste differences. Although the Sinhalese are generally Buddhists and the Tamils are generally Hindus, these clear markers of ethnicity are clouded by several facts: (1) a number of both Sinhalese and Tamils are Christians, as a consequence of colonialism; (2) as mentioned, a considerable number of Muslims also speak Tamil, though this does not qualify them as Tamils; and (3) even today, but more significantly at the time of independence from colonialism, a small minority (4 to 5 percent) of both Sinhalese and Tamils speak English, largely or exclusively, which has further exposed them to English education, economics, and politics. It is also highly consequential, as I will argue, that Tamils in the north were especially successful in availing themselves of English-language education and entering the British colonial administration as well as other opportunities presented by Western education.

There are also regional differences within the ethnic groups of Sri Lanka. For instance, the Sinhalese could be reasonably viewed (and have at times viewed themselves) as two less-than-homogeneous groups, and the Tamils are justifiably analyzable into three. In the former case history and geography conspire to distinguish a central-upland Sinhalese society from a coastal one. The central-upland group, living in the region farthest from colonial impact, has maintained the strongest traditional culture and, even more important, the strongest *sense* or ideology of traditional culture and of themselves as possessors and guardians of that culture; as an indication, they are referred to by the name of the last Sinhalese kingdom to fall to British control in 1815, Kandy, hence being known as Kandyan Sinhalese, constituting less than half of the total Sinhalese population. The symbolic value of Kandy in contemporary Sinhalese identity should not be underestimated; as Tambiah writes: "To modern-day Sinhalese, the Kandyan kingdom represents their 'traditional past'" (1986, 97). The coastal group, basically on the west and south coasts, was more affected by colonial contact and accounts for most of the Sinhalese population and most of the English-educated Sinhalese; this segment of the population is known as the Low-Country Sinhalese.

The Tamils have a different and both older and newer pattern of regional diversity. First, northern and eastern Tamils differ culturally, and the two areas "had neither strong social interconnections nor acted as political collectivities," whether we consider the pre- or postcolonial periods. Daniel, in fact, argues that the eastern Tamils not only distinguish themselves from the peninsular or "Jaffna" Tamils but actually resent the dominance of the latter in Tamil politics and nationalism. Collectively, however, these Tamils are known as "Ceylon Tamils" because of their long habitation of the island, long enough to think of themselves, and *usually* to be thought of by others, as indigenous to the island. But there is another group of Tamils in Sri Lanka called the "Indian Tamils" or sometimes the "estate Tamils." The majority of the world's Tamils—some thirty to forty million—live in south India, not Sri Lanka, and the connection between the two localities of Tamils has always been active, from ancient south Indian invasions and interventions in Sri Lankan political affairs to more modern economic and cultural exchanges; this is illustrated by the fact that, until the late nineteenth century, an equal or greater number of Ceylon Tamils migrated to Madras in search of work as migrated to Colombo. This Indian-Ceylon Tamil relations alone is sufficiently suspicious to the Sinhalese to be a factor in the latter's animosity toward the Tamils.

Yet a culturally more threatening factor has been the presence of recent Tamil immigrants from south India, who can make no claim to Sri Lankan nationality. As a result of colonial development, namely plantation estate development in upland parts of the island, and in conjunction with British imperial domination of India, large numbers of Tamils from India were introduced into Sri Lanka in the nineteenth and twentieth centuries as laborers. From 1871 to 1881, during the coffee boom, 24,000 Indians per year were brought to Sri Lanka, and during the tea boom, from 1891 to 1900, 34,000 annually, adding 10 percent to the population of the island. The very height of this labor importation came in the years 1923–28, during peak years of rubber production, when yearly Indian

Tamil immigration averaged 60,000. By 1953 Indian Tamils outnumbered Ceylon Tamils slightly, 984,327 to 908,705, almost all located in traditionally and strongly Sinhalese areas in the central part of the country, right in the midst of the old Kandyan kingdom, yet almost totally unintegrated with the rest of the society. And, finally, little or no kinship was felt between Ceylon Tamils and this new constituency of Indian Tamils. Daniel even finds a certain amount of hostility and resentment between the two groups; for example, each group has pejorative nicknames for the other and criticizes the dialect of the other (1996, 18).

Perhaps most interestingly, Sinhalese and Tamil societies are internally differentiated by caste. The Tamil caste system is clearer, is more affected by concepts of purity or cleanliness, and has arguably been less challenged by social change than the Sinhalese, yet caste is an important feature for both, and both systems are distinct in ways from the Indian caste system. In Sinhalese society one special feature is the absence of a Brahmin category; instead, the highest caste is the *goyigama* (or *goigama*), the farmer category. It is the majority caste, at around 60 percent, although not all *goyigamas* are actually farmers, and not all farmers are *goyigamas.* Within the caste are various grades, *radalas* being the highest among Kandyan Sinhalese and *mudalis* highest among Low-Country Sinhalese. Next in rank after *goyigamas* is the *karava,* or fisherman caste; the *salagama,* or cinnamon peeler caste; and the *durava,* or toddy tapper caste. After this collection of categories come the *navandannas* or *achariyas,* the artisans and smiths. In the case of Tamil castes, in accordance with the importance of "cleanliness," or "ritual purity," the highest caste is Brahmin, but the majority caste, as with the Sinhalese, is the cultivator, or *vellala,* caste. Also in the category of "clean castes" are the *karaiyars* and *mukkuvas* (fishers) and the *koviyars* (laundrymen), and so on. At the bottom are the "unclean castes," essentially untouchables, including the *pallars* and *Nalavars.*

The first thing to consider in unpacking this diversity and its role in contemporary ethnic affairs is that Sinhalese *karavas* and *salagamas* benefited inordinately from Western contact and the economic opportunities presented thereby. Many *karavas* and *salagamas* became wealthy, often surpassing their caste superiors. Furthermore, many *karavas,* in particular, converted to Christianity, while most *goyigamas* remained Buddhist. Thus, a potentially significant intraethnic rift was created in terms of economics and religion. Also, rather than assimilating to the *goyigama* caste, which may have been ideologically impossible anyway, the lower but economically mobile castes "maintained their caste solidarity, and kept their wealth within the caste by arranging suitable marriages" (Farmer 1963, 49). And, although many adopted European names and other superficial aspects of Western culture, they did not attempt to use Western ideology to undo the caste system; instead, they used caste ideology, specifically genealogies, to establish their *kshatriya* (warrior) origins and therefore their superiority to the *goyigamas,* to explain and enjoy fully their new-found wealth and status.

Predictably, this pitted the nouveau riche *karava* and *salagama* castes "politically"—that is, not only for political office but for social power and recognition—against the traditionally high-status *goyigamas;* in fact, before about 1925 some of the bitterest competition in Ceylon was not intercommunal but intercaste. This differentiation and competition took place both in the religious and political realms. In terms of religion the very Buddhist priesthood was split more or less along caste lines by the nineteenth century: the older *siam nikaya* sect, essentially a brotherhood of *goyigama* monks, was joined and challenged after the turn of the century by four *amarapura nikaya* sects drawn principally from the lower castes.[1]

The challenge of the lower castes to their traditional betters also took political and polemical form. During the period when Christianity and Buddhism as a whole were in competition for the soul of Ceylon, the castes entered into a similar debate, particularly in the years 1868–70. In 1876 a *karava* monk named Weligame Sri Sumangala Thero published a treatise known as *Itihasa* arguing for the superiority of his caste over the *goyigamas.* Over the following decade some seventeen pamphlets appeared out of various castes contributing to the controversy, and this issue lived on at least into the early 1900s. In politics proper the lower castes, especially the *karava,* openly competed with the *goyigamas* for office: when the 1911 Legislative Council elections permitted the seating of one Sinhalese member, the *karava* caste put forward its own candidate, H. Marcus Fernando, which led the *goyigamas,* who perceived that they could not defeat this action alone, to support the Tamil candidate, Sir Ponnambalam Ramanathan. In other words, not only were Sinhalese pitted against Sinhalese, but same-status castes *across* ethnic boundaries still recognized some common cause and allied themselves in disregard of ethnicity in favor of caste interests; as a contemporary observer, Sir Hugh Clifford, described it, the campaign of 1911 "was fought purely on caste lines, a

1. Dharmadasa (1992, 88) gives the names Mulavamsa, Saddhammavamsa, Dharmaraksitvamsa, and Kalyanavamsa and describes them as "of Burmese inspiration."

high caste Tamil being chosen with the aid of the high caste Sinhalese vote, caste prejudice thus proving to be a stronger passion than racial bias" (qtd. in Ludowyk 1966, 154). Even after independence, caste interests were still powerful enough to have implications for party politics: the *salagama* faction within the United National Party (UNP) defected from the party in the 1950s and helped bring it down and precipitate the SLFP victory in 1956 that empowered Sinhalese nationalism with government authority, and later the same caste played a part in bringing down the Sri Lanka Freedom Party (SLFP) government. In addition, Ponnambalam (1983) asserts that the *karavas* helped and organize and agitate for the Sinhala-only policy in order to break the power of Tamils and the *vellala-goyigama* alliance.

Within the Tamil community the caste picture is perhaps even more complicated and contentious. Like the Sinhalese case, Tamil caste creates an intraethnic element of rivalry, particularly between two upper-caste groups (the *vellela* and the *karaiyars*) and between the upper-caste and the lower-caste categories in general. Tambiah notes that recently, and "ironically," tension between *vellelas* and *karaiyars* has "surfaced at the time of the political mobilization of all Tamils." Yet to me this seems not at all ironic, since the moment of mobilization is also the moment of decision about the definition and direction of that movement, when intracommunal cleavages must and will show themselves. There is no reason to presuppose that ethnic identities will triumph over other types of identities. In regard to the lower or untouchable castes we see here an illustration of how such striations within an ethnic group may actually shape or impede common ethnic consciousness.

This process of internal differentiation and contradiction is brought out well in Pfaffenberger's (1994) discussion of an incident in 1968 between *vellelas* and the lower *Nalavars* and *pallars.* Two points need to be made first. One is that the Jaffna area contains a particularly large segment of these "outcastes," while *vellela* dominance is nearly complete. The other is that extensive restrictions, called "sumptuary restrictions," control the lives and conduct of the outcastes. For example, they were at the time forbidden to attend school, to sit on a bus, to own a car or bicycle, to wear shoes, to cremate their dead, to use laundries, cafes, or taxis, or—the subject of the present case—to enter temples.[2] The incident under consideration was a confrontation over the restriction against temple entry. The

2. See Pfaffenberger 1994, 148, for a complete list of caste restrictions.

instructive element for us, however, is that, in the process, caste became an issue in ethnic identity: some *vellelas* denied that *Nalavars* and *pallars* were "really Tamils," while *Nalavars* and *pallars* would use the designation "Tamil" only to refer to *vellelas.* In other words, speaking the same language, observing the same religion, inhabiting the same region, sharing the same "racial" qualities—sometimes all of these are still not enough to create ethnic solidarity and to embrace subgroups under the same ethnic rubric. Ethnic categories are, and certainly were in this case, more volatile and particularistic than that; here the term and the identity *Tamil* had a much restricted meaning and referent *for both subgroups* than it has or has come to have in conventional social and political parlance.

We can see then in the Sri Lankan ethnogenesis—that is, castes coming together to form ethnic groups or pulling apart to form schisms within ethnic groups—a hint of the general process of "differential incorporation" to which Tambiah has alluded. In south Asian societies as a whole he identifies a phenomenon by which societies incorporate new and alien groups such as the waves of migrants who came to and settled in Sri Lanka over its 2,500-year history. In this process the groups are absorbed by "inferiorization": they are first aggregated from disparate communities into a caste and then assigned to a place in society, but an *inferior* place, in keeping with the hierarchical ideology of the caste system. By doing so, he suggests, "the numerous migrations and infusions of South Indian peoples . . . were later aggregated as the *karava* caste, the *salagama* caste, and so on" (1986, 101) and integrated into Sinhalese society, but in a subordinate position.

Roberts, in his extensive discussion of caste change and conflict, develops this point further, maintaining that the *karava, salagama,* and *durava* castes are, for the most part, relatively recent immigrants to the island, arriving between the thirteenth and eighteenth centuries. He also asserts that they are of Dravidian origin, making them kin to the Tamils, but that they were eventually fitted into the *rajakariya* system and amalgamated and accepted as Sinhalese castes. Even more interestingly, he identifies more modern processes, including colonial ones, which have altered the definitions and fortunes of these groups. For instance, although the three lower castes were not each confined to any single occupation traditionally, the European (initially Portuguese) practice of classifying groups according to occupation led the *karavas* to be designated as "fishers" synonymously with the *kevullo* category, such a low-ranking status that the equation "was not merely derogatory, but carried damn-

ing status implications" (1982, 56). The dominant *goyigamas* apparently were more than happy to see this affront to *karava* social rank, leading Roberts to refer to the entire episode as a case of "attempted murder by classification." On the other hand, as is often emphasized, the changes that colonialism, European rule, and economic modernization brought also acted as "partial solvents of the status quo," offering previously nonexistent avenues of protest, advancement, and competition.

The Historical Is the Political

We have been struggling so far with the conventional idea that the Sinhalese and Tamils are two distinct and homogeneous nations. But what of the other typical notion, that they are historically, even primordially, opposed to each other? Somehow out of all this diversity, with various potentialities for ethnic identity formation, the identities on the island have coalesced into only two, and two very conflictual, options. In Sri Lanka history plays a particularly critical role in ethnogenesis, partly because the Sinhalese are characterized by an unusually productive historical consciousness and partly because of the antiquity and extent of the literate tradition on the island. As we discussed in the first chapter, however, history is open to various interpretations and to various uses, especially when that history is at least in part mythological.

For the Sinhalese their national identity and political history (and future) are invested in their special historical relation, even mission, in regard to Buddhism and the epic struggles in which they have engaged to preserve Buddhist culture on the island. The historical charter text is the *Mahavamsa,* and to a lesser degree the *Dipavamsa,* the *Culavamsa,*[3] and the *Rajavaliya,* the ancient chronicles of the Sinhalese Buddhist kingdoms. The *Mahavamsa* in particular tells the tale of the establishment of the Sinhalese and of Buddhism on the island and of the subsequent fortunes of Sinhalese Buddhist civilization under the impact of various settlers and invaders. In the chronicle the island of Lanka was originally uninhabited by humans but was populated by demons called *Yakkhas* and *Nagas* and was ruled over by the demon-king Ravana (of Ramayana fame). Meanwhile, in northern India the daughter of the king of Vanga was attacked by a lion (*sinha*) who abducted her and impregnated her, leading to the birth of two children—a son, Sihabahu, and a daughter, Sihasivali. The two sib-

3. Kemper (1991) maintains that the name Culavamsa makes an unnecessary distinction between the earlier and later chronicles, all of which he posits are genuinely *Mahavamsa.*

lings ruled as king and queen of a city called Sihapura and had sixteen pairs of twin sons, of whom the eldest son was named Vijaya. Vijaya, the chronicles assert, was violent, demonic; according to the *Dipavamsa,* "he committed most wicked and fearful deeds, plundering the people." Finally, he and seven followers were exiled to the land of Lanka.

We can determine the timing of these events because the chronicles posit that on the very day of Vijaya's arrival on Lanka the Buddha died but not before uttering these words in the *Mahavamsa:* "Vijaya, the son of king Sinhabahu [*sic*], is come to Lanka from the country of Lala, together with seven followers. In Lanka, Oh lord of Gods, will my religion be established, and carefully protect him with his followers and Lanka." We can therefore set the date of the first "human" settlers on Lanka at 543 B.C.E.[4] To return to the tale, which differs in details in the various documents from this point, Vijaya, with the direct or indirect aid of the Buddha (who in one version makes a personal appearance on the island), vanquished the demonic inhabitants with the help of one of the *yakkhini* (female demons) named Kuvanna, whom he married. Thus were born the Sihala, the "people of the lion." Note that this story of Vijaya is not the only tale about the colonization of the island. Gunawardana (1990) mentions other myths that assign the origin of the civilization to a merchant or traveler named Simhala.

In any event, while Buddhism was prophesied for Lanka, it did not arrive until the rule of Asoka (ruled 274–237 B.C.E.), the great Buddhist Indian emperor, who sent a mission there headed by Mahinda; Mahinda and four other *thera* (elders) reportedly arrived in the air at the city of Anuradhapura and converted the king, Devanampiya Tissa. As a Buddhist kingdom, Anuradhapura thrived and grew, until some south Indian (Dravidian or Tamil) ruler usurped the throne. Thus commences one of the other great recurrent—and politically evocative—themes in the mythological texts: the interruption and ruination of Sinhalese Buddhist society by non-Sinhalese, non-Buddhist interlopers and the continuing necessity to oppose and eliminate this interference. In other words, a pattern becomes evident in Sir Lankan history, which emerges "as a great apocalyptic clash between the Sinhalese, who possessed the island and the Tamils (Dravidas), who came seeking to dispossess them" (Arasaratnam 1987, 34).

4. The date of the Buddhas life, and therefore death, varies according to various traditions. In Sri Lanka the traditional date of his death is 543 B.C.E., as evidenced by the celebration of the 2,500th anniversary of the event in 1956. In India the date is often identified as 486 B.C.E. and in China as 947 B.C.E.

The first, and most commonly referred to in modern discourse, round of this cosmic struggle occurred between the Tamil king Elara and the Sinhalese Buddhist culture hero Dutugamunu (which is transliterated in a variety of phonetically similar ways), or "Gamani the Angry." In the *vamsa* texts King Elara, who ruled for forty-four years, was admittedly a foreign ruler but a righteous one: he ruled "with even justice toward friend and foe" and was "a protector of [Buddhist] tradition," speaks the *Mahavamsa.* In fact, this is one of many occasions when Sinhalese and Tamils lived together in relative ethnic harmony. Yet Dutugamunu and his army of ten champions—each of whom possessed superhuman qualities and some of whom are reckoned as demons even today—defeated Elara and took control over the kingdom in the name of Buddhism. Says the *Mahavamsa* of Dutugamunu: "His war-cry was 'Not for kingdom but for Buddhism.'"

In the process of winning back the kingdom for Buddhism, Dutugamunu's actions also accomplished another crucial and fateful goal, which was to unify purportedly the entire island under one polity for the first time in history. From this point on Sinhalese Buddhists can and do claim title to the whole island, regardless of who "temporarily" wrests control of what part of it from them. This unified Lankan polity was centered on the north-central city of Anuradhapura, which claimed (and sometimes but not always exercised) sovereignty over the total island; the region around Anuradhapura was known as the King's Country, "Rajarata." The pattern set in these early events was repeated with sufficient regularity to affect the historical consciousness of the chroniclers and their descendants. In the fifth century C.E. an invasion from south India resulted in the conquest of Anuradhapura, which was "liberated" or reconquered by Dhatusena twenty-five years later. Again in the ninth century the same Pandyan kingdom of south India sacked Anuradhapura for the first but not last time; in 993 the Chola empire annexed Rajarata.

As a result of these conquests, the Sinhalese kingdom began to recede to the south and west from Anuradhapura. Sinhalese Buddhist power revived briefly under Parakramabahu (1153–86), who is the main subject of the first update of the *Mahavamsa* tradition and is second in legendary fame only to Dutugamunu, but after this time a long protracted decline of Sinhalese Buddhist civilization set in. By the early thirteenth century Sinhalese Buddhist power had removed itself to the far southwest of the island, and a separate Tamil kingdom was established at Jaffna in the north, which lasted continuously (with the exception of a seventeen-year period when Sinhalese prince Sapumal seized it [1450–67]) until the arrival of the Portuguese in the early seventeenth century.

Two themes rise immediately from this tale. One is that Sri Lanka has always been closely linked to the civilizations of India, even of south India, whether by choice or by force. Sinhalese royalty often took wives from south Indian kingdoms and were often militarily allied with them, either requesting or sending soldiers in times of mutual need. Their contact, then, although often hostile, was also often friendly. The other theme is that south Indian / Tamil hostile contact has been regular enough and jarring enough to serve as a cause—or at least an *explanation*—of the decline of Sinhalese Buddhist civilization in general; Sinhalese misfortune could be and was blamed on south Indian interference and (by the Buddhist monkish chroniclers) on Sinhalese religious infidelity. As a thirteenth-century Sinhalese document maintains:

> This island belongs to the Buddha himself . . . therefore, the residence of wrong-believers in the Island will never be permanent, just as the residence of the Yakkhas old was not permanent. Even if a non-Buddhist ruled Ceylon by force for a while, it is a particular power of the Buddha that his line will not be established. Therefore, as Lanka is suitable only for Buddhist kings, it is certain that their lines, too, will be established. (Qtd. in Little 1994, 29)[5]

Let us, then, emphasize these key points: (1) the Sinhalese can and do argue that the island is theirs by right of priority, as they were the first (or at least the first *human*) inhabitants of Sri Lanka; (2) they can and do argue that the island is theirs by right of the unique dispensation of the Buddha himself and by the world historical mission of Lanka in Buddhism; (3) they can and do argue that they once ruled the entire island politically and that therefore the island is historically theirs by the right of precedent; and (4) they can and do argue that all of their tribulations come from south India in general and from Tamils in particular and that they are in constant or recurring danger from that place and those people.

---

5. It is reported that early Sinhalese nationalist Anagarika Dharmapala loved to quote this passage.

The link between this mythological history and historical consciousness on the one hand and more contemporary ethnic developments on the other has been made in two ways: in terms of the ethos that this religiocultural vision imbues in the Sinhalese and in terms of the subsequent political uses, beginning in colonial times and extending into the present, to which they have been put in the process of "inventing" a Sinhalese (and an opposing Tamil) group and in wrestling over the social and economic resources of the modern state. In a controversial exegesis Kapferer suggests that the religious ethos of Sinhalese Buddhism embodies a cosmology that emphasized and conjoins two critical ideas, evil and the state. "The violence of Dutugamunu—and of Vijaya—is the violence of the sacred. It is the violence of opposition, of birth, and of recreative transformation," argues Kapferer (1988, 62). In the *vamsa* literature the state is the vessel of the culture and religion, especially the *sangha,* and it is the state (directly; the *sangha* and religion indirectly) that is portrayed as under assault in the chronicles. In other words, the state is continuously exposed to evil, the evil of "destructive fragmentation," of "decline, reformation, and re-creation." Furthermore, he asserts, the state and the nation (the Sinhalese people) are in "dangerous reciprocal conjunction," such that an attack on one is an attack on the other, and therefore the nation takes "very personally indeed any opposition to the state by persons who are ontologically foreign and threatening" to the state, its institutions, and its order (100–101). Thus, in his most interesting and controversial analytical move he likens Sri Lanka's ethnic violence to "a gigantic exorcism"; the "passion of ethnic violence" is related to "the passion of sorcery." Contemporary ethnicity is myth become historical reality, with all of its attendant energy. As one of his more convincing bits of evidence, he mentions the Asala festival, an annual Sinhalese ceremony of Kandyan kinghood and statehood; he notes that the most vigorous modern rioting, in 1977, 1981, and 1983, all occurred at or after the time of Asala.

On the other hand, Kemper analyzes the *Mahavamsa* literature in terms of the salience of two themes: unity and heroic leadership. The three great heroes of the chronicles—Vijaya (whose name means "victory"), Dutugamunu, and Parakramabahu—are all great unifiers of the people and the island, carriers of important cultural-historical missions. Unity itself has been a fragile commodity through the centuries, coming and going with the vicissitudes of politics and culture. This fact leads to the Sinhalese historical self-image of "having been repeatedly threatened through their history by outside forces, occasionally saved by heroic leaders, and now left defenseless" (1991, 207).

Reviving—or Creating—History

Sinhalese historical consciousness provided a fertile raw material for nation building, but to become such a force it required a catalyst. After all, the texts upon which this memory was based were monkish and not popular ones before the eighteenth century or so, which means that the stories were told from a distinctly monkish point of view and that the texts themselves were not thoroughly known to the masses nor even to all *bhikkhus.* Lay people knew bits and pieces of the tradition the way medieval Christians knew bits and pieces of the Bible without actually seeing one, but the text itself was "more a cultural object to be treasured than a book to be read" (Kemper 1991, 191). Colonialism, however, would change all that.

Sinhalese "cultural revival" began under the forces of colonialism not as a reaction to Tamil ethnicity or Hinduism but to Christianity. Reacting to the decline of Buddhism under European missionization, a Buddhist revival was attempted as soon as the late eighteenth century, when *bhikkhus* were brought from Thailand and Burma to rejuvenate the *sangha* and the king had Buddhist temples rebuilt and texts copied—and this king (named Kirti Sri) was not even a Sinhalese but a Tamil. The most important and sustained revival, however, and the one that most influenced modern ethnic consciousness began in the mid-nineteenth century and was a by-product of British colonialism and Hindu reform movements in India. Even before the British printing presses had made their way to Ceylon, and the first books in Sinhalese and Tamil were published, mostly Bibles and catechism books; having texts, even foreign subject texts, in indigenous languages helped to strengthen both languages but especially Tamil, due to the quantity of work devoted to it in both Ceylon and southern India. For the Sinhalese Buddhists autonomous publishing began in the mid-nineteenth century, with the first Buddhist newspaper, *Lak Mini Pahana,* commencing in 1862. In the decade 1860–70 ten new Buddhist periodicals were opened, and by 1890 there were nineteen such journals, as compared to nine Christian publications. Altogether there were over 150 Sinhalese newspapers and periodicals (Dharmadasa 1992, 170).

But at least as important as the very existence of these media were their contents. They covered topics from Oriental literature to Ayurveda and astrology to Buddhist and Pali philology to affairs concerning the "welfare of the Sinhalese people." They reflected a widespread and focused new revival of Sinhalese Buddhist culture, very largely under the aegis of the political *bhikkhus,* who, since the *Mahavamsa* days, had seen it as their right and duty to be active in the preservation and promotion of the religion. Buddhist *samagamas* (associations) were formed, such as *Sarvagna Sasanabhivruddhi Dayaka Dharma Samagama* (Society for the Propagation of Buddhism) in 1862. This activity reflected a clear modernization of culture that had no counterpart in Sinhalese tradition; as Dharmadasa writes, "In place of the primordial social relations based on tradition and sentiment, associative social relations were being formed—based on reasoned deliberation and personal choice" (1992, 131–32).[6]

From the 1860s on the struggle between Buddhism and Christianity was active and articulate. Activist *bhikkhus* were necessarily at the center of it; for example, one of them, Walane Siddhartha, was the founder of *Lak Mini Pahana.* Another was Batuwantudawe, who wrote *Kristiani Prajnapti Khandanaya* (The Tearing Asunder of the Evidence and Doctrine of Christianity) in response to an influential pro-Christian tract. Most important, there was Migettuwatte Gunananda, *salagama* monk and leading spokesman for Ceylonese Buddhism. It was he who founded the *samagama* mentioned previously and who engaged in a public debate with Christian Sinhalese in 1873, which was attended by ten thousand people who generally agreed that Gunananda had won. In this and many other ways Buddhism was proving its value and validity vis-à-vis the foreign dominant religion, even as a Buddhist constituency or nation was being constructed.

Yet neither the interest in nor the structure of Sinhalese Buddhist studies at this time was completely autochthonous. British scholarly research in the fields of history and linguistics played a substantial role in enhancing the interest in and defining the parameters of knowledge in Ceylon as in most parts of the empire. This scholarship "discovered" or injected two elements into the cultural mix in Ceylon: the notion that Sinhala is derived from Sanskrit and therefore that it is an Indo-European or Aryan language (in distinction to the non-Aryan Dravidian roots of Tamil), and the general conception of race, namely as a device to understand linguistic and cultural differences (i.e., that each language group is a race group). The logical connection between these two notions was made by a Sinhalese scholar, James D'Alwis, who in the 1850s and 1860s placed Sinhala in the Aryan language family and, by extension, "placed the Sinhalese on the side of the light against the putative darkness and primitivity of the Dravidian presence" (Pfaffenberger 1994, 21). D'Alwis's most enduring con-

6. Dharmadasa also provides an extensive list of such *samagama* organizations.

tribution was the translation of the *Sidat Sangarava,* a medieval Sinhalese grammar, which not only helped revive interest in Sinhalese language and literature but which aimed to glorify that language and literature as ancient, pure—and threatened.

One other unmistakable influence came directly out of the West, and that was the neo- or pseudo-Eastern Theosophical Society. Madame Blavatsky and Henry Steele Olcott took an active interest in Sinhalese Buddhism and even traveled there for a series of public lectures in 1880. Gunananda, of Christian-Buddhist debate fame, was in contact with them and introduced a young man named Anagarika Dharmapala to them. This was to be a momentous event, as Dharmapala went on to become a champion of Sinhalese Buddhist civilization. But the initial action were all Olcott's. It was he who published *The Buddhist Catechism,* organized the Buddhist Theosophical Society and a number of BTS schools (that reached 225 by 1910), and encouraged Dharmapala's curiosity into traditional Buddhist culture. From this time on Buddhist revivalism took on a distinctly Western hue, from the formation of the Young Men's Buddhist Association (YMBA) to the catechistic nature of the new Buddhist teaching and the Western-style organizational structure to the racial and nationalistic facets that infused it. The journal of the BTS, *Sarasavi Sandarasa* (started in 1880), offered the "most persistent and vociferous enunciation of the Sinhalese-Buddhist identity" among the organs of early Sinhalese nationalism and emphasized the issue of cultural authenticity" (Dharmadasa 1992, 121). Other Sinhalese journals, like *Lankapakaraya,* and the newspaper *Lak Mini Kirula* (both 1881) also published articles dealing explicitly with Lankan/Sinhalese history and highlighting the sanguine role of Buddhism in this history: the former, in its first editorial, wrote, "although Lanka is a small country it was shining brightly during the time of our monarchs because of the all-around welfare of the people in the spheres of various arts and the Buddhist religion" (qtd. in Dharmadasa 1992, 120). This history also was interlaced and informed by excerpts and tales from the chronicles, such as the following comments from the newspaper *Lak Mini Pahana.*

> Although the cruel king named Elara came here hoping to uproot the Sinhalese nation and waged war, as the Sinhalese royal family remained safe in the southern region, the fortunate prince Dutthagamini [*sic*] came forth and destroyed the Tamils and constructed the great edifices which can still be seen in Anuradhapura, thus making it possible to be

> said that the Sinhalese were a great nation. (Qtd. in Dharmadasa 1992, 140)

This represented, as Tambiah has suggested, a "popularization" of a high mythohistorical tradition, which began to make ancient monkish knowledge an aspect of general information and discourse and to equate mythic chronicle with empirical history.

This popularization, and concomitant Westernization, took numerous forms, some of which we have already mentioned. Besides newspapers, journals, and *samagamas,* drama societies, social movements, and "popular art" functioned to elevate or create, objectify, and ultimately sanctify Sinhalese Buddhist culture. The Sinhala Naya Samagama (Sinhala Drama Society) formed to work for "the honour of the Sinhala race," as did the aptly named Drama Society for the Adornment of the Sinhala Language and the Drama Society for the Edification of the Sinhala Aryans. And the glorification of Sinhalese culture, at this time, entailed a criticism or rejection of Western culture, as in temperance movements like the Colombo Total Abstinence Union and in literature like the novels of Piyadasa Sirisens, the first of which was, again, serialized in a Sinhalese newspaper. M. J. de Silva, whose early-twentieth-century plays dramatized moments from Sinhalese history, made it his deliberate aim "to propagate once again the Sinhalese music that has gone into abeyance; to depict the ancient customs, dress, ornaments, etc.; to censure the evil habits among our people today; to re-create the national awareness that has been of yore; and to foster a love for the Sinhala language among the younger generation who now find it distasteful" (qtd. in Dharmadasa 1992, 128).

It should be evident that Sinhalese national consciousness, at least as it exists today, did not exist before this period but was intentionally and strenuously created through the activities of nationalist-minded elites who selected and manipulated cultural resources (like history, culture, and literature) for distribution to an ever-increasing audience for politicocultural reasons (initially, to resist British domination; later, of course, to root out and oppose Tamil / south Indian threats to national sovereignty, economic success, and cultural honor). In this process Dharmapala (1864–1933) holds a place of singular influence. Being himself, to a degree, a product of Westernized Buddhism in the form of the Theosophical Society, he became the leading spokesman for Sinhalese Buddhist nationalism and helped frame the discourse that energized that nationalism through the 1950s to the 1980s and even to this day.

Let us remember that Dharmapala's, as most Sinhalese nationalists', main goal was to discredit and undermine Western imperialism. And, as in most early anti-imperialist movements, the language of resistance was religious more so than political or economic; in this case the Sinhalese nationalists' unique relationship to Buddhism made Western interference untenably offensive. Added to this was the fact that the Sinhalese nation was itself unique in all the world, having no homeland other than its island.

> The island of Lanka belongs to the Buddhist Sinhalese. For 2455 years this was the land of birth for the Sinhalese. Other races have come here to pursue their commercial activities. For the Europeans, apart from this land, there is Canada, Australia, South Africa, England and America to go to; for the Tamils there is South India; for the Moors . . . Egypt; the Dutch can go to Holland. But for the Sinhalese there only this island. (Qtd. in Dharmadasa 1992, 138)

And, consequentially, Dharmapala incorporated the new racial arguments that Western influence made available:

> the Aryan race is the only race with noble customs handed down from tradition. . . . [therefore] the Sinhalese (who are Aryans) should cultivate ancient codes of conduct, Aryan customs and Aryan dresses and ornaments. . . . The Sinhalese first came to this country from Bengal and the Bengalis are superior in their intelligence to other communities in India. (145–46)

The ethnic implications of this position are clear enough: the Europeans have ruined Sinhalese culture and dragged it and the Sinhalese people down to the level of the "lower races": "From the day the white man set foot on this island, the arts and sciences and the Aryan customs of the Sinhalese have gradually disappeared and today the Sinhalese have to kiss the feet of the Moor [and] the dastardly Tamil" (138). This pits the Sinhalese and the Tamils (and we should not forget the Muslims) in a way that is not altogether traditional in Ceylonese experience.

Even so, there was a tradition upon which Dharmapala could call and from which he could extract ethnonationalist meaning, and this is the *vamsa* literary tradition. The chronicles were evidence of "the inseparable connection between state and *sangha*," telling a story that was as relevant and true now as then. In it he and like-minded nationalists found support for racial interpretations of Sinhalese identity, Vijaya being the "progenitor of the 'Aryan' Sinhala people," and for the interpretation of Sinhalese history as a continuous and unified struggle against foreign enemies bent of the destruction of Buddhism and Sinhalese sovereignty. In this latter cause Dharmapala's favorite historical character was Dutugamunu, the "righteous" king who fought for and restored Buddhism to its foremost place in Lankan civilization. Even more, the same struggle was under way at present, and the same—or an even greater—cultural effort was called for: "During king Dutthagamini's [*sic*] time the Sinhalese had only one enemy. In the present day there are several races who are prepared to destroy the Sinhalese people: the English, Tamils, Muslim, Malay, Parsee, Bombay [*sic*] and Kabul" (qtd. in Dharmadasa 1992, 141). That the Sinhalese nation had survived all of these assaults and insults was part of the testimony of its greatness.

While Dharmapala's works were not a focused assault on Tamils in Ceylon, they provided what Little has called "a warrant for intolerance" and "all the essential premises" for a modern crusade against the Tamils: "the racial and religious purity and superiority of the Sinhala; their incontestable sacred and historic right to rule, the need to contain and control the always menacing, barely tolerable non-Sinhala minorities of the island" (1994, 36). For him and subsequent Sinhalese culture revivalists, the vision of Ceylon did not include a notion of a multiethnic society; Ceylon (and later Sri Lanka) was Sinhalese.

No doubt, Tamil opinions on such questions were different, and we can follow a parallel but often interacting development of Tamil historical consciousness and "ethnic mobilization," even ethnogenesis, throughout the same general period and under the impact of the same general forces. Not only were the interpretations of group identity different, however, but also the locus was: while the Sinhalese emphasized history, the Tamils emphasized "heritage" (Daniel 1996), that is, their actual or potential present and past cultural characteristics. Thus, early Tamil ethnic mobilization took the form of "an indigenous literary and cultural movement among the Tamils dedicated to the antiquity, originality, and preeminence of Dravidian culture" (Little 1994, 38). Ceylonese Tamils identified with and followed the lead of South Indian revivalism, recognizing close cultural, social, and language links, celebrating their history and culture, and distinguishing themselves from the Sinhalese in the same way that southern Indians distinguished themselves from northern Indians. Tamils also organized parties and groups like the Justice Party, the Madras Presidency Association, and the Self-Respect Movement.

To illustrate the cultural focus of Tamil nationalism we can consider the Tamil counterpart to the Sinhalese Dharmapala, a man named Arumugan Nalavar, who founded Jaffna Hindu College. His aim, as he expressed it, was "to return the people to a strictly textual religion bereft of both the deviations that carelessness had wrought in the practice of Saivite religion and the vulgarizations of the folk cults—the cults of goat sacrifice, nautch dancing, and wordless pujas performed by the 'unclean' and the uninitiated" (qtd. in Tambiah 1986, 107). Tambiah goes on to assert that the educated Jaffna Tamils became the champions of traditional Tamil culture, including classical Tamil language, music, and dance. These markers, more than dynastic history, set Tamils apart from Sinhalese in Ceylon.

Even so, Tamil identity gradually became more "historicized," and when they sought to articulate their history the Tamils turned in part to the same source that the Sinhalese did—the *vamsa* literature. In it they found many elements that could be used to highlight either the often close and cordial relations between Sinhalese and Tamils or the independent glory of Tamil civilization on the island. In the area of the former they could point to the facts that Vijaya married a south Indian princess, that Sinhalese kings regularly took brides from south India, that Tamils are acknowledged as inhabitants of Lanka for about as long as Sinhalese have been there, that some Tamil rulers (even Tamil rulers over Sinhalese populations) like Elara are praised for their justice and protection of Buddhism (and that "Sinhalese" heroes like Dutugamunu were actually opposed by many Sinhalese), and that the last Sinhalese kingdom, Kandy, was ruled near the end by Tamils kings (the Nayakkars from South India). As far as the latter is concerned, Tamils take heart from the south Indian, especially the Cholan, invasions of Lanka, with whom they identify (although the Tamils on the island had been away from southern India for a long time before the Cholas arrived); perhaps most significantly, they emphasize the sovereign Tamil kingdom centered in Jaffna since the thirteenth century.

Thus, both Tamils and Sinhalese nationalism came to take history seriously, in an effort to prove who was there first, who has done injustice to whom, and who has the right to rule what part of the country; they have even, in part, turned to the same historical materials, which they interpret in very different ways. Yet this is not the whole of the Tamil position. For one thing, they have their own documents to turn to, most important the *Yalpana Vaipava Malai* (The Garland of Jaffna Events [*YVM*]), a chronicle of Tamil history in Jaffna that was only compiled in the early eighteenth century by a Jaffna Tamil, Mayilvakana Pulavar, at the request of the Dutch governor at the time; this document, which became the standard and accepted history of the Tamils throughout the nineteenth century, was a collection of "oral traditions, palm leaf manuscripts of uncertain date, and 'lost works' only preserved in memory" (Hellman-Rajanayagam 1990, 108).

According to the *Yalpana Vaipava Malai,* Rama (the hero of the Ramayana) defeats the *yakkhas* (demons) of Lanka and particularly his enemy, the demon Ravana, and established Ravana's brother Vikhishana as ruler. This is followed by an account of Vijaya, except that Vijaya is a Saivite Indian prince, and he and his men are married to Tamil wives. Upon arrival Vijaya marries Kuvanna, or Kuveni, as in the *Mahavamsa.* Vijaya builds Saivite temples before Buddhism comes to the island. Then the chronicle switched to a history of Chola relations with Lanka; Chola kings settle the first Tamils, the *Vanniyars,* in eastern Lanka (not Jaffna) and rebuild the ruined temple at Trincomalee. A vague reference is made to Elara, although by the name of Manuniticolan. The story of the establishment of Jaffna comes next, at which point the narrative becomes a fairly straightforward history of Jaffna dynasties, with the important note that the Sinhalese and the *Vanniyars* are portrayed as the source of trouble to the kingdom. The origins of various Tamil castes are recounted, as is the arrival of the Portuguese (who are viewed negatively) and finally of the Dutch (who are viewed somewhat more positively). At that point the tale closes.

This "history" became the basis for study and debate by Tamil historians throughout the colonial period. For example, the historian Muttutampipillai in 1912 dated the reign of Elara to a time well before Vijaya ever stepped foot on the island. The Tamils, however, had a *choice of pasts* that made them "free to view and define their identity in quite different ways, *without losing their identity as Tamils,* whereas for the Sinhalese there has been one history available" (Hellman-Rajanayagam 1990, 113). Principally, they could emphasize their Sri Lankan connection or their south Indian connection: they could distinguish themselves as a unique population of Ceylonese, or identify as part of a larger social whole, or simply point to their heritage as an offshoot of that larger Dravidian society. As a result, Tamil claims to identity emphasized culture more than history and took an ambivalent and varying stand in regard to history.

Subsequently, the attitude toward and content of Tamil ethnic history also underwent a major change around 1930. Before 1930 they used their history in what has been labeled an "inclusive strategy," in which they argued that they and the Sinhalese were not so different and incompatible, both being of south Indian derivation (i.e., denying the Sinhalese claims to "Aryan" status). After 1930, however, and probably from the pressure of Sinhalese nationalist agitation, the Tamil position began to become more exclusive, asserting the distinctness, superiority, even priority of Tamils over Sinhalese. The most interesting manifestation of this position was the claim that, in fact, Tamil had been on Ceylon before the Sinhalese or even that the Sinhalese *were* Tamils. As a Tamil memo to a Ceylonese governor in 1935 stated: "The Ceylon Tamils were the original inhabitants of this island and the Sinhalese people of old regarded themselves as an off-shoot of the Tamil nation." Similarly, a Tamil politician in 1939 maintained: "The greatest Sinhalese kings are Tamils. The Tamils had an unparalleled history and an unequaled traditional culture . . . [whereas] the Sinhalese were a nation formed from the hybridization of a small class of people from north India; they were a nation of hybrids without history" (qtd. in Dharmadasa 1992, 294). Whether or not this constitutes a consensus sentiment, it certainly represents a new attitude in Tamil-Sinhalese relations.

Of course, to secure this claim history needs to be re-read and reinterpreted, which happened accordingly. For historically minded Tamil nationalists, Tamils could be located in the pages of the *Mahavamsa* from the first—in fact, in the boldest interpretation the indigenous "demon" population *was* the Tamils. Ponnambalam writes that for centuries before Sinhalese arrival there were two Naga kingdoms on Ceylon, one in the north, called Naga Tivu in Tamil and Naga Dipa in Sanskrit (note the discrediting of the Sinhala language), and one in the southwest, known as Kelaniya. Sinhalese invaders later defeated the *Naga* and *Yaksha* people, who were recast in the myths as nonhumans, snakes, and demons. This theory of a mythical "misinterpretation" is supported by the fact that the later *vamsa* literature attributes devil-like qualities to the Portuguese, who are said to drink blood and eat stones and make noises louder than thunder.

The rhetorical implications of this version are that the Sinhalese are not a superior people—not even a distinct people—but merely "Tamil people who adopted a language which developed from Pali" (20). "Racially" or by descent, they are a mixture of the indigenous people of Ceylon and subsequent invaders and settlers, both Aryan and Dravidian. Culturally, they are corrupted or inferior Tamils: "The truth is that there is no aspect of Sinhalese-Buddhist culture . . . which is not foreign or borrowed" (Ponnambalam 1983, 230). There was no "great and glorious Sinhalese-Buddhist civilization" in ancient times; in a word, "the 'identity problem' of the Sinhalese was really the absence of an identity. Therefore, what was being sought was a new identity" (237).

What is interesting and important about this polemic is not its veracity, which is unestablished (as is the Sinhalese counterpolemic) but the very terms in which it is conducted. Both sides end up invoking history, and mythical history at that, as the substance of their claims to a political stake in Sri Lanka's present and future. In this way history itself becomes political in the service of ethnic differentiation, unification, legitimation, and mobilization. Thus, vernacularization and transmission of mythohistorical themes to as wide a political audience as possible is to the advantage of both groups. For example, episodes from the *vamsa* literature, like the adventures of Vijaya or Dutugamunu, are not only reproduced in political dialogue but also in school textbooks and presented as factual evidence of "Sinhalese identity and Sinhalese political rights." Furthermore, debunking the accuracy of the other group's history becomes a major activity, taking various forms: attempts to show inconsistencies in the chronicles that undermine their credibility; exegesis that emphasizes otherwise "silent" (ethnically nonselected) passages or themes in the historical literature, such as that Dutugamunu was resisted by many Sinhalese princes and aided by some Tamil ones; construction of alternative histories, as we have seen in the *YVM* and subsequent Tamil histories; and the politicization of the evidence that would support one ethnic version over another. This includes not only textual evidence but material evidence as well, such as that collected by physical anthropology and archaeology; the former would establish biological/racial similarities and differences between groups that one group or the other would contest, while the latter would substantiate historical claims with real artifactual evidence.

Therefore, we see the escalating tension between Sinhalese and Tamils accompanied by "rhetorical wars fought over archaeological sites, place-name etymologies, and the interpretation of ancient inscriptions" (Spencer 1990, 3). These wars even take the form of the destruction of newly discovered archaeological sites that indicate the antiquity of one side or the other. Since the Sinhalese gained control of the post-independence government, officially sponsored archaeology "virtually equates that field with the digging of Buddhist sites and the restoration of Buddhist monuments"; with few exceptions there has not been any significant interest in "breaking the Buddhist time barrier" (Tambiah 1986, 88) that might provide ammunition for the Tamil claim that there was a Ceylonese civilization before Buddhism or even before the Sinhalese.

Background to the Conflict: Colonialism, Constitutions, and Communalism

We have been observing how historical claims evolved into cultural contestation. It remains for us to see how this cultural contestation was transformed into ethnic conflict, especially under the forces of colonialism and then electoral politics. Colonialism, even before but especially with the British, brought important and lasting changes to Ceylon, most notably Western language and education, Christianity, and the "spoils" of Western administration (jobs, offices, economic opportunities of various sorts). As early as the Portuguese period (1505–1638), the differentiation between the Low-Country Sinhalese and Kandyan Sinhalese had begun, Kandy being an area that the Portuguese never conquered or never held for long. Portugal also introduced Christianity in the form of Roman Catholicism, Portuguese names, and a new kind of racial diversity in the mixed marriages that produced the first mixed children, or Burghers. Finally, as in so many colonial contexts, the intervention of European administration actually strengthened the positions of certain local chiefs, largely Sinhalese, whose powers had been traditionally defined and delimited.

Change continued apace under the Dutch (1638–1794), who established a firmer administrative control over Ceylon. Protestantism was introduced and Catholicism persecuted, and to compensate for a shortage of labor south Indians and Indonesians (Javanese, Amboinese, and others), were imported to Ceylon, and Tamils from other parts of the island were moved into more inland (and therefore more Sinhalese) areas. This began the assemblage of the more complicated ethnic situation in Sri Lanka today. Yet it was the British who left the most important and enduring impact on Ceylon, seeing the island ultimately to independence. It was the British who finally subdued the last autonomous kingdom of Kandy in 1815, creating for the first time in the modern age a single united Ceylonese society. South Indian Tamil labor was recruited at an accelerating pace to service the expanding plantation system, creating enclaves in central Ceylon, where Indian Tamils constituted up to 75 percent of the population. The two most serious changes, however, took place in education and political organization.

Almost immediately after the establishment of the Crown Colony of Ceylon, missionary societies were permitted to enter and set up shop. The London Missionary Society (1805) was followed by the Baptists (1812), Wesleyan Methodists (1814), and Church Mission (1818); one non-British organization, the American Missionary Society (1813), was allowed to participate, though not in Colombo but only in the harsher and less desirable area of Jaffna. All missionary organizations concentrated on education in English as their main activity. The AMS was particularly successful in its mission of educating Jaffna Tamils in English, so much so that Tamils began to outdistance Sinhalese in their command of the language and therefore in their preparedness for service in colonial administrative posts. This marketable skill, plus the comparatively unfavorable environment of the arid northern peninsula, led many Tamils to migrate south and take a disproportionate percentage of jobs in what was traditionally Sinhalese country. In this way the Ceylon Tamils came to occupy a significant position in the economy and bureaucracy of Ceylon.

Beyond this, English-language education had the added effect of creating in essence a new class of Ceylonese, who were sometimes called, rather condescendingly, the "educated Ceylonese." What was interesting and important about this group was their intellectual and emotional distance from traditional Ceylonese culture and their intercommunal (and therefore noncommunal) character. Arasaratnam calls this English-educated elite "the first integrated national social class" in Ceylon, while he as well as Dharmadasa maintain that this new class had little knowledge or concern about indigenous culture, history, or literature and that they adopted Western worldviews, modes of dress, and lifestyles. Finally, this new elite was not a communal or ethnic class but rejected communalism as a solution to the problems of Ceylon and as a viable source of national identity for Ceylonese. While cooperation between ethnic communities within this elite may not have been perfect and was certainly not permanent, it was general, and the English-educated elite concept of nationality for Ceylon was "Ceylonese" rather than Sinhalese or Tamil. The result of this disparity between a small minority (4–5 percent) of "educated Ceylonese" and the rest of the island's population was the introduction of a new, powerful, and pregnant social fissure in the society.

Nevertheless, communalism was incorporated into the early administrative structure of British colonialism. Unified government of Ceylon was established in 1833, and the first Legislative Council was assembled. This council included nine official and six unofficial members, three of the latter of whom were Ceylonese—one Low-Country Sinhalese, one Tamil, and one Burgher. In 1911 the Legislative Council was reformed to include elected unofficial members, with rural Europeans, urban Europeans and Burghers, and educated Ceylonese each choosing one member; there were also six nominated members, two representing Low-Country Sinhalese, one for Kandyan Sinhalese, two Tamils, and one Muslim. The formation of the Ceylon National Congress (CNC) in 1919 brought together major Sinhalese and Tamil organizations; in fact, the president was a Tamil, Sir Ponnambalam Arunachalam. The CNC resisted communal representation in Ceylon as an attempt to divide the Ceylonese people and sought constitutional reform but especially the enhancement of the status of the elite, who had begun to realize the limitations on their economic and social advancement under the colonial system.

Constitutional reforms begun in 1920 had the effect of straining and eventually rending this intercommunal cooperation. Territorial representation necessarily put Sinhalese in a position of strength and Tamils in one of weakness: before 1920 Tamils held an equal number of seats as Sinhalese, but after 1920 the Sinhalese outnumbered the Tamils thirteen to three. The former used their majority to block the nomination of Sir Arunachalam for the legislative seat for Colombo. As a consequence, the Tamils withdrew from the CNC and formed their own party, the Tamil Mahajara Sabha, leaving the CNC as an essentially Low-Country Sinhalese organization. Continuing communal pressures were exercised during the deliberations of the Donoughmore Constitutional Commission (1928–29). Many groups, and not just the monolithic ethnic groups of Sinhalese and Tamil, came before the commission to make their case for special recognition, representation, or protection; some Kandyan Sinhalese organizations maintained that Kandyan and Low-Country Sinhalese were distinct peoples and asked for autonomy in a three-way federation of Kandyan Sinhalese, Low-Country Sinhalese, and Tamil provinces. Clearly, the modern ethnic groups, as we know them, had not at this stage of social evolution coalesced.

The final recommendations of the Donoughmore Commission, which were incorporated into the so-called Donoughmore Constitution of 1931, rejected ethnic and communal representation in favor of territorial representation. The commission's report put it thus:

> Not only is the population not homogeneous, but the diverse elements of which it is composed distrust and suspect each other. It is almost true to say that the conception of patriotism in Ceylon is as much racial as national and that the best interests of the country are at times regarded as synonymous with the welfare of a particular section of its people.

After a brief attempt to boycott the new constitution, the Tamils joined the new government and cooperated with Sinhalese leaders.

The new political structure encouraged the growth of new political parties, which had been relatively absent previously. In 1935 the Lanka Sama Samaja Party (LSSP), a leftist party, was formed, and around the same time the soon-to-be important Sinhala Maha Sahba (SMS, or Great Council of the Sinhalese) was founded by Solomon West Ridgeway Dias Bandaranaike, as a specifically Sinhalese party, out of the CNC. Bandaranaike expressed his reasoning for initiating the party as providing unity to otherwise disunited Sinhalese:

> We [the SMS] saw differences amongst our own people—caste distinctions, up-country and low-country distinctions, religious distinctions, and other distinctions—and we therefore felt that we should achieve unity, which is the goal of us all. Surely, the best method was to start from the lower rungs: firstly, unity among the Sinhalese; and secondly, whilst uniting the Sinhalese, to work for higher unity, the unity of all communities. (Qtd. in Ponnambalam 1983, 61)

Yet there was by this time an untapped, and partially undeveloped, frustration on the part of many Sinhalese, especially Sinhala-speaking Sinhalese, regarding the current state of affairs in Ceylon. They felt outside of the political system, unrepresented by the English-educated elite, who were not in touch with more traditional Sinhalese culture and interests, and threatened by the disproportion of Tamils in high places and Tamil demands for protection of those places. The Sinhalese community as a whole was on the verge of becoming "a majority with a minority complex," as Tambiah has phrased it, as if they were in danger of losing their autonomy, their birthright, their very culture, if things continued in the direction they were heading.

Communal lines began to emerge more clearly, though not yet violently, in the final decade before independence from colonialism. Two important developments in 1944 were the formation of the Ceylon Tamil Congress and the beginning of the Constitutional Commission (known as the Soulbury Commission), which eventually drafted the constitution that carried Ceylon to independence. The CTC presented an argument to the Commission for balanced or "50/50" representation for Tamils and Sinhalese on the basis that Tamils would suffer discrimination from a Sinhalese-dominated government. The commission, however, rejected the very principle of communal representation and reaffirmed the administration's commitment to territorial representation and in fact found no evidence of prior legislative discrimination and actually claimed to perceive the beginning of the erosion of communal lines under the growing force of common social and economic interests. Even so, certain provisions were included with an eye to securing minority rights and participation; for one, a section of the constitution prohibiting discriminatory legislation was inserted, and, for another, apportionment scheme based on a combination of areas as well as population was worked out that seemed to favor both Tamil and Muslim settlements in the north and east (Farmer 1963, 57). Lord Soulbury himself later expressed the opinion that the constitution "had entrenched all the protective provisions for minorities that the wit of man could devise" (qtd. in Ponnambalam 1983, 63).

The draft constitution was presented to the Ceylon state council in late 1945, and its leader, D. S. Senanayake, reassured the Tamils of the goodwill of the CNC and the Sinhalese. Under this new structure elections were held in August and September 1947. For the election D. S. Senanayake reconstituted the CNC into a new party, the United National Party (UNP), which included Sinhalese, Tamils, and Muslims (it was a united front of the CNC, the Sinhala Maha Sabha, and the Muslim League), mostly from among the English-educated elite; the main adversary of the UNP was not an ethnic party but the leftist LSSP, turning the election into more of an ideological battle than an ethnic one. The UNP won a plurality of seats, and a few months later, on February 4, 1948, Ceylon gained independence, and the UNP government under Senanayake became the sovereign government of Ceylon.

Culture Becomes Conflict

> *Not until 1956 did we really believe that we were second-class citizens. Until then all we were engaged in were preventive measures, which we thought would hold.*
>
> —Tamil United Liberal Front leader Appapillai Amirdhalingam

Effectively, then, political power in Ceylon was transferred peacefully, without popular mass mobilization, to the old elite of earlier-twentieth-century vintage. Because independence had come so peacefully, there was "no occasion to associate and involve the masses in the struggle and to infuse in them the nationalistic emotion" (Arasaratnam 1964, 7). In other words, no overarching and generally shared conception of national identity had been generated or embraced by the disparate communities of Ceylon, and what differences existed had been largely unexploited and unacknowledged by the leadership of the new state. Fatefully, the UNP and its principles "left completely cold all of those who did not belong to the *elite,* particularly those who in the upper levels of the Sinhalese-speaking intelligentsia were reckoned persons of consequence: the *bhikkhu* (Buddhist monk), the village teacher, and the Ayurvedic physician" (Ludowyk 1966, 240). It was to be largely these groups, especially the *bhikkhus,* who would figure significantly into the ethnic mobilization and escalation to come.

Ethnic irritants were not long in appearing. Even before independence an issue arose over the design of the national flag, on which the Sinhalese wanted a lion symbol to dominate. An infinitely more urgent problem, however, came in the form of the Ceylon Citizenship Act No. 18 of 1948, with which all Indian Tamils were deprived of citizenship in Ceylon, even if they had been born or had lived for a long time on the island. In 1946 there were some 666,000 Indian Tamils identified as inhabiting Ceylon, mostly working on up-country plantations; they had received the vote under the Soulbury Constitution and even representatives to the new parliament. On the supposition, however, that Indian Tamils were not actually Ceylonese but Indians, and therefore not permanent but temporary members of Ceylonese society, the Citizenship Act (in effect on September 21, 1948) established criteria for citizenship that most Indian Tamils could not meet. Specifically, an individual born in Ceylon before October 15, 1948, qualified only if his or her father was also born in Ceylon or if his or her paternal grandfather and great-grandfather were born there; in other words, two generations of Ceylonese descent were required. For those born outside Ceylon, again two paternal generations of Ceylonese descent were necessary. And even a person born in Ceylon after October 15, 1948, still needed a father's citizenship to be eligible for citizenship by descent. There was also a provision for citizenship by registration.

Upon this foundation the Senanayake government delivered the coup de grace to Indian Tamils in the Ceylon (Parliamentary Elections) Amendment Act, No.48 of 1949, which made enfranchisement contingent upon

Ceylonese citizenship. Thereby, with this sequence of legislation, most Indian Tamils were deprived of the right to vote in Ceylon. Beyond sounding the alarm for many Tamils, who nevertheless continued to attempt to work with the Sinhalese within the system, the legislative moves created out of the Indian Tamils "a community of 'stateless' people since India also refused to grant them citizenship, and it opened an important rift between Ceylon and India, arousing anti-Indian sentiment in segments of the Ceylonese population" (Arasaratnam 1964, 18). As a final insult, in 1951 the study of the Sinhala language was made compulsory at the secondary school level. Arguably, this initial step in the language controversy was not as malignant as might appear or as would follow. The ruling UNP was still at this time "explicitly an intercommunal and interfaith party" (Wriggins 1960, 116), seeking to align all groups against the perquisites of foreign power and influence. As such, the enemy of Sinhala was not so much Tamil as English, and the party and government held up the principle of *swabasha* (mother tongue)—that is, the two native languages of Ceylon as opposed to English or only one or the other of the native languages—as the ideal for society. No doubt, laws to advance Sinhala could be and were seen as slights to Tamil, even if their (main) objective was to displace English. But by this juncture most every action by Sinhalese or Tamil was coming to have ethnic import.

As an illustration, by 1949 the Tamil Congress had split between those who could countenance continued cooperation with the UNP-dominated government and those who could not, the Indian Tamil issue being the primary wedge between them. The dissenters formed a new party, known generally as the Freedom Party (although the Tamil name is Tamil Arasu Kadchchi, or "Tamil Rule Party"), which held as its main platform the call for a federal state with an autonomous Tamil province in the north and east of the island. Even more consequentially for the future of Ceylon, in 1951 S. W. R. D. Bandaranaike, who had earlier organized the Sinhala Maha Sabha (and, although he had entered the coalition to form the UNP, had simultaneously kept together his distinct party structure), left the UNP and founded a new party, the Sri Lanka Freedom Party (SLFP). The SLFP was originally also intercommunal and endorsed the swabasha policy, as indicated by this passage from the party manifesto:

> It is most essential that Sinhala and Tamil be adopted as official languages immediately, so that the people of this country may cease to be aliens in their own land, so that an end may be put to the inequity of

> condemning these educated in Sinhala and Tamil to occupy the lowest walks of life, and above all that society may have the full benefit of the skill and talents of the people. The administration of the government must be carried on in Sinhala and Tamil. (Qtd. in Ponnambalam 1983, 84)

Thus, the SLFP's target was initially and explicitly English, or, better yet, the English-educated elite who had dominated Ceylon from before independence; its interest was the promotion of native languages, or, better yet, of those persons whose education was in native languages. Then, suddenly, in 1952 D. S. Senanayake died in an accident, and the party reemerged in May 1956 as a more distinctly partisan Sinhalese party. As Arasaratnam writes, this introduced a new kind of ethnic nationalism into Ceylon politics that

> was intended to bring the Sinhalese into a consciousness of their nationhood that would not be linked to a hybrid Ceylonese concept, which he dismissed as Western and middle class. The Sinhala nation were to come forward from the villages to assert themselves and wrest power from the English-educated, urban elite, who were anti-national in outlook. The Sinhala language and the Buddhist religion were to be raised in status. (1964, 25)

This new approach appealed to many Sinhalese, not least the rural population, who were particularly exposed to the politics of the Sinhala-educated upper classes like the *bhikkhus,* the teachers, and the Ayurvedic doctors, in whose interest the SLFP seemed to be working.

Of singular importance were the *bhikkhus,* who cherished a tradition of political activism in Sinhalese society and who had been involved for decades in efforts to revive and reform the Buddhist religion and Ceylonese society in general. As early as June 1946, a group of the so-called political *bhikkhus* had organized themselves into a political force in the Lanka Eksath Bhikkhu Mandalaya (LEBM, or Ceylon Union of Bhikkhus). One of the leaders of this movement, Walpola Rahula, saw its goal as "the great reawakening of the *bhikkhus* and laymen regarding current religious, social, economic, and political problems" and projected *bhikkhus* into the debate as a serious political force (Tambiah 1992, 27). *Bhikkhu politics* and *political bhikkhus* became watchwords of the emergent polity of independent Ceylon.

As we saw, however, *bhikkhus* and other traditionally high-status Sinhalese were not accorded much power or respect in the first UNP governments of Ceylon. Yet in 1956, the same year as the election that would carry Bandaranaike's nationalist SLFP to power, the All Ceylon Buddhist Congress, having failed to convince the government to appoint a commission of inquiry into the state of Buddhism in Ceylon, appointed one of its own. Its report issued in the same year, entitled "The Betrayal of Buddhism," embodied many of the historical and cultural elements discussed here and raised them to the level of political discourse. The report begins "with a tragic sketch and beleaguered view of Sinhala Buddhist history," the interpretation of which is implicit in the *vamsa* literature. It further emphasizes the historical interrelation between the state and the *sangha* in which the *bhikkhus* played a key role in maintaining religious and cultural purity, while the righteous king protected and followed the religion:

> Throughout their history, the stimulus to action, for the Sinhalese, was the ideology that they were a nation brought into being for the definite purpose of carrying, "for full five thousand years," the torch lit by the "Guide of the World" twenty-five centuries ago; and the structure of Sinhalese society has been shaped in pursuance of this ideology. Buddhism was the State Religion. The chosen king was always a Buddhist, and the people supported him with wholehearted loyalty, because he, as the chief citizen of the country, was the leader in shaping and sustaining their ideology, and the protector of the national faith. The temple became the center from which radiated learning, arts, and culture. The Sangha were the guides of the king's conscience and the mentors of the people, whose joys they shared and whose sorrows they assuaged. (Qtd. in Tambiah 1992, 38–39)

The report contains specific recommendations to the government as well, such as the withdrawal of state aid to Christian schools and the eventual takeover of the education system and the government enactment of a Buddha Sasana Act, which would reinstitute the traditional relation between state and *sangha.* As we have seen, this and many similar actions were in fact taken by the Bandaranaike and subsequent Sinhalese Sri Lankan administrations, to the dismay and aggravation of the Tamil observers. In this and other ways Buddhist mythohistorical ideology and imagery began to become political ideology; Bandaranaike's first political party, the Sinhala Maha Sabha, was a deliberate attempt "to establish

Buddhism and Sinhala culture as the foundation of Sri Lanka's identity." It is no coincidence, ultimately, that 1956 was also the year of the Buddha Jayanti, the 2,500th anniversary of the Buddha's death—and, concurrently, of Vijaya's arrival on Lanka. Attention was focused in a heightened manner on the religion and history of the Sinhalese Buddhist people at that time, and, according to de Silva, this attention and the energy it engendered "became, in the messianic atmosphere of the Buddha Jayanti, the prime determinant of the process of change" (qtd. in Little 1994, 66). Under the new Sinhalese nationalist government of Bandaranaike these energies were translated "into concrete policies and programs of language, education, employment, peasant resettlement, territorial control of the island, and so on" (Tambiah 1992, 58). The past, or a version of it, had become contemporary politics.

As far as ethnic irritants go, the key plank in Bandaranaike's platform (his SLFP having formed itself into the Mahajana Eksath Peramuna [MEP, or People's United Front]) was "Sinhala only," although he allowed the possibility of "reasonable use of Tamil." In fact, Bandaranaike promised that, if elected, he would introduce a Sinhala-only bill the next day. Another of his colleagues in the MEP also committed to "the wholesale repatriation of Indian Tamils if he came to power" (Ponnambalam 1983, 120). In total the position of Bandaranaike and his party was, for the first time in Ceylonese electoral politics, not just to advance Sinhalese but to advance *only* Sinhalese; "for the ordinary Sinhalese the enemy became not merely English but Tamil as well" (Arasaratnam 1964, 27). Second to the language issue came the religious issue, with a warning that Buddhism was in danger. Furthermore, anyone opposed to this position, including the UNP, could be branded as a traitor to the Sinhalese people. With the assistance of the *bhikkhus* and village leaders, who delivered their block votes, the MEP carried an absolute majority of seats in the new government (51 out of 95) and had a clear mandate to implement its program.

So, "Ceylon entered a new era in which the establishment of Sinhala hegemony was followed by Tamil resistance" (Arasaratnam 1987, 37). First, Bandaranaike made good on his promise to introduce Sinhala-only legislation, which he did on June 5, 1956. By this time the UNP had come around to support the policy of Sinhala as the only official language of Ceylon. The Official Language Act, No. 33 of 1956, which made Sinhala the only official language, also allowed a period of over four years to implement the change, during which time other "languages hitherto used for [official] purposes may be continued to be used." Even so, Tamil members of parliament voted against it. On the day of introduction of the bill the leader of the Freedom Party, S. J. V. Chelvanayakam, organized a *satyagraha* (peaceful sit-down protest) of three hundred Tamils outside the Parliament House. The first modern ethnic conflict in Ceylon ensued, as a march of political *bhikkhus* and supporters of the bill, protesting any concession to Tamil, attacked and beat the Tamil protesters. Some were thrown into a nearby lake. From there several days of rampage, rioting, and looting against Tamil individuals and businesses followed, in which 150 people died.

The language issue was not, however, the only affront to Tamil sensibilities. The government also established a ministry of culture "to direct and subvent" the revivalist Buddhist activity that was coming so strongly from the political *bhikkhus* and the villages. In addition, the government had been for some time pursuing a policy of resettlement, mainly of Sinhalese peasants and mainly onto the thinly populated lands that Tamils considered their own; already by independence the Sinhalese proportion of the population of some northern and eastern areas had increased, while the Tamil proportion had decreased, particularly noticeably in the Trincomalee District, which was 3 percent Sinhalese and 55 percent Tamil in 1921 but over 20 percent Sinhalese and just over 45 percent Tamil twenty-five years later. The Freedom Party demanded an end to this resettlement scheme, or "colonization" in its words, which would dilute Tamil claims to those areas and create dangerous mixes of ethnic groups in which conflict could easily be sparked.

There is reason to believe, furthermore, that Bandaranaike was more an ethnic opportunist than a hard-line partisan on the language issue; before the language bill was passed he expressed tolerance for Tamil, and in early 1957 he proposed a system for the "reasonable use of Tamil" that would have weakened the act considerably. For example, he proposed education in Tamil, public service exams in Tamil, and official government business in Tamil for Tamil speakers. These concessions led to a meeting with the Freedom Party and its leader, Chelvanayakam, and ultimately to an agreement known as the Bandaranaike-Chelvanayakam Pact on July 26, 1957, which, in allowing both Sinhala and Tamil recognition, implied to many Sinhalese nationalists the acknowledgment that Ceylon was in reality a plural society. Tamil was accepted as "the language of a national minority of Ceylon, and . . . the language of administration in the North and East Provinces"; additionally, the pact reopened the question of Ceylonese citizenship. In return the Freedom Party agreed to call off a *satyagraha* and drop its demand for linguistic parity.

The reaction of radical Sinhalese and Buddhist nationalists was swift and vociferous. *Bhikkhus* conducted their own very public *satyagraha* in protest, and opposition Sinhalese leaders like Senanayake and Jayewardene called the pact an "act of treachery" and a "betrayal of the Sinhalese," respectively. This was the first instance of a poisonous and self-destructive pattern that was to be repeated in Ceylon politics, in which, as Manor has characterized it: "The party in power strives to foster communal accommodation. The major party in opposition manipulates Sinhalese parochialism to wreck that attempt" (qtd. in Tambiah 1992, 48–49). Under this virulent nationalist attack Bandaranaike canceled the pact and set the stage for the next outbreak of violence.

Festering ethnic frustration exploded again in May 1958, when rumors and exaggerated stories led some Sinhalese to gather at the Polonnaruwa train station and assault the incoming train, killing three people. Also a Sinhalese farmer was killed by his own personal enemies, and this was blamed on Tamils, but the wildest (and, as Farmer suggests, carefully calculated) rumor was that a Tamil invasion was heading toward Polonnaruwa from Trincomalee and Batticaloa. Thus aroused, gangs of Sinhalese attacked Tamils, touching off four days (May 24–27) of "mob law and racial violence as had not been thought possible in Ceylon" (Ludowyk 1966, 250). The aggressors, as Tambiah asserts, were largely Sinhalese from the resettlement areas, but the violence spread as far as Colombo, and it was not, in all appearances, spontaneous. Rather, instigators, often dressed as *bhikkhus,* circulated among the crowds inciting racial hatred and deliberately spreading false information, all the while profiting from the carnage.

Bandaranaike's government was slow to respond, and it was in fact Governor-General Goonetilleke who finally declared a state of emergency that lasted from May 27, 1958, until March 1959. Government troops were called out to stop the rioting, which meant fighting and arresting Sinhalese by and large, and for this the government drew bitter criticism for using its power to help Tamils and kill Sinhalese. In the final sad chapter of this initial period of the formation of ethnic conflict in Ceylon, Bandaranaike was himself assassinated on September 25, 1959, by a *bhikkhu* in what appears to have been an extremist-Buddhist plot. As an ironic result, the political *bhikkhus* were sufficiently discredited that a period of seventeen or eighteen years followed (1960–77) without serious interethnic violence. Tambiah basically argues that the cessation of violence was related to the satisfaction of the demands of the Buddhist activists in regard to the place of Sinhalese Buddhist culture in Ceylon politics. At the same time, according to Horowitz, the Tamils endured the indignity and deadly force of the 1956–58 period "without demanding anything more than a mild federalism" (1985, 244), so that Tamil ethnic demands did not escalate, certainly not to the level of separatism.

This is not to say that Sinhalese ethnic pressures abated nor that Tamils had either capitulated or adapted to a Sinhalese Buddhist–dominated society. Bandaranaike was succeeded as prime minister by his widow, Mrs. Sirimavo Bandaranaike, who was, if anything, more unyielding and systematic in her ethnic dealings than her husband. Under her two administrations (1960–65 and 1970–77) the "fires of communal and religious conflict were ingenuously fed for short-term political advantage" (Wriggins 1960, 123), provoking and teasing fears of Tamils and branding opponents as sympathizers of Tamils (and of Christians). Further, the reach of the state over economic institutions like transportation, wholesale trade, the plantation system, and a number of key industries and then over the education system also increased in these years, making Sinhalese domination of the society more effective. Unrest in this situation was evident, as in the 1962 failed coup by the military; interestingly, however, the leaders of the coup were not Tamils but Christians, and its failure led to the elimination of Christians from both military and police.

In 1964 a long-standing Sinhalese promise to begin repatriation of Indian Tamils to India was fulfilled, when the Indo-Ceylon Agreement (or the Sirima-Shastri Agreement) was reached between the two governments in October 1964. The agreement provided for the return of 525,000 Indian Tamils over fifteen years, while 300,000 would be granted Ceylonese citizenship over the same period, giving a ratio of seven-to-four for Indian citizenship as opposed to Ceylonese citizenship. Although the terms were slow to be realized, it was yet another piece of evidence that Sinhalese were serious about reducing or extinguishing Tamil power in Ceylon.

The 1965 election turned out Mrs. Bandaranaike and the SLFP government and replaced it with the UNP in a campaign that, according to Ludowyk, "was conducted on a level of hatred and vituperation not exceeded before" (1966, 265). The new prime minister, Dudley Senanayake, who had been one of the main critics of the Bandaranaike-Chelvanayakam Pact and therefore had helped cause its nullification, ended up making a pact himself with the same Chelvanayakam on virtually the same terms. Senanayake agreed to recognize Tamil as the official language of the north and east provinces, to devolve some powers to Tamil areas in the form of district councils, and to dilute the resettlement schemes long under way by giving local Tamils the first right to settle on these open lands before other citizens were given the opportunity. The new agreement, like its predecessor, was undermined and eventually nullified by extremist pressure.

The period 1965–70 is perceived as a time of relative reconciliation between Sinhalese and Tamils, but this period came to an end with the return of Mrs. Bandaranaike and the SLFP to power in 1970. Winning an absolute majority in Parliament, she was freer to move on her agenda, which included drafting a new constitution. Again, she was not without her strenuous opponents, but again they were not initially principally Tamil; in 1971 another armed coup, this time by the Janatha Vimukti Peramuna (JVP, or People's Liberation Front), which consisted mainly of second- and lower-caste Sinhalese youths who resented upper-caste and Christian influence in national politics, was put down with the assistance of the Indian army. Discontent and conflict was not, therefore, strictly interethnic but also intercaste and intraethnic.[7]

In the realm of Sinhalese-Tamil relations two fatal blows were struck in the early 1970s, one educational, one constitutional. In 1971 a system of preferential university admissions, under the characterization of "standardization" was introduced, to be developed and expanded over time. By 1970 Tamils, at around 20 percent of the population, composed nearly 50 percent of all admissions to medical and engineering schools. The first step in the standardization scheme was to scale the raw scores of university admissions tests according to the *three* test language media—Sinhalese, Tamil, and English—so that the number of admissions in each media would be proportionate to the number of students taking the test in each medium. this should, theoretically, establish a preference for Sinhalese students, as they are a majority of the populations, allowing a Sinhalese student to gain admission with a raw score of only 90 percent of the minimum Tamil required score. The effect, however, was not great enough, since Tamils still *took* the tests in greater numbers than their share in the general population and *passed* the tests at a higher rate, so a second tier of preferences was added.

The second tier of preference was based on district share of population.

---

7. For more on the JVP, see Samaranayake 1987.

At first 70 percent of admissions were based on standardized scores and 30 percent on district quotas, but subsequently the system was expanded so that only 30 percent of admissions were based on test scores, 55 percent on district quotas, and the remaining 15 percent were set aside for "educationally backward districts." The results were as expected and hoped: the percentage of Tamils admitted in 1974 to medical school dropped to 26 percent and to engineering school to 16 percent. Overall, the percentage of Tamils with college degrees dropped to almost one-quarter of the level a decade earlier. Predictably, "Tamil prospects for government service and the professions dwindled" (Horowitz 1985, 249).

The kind of direct and palpable assault on the economic and social fortunes of the Tamils was coupled with constitutional changes that secured the political and cultural hegemony of the Sinhalese. In 1972 a new constitution was introduced that delivered "a decisive symbolic rebuff" to Tamil culture and aspirations of autonomy and in fact to the very notion of Ceylon as a plural society. The constitution, enacted on May 22, 1972, created the Republic of Sri Lanka (*Lanka* being an ancient name for the island and *Sri* a word meaning "blessed") and enshrining the position of the Sinhala language and Sinhalese Buddhist culture in the state. Sinhala was reinforced as the official language of administration throughout the island, federalism or any type of devolution of power was rejected, and Buddhism was accorded a "foremost place" among the religions of the polity, which the state was "to protect and foster." In fact, the second chapter of the constitution is entitled "Buddhism." Ethnic lines were clearly being emphasized again and ethnic animosity building. In January 1974 police in Jaffna attacked a crowd at a meeting of the Fourth International Conference of Tamil Studies, killing eleven and touching off several days of brutality committed by police and civilians. Mrs. Bandaranaike's government also banned the importation of Tamil films, books, magazines, and such from India's Tamil Nadu state and such organizations the Tamil Youth League.

Incidents and policies like these "left the Tamils with a feeling of insecurity and helplessness" (Arasaratnam 1987, 45) and contributed to the growth of extremism of Tamil sentiment and the coalescence of ethnic boundaries. In particular, Tamil leaders, who had attempted to work within the Sinhalese system to ensure Tamil rights, now began to move definitely in the direction of Tamil nationalism and even separatism. In 1975 the Freedom Party reorganized itself as the Tamil United Liberal Front (TULF) standing on a platform of separate Tamil nationhood and the establishment of Tamil sovereignty in the areas in the north and east, which were designated as the distinct state of Eelam. Chelvanayakam himself, the representative who coauthored two pacts with Sinhalese governments to protect Tamil rights, now repositioned himself "as an uncompromising Tamil separatist" (Little 1994, 78).[8]

The year 1977 marked the end of any semblance of civility between the Sinhalese and Tamil communities and anticipated the days of explicit violence ahead. A national election was held in July 1977, in which the UNP, led by J. R. Jayewardene, won a commanding majority of 140 out of 168 seats. The TULF ran candidates in the north and east provinces, painting the election as a referendum on Tamil sovereignty, and carried 60 percent of the vote there, although they were stronger in the north than in the east. The overwhelming success of the UNP left it with very little opposition in the government, mainly in the form of the TULF, with a mere 18 seats. The "ethnicization" of politics was evinced in this split as well as in the more conspicuous images of the island's Buddhist culture and history employed by Jayewardene, who referred to himself as Sri Lanka's 193d head of state, "the inheritor of the Sri Lankan monarchy," and deliberately made comments and speeches reminiscent of those of past Sinhalese Buddhist kings. He advocated the establishment of a *dharmista* ("righteous society," in Buddhist terms) and set about having the *Mahavamsa* updated to the year 1977.

His use, however, of the Sinhalese Buddhist past in his contemporary politics did not end there. The parliament was moved to the old center of Kotte power. He created a Department of Buddhist Affairs and planted a sapling of the bo tree at the spot where Buddha supposedly left his footprint. He deigned to be addressed by the title *devavahanse,* a term with kingly or divine connotations, and invoked the name of Asoka in speeches—all "part of a process by which the new government created Buddhist culture" and anchored itself to that culture. Even the resettlement program that brought large numbers of Sinhalese into Tamil majority areas (and tipped the demographic balance against Tamils) was conceived, or at least rationalized, as a restoration of the past—a reversal of the southwestward migration begun in medieval times—when Sinhalese people and power pervaded the island and the community was prosperous and great. Rural development took the form of a "Village Re-awakening"

8. For the complete TULF manifesto, see Ponnambalam 1983.

program that would "help peasants re-discover the traditional values and forms of social organization of their Sinhala-Buddhist ancestors" (Woost 1990, 164). The rhetorical use of mythohistorical imagery is clear in some of the remarks that accompanied the inauguration of one particular project in 1986:

> I remember talk about the great irrigation works of the ancient kings like Dutugamunu [*sic*] and Parakramabahu. Some say these works could only be done with the help of giants, that common people could not accomplish such great feats. . . .But our works . . . show that we are the giants of today. Impossible works, you ask? There are no impossible works for the Sinhala people.
>
> The ethical and hard-working qualities that have been revealed here in this village are indicative of the personalities of people born and brought up in our villages. No other country in the world has the spiritual development that we have, and here we are making it known to the world that it is the Sinhala Buddhists who have . . . had a spiritual superiority for over 2,500 years. For that reason . . . [the community that] can protect the Sinhala nation and Buddhism is the Sinhala nation with its historically important human qualities and superiority.
>
> This is indeed a historical landmark when one thinks of the . . . 2,500 years since Prince Vijaya came and established our nation. All of those who came with him were small farmers just like yourselves. . . . Thus this conference marks only the second time since Vijaya's arrival that there has been such a conference of small farmers. . . . Indeed this events turns a new page in our history as a people. (Qtd. in Woost 1990, 176–78)

Perhaps the best summary and explanation for this kind of hortatory speech making is contained in one of the speeches itself: "It does not matter if some already know this history, for hearing it again, over and over, will only strengthen their pride in the nation. Then the seed of pride in the nation would undoubtedly germinate in their minds" (qtd. in Woost 1990, 178). Indeed, we might look upon the entire course of the ethnic conflict in Sri Lanka as the germination of such a historical and cultural seed of pride.

What we have, then, finally by the late 1970s and through the 1980s is a "formulaic Buddhism" that equates the Sri Lankan present with the Sinhalese Buddhist past, which defines being Sri Lankan as being Sinhalese and being Sinhalese as being Buddhist, and which makes "a total claim—territorially and politically—over Sri Lanka." This hardening of the Sinhalese position, this crystallization of ethnic boundaries, represents not just an appropriation or activation of the past and of traditional culture but an interpretive or selective use of that past and culture, under the impact of colonial and modernizing influences and present-day economic and political forces. It further, whether it advocates or inevitably inspires intolerance and violence, certainly provides the conditions for—a "warrant" for—such attitudes and actions. Finally, by drawing and enforcing ever more exclusive and militant ethnic boundaries, this process has contributed to the radicalization of Tamil ethnicity, which was not present in the same quality and quantity even fifty years ago and which, through the process, has acquired a "symmetry" with Sinhalese ethnonationalism; the result is that both groups (now defined as totally and primordially exclusive nations) occupy the same "rhetorical space" of history, religion, and culture—in which these latter elements, and the violence they spawn, are the stuff of politics.

Ethnic Conflict Becomes Separatist Nationalism

As if these developments were not ominous enough, in the same year the old Tamil statesman Chelvanayakam died, who had perhaps been the only one of the moderate Tamil leaders with "sufficient *gravitas* to persuade the restive, radical youths to give electoral politics one more try" (Pfaffenberger 1994, 10). The vacuum of restrained leadership let loose the accumulated grievance of the younger generation, who were less willing to trust Sinhalese promises and more willing to entrust their future to activism and even violence. By mid-August, and for two weeks, Sinhalese conducted anti-Tamil riots, in which over a hundred Tamils were killed, Tamils houses and shops looted and burned, and some fifty thousand left as refugees. Large numbers of young Tamils were arrested, tortured, and released without charge, according to Tamil sources. Even more significantly, organized Tamil extremists and guerrilla groups now formed, most notably the Tamil New Tigers, or, as they eventually came to be known, the Liberation Tigers of Tamil Eelam (LTTE) or simply the Tamil Tigers. The LTTE emerged after a time as the largest and most successful nationalist group, drawing on traditional Tamil culture and symbols (such as the tiger, a royal symbol of ancient Indian [Chola] Tamil kings) and aggressively eliminating most of their rivals with the Tamil community. Nevertheless, other groups such as the Eelam People's Revolutionary Liberation Front (EPRLF), the Eelam Revolutionary Organization of Students (EROS, which is largely under the control of LTTE), the Tamil Eelam Liberation Organization (TELO), and the People's Liberation Organization of Tamil Eelam (PLOTE) continue to exist with varying ideologies and levels of activity and success.

In 1978 the armed insurrection of Tamil separatists against the Sri Lankan government began in earnest. Time had run out for a political solution, and three decades of frustration and escalating ethnic sensitivity boiled over. As Arasaratnam writes, this completed the transformation of Sinhalese-Tamil relations "from competitive coexistence to intense conflict and even racial warfare" (1987, 51). In the face of mounting violence, the government first enacted the Proscribing of the LTTE Law, No. 16 of 1978 and then replaced it with the forceful Prevention of Terrorism Act, No. 48 of 1979, allowing for the abrogation of many civil rights and aspects of due process. For example, an individual suspected of being "connected with or concerned in any unlawful activity" could be detained and held without trial for eighteen months; police were granted extreme powers of search and seizure; writ of habeas corpus was denied; and *unlawful activity* was given the widest possible definition. Jayewardene subsequently declared a state of emergency, ordered the army in Tamil territory with orders to "wipe out" the terrorists, and initiated a "reign of army terror" in the Jaffna Peninsula (Ponnonbalam 1983, 202–3).

Violence was met with violence, the LTTE killing some twenty police officers over the following months. In the summer of 1981 another explosion of communal hostility erupted, which led to a meeting between the government and the TULF in which the government accepted several demands including recruitment of Tamil police to serve in Tamil areas, a review of the standardization system, decentralization of administration to district development councils, and the prosecution of police involved in the recent violence. Yet the TULF neither spoke for nor controlled the guerrilla groups like the LTTE, which kept up its campaign for a more radical nationalist solution in Sri Lanka. Ultimately, the greatest conflict yet began in the summer of 1983. On May 18 "marauding gangs of army personnel" set Jaffna on fire. LTTE attacks on police and soldiers in turn resulted in the deaths of thirteen soldiers whose bodies were brought to and displayed in the capital city on July 23. Emotion, running high due to the funerals and the inciting coverage by the media, ran over, and the crowd went on a rampage of looting, burning, and killing of Tamils in the city. The conflagration lasted for nearly two weeks, until August 5, and was unlike previous riots in a number of ways. First of all, the scale was much larger; second, earlier riots had not commenced in Colombo. Third, and most ominously, the rioting seemed organized and planned: rioters reportedly carried lists of voter registration and addresses so that they could immediately identify Tamil homes and businesses. Sinhalese gangs were well armed and traveled by bus and train to their destinations. Furthermore, the riots were aided and abetted by "the active participation or passive encouragement of the ultimate guardians of law and order—the police and the army" (Tambiah 1986, 24). Finally, the destruction caused by the riots was not limited to Sri Lankan Tamil homes and businesses but was more widespread, affecting Indian enterprises in Colombo such as the Indian Overseas Bank and even industries that employed many Sinhalese.

In the aftermath of the 1983 riots Jayewardene condemned and then effectively banned the TULF by endorsing the Sixth Amendment to the Constitution, which read: "No person shall, directly or indirectly, in or outside Sri Lanka, espouse, promote, finance, encourage, or advocate the establishment of a separate State within the territory of Sri Lanka." The Sinhalese-Tamil struggle was no longer (if it ever had been) a completely internal domestic problem, however, as India and the government of Indira Gandhi took greater interest. Apparently, India had been arming and training Tamil guerrillas for some time, and the new riots, together with the potential for one hundred thousand or more Sri Lankan Tamil refugees to flee to India, strengthened her determination to support the guerrillas "as well as to help arrange a settlement that would, in her eyes, protect Tamil interests in Sri Lanka" (Little 1994, 7). The motivation may have been to appease the large Tamil community in India, or it may have been to keep the government of Sri Lanka off balance, but it led eventually to an intergovernmental agreement and Indian intervention in Sri Lankan ethnic affairs.

By 1987, Little maintains, "there was widespread Sinhalese pressure for total war against the Tamil minority" (1994, 7). Tamils, in particular the LTTE, had taken virtual control of Jaffna Peninsula, acting with pseudo-governmental powers to collect taxes, run radio and television stations, and regulate some industries. This upcoming ethnic war, however, was not to be fought by government forces alone but with the assistance of the Indian army. On July 29, 1987, the two states sealed the Indo-Sri Lankan Agreement to Establish Peace and Normalcy in Sri Lanka, which called for a negotiated solution to the ethnic conflict to be enforced by Indian military power. The Indian army, or Indian Peace Keeping Force (IPKF), was injected into Tamil areas to pacify Tamil guerrilla groups and establish order, after which a set of ethnic compromises would be set in motion. For example, Sri Lanka would be acknowledged as a plural society, multiethnic and multilingual, including recognition of the northern and eastern provinces as historically Tamil; accordingly, Tamil (and English) would be granted official language status along with Sinhalese. Also, the two Tamil provinces would be united under a single provincial council with powers of state (an effective devolution of state authority). For their part Tamil militants would be required to accept a cease-fire and to disarm.

The reaction to this agreement was predictable: Tamils at first welcomed it, while Sinhalese met it with shock and resentment and then two days of rioting, as an affront to national sovereignty and Sinhalese Buddhist culture. Within days 3,000 Indian troops were in northern Sri Lanka, and within a month that number was up to 10,000. Soon Tamils too were aggrieved by the IPKF, which essentially conducted a war in northern Sri Lanka, and Tamil guerrillas inflicted heavier-than-expected casualties on the force, killing as many as 150 Indians and wounding another 500 before the whole exercise was over. At its peak in mid-1988 the IPKF reached over 50,000 members, until it was finally withdrawn in early 1990. The Tamil National Army set up and left behind to safeguard the Tamil regions quickly collapsed, and the LTTE benefited from the former's abandoned or captured weapons and supplies. The conflict then settled into a local but "expensive and bloody, civil war" between the LTTE and the Sri Lankan army. Yet one last international repercussion was the assassination of Rajiv Gandhi, Indira Gandhi's son and successor, in May 1991. By early 1993 government forces were gaining ground on the insurgents, and the LTTE hinted that it may been willing to compromise on its demands. Even so, in May 1993 Sri Lankan president (the political structure of Sri Lanka having been changed from a parliamentary to a presidential one) Ranasingha Premadasa was assassinated in an LTTE plot, and at last report the armed struggle continues. The head of the LTTE, Vellupillai Prabhakaran, who orchestrated Rajiv Gandhi's assassination, broke the latest cease-fire in April 1995 and is again fighting the Sri Lankan government and its new president, Chandrika Kumaratunga. The LTTE runs a tight administration in Jaffna, which has been called "a rule of terror," and maintains itself through an international network with offices in London and Paris and through the financial contributions of expatriate Tamils all around the world.

Conclusion

In this chapter we have seen the emergence, out of certain preconditions, interpretations, decisions, and events, of not only ethnic conflict in Sri Lanka but of the very ethnic identities and ethnic groups that sustain the conflict. We have seen that nationalism in Sri Lanka "is not a pre-existent fact, a 'given' upon which politics builds; it is a process, characterized by argument and assertion, itself deeply tied to local politics" (Spencer 1990, 11). Nationalism and ethnic identity clearly are not constants: the nationalism that launched Sri Lanka, "Ceylonese nationalism," is not the same as the Sinhalese nationalism of the 1950s (which was "couched and implemented in ways that could be seen as the strengthening of Buddhism and the eradication of inequalities resulting from colonialism"), nor is either of these the same as that of the 1980s (which emphasized "the unity and sovereignty of the 'motherland,' and their major identity . . . as 'sons of the soil,' whose political legacy was Buddhism" [Tambiah 1992, 91]). Similarly, Tamil nationalism grew, partly in response to challenges from the Sinhalese, from a call for respect and inclusion to a demand for protection to an armed separatist struggle for a sovereign homeland. Along the way both groups have invoked the same kinds of evidence and have constructed an arena of discourse as they have battled in their political and ethnic arena.

In fact, before the modern (i.e., colonial and postcolonial) period Sinhalese and Tamil ethnic identity did not exist as it does at present; Kemper maintains, for instance, that until the tenth or eleventh century it was still possible to be Buddhist and Tamil. Thus, the interpretation of the Sri Lankan, especially the Sinhalese, "national past as a history of warring 'communities,' 'races,' or 'ethnic groups,'" is not a fact but, rather, "a product of colonial readings of the available sources on the Sri Lankan past" (Spencer 1990, 5). For instance, Pfaffenberger argues that the *Mahavamsa* episode in which Dutugamunu fights and eventually vanquishes Elara was not originally "a struggle against the Tamil ethnic group [but] it was a struggle against a particular group of Tamils"; this is supported by the fact that some Tamil nobles allied themselves with Dutugamunu and some Sinhalese opposed him. In fact, Tennekoon describes the popular and scholarly debate of 1984 that not only evoked Dutugamunu but redefined his adventures "from a conscienceless war against Tamils to the (morally justified) war of unifying a divided country" (1987, 23). The "extension" of a conflict between *some* Tamils and *some* Sinhalese to a conflict between *Sinhalese* and *Tamils* is a new and invented tradition. And, if ethnic identity and ethnic solidarity did not exist in this premodern day, certainly the phenomenon we call nationalism did not; it had to await the formation of the nation.

The recognition of the construction, the invention, of Sri Lankan ethnicity and conflict is not to say that there are no real differences in Sri Lankan society. There are, in fact, as we have seen, more differences than are currently actually used (or at least welcomed) by nationalists on either side. What is important and instructive is the fact that "pre-existing differences were re-interpreted in a new fashion that emphasized antagonism and hostility instead of tolerance and exchange" (Hellman-Rajanayagam 1990, 119). In this reinterpretation real, deep, and sometimes even ancient beliefs, themes, and identities are combined with modern factors such as colonialism and economic opportunities and competitions to produce the ethnicity that we see today. As a case in point, Nissan and Stirrat find it to be no coincidence that "the boundaries of 'ancient Tamil Eelam' follow the administrative boundaries of the colonial era with uncanny exactness." As we have also seen, foreign concepts or practices such as race theory, Western education, religious conversion, and representative democracy exacerbate or create differences or conflicts over old differences.

Finally, then, it is evident in the case of Sri Lanka how the ethnic conflict between Sinhalese and Tamils is informed by and carried out in the language of culture and history but is actually a product of recent and contemporary circumstances. In the process of creating a state and distributing the economic resources and spoils of that state, and by way of the manipulation of cultural and historical resources and of decisions and actions by various individuals and constituencies with varying interests and varying definitions of what the state should be, there was created as well a nationalist consciousness, an ideology of nationalism, and even the very nations that would bear and contest that nationalism. In Sri Lanka, as Little writes, "Nationalism radically transformed communities traditionally diffused and dispersed into consolidated, inclusive, standardized 'mass societies' bound together by a shared sense of being a people, of having a distinctive national identity" (1994, 31).

Chapter 4

The Kurds: Frustrated Nationalism

If only there were harmony among us,
if we were to obey a single one of us,
he would reduce to vassalage
Turks, Arabs, and Persians, all of them.
We would perfect our religion, our state,
and would educate ourselves in learning and wisdom.
—Ahmad-i Khani, "Derde me," preface to *Mem u Zin*

In 1991, in the aftermath of the Persian Gulf War, in which the United States evicted Iraq from Kuwait, the Kurds captured world attention as an ethnic group struggling for security, self-determination, and even statehood. The United States welcomed and even helped instigate the 1991 Kurdish uprising, as well as that of the Shi'ites of southern Iraq, in an effort to destabilize, if not topple, Saddam Hussein's regime. For a brief time, around March 1991, the Kurds controlled nearly all of what they consider their "homeland," Kurdistan, in Iraq, but soon the government threw all of the technology of modern warfare, freed up by the surrender to the "Coalition" forces, at the rebels. Within a month government troops had pacified large areas of Kurdish resistance, and thousands of Kurds were on the retreat; by some accounts as many as a half-million Kurds fled to Turkey and 1.5 million to Iran, both of which countries contain substantial Kurdish populations and both of which were recently or currently (and traditionally) enemies of Iraq. Kurdish aspirations for an independent homeland were dashed—once again.

This episode is only the most familiar, and not even the latest, in a long story of Kurdish struggle for autonomy and freedom from discrimination and repression, going back at least to the early nineteenth century and, if seen in a certain light, much further than that. This episode also ended as all previous ones have ended—with the defeat and dispersal of the Kurds. In the present chapter we will discuss the source and course of Kurdish ethnicity and nationalism and the conflict in which the Kurds have engaged not only with Iraq but also with Turkey, Iran, and often each other. As the title of the chapter suggests, Kurdish nationalism has been repeatedly frustrated in the sense that its efforts have been defeated in every instance. Yet mere military failure is not the only cause of their frustration, and the explication of the other dimensions that continuously undermine the realization of Kurdish national goals, and even the realization of a unified Kurdish ethnic identity, will be our main concern. The two critical factors to consider are, first, international politics and the interests and actions of other larger players on the world stage and, second, the internal cultural and political divisions among the Kurds themselves, which impede effective organization and mobilization and even a firm sense of shared interest, identity, and destiny.

In the process of analyzing these elements, we will also have the opportunity to consider once again the construction and circumstantial nature of ethnicity and ethnic conflict and the diversity within the categories "ethnic group," "ethnicity," and "nationalism." Ethnicity has not derived from the same origins for the Kurds as for, say, the Sinhalese or Tamils, nor has it taken the same shape nor yielded the same results. Some aspects of the cases are comparable—for example, the formation of political parties and the role of cultural preconditions and such modern factors as print and literacy—but the unique set of the cultural preconditions and the contemporary and historical circumstances make ethnicity among the Kurds very different than among other ethnic groups.

A Kurdish Nation?

There is clearly a group of people in the world who call themselves Kurds. As I have argued throughout, however, a group must fulfill three requirements to be a nation: a common culture, a consciousness of shared identity, and political organization toward a national goal. All three of these the Kurds have lacked almost entirely until late last century or even early this century and still lack to a certain extent. In fact, even culturally "Kurdish society remains heterogeneous in almost all those aspects that normally form the basis of an ethnic identity, such as religion, language, modes of economic production, and coherent homeland" (Izady 1992, 185).

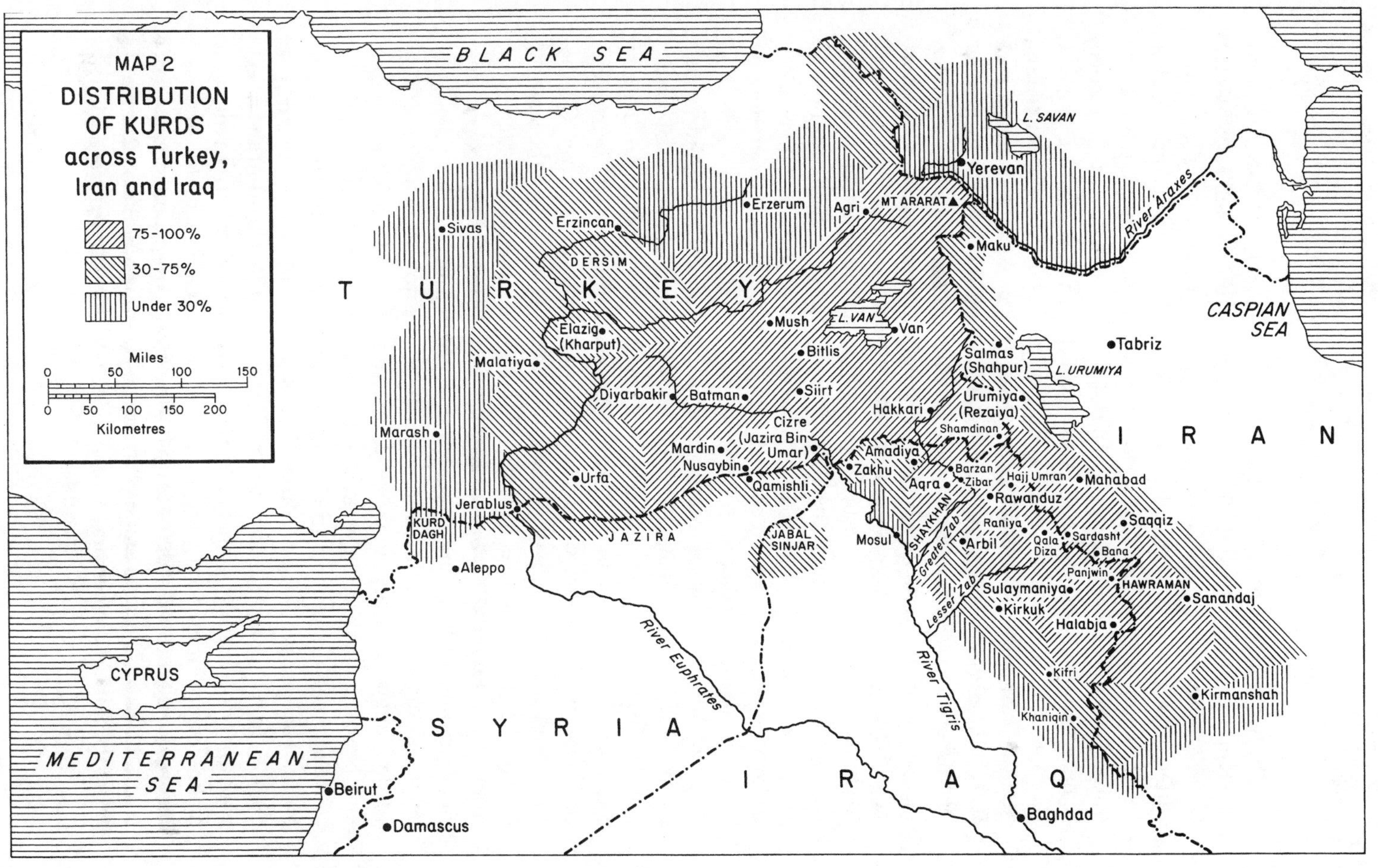

Kurdistan. (Reprinted from *A Modern History of the Kurds,* by David McDowall [London: I. B. Tauris, 1996], by permission of the publisher.)

The two elements of culture that might seem most immediately to bond the Kurds are language and religion; generally, Kurds speak Kurdish and are Muslims. Yet here already we encounter important and consequential differentiation within the Kurdish protonation. For example, the Kurds, a small nation of some twenty-five to thirty million, exhibit significant linguistic variation. The "Kurdish language" is actually a set of related dialects and languages within the West Iranic family of the Indo-European language group. The main division may be made between Kurmanji and Sorani. Kurmanji is the majority language of Kurds, spoken by around three-fourths of the population, and is predominant in the Kurdish areas of Turkey, Syria, and the former Soviet Union. It has also produced the largest and most prestigious body of Kurdish literature and is sometimes held to be the "true language" of the Kurds, although this status is relatively recent, having been established only around the sixteenth century (Izady 1992, 173). Sorani is the largest language among the Kurds of Iran and Iraq. Whether these two tongues are dialects or separate languages is debated, but they have been compared in distinctness (at least grammatically) to English and German.

Three other tongues are identifiable in Kurdish country. Gurani (whose speakers call their language Kurdi) is most common in pockets of southern Kurdish areas in Iran and Iraq. Zaza is spoken in enclaves in Turkey and northern Iraq. Finally, a Persian-like dialect can be found in extreme southeastern Kurdistan, which falls in or near Iranian territory. On the whole Kurmanji has been displacing the other languages over the last few centuries, but it has not yet achieved the level of a national language. Naturally, then, no standard written Kurdish language exists as of yet. Some small amount of literature appeared in Kurmanji before the nineteenth century, but, as Kreyenbroek points out, it was not normally used as a written language at that time (1992, 69). Even today Kurdish languages may be written in three different scripts—Arabic, Latin, and Cyrillic.

Religion is the other critical domain, and again a similar situation holds. The vast majority of Kurds are, of course, Muslims—a sufficient number to recognize it as the "normal" religion of Kurds—but the internal variety of Islam, together with the persistence of minority religions, make religion imperfectly unifying and occasionally actually divisive. About three-fourths of Kurds are Muslims, and with the introduction of Islam the Kurds became among "the most vigorous and devoted defenders of the faith" (Bulloch and Morris 1992, 60), often recognizing religion as a more effective identifying and mobilizing force that any other aspect of their culture, even into the twentieth century, as we will see.

The same basic schism that divides all of Islam exists in Kurdish Islam, however, and in roughly the same proportion. Some 60 percent or more of Kurds are Sunni Muslims, particularly of the Shafi'ite school, while another 6 to 7 percent are Shi'ites. As would be expected, the Sunnis predominate in western Kurdish lands (Turkey and Iraq), while the Shi'ites are most numerous in the east, especially Iran; there are, however, pockets of each sect in areas dominated by the other. There has not tended to be great conflict between the two denominations, no greater than in Islam as a whole, but neither has there been great cooperation and shared identity. In fact, in some areas, such as Kermanshah (in Iranian Kurdistan), provocative anti-Sunni behavior is a part of some Shi'ite festivals (Izady 1992, 136).

Muslim Kurds are further differentiated by their participation in various religious orders, especially Sufi brotherhoods (*tariqas*). Each *tariqa* is headed by a master, or *sheikh,* who has substantial power and influence over his followers, or *murids,* and often comes to be seen as a savior-figure, or messiah (*mahdi*), by them. *Sheikhs* may be called upon to perform an assortment of social functions, religious, medical, and legal; in addition to their spiritual leadership roles, they may be recognized as shamans to heal illness and even perform miracles, and some are revered even after death, their tombs becoming important prayer or pilgrimage sites.

In their history *sheikhs* have also exercised influence through economic means. By way of marriage alliances and reciprocity for religious services they could accumulate considerable resources of land, livestock, and money. In addition, *sheikhs* sometimes controlled religious organizations called *waqfs* (charitable trusts left to provide income for religious and public works as well as for the donor's family) and have often used *waqf* property as if it were their private property. As an effect of all these points, *sheikhs* could be and have been significant political figures. Together with *mullahs,* the village-level teachers and representatives of orthodoxy, local religious authorities often commanded extreme loyalty within the vernacular of religious belief and symbolism and in fact regularly served as the only serious center of "mass" mobilization and legitimate leadership. Accordingly, as I will discuss shortly, the major figures of early modern Kurdish nationalism (in the nineteenth century) and even of some relatively recent nationalist movements were almost all religious leaders, especially sheikhs. Secular, political party–based ethnic organization has been much slower to develop and is not fully developed yet.

The two major Sufi orders among the Kurds are the *Qadiri* and the *Naqshbandi.* The older of the two is the *Qadiri,* which was founded around the year 1100, although it has been in decline relative to the *Naqshbandi* for the past century or two. The *Naqshbandi* was not indigenous to the Kurds but originated in Central Asia in the fourteenth century and enjoyed its greatest rise in Kurdistan in the nineteenth. It predominates in northern and western Kurdish regions, while the *Qadiri* areas tend to be the center and east. In addition to Islam, Judaism, Christianity, and Baha'ism are all practiced in Kurdistan. Most non-Muslim Kurds follow not one of these world religions, however, but one of heterodox religions like Alevism, Yazidism, or Ahl-i Haqq.

Alevism is significant both for its numbers and its relations to the majority Kurdish society. There are three million Alevis, mostly in eastern and southeastern Anatolia, although there are many in Syria. Only about one-third of Alevis are Kurds (which still leaves about one million Alevi Kurds, or between 4 to 6 percent of all Kurds), but a majority of the *Dimili-* or *Zaza*-speaking Kurds are Alevis; this adds a second layer to their distinctiveness from majority or "normal," or "real," Kurds. Alevis compose over 13 percent of the Syrian population, including many Arabs (Izady 1992, 152). Alevis have also been known by the names *Qizilbash,* a Turkish term for "red heads," referring to their characteristic red headgear, and *Alawis,* or "followers of Ali." Ali, who is the key figure in the historical schism between Sunnis and Shi'ites, is also the highest avatar of divinity for the Alevis, which allows them to claim a relation to Islam. Alevis, however, do not follow the basic tenets of Islam, such as the five pillars of faith or ritual ablution, nor do they build mosques or veil their women; furthermore, they practice many unorthodox behaviors, such as veneration of trees.

Because of their heterodox beliefs and practices, Alevis have been the target of historical and recent oppression: Alevis sided with the Persian Empire against the Ottoman Empire in the epic struggle between the two in the early sixteenth century, and, as a consequence, forty thousand Alevis were killed by the Ottomans in 1514. Since the 1970s they have been attacked on several occasions, once resulting in at least one hundred (and maybe several hundred) deaths, and the Turkish government had actually sought to resettle them. Some orthodox Sunnis assert "that Alevis are little better than animals and that it is acceptable and even meritorious for Muslims to kill them" (McDowall 1992b, 60).

Yazidis, who make up over 5 percent of the Kurdish population, have, if anything, come under more pressure than the Alevis, for they are commonly considered devil worshippers. Yazidis practice a mixture of Islamic, Christian, Jewish, and pagan beliefs with a clear dualistic aspect; in addition to God they recognize "The Peacock Angel" (*Malak Tawus*), which is often mistaken by outsiders as Satan. Also, what Izady calls a "faulty identification" between the name Yazidi and that of the Umayyad caliph Yazid ibn Mu'awiyya (680–83) has had important ethnic consequences. For one, the more successful and notable Yazidi leaders tend to adopt Arab dress, names, and language rather than Kurdish; besides the obvious loss of "potential Kurds" to a different ethnic group, this phenomenon adds a "class" dimension to the question of Kurd/Arab identity, at least in some cases—wealthier Yazidis shedding their Kurdish identity and culture, while poorer ones maintain Kurdish names and norms. For another, both Syria and Iraq, which hold large numbers of Yazidi Kurds, encourage this identification in an effort to detach them from their Kurdish identity and to assimilate them to an Arab identity; accordingly, the governments of Syria and Iraq now call Yazidis "Umayyad Arabs." Although most Yazidis live in Syria, the second largest concentration is in the Caucasus, to which they retreated after a series of massacres; there up to one-half of the local Kurds are Yazidis. In Iraq the Yazidis mainly inhabit the area north of Mosul.

Finally, Ahl-i Haqq might be considered an extreme version of Shi'ism, which reveres Ali but goes further afield in its heterodoxy by worshiping various avatars of Ali, including its own founder, Sultan Sahak. Being the most common in southern Kurdistan, van Bruinessen maintains, the sect emerged among Gurani speakers, and Gurani continues to be its sacred language. Like many of the other minority sects in the region, Ahl-i Haqqs are not exclusively Kurds, including some Turkomans in the ranks. Thus, religion and language cross-cut ethnicity.

In addition to the linguistic and religious facets of culture, Kurdish social organization has been, and to an extent continues to be, an obstacle to national consciousness and mobilization. In a word this organization has traditionally been essentially tribal and *feudal* in nature. The Kurdish tribe—an imprecise word for an imprecise entity—known by such terms as *ashira, tira, taifa,* and others (McDowall 1996, 13),[1] has tended to be a fluid, mutable, territorially oriented, at least quasi–kinship group. It is "in the middle" of a segmentary social system, such that it may be composed

1. See Izady 1992, 78–85, for a list of tribes.

of smaller units down to the clan and family and may be a constituent of larger units up to the tribal confederacy and ultimately the nation. Many of today's clans and tribes can be traced back hundreds or thousands of years, while others are comparatively recent in origin, and others have been absorbed and lost their distinct name; also, tribes of some antiquity may or may not be living at present in the same territory as in past epochs. Tribes have tended to be pastoral and nomadic or seminomadic, although this lifestyle is on the wane in relative terms in the contemporary scene.

Each tribe was led by a ruling family, whose headman used the title *agha.* The *agha* functioned as something of a chief or feudal lord, leading warriors, extracting wealth, and demanding loyalty. Tribes, or even more so their *aghas,* were fundamentally in competition with other tribes and other *aghas.* Each had specific interests, in the form of land, wealth, power, or prestige, that may coincide with the interests of the nation or that may act directly against the interests of the nation. As in all segmentary societies, tribes could unite to form confederations, especially in times of mutual threat, but such confederations were always tenuous, and they were not the inevitable response to shifts in political winds. It was just as likely that a tribe or *agha* would seize a crisis moment as an opportunity to advance parochial interests, and the rise or preeminence of one tribe is a perennial challenge to others. In the end "the play between the tribes is one of perpetual competition and potential opposition. This excludes any strategic external alliance. The preferred option is a series of manoeuvres aimed more at weakening rather than destroying an enemy. Allegiances can therefore fluctuate, but division itself, as a ground rule, remains a constant" (Chaliand 1994, 22).

Fredrik Barth's ethnography of southern Kurds helps us to understand the social principles behind this phenomenon. He attributes Kurdish localism and competitiveness to kinship and marriage practices (which make each local group essentially an enclosed kinship group) and the lack of formalized offices or even formalized scales of hierarchy. The social enclosure of local groups means that such groups have few important connections with other groups and certainly recognize no authority outside the group, and the very conception of authority and power—as vested in individuals, not offices, and as shifting and indefinite—makes leadership and loyalty personal and questionable. Multiple "scales of hierarchy" exist within society, and no one hierarchy or status predominates, at least not permanently. In other words, there is no "normatively or legally defined 'right' state" of authority or power; "in that sense, all persons with power are usurpers" (1953, 125). Hence, any leader's claim to power can be challenged, and a conflict or rebellion can occur "where either the subject individuals do not recognize or are suspicious of the actual status and powers of the supraordinated person, or where the latter incites a person or group against him by overstepping his 'reasonable' area of free grace in his relation to them" (125–26).

Accordingly, when one tribe or tribal leader has mounted a revolt against central authority, of whatever sort, it has not been uncommon for other tribes and leaders to fail to support or actually to oppose the movement—to the point of siding with a foreign power against the rebelling fellow Kurds, just to restrain the ascension of the leading tribe or to avenge for slights or insults in the past. And, while this behavior seems counterproductive and self-destructive from a national standpoint, it must be remembered that the motivations of the rebellion may not be altogether national themselves: especially in the early modern period of Kurdish nationalism and even into the recent period, the leaders of "nationalist revolts" tended to be, if not *sheikhs,* then tribal leaders, and their revolts were often not national in any serious way but personal or provincial, aiming at the aggrandizement of the tribe or leader or at "the desire to get rid of some local administration which hampered them in their lawless ways, or was rapacious and extortionate" (Arfa 1966, 155).

In other words, rival tribal leaders, observing other notables organizing revolts, were often *not wrong* in their assessment that the activity was for the local benefit of the organizers and not for the Kurdish nation. Or, even if the revolting tribe acted out of genuine nationalism, there was the chance that its success would catapult it into greater power and prestige or give it preeminence in any new Kurdish polity that might be won in the contest. Both of these situations would be perceived as a threat to the observing tribes and *aghas* and might lead to the not irrational decision to boycott or resist the movement. This predicament has gone so far as to pit Kurdish tribe against Kurdish tribe in what could have been a struggle for Kurdish autonomy from a shared oppressor. There are many instances of such behavior, some of which I will examine in subsequent pages. Let it be said for now, in summary, that tribalism "seems to have been the main barrier to the emergence of a national consciousness" among the Kurdish people (Kendal 1993a, 15–16).

It is necessary to realize, however, that not all Kurds today are (nor in the recent past were) tribally organized, nor are they all nomadic, although this notion dominates our typical image. First, they have a long history of sedentism, agricultural, and even urbanism; in fact, some of the world's oldest urban sites are located in Kurdistan, and that city culture declined as nomadism increased only in the last millennium or so. Cities with histories of two to four thousand years were reduced to "strongly fortified and shrunken urban islands in a vast area of overtly anti-urban pastoralists" (Izady 1992, 121). Today, although Kurds are less urbanized than neighboring groups, there are still several large urban centers in Kurdistan, one with almost a million residents, two with around one-half million, and so on, down to eighteen with 100,000–500,000.

Into the recent past much of this urbanism was of a feudal nature, with citydwelling lords or *begs* holding land that tenant farmers worked. In the urban centers tribal affiliation was often weakened if not lost, so that there are large numbers of Kurds who are not and do not consider themselves tribal. The distinction between tribal and nontribal Kurds is even marked in Kurdish nomenclature for themselves; for instance, nontribals are called *Kirmanj* in Mosul and Arbil, *Miskem* in Kirkuk and Suleymaniye (or Sulaymania), and *Goran* in parts of Suleymaniye. In this century Kurdish notables, including *begs, aghas,* and *sheikhs,* have increasingly migrated to cities, as have a substantial number of working-class people in search of jobs or refuge from rural violence. An urban Kurdish intelligentsia has been comparatively slow in developing but has been present in major Near East cities for at least one hundred years. As is to be expected, this elite has been fairly disconnected from the rural/tribal scene; yet, unlike many regions undergoing ethnic conflict, it has been the rural rather than the urban elite that has been behind most of the ethnic activity.

One final consideration to make in terms of Kurdish disunity and the obstruction of national consciousness is the political-territorial element. That is, virtually throughout their history, and certainly for the last five hundred years or more, the Kurdish population has spilled across state boundaries—sometimes two (as with Persia and the Ottoman Empire), sometimes more (as at present with Turkey, Iraq, Iran, Syria, and Russia). *Kurdistan* is only a geographical designation and has never been the name of a state. Within the borders of each of the states that harbor or have harbored them, Kurds have met with different circumstances and pressures, leading to further cultural and political separation from their brethren across the frontiers. For this reason, and together with the essentially local and segmentary nature of Kurdish society, "no cross-border culture has emerged" (Bulloch and Morris 1992, 221). This fact has not only perpetuated or even created social and cultural differences between separate Kurdish enclaves, but it has also interfered with the development of a pan-Kurdish nationalist movement. Instead, state-bounded Kurdish communities have tended, for internal and external reasons, to struggle separately against their particular central state authority. The internal reasons have already been discussed; the external reasons have to do with the state and international response they expect and typically get if rebellion is seen as a real pan-Kurdish nationalist movement rather than as a domestic affair. As long as Kurdish activities are perceived as seeking no more than civil rights or at most autonomy within the existing state structure, they are often met with a less harsh and concerted response. Even if only one state-bounded Kurdish population appears to aim at statehood, this causes fear in the neighboring states that "their" Kurds may seek to join the movement, in which case international rivals or even enemies (such as Iran and Iraq) may actually unite or cooperate to smash Kurdish nationalism. Accordingly, having learned their geopolitical lesson the hard way, "the Kurds have generally gone out of their way to make clear that, in each state, they are fighting separate campaigns against different enemies" (Bulloch and Morris 1992, 220). Occasionally, this situation has led to the incongruous outcome that one state-bounded Kurdish contingent (say, Iraqi Kurds) cooperates or allies with the central government (e.g., Iran) of the enemies of fellow but out-of-state Kurds (in this case, Iranian Kurds) to get support for their campaign against their own centralized state enemy (in this case, Iraq).

Kurdish History and Kurdish Identity

Despite all of these forces to the contrary, the Kurds are generally thought of, and try to think of themselves as, a distinct people and not just a set of minority populations within pluralistic states. And there is in fact an ancient history and culture that they can claim to substantiate their demand for peoplehood, if not nationhood. Groups that have been identified as the Kurds or the ancestors of the Kurds appear as much as four thousand years ago in Sumerian inscriptions; these writings refer to a country called Kardaka and recount how King Tigleth Pileser fought a tribe known as Kur-ti-e. A kingdom by the name of Gutium is also mentioned, based in modern-day Kurdistan, and, according to history, the king of Gutium conquered Babylonia over four thousand years ago.

Later, when the Greeks (the famous "10,000") passed through the Kurdish mountains, Xenophon tells of a tribe that he calls Kardukai or Kardoukhi that savagely harassed the retreating army.

Whatever the veracity—or relevance—of these ancient references, it does seem that a name and a group of great antiquity can be and have been linked to the Kurds of today. It is doubted, however, that these ancient Kurds were a single race or ethnic group in the modern sense but, rather, an amalgamation of various waves of immigration over centuries. Many contemporary Kurds believe that they are descendants of the Medes, an Indo-European people who migrated from the Caucasus into the Iranian plateau three thousand years ago or more, but McDowall posits that, if the name ever referred to one particular ancestry, *Kurd* eventually became a generic term for a mixture of Iranian, iranicized, and other (including Semitic) peoples (1992a, 11).[2] By the time of the Arab conquest of the Near East, the name *Kurd* was a term for the peoples living in the Zagros mountains of northwestern Iran, and the Arabs continued the use of the word as basically a regional or even socioeconomic term—meaning something like "mountain people" or "nomad"—rather than an ethnic one. Accordingly, there are mentions of entire tribes converting from Kurdish to Arab, or vice versa; some Kurds today apparently insist that they were originally Nestorian Christians (Van Bruinessen 1992a, 46).

Under the Seljuks around the turn of the eleventh century the intermixing and assimilation of Kurds and Turks continued as it had in the past with Kurds and Arabs; "some ethnically Turkish tribes became Kurdified, while Kurdish tribes became Turkified. Kurds became vassals of Arab chieftains and vice versa, and Arab and Turkish words entered the vocabularies of the Kurdish dialects" (Bulloch and Morris 1992, 58). Like Sri Lanka at roughly the same time in history, the political organization of this Seljuk empire was feudal and dynastic, not ethnic. The Seljuks used the name Kurdistan to refer to one of their *sanjaks,* or provinces, extending from Kermanshah to Sinjar, rather than to an ethnic or racial group or region. Unfortunately for the Kurds, Kurdistan became a main battleground between the Seljuk Turks and the Byzantine Empire. Yet this crisis also produced the Kurds' greatest son, Salah-ed-Din (or Saladin), born in 1137 at Tikrit. Being the Muslim leader who recaptured Jerusalem from the Crusaders, he "did not accentuate his Kurdishness; Saladin was not himself a Kurdish tribal leader, as were many of his generals, and the armies he commanded were predominantly Turkish" (67).

---

2. McDowall even claims that some Jews in Israel presently call themselves Kurds.

By the thirteenth and fourteenth centuries the Kurds had extended their territory down into the Iranian plains to near present-day Teheran. The invasions of the Mongols and Timur or Tamerlane, however, pushed the Kurds back into the mountains (and, consequentially, into Armenian territory) and off the plains where settled agricultural communities existed. Timur took Mosul in 1394 and went on to Diyarbakr (or Diyarbekir), devastating the urban centers and facilitating the conversion from sedentary to nomadic ways for many Kurds. Thus, with the uprooting and destruction of agriculture, large areas became available and were appropriated for pastoralism, providing the opportunity for the development of what is commonly thought of as traditional Kurdish culture. In other words, Kurdish culture may have been essentially or exclusively nomadic and pastoral at some point in the distant past, but a long tradition of urbanism and agriculture was interrupted and overturned only lately by historical circumstances to produce a new traditional culture.

Kurdish Pre-Nationalism and Early Nationalism

Early modern Kurdish history, and the background for modern Kurdish ethnic struggles, begins in the sixteenth century with the clash between the two rival empires astride Kurdish territory, the Safavid dynasty (in Persia) and the Ottoman Empire. These two great powers wrestled over their middle ground until the decisive Battle of Chaldiran in 1516, when the Ottomans defeated the Persians. As a result, most of Kurdistan was annexed by the Ottomans and divided into three *vilayets,* and the *aghas* of the Kurdish tribes that sided with the Turks in the war were rewarded: the Sultan recognized the essential autonomy of those tribes and guaranteed the hereditary rights and privileges of the traditional Kurdish leaders, who were bestowed with the status of Kurdish *hukumats* (governments), "liable only to an annual nominal tribute, and the levy of a fixed number of armed and mounted recruits in the event of war" (Safrastian 1948, 40). Sixteen of these virtually independent principalities were established, their rulers bearing the title of *emir;* van Bruinessen (1992) has characterized these emirates as "the most 'advanced' forms of autochthonous political organization" that the Kurds achieved in recent centuries, perhaps ever. In addition, the Ottoman government moved several clans and tribes, especially to key border locations, where Kurds would act as buffers and advance guards against future Persian aggression; the tribes were enticed with promises of fiefs, privileges, and administrative offices, and in fact some fifty Kurdish fiefdoms were created or recognized. But the price that the

Kurds paid was high: to be used as pawns in the larger international machinations of a greater power. On the other side of the border the Safavids were doing essentially the same thing in a struggle that did end with Chaldiran. Nor would this be the last time that the Kurds got caught up in, and chewed up in, other states' politics.

The international competition over the Kurds aimed at more than their service, however, but at their very identity. The Safavid emperor Shah Abbas II (1585–1628) commissioned a history of the Kurds, which was written by Sharaf-ed-Din (also known as Sharaf al Din or Sharaf Khan) in 1596 and is called the *Sharafnameh.* The document is an aristocratic history of the Kurds up to the sixteenth century, focusing on the noble families but tracing the nation back to its purported origin to the earliest tribes, the Bajnavi and Buhti, and their first homeland south of Lake Van (near the Ottoman-Safavid border). This chronicle was predictably written in Persian, but it had more than purely historical or scholarly import: the Shah's larger aim was, Safrastian argues, "to arouse the hereditary pride of the Kurds to recall their ancient associations with Persia and the East, and thus divert their attention from the Ottoman Empire" (1948, 42). It was, in other words, a political document—an ethnopolitical document—attempting to define Kurdish identity in such a way as to sway it loyalty. Even that long ago, it seems, parties were trying to define and attract and use the Kurds and found national history and national dignity expedient and exploitable devices.

But, just as the Safavids and Ottomans tried to play the Kurds against each other, so the Kurds tried to play the two great regional powers to their own advantage, which was basically to maintain as much autonomy and privilege as possible—that is, to escape the mandates and exactions of either central government if they could. When the demands of their overlords became inescapable or unbearable, however, the Kurdish chiefs and *emirs* (rather than "the Kurdish people") revolted; if their revolt was successful, "they tried to make the best bargain from their momentary success; if not, they crossed the unguarded border into a neighboring state and took shelter with the Kurdish tribes living in that country, remaining there until more auspicious times" (Arfa 1966, 16).

By 1800 the Ottoman Empire was in steep decline, so to attempt to arrest and reverse this process the Ottoman government tightened its control over formerly autonomous areas, including the Kurdish areas. This entailed first of all the extension of direct imperial rule into the functionally independent Kurdish emirates and the establishment of state bureaucratic devices to replace Kurdish petty princes and chiefs and to integrate these regions more completely into the Ottoman polity. Specific policies included a more effective military draft and taxation and forced sedentarization. These reforms were perceived by the *emirs* as infringements upon their sovereignty and privilege, and they were resisted accordingly. So commenced the first series of modern Kurdish uprisings that are sometimes but inappropriately deemed to be the beginning of Kurdish nationalism; instead, as the risings were not coordinated, nor based on culture, nor motivated by the interests of the Kurdish masses or nation, these early activities would be more accurately seen as private affairs of *emirs, aghas,* and *khans* to improve their individual situation vis-à-vis the Ottoman authorities.

The first major Kurdish insurrection came in 1806 in the emirate of Baban, based in the city of Suleymaniye. The second and more serious uprising began in 1826, when Mir Muhammad, the prince of Suran in southern Kurdistan, declared independence from the Ottoman government and opened an armaments factory to prepare for war. By 1833 he had thirty thousand well-armed men under his command, and he led a large-scale rebellion until 1836, when the government used the Kurds' religious faith against them: it called upon a Kurdish *mullah,* Mullah Khati, to issue a *fatwa,* or religious decree, that any soldier who fought against the army of the Caliph would be considered infidel. This made it impossible for Mir Muhammad to spur his men to the attack, and the rebellion was broken.

Sporadic revolts by *emirs* and *begs* continued throughout the middle of the century: Badr Khan Beg (1840) and Yezdan Sher (1855) are the two most notable cases. By mid-century the Ottoman authorities had succeeded in breaking the backs of the independent Kurdish principalities but at the cost of great resentment by the Kurdish people. And, especially after the Crimean War (1854–56), the authorities sought to settle nomadic tribes in agricultural communities on state land. Yet the atomization of the Kurdish polities from relatively large principalities to smaller collectivities, tribes, and villages left a power vacuum in Kurdish society that other traditional Kurdish leaders stepped up to fill. These were, in particular, the religious and tribal notables, the *sheikhs* and *aghas.* Kurdish nationalism or ethnic conflict from the late nineteenth century to at least the mid-twentieth is dominated by the figures of religious leaders and tribal chiefs; almost all ethnic or national activity has been led by or has centered around one of these kinds of personages. Interestingly, *sheikhs* emerge as the first more or less nationalist—or at least pantribal—organizers, which is comprehensible as they, unlike *aghas* or even emirs, had a more (but not completely) pantribal and "universal" appeal and vision based on their spiritual authority and powers.

Yet another war between Russia and the Ottoman empire (1877–78) and the resulting peace led Sheikh Ubayd Allah (or Ubaidullah) to instigate the first real Kurdish nationalist movement in the modern sense. The Treaty of Berlin in 1878, which concluded the war, stipulated that the Ottoman government would undertake efforts to protect and reform *Armenian* (i.e., Christian) areas and "to guarantee their security against the Circassians and Kurds." This was seen by the *sheikh* and other Kurds as a virtual promise that Armenians would receive a state, on Kurdish land, while the Kurds would not. Thereupon, he did something that no Kurd had done before: he "launched a sophisticated diplomatic strategy that included the creation of the Kurdish League—the first Kurdish alliance of its kind" (Olson 1989, 6). And, while the Kurdish League did not last long,[3] the *sheikh* had the effect of bringing the Kurds' grievances to international attention (for the Kurds, always a mixed blessing) and of defining the "the first clear statement of modern Kurdish nationalism." He opened contact with Mecca and Egypt and sent representatives to the Russians and British; the British began thereafter to supply weapons to the Kurds. In his letter to the British vice-consul in July 1880, he issued these nationalist-sounding words:

> The Kurdish nation is a people apart. Their religion is different (to that of others), and their laws and customs are distinct. . . . The chiefs and rulers of Kurdistan, whether Turkish or Persian subjects, and the inhabitants of Kurdistan, one and all united and agreed that matters cannot be carried on this way with the two governments, and necessarily something must be done so that the European governments having understood the matter, shall inquire into our state. . . . We want our affairs to be in our hands. . . . Otherwise the whole of Kurdistan will take the matter into their own hands, as they are unable to put up with these continued evil deeds, and the oppression which they suffer at the hands of the two governments of impure intentions. (Qtd. in Olson 1989, 2)

3. In fact, McDowall (1996, 58) suggests that the Kurdish League may have been merely a rumor and that it certainly never accomplished anything nor made any statements.

Sheikh Ubayd Allah had the enviable position of being not only an articulate nationalist but a revered spiritual guide of the *Naqshbandi* order. His religious status gave him appeal on both sides of the Ottoman-Qajar (the Qajar dynasty having replaced the Safavid in 1794) border, and his goal was a unified Kurdish state encompassing Kurds within all existing state boundaries; however, whether this was a nationalistic goal or a personally aggrandizing one is open to discussion. The Ottomans even supported the *sheikh* for a time, in hopes of using the Kurds to get leverage against the Azeris and Persian Kurdistan and, of course, as always, their nemesis the Russians. In 1880 the *sheikh*'s forces attacked Persia with eighty thousand men and took Mahabad and came near Tabriz (the capital of Azerbaijan). The shah's army, supplemented by rival Kurdish tribes, as well as the now alarmed Ottoman army, caught the Kurds in a vice and forced them to withdraw. The *sheikh*'s followers returned to Anatolia where they were not immediately disarmed, as the government saw the force as a potential weapon against Persia. But when the *sheikh* was detected making overtures to the Russians in 1882, he was exiled to Mecca, where he later died.

Thus, by the end of the nineteenth century incipient Kurdish nationalism had shown itself, but it was still far from mature and far from unified. It could be said with some justification that a modern ethnic group or nation did not exist among the Kurds before 1880 and probably much after. Yet there were some distinctly modern ethnogenetic processes at work with a few years or decades. For example, nationalist voices like the poet Haji Qadir (1817–97) had appeared to give form to Kurdish identity and consciousness. Haji Qadir's poetry has a clear nationalist flavor, advocating such things as the use of the Kurdish language over Turkish or Persian and urging the various tribes to "transcend regionalism and narrow provincialism, and unit for the greater cause of Kurdish nationalism" (Entessar 1992, 49). He criticized Kurdish traditional religious leaders for going too far to accommodate their foreign superiors, and he invoked a traditional Kurdish culture and literature, including the seventeenth-century national epic *Mem u Zin* (the "Kurdish *Romeo and Juliet*"), to reveal to Kurds their historical and cultural identity.

Even more instrumental to a modern type of ethnicity was the establishment of ethnic associations, publications, and parties. The first of these to appear was the journal *Kurdistan* in April 1898, published by Midhad Badr Khan Bey, whose family was to be prominent in early Kurdish nationalism; the journal was bilingual (Kurdish and Turkish) and "mainly cultural and educational in tone." After 1908 and the Young Turk revolution, for a time Kurdish self-expression was tolerated and even supported; that year saw the emergence of the Kurdistan Ta'ali wa Taraqi Jamiyati (Society for the Rise and Progress of Kurdistan). The founders of the group included Emir Ali Badr Khan, General Muhammad Sharif Pasha, and Sheikh Abdul Qadir (son of Sheikh Ubayd Allah). The society also established a cultural association, Kurt Neshri Maarif Jamiyati (Society for the Propagation of Kurdish Education), which opened a Kurdish school in Istanbul. Several other newspapers and journals debuted over the next few years, including *Kurd, Rozhi Kurd, Heviya Kurd,* and *Zhin.*

Yet external interference and internal division again bedeviled the Kurds. In 1910 the Young Turk government closed down the society, and three years later a second and rival organization, Hevi-i-Kurt Jamiyati (Kurdish Hope Society), was created by Kurdish urban students, sons of *sheikhs, emirs,* and other notables who had left behind the rural, tribal life of most Kurds. This transitional moment is reflected in the demands that two *sheikhs* presented to the Young Turk government; the seven demands included four nationalistic ones (Kurdish administration, Kurdish instruction, Kurdish officials, and Kurdish revenues) and three religious ones (administration according to the Shari'a, positions to be filled by religious authorities, and taxes according to the Shari'a). It is impossible to say what direction Kurdish ethnicity may have taken at that point, for World War I was to intervene.

World War I has been called an imperialist and nationalist war, and at least from the perspective of the Near East it was both. By the early twentieth century all European powers had their sights on the decaying Ottoman Empire, and much of the Eastern theater of the war was fought across Kurdistan, resulting in 600,000 to 700,000 or more Kurdish deaths, in addition to over one million Armenians; in fact, of the 2.5 million Muslims who died, almost 42 percent were in the six *vilayets* of eastern Anatolia. What is more, many of the casualties were not caused by the Allies: ethnic groups took their revenge against one another for past wrongs, such as Armenians who set upon Kurds for the Kurdish massacres of Armenians in the 1890s.

With the Turkish defeat, Britain occupying most of the Near East, various groups advancing their claims to sovereignty and statehood, and a sympathetic international community, now was the time for Kurdish nationalism to achieve its goals. Instead, yet again, external machinations and internal rivalries were to stifle the Kurds' wishes. At this time Kurdish nationalists were active: the first organization to appear was Istiqal-i Kurdistan (Liberation of Kurdistan) led by Seyid Abdullah, grandson of Sheikh Ubayd Allah. Kurds in Paris established Hoyboun, or Khoybun (Independence), the first modern Kurdish political party, which was to declare itself the Kurdish government-in-exile in 1927. The most important of the groups, however, was Kurdistan Ta'ali Jamiyati (Society for the Recovery of Kurdistan), an Istanbul-based organization that sought self-determination on Wilsonian principles. This and other groups took heart from Wilson's Fourteen Points (January 8, 1918), especially the statement: "The Turkish portions of the present Ottoman empire should be secure in sovereignty, but the other nationalities which are under Turkish rule should be assured an undoubted security of life and an absolutely unmolested opportunity of autonomous development." In fact, the King-Crane Commission, which assessed the situation of postwar Turkey, recommended to the Peace Conference the creation of three states: one Turkish, one Armenian, and one Kurdish. The subsequent treaty, the Treaty of Sevres (August 10, 1920), contained three articles providing a mechanism for the establishment of an independent Kurdistan.

In the meantime it became clear that Britain and France did not intend to vacate their mandated areas right away, in particular, as far as the Kurds were concerned, the *vilayet* of Mosul. This triggered a spate of uprisings by Kurds (and other groups), most notably by Sheikh Mahmud Barzinji, whom the British had appointed as governor of Suleymaniye. Resenting British limitations on his autonomy (not unlike Kurdish petty chiefs and lords throughout history in relation to their overlords), he led a revolt in the spring of 1919, captured a large region north of Mosul, and declared it independent with himself as ruler of all Kurdistan. McDowall interprets this event also as less than nationalistic, however: "He appealed for a jihad, not a national liberation struggle . . . his style was to use kin and tribal allies and his aim was the establishment of a personal fiefdom" (1996, 158). The rebellion was beaten back with bombing from the British Royal Air Force, but Sheikh Mahmud remained at large and active into the 1930s.

The Treaty of Sevres was never implemented, as it turns out, because it was never ratified; the Turkish government that signed it was deposed and replaced by Mustafa Kemal and a new and more vigorous Turkish nationalism, which led to nullification of the treaty. Kemal (also known as Ataturk, or "Father of the Turks") insisted that the Mosul area was Turkish territory and be returned to Turkey, but, instead of letting this happen or making a Kurdish state there, the British attached it to the new state of Iraq, within which Kurds would have the right to establish an autonomous government. This despite the findings of a League of Nations Commission that, "if the ethnic argument alone had to be taken into account, the necessary conclusion would be that an independent Kurdish State should be created, since the Kurds form five-eighths of the population" of the Mosul province (qtd. in McDowall 1992b, 81). Obviously, though, this time, as so many times previously and subsequently, the ethnic argument alone was not to be taken into account. As for the British, their main interest was the new pro-British government in Iraq, to which they were willing to sacrifice the interests of the Kurds.

The ultimate legal resolution of the Kurdish question, and of postwar Near Eastern politics in general, came in the Treaty of Lausanne, released on July 24, 1923. Most of the Kurdish territories were officially recognized as within the new state of Turkey, the rump of the old Ottoman Empire; the Turkish government representatives to the treaty negotiation had maintained that Turks and Kurds would be partners in the new state, that "the Government of the Great National Assembly is the Government of both Turks and Kurds" and that, "although Turks and Kurds may speak different languages, these two peoples are not significantly different and form a single bloc from the point of view of race, faith, and custom" (qtd. in Kendal 1993b, 49). The treaty did not refer to the Kurds specifically but did provide articles aimed at the protection of "minorities," by which it meant non-Muslim minorities such as Greeks and Armenians but not Kurds.

From this time on, the Kurds were in new waters although still surrounded by some of the same old sharks. From at least 1923 the Kurds found themselves divided across three major state boundaries (Turkey, Iraq, and Iran) and trickling over at least two more (Syria and the Soviet Union). Kurdish nationalism had shown itself for the first time but was still far from fully developed and even farther from success. Subsequent discussion of Kurdish nationalism and ethnic conflict must take into account these new political circumstances as well as the more remote great power games being played at first between the three main Near East states and also between them and the British and later between the United States and the Soviet Union. Therefore, we will proceed by considering the separate Kurdish struggles with Turkey, Iraq, and Iran, illustrating once again that Kurdish nationalism is not a unified force but a traditionally and strategically divided yet interdependent one. But, before doing this, let us explore more fully the other factor that has perpetually undermined and blocked Kurdish interests, that is, the interests and actions of external powers.

The Kurds and International Politics

Kurds as a nation have always straddled two or more state boundaries and thus fallen under the influence of two or more political systems. In actuality, "Kurdistan" has occupied a crucial historical position between Near Eastern empires for centuries, if not millennia, so Kurdish history and ethnicity are profoundly linked with international forces. Kurdistan was the frontier, and often the battleground, between the Byzantine and Arab Empires, the Byzantine and Ottoman Empires, and the Ottoman and Safavid/Qajar Empires. Under foreign influence Kurds reached their highest level of political integration so far in the form of the semiautonomous principalities and *emirates*. Yet foreign powers give with one hand, while they take with the other.

The dismantling of the principalities in the nineteenth century constituted a social *devolution* in Kurdistan. But foreign forces had an even more enduring impact on social patterns and structures: the tribal organization as we know it today is "in a certain sense" a product of the state systems that overarched Kurdish society. In moving and resettling tribes, the states encouraged or facilitated new tribal arrangements, affiliations, or even confederacies while breaking up others and also engendering new tribal rivalries and hostilities. Since then "the largest and most complex tribes also have fallen apart or, at least, do not function as corporate units any more (if they ever did)" (Van Bruinessen 1992, 133).

World War I brought new foreign armies and governments with new interests into the scene. It is important to remember that the interests of the new great powers in the Near East were imperial, economic, and geopolitical. First, they wanted to establish spheres of influence and friendly and pliable states. Iraq was such a state, created by Britain and governed by a king (Faisal) whom the British installed, as was Syria for the French; the continued existence and sympathy of these states thus naturally became a larger concern than other small stateless groups, and, hence, Mosul could be fairly easily absorbed into Iraq and other Kurdish areas into Syria without much distress to the imperial powers. With such political commitments it became incumbent upon the new powers to oppose Kurdish (and other) nationalist independence movements and even to discount the validity of such movements. Hence, the British could suggest, as they did in a memorandum to the League of Nations, that "Kurdish independence is outside the realm of practical politics." The letter continues:

> On political grounds . . . the conception is almost fantastic. Although they admittedly possess many sterling qualities, the Kurds of Iraq are entirely lacking in those characteristics of political cohesion which are essential to self-government. Their organization and outlook are essentially tribal. They are without traditions of self-government or self-governing institutions. Their mode of life is primitive, and for the most part they are illiterate and untutored, resentful of authority and lacking in sense of discipline or responsibility. (Qtd. in Bulloch and Morris 1992, 95)

In conclusion, they determined that it would be "unkind to the Kurds themselves to do anything which would lend encouragement to the sterile idea of Kurdish independence."

The key economic interest in the Near East, then and now, is oil. Despite the fact that the Mosul Commission found "a Kurdish national feeling which, though yet young, was reasonable enough" (qtd. in Edmonds 1957, 423) in this area of Kurdish concentration, it was decided to attach the oil-rich former Ottoman *vilayet* of Mosul to the other two former *vilayets* (Basra and Baghdad) that would make up Iraq. It was deemed that an Iraq without Mosul and a Mosul without Iraq would be unviable. Thus, over the protests of the Mosul and Kirkuk Kurds, the region was affixed to the new state. Since then, oil has continued to figure into and hound Kurdish aspirations.

Of all the interests at work in Kurdistan, however, the most enduring and pernicious is geopolitics. The Kurds, being cursed with their pivotal location, are too well placed and too available to be overlooked in international contests of strength and will in the region. First, there was Turkey, the heir to Ottoman Anatolia, although that inheritance had to be claimed and defended. Among the Allies' geopolitical interests was the weakening, perhaps even the dismantling, of Turkey after the war, such that they supported a Greek invasion of western Anatolia in May 1919; it was only in the summer of 1922 that the Turks were victorious, and the Allies had to accept the existence and sovereignty of this new Turkish state. As a direct result of this and the emergent nationalism in Turkey, they were compelled in the Treaty of Lausanne to recognize the territorial integrity of Turkey, including the major portion of Kurdistan. Subsequently, the Turkish government, more thoroughly and effectively than any other in the region, suppressed Kurdish nationalism and even defined away Kurdish language, culture, and identity, as we will see; at the same time, in its Near East geostrategy, the British policy after 1924 included "utilizing the Kurds as a diplomatic, political, and military instrument against the Turks" (Olson 1989, 52).

An old problem with a new face was Russia, or, after 1917, the Soviet Union. Now, as not only an expansionist power but a communist and "liberationist" and anti-imperial one, it was a special concern to the Western Allies, who took every precaution to obstruct it. Soviet interests were not exclusively focused on the Kurds—Armenians and Azeris were more immediately important to them—nor was the Soviet threat as great after World War I as after the second, but the USSR was significant as a player and as a foil right from the start. One prime concern of the West was that Persia, or Iran as it eventually came to be called, not fall into Communist hands. In 1925 Reza Khan of Iran became Reza Shah and set about, with Western support, to create a centralized state based on the unity of the various nationalities under a Persian consciousness.

It was Soviet intervention that led to the rise of the only real Kurdish state in modern times, Mahabad, within the territory of Iran. We will discuss Mahabad more fully in the section on Kurds in Iran, but we can explore the Soviet role here. During the war some middle-class Iranian Kurds had formed a group known as the Komala (Committee), short for Komala-i Jiyanawi Kurdistan (Committee the Revival of Kurdistan), which came to be recognized and supported by the USSR. Chaliand reports that by 1944 Kurdistan and Azerbaijan were full of Soviet agents, mixing among the tribes and initiating contacts. A "Kurdish-Soviet Cultural Relations Society" was even opened in April 1945 as a front and meeting place for the Komala. Yet the Kurds and the Soviets had different ideas of what this relationship and movement should come to: the Komala sought, first, autonomy for the Iranian Kurdish territories and, ultimately, the unification of Kurds across state borders into a single independent Kurdistan, while the USSR's interests were more varied and complicated—and selfish. For one, they wished to weaken and pressure Iran into concessions; in this effort the entire Kurdish matter was a mere tool. For another, they aimed to help bring to life a government that would be sympathetic, if not subservient, to them. At the same time, they hoped to unify

Kurds and Armenians into at least a cooperative relationship, if not a single state, leaving Kurds with something less than the full autonomy they sought.

At any rate the Soviets supported the Kurds with a printing press, weapons including tanks, and military training. Kurdish leaders were taken to Soviet territory to learn and plan. The most important of these was Qazi Muhammad, a highly respected Kurdish religious figure; the Soviets were not entirely satisfied with him as a nationalist leader, because of his religious conservatism, but they recognized his value to a Kurdish national struggle and convinced the Komala to accept him. So the Soviets, for their own reasons, played on Kurdish religious commitment to strengthen a nationalist movement that would have had considerably less appeal to traditional Kurds had it been couched in secular leftist terms.

Late in 1945 Soviet agents among the tribes told them to prepare for combat and ordered the *aghas* to gather in Mahabad. Again, impetus for Kurdish action came from outside Kurdistan: on December 10, 1945, the Azeris moved and captured Tabriz and declared the "Azerbaijan People's Government," and on this cue Qazi Muhammad and the Komala, which had been reorganized as the Kurdish Democratic Party (KDPI, to distinguish it from the KDP in Iraq), declared their own independence on January 22, 1946. Having taken the first steps toward self-determination, the perennial enemies of Kurdish national interest, internal divisiveness and outside interference, reared up as usual. The great Iraqi tribal leader Mullah Mustafa Barzani had arrived in Mahabad in October 1945 with his men, who became the backbone of the small state's armed forces. Yet the tribal forces and the town-based government never really trusted each other, as is evident from the fact that Qazi Muhammad kept Mullah Mustafa Barzani and his people outside the city and tried to create his own state military force. Also, partly because of their animosity to *any* central government, foreign or domestic, and their suspicion of Qazi Muhammad's connections to the Soviet Union, almost all of the tribes surrounding the Mahabad region failed to rally to the new republic and some actually sided against it. And, when Iran complained to the United Nations of Russian activities within its territory, the West pressured the latter to withdraw, which they did by May 1946. Thereupon, the Iranian army launched its offensive against both Azerbaijan and Kurdistan; Azerbaijan fell on December 17, 1946, and Mahabad soon after. Qazi Muhammad and other leaders were arrested and later hanged for treason. Mullah Mustafa Barzani and his entourage, however, escaped into the USSR, where they remained for eleven years, only to reemerge when the times were right in Iraq.

This is hardly the only or last episode of Soviet influence on Kurdish affairs; naturally, much of United States and Western policy in Kurdistan, as elsewhere, was motivated by the general containment policy toward the Soviets. Let us, however, quickly consider some other dimensions of the international forces impinging on Kurdish ethnicity and nationalism. One obvious dynamic is the rivalry between Iraq and Iran, which each shelter large Kurdish populations and have plenty of other differences aside from that, from water and coastal disputes to competing desires for regional domination. Kurdish struggles have continuously taken advantage of, or been exacerbated by or been frustrated by, this international rivalry. For example, in an age-old pattern suppressed rebellions often lead to a Kurdish group crossing the border from one state to the other; often these Kurds are even welcomed as enemies of the enemy and therefore as friends. Sheikh Mahmud, who was defeated in Iraq, crossed into Iran. But, rather than let "foreign" Kurds make trouble in their state, especially the trouble of pan-Kurdism, the "host" state is eventually typically driven to oppose the refugee Kurds, as occurred in the case of Sheikh Mahmud. Or, if not that, then the refugee Kurds are sacrificed on the altar of "improved international relations" with their on-again, off-again rival state.

Iran and Iraq have been at war intermittently for the last twenty years or so. One such war occurred in 1974–75, primarily over the Shatt-al-Arab waterway. During the war Iran incited the Iraqi Kurds to resist the Iraqi government, providing them with supplies and logistical support to do so. On March 5, 1975, however, the Algiers Agreement brought an end to this round of hostilities between the two states (and settled the Shatt-al-Arab dispute in Iran's favor, which would return to haunt the Near East another day). In return Iran agreed to discontinue support to the Kurds and to close its border to them, whereupon the Kurdish revolt collapsed again; a major Iraqi offensive into Kurdistan followed immediately upon Iran's withdrawal. Incredibly, the same scenario was to play out again when yet another war broke out in 1980 after Saddam Hussein denounced the Algiers Agreement.

Once the war began, both sides used the Kurds as an excuse and a weapon for fighting. Iraq opened relations with the Kurds in Iran, and Iran sought and received the support of Iraqi Kurds of both major political parties (the KDP and the PUK). The tragic and near-farcical upshot of this situation was the Kurds were supporting *both* sides and opposing *each other*—Iraqi Kurds seeing Iran as friend and ally, Iranian Kurds seeing Iraq as a friend and ally. Perhaps no incident illustrates the "nationally illogical" behavior of the Kurds more clearly as well as the eagerness of regional states to exploit that behavior; yet, on the level of local/personal interest on the parts of particular Kurdish communities or leaders, the decisions make a certain amount of sense. Simultaneously, having been mobilized in a Kurdish struggle, if not exactly a nationalist one, the Kurds extended their activities into Turkish territory; in early 1983 Iraq made an arrangement with Turkey to allow Turkish troops to cross into Iraq in "hot pursuit" of Kurdish insurgents, and by the summer Turkish and Iraqi forces were cooperating in pacifying the Kurds.

The United States and its allies have also had a frequent hand in the region, not least in the recent Gulf War. War, or at least state interest, could not make stranger bedfellows than in this regard. U.S. interests including as they did both the security of Israel and the alliance with Iran (up to 1979); Israeli interests concentrating on its own security vis-à-vis the Arab threat; Iranian interests leaning toward anything that might weaken its rival Iraq and cement its relation with the United States (up to 1979); and Kurdish interests as always focused on "local" if not national self-determination and any friendly outsider who might assist at the moment—all these coincided in a machiavellian web such that Iran, in conjunction with Israel and the United States, recruited and backed Iraqi Kurds in an effort to destabilize the Iraqi regime. As early as 1963, Israel was sending substantial aid to Mullah Mustafa Barzani by way of SAVAK, the shah's secret security organization. In 1965 Israeli-backed training camps were established, and after the 1967 Arab-Israeli War military aid to the Kurds was stepped up. In fact, Mullah Mustafa Barzani visited Israel himself in September 1967. By 1968 and the second Ba'ath revolution in Iraq the United States also came to see Iraq as a regional danger and the Kurds "as a strategic asset to be used in keeping the Iraqi regime at bay" (Entessar 1992, 119).

The United States now began to dabble, too, in Kurdish national matters, according to the Pike Report to Congress, providing some sixteen million dollars in secret funds to Kurdish leaders from 1972 to 1975. As a result, Kurdish forces were militarily transformed, from guerrilla, ambush-and-retreat fighters into a well- and heavily armed force "able and willing to engage in set-piece battles with their enemy" (Bulloch and Morris 1992, 136). U.S. intelligence reports credited this aid and logistical support (such as the openness of Iran's borders to Kurdish rebels) for the Kurds' ability to withstand major Iraqi offensives. It was a precarious alliance for the Kurds, since it was an alliance of convenience for all sides, one that would shift or cease as circumstances and interests warranted; when United States or Israeli or Iranian interests were no longer served by the association, they could extricate themselves fairly easily (as Iran did after the Algiers Agreement), leaving the Kurds alone to face the consequences. The same outcome can be seen in the aftermath of the recent Gulf War.

It is clear, then, that Kurdish nationalism, and at times also Kurdish internal division, has been exploited and therefore to an extent determined by the strategic interests of outsiders who are not, to put it kindly, deeply committed friends of the Kurdish people. Thus, the Kurds have been repeatedly frustrated and abandoned by their would-be benefactors, to be beaten down into a sullen submission until the next time. By being used in this way, Kurdish nationalism has developed unevenly and only slowly. It remains for us, then, to investigate the conflicts between Kurds and their major host states—Turkey, Iraq, and Iran—with an eye to how the activities and results of the Kurds have been affected by each specific sociopolitical setting and how each state's policy toward the Kurds has been shaped by a combination of internal/cultural and international/strategic factors.

Kurds in Turkey

The largest community of Kurds in the world (nine to ten million) is found in Turkey, the Anatolian remnant of the Ottoman Empire; this also amounts to a substantial portion (about 20 percent)of Turkey's overall population. Turkish Kurdistan is an area of some 80,000 square miles, or 30 percent of Turkey's total area, divided into eighteen *vilayets.* Conversely, the population of Kurdistan is not 100 percent Kurdish, but it is over 80 percent Kurdish (although all demographic statistics for Kurds and Kurdistan are subject to a considerable range of error). Kurdistan is still mostly rural, but sizable communities of Kurds live outside Kurdistan in major Turkish cities like Istanbul and Ankara.

Modern Kurdish nationalism rose from the ashes of the Ottoman Empire after World War I. It was faced and opposed, however, by a muscular *Turkish* nationalism, as expressed by the early theoretician of "Turanism," Ziya Gokalp, and as practiced by the "father" of modern

Kurdish Areas in Turkey. (Reprinted from *The Kurds: An Historical and Political Study*, by Hassan Arfa [London: Oxford University Press, 1966], p. 35, by permission of Oxford University Press.)

Turkey, Mustafa Kemal Ataturk. During Ottoman times *Turk* had been something of a derogatory term, not one of national pride and not one that was promoted by the state. Yet, in the postwar state-building process, a nationalist ideology would serve well. Gokalp captured the post-Ottoman, pan-Turk nationalism in his words: "The country of the Turks is not Turkey, nor yet Turkistan. Their country is a vast and eternal land: Turan!" (qtd. in Gunter 1990, 7). Gokalp's notion of Turanism was not racial but cultural (he himself was of Kurdish lineage), that is, anyone raised with Turkish culture was a Turk. This view eventually gave way to a race ideology, however, and Turkey was to be the national home of this race exclusively: Ismet Inonu, one-time prime minister of Turkey, maintains: "Only the Turkish nation is entitled to claim ethnic and national rights in this country. No other element has any such right" (qtd. in Entessar 1992, 81). And minister of justice in the 1920s, Mahmut Esat Bozhurt, was more emphatic: "I believe that the Turk must be the only lord, the only master of this country. Those who are not of pure Turkish stock can have only one right in this country, the right to be servants and slaves" (qtd. in McDowall 1992b, 38).

Understandably, this attitude was intolerable to the Kurds, who could see their future under Turkish domination as either to be stripped of their distinct Kurdish identity or to be reduced to "servants and slaves" in a land not of their own. Then, in 1924, the caliphate was formally abolished, breaking perhaps the main link between the devout Muslim Kurds and state; shortly thereafter, Shari'a courts were abolished in favor of civil courts. Finally, the series of legislation set restrictions and prohibitions directly in the way of Kurdish nationalism, in fact, even of Kurdish identity and cultural distinctness. The Kurdish language was outlawed and Kurdish organizations banned, while Kurdish land could be expropriated and used to settle Turks. The administration of Kurdistan became increasingly militarized.

These frontal assaults against Kurdish ethnicity touched off a series of revolts, mostly under the leadership of traditional Kurdish elites. Clearly, these elites—*mullahs* and *sheikhs, aghas* and *begs*—had the most to lose in the short run from the attacks upon Kurdish religion and property. The first great uprising was led by Sheikh Said, a Naqshbandi authority and one of the most prominent members of the new Azadi (Freedom) organization. Throughout the early weeks of 1925 Sheikh Said traveled around Turkish Kurdistan, issuing *fatwas* and giving speeches against the secular Turkish government. By the time the rebellion broke out, on February 8,

1925, the movement had raised fifteen thousand fighting men in the cause of Kurdish national independence. The Kurdish rebels attacked Diyarbakr on March 2 but were defeated by a Turkish force. By April Sheikh Said was apprehended and eventually hanged.

The insurgency was hobbled, as usual, by Kurdish disunity. While the rhetoric of the "movement" was national, tinged with religious elements, it did not attract or hold the various Kurdish constituencies into a solid front. For one thing, Sheikh Said's revolt was primarily tribal; it did not appeal to or mobilize nontribals from the plains nor the urban populations of such key centers as Diyarbakr. In fact, Entessar reports that some city-dwellers turned against the rebels because of the latter's looting and other nonnationalistic excesses. Even more, not all tribes participated: participation was largely limited to the smaller and *Zaza*-speaking tribes so that, although nearly 100 percent of such tribes were involved, still they constituted only a fraction of the potential Kurdish force. Alevis also did not join, as they did not wish to contribute to the creation of a Sunni-dominated state in which they would be a discriminated minority, even if it were to be a Sunni *Kurd*-dominated state; this was tantamount to tacit support for the Turkish government, which could operate in and around Alevi territory without fear of resistance. And in some cases, when tribes, such as the Sasunah and Tatukan, refused to join his movement, Sheikh Said had his armies attack them, fellow Kurds though they were.

The impact of the failure of the Sheikh Said rebellion was twofold. First, it marked a change in the nature of Kurdish ethnic activity, from religious in character to more strictly secular and political, although still not fully national. Second, it discredited the moderates and leftists among the Turks in the eyes of the regime, people who might have been sympathetic to Kurdish grievances and might even have had some influence on minority policy, giving the Kemalists the motive and the opportunity to push on with more, and more extreme, measures against the Kurds.

This phase of Kurdish nationalism in Turkey, however, was not effectively suppressed until the late 1930s. Before that was accomplished, two other noteworthy uprisings, the Mount Ararat and the Dersim revolts, broke out and were crushed. The Mount Ararat revolt was a combined outcome of activities by *Khoybun,* the expatriate Kurdish party that had earlier declared itself a government-in-exile, and survivors of the 1925 failed movement who had fled to Iraq and Iran and eventually gathered near the mountain. The head of this new agitation was Ishan Nuri, who by 1929 controlled a sizable area and was indirectly aided by the shah of Iran (who sought to use the "Kurdish card" in his ongoing border disputes with Turkey). As usual, the two major states reached an understanding, this time exchanging some territory, and Iran withdrew its support, leaving the Kurds to be surrounded and beaten by the Turks. The Dersim (or Tunceli, as it is known since Kurdish town names were Turkified) revolt erupted as an effect of the aftermath of the 1930 defeat of the previous uprising. In 1932 the Turkish government established "zones" in Kurdistan in which different policies regarding Kurdish populations were to apply. Dersim fell within a zone where populations were to be totally evacuated, so between 1936 and 1938 the Turkish army struggled with the resistance against the forced removal, eventually committing sixty thousand troops, until it was broken.

After Dersim no major Kurdish uprisings took place in Turkey until after World War II. The Turkish authorities set about a very successful campaign of suppression and even eradication of Kurdish culture and identity. This campaign entailed mass deportations, exiling of Kurdish *aghas* and *sheikhs,* and drafting of Kurdish youths into the Turkish army. Turkish Law No. 2510 (June 1934) provided a legal basis for some of these actions, stating that a person "whose mother tongue is not Turkish may be resettled for military, political, cultural, or security reasons if the Ministry of Interior deems it necessary for the good of the country" (qtd. in Entessar 1992, 106). The penal code of 1938 criminalized "Communist" or "separatist" organizations and propaganda as well as "insulting" behavior toward the government and its officers. The ban on Kurdish language was extended to Kurdish traditional dress, and even the names *Kurd* and *Kurdistan* disappeared. Kurdish identity was defined away, Kurds being considered merely another Central Asian / Turanian tribe and therefore *Turks,* the Kurdish language being merely a corruption of Turkish. Kurds were officially recognized as "mountain Turks," and *Kurdistan* ceased to exist as a political term; henceforward, the region was simply the "East" of Turkey.

The (first ever) Turkish free elections in 1950 and U.S. influence in the form of the Marshall Plan brought a liberalization of political and ethnic life. Kurds had supported the successful Democratic Party, and several Kurds received positions, even cabinet positions, in the new government; many former exiles were allowed to return home. Even so, the assimilation of Kurds was already well advanced; in particular, traditional leaders had largely been urbanized and co-opted into the mainstream and become more modern and bourgeois, an absentee landlord class dissociated from the peasantry. From this new "class" rose the next phase of Kurdish nationalism in Turkey, known as "Eastism."

Again, Kurdistan had officially ceased to exist, so Kurds could only refer to their land as "East" and could only refer to its problems as economic ones within the Turkish system. "Eastism" (*Doguculuk* in Turkish) was a movement stressing the economic issues and development of the region, which was officially recognized as an "underprivileged area." The movement began in late 1958, when Kurdish-language broadcasts from Radio Baghdad and other sources rekindled Kurdish feelings in Turkey. The Eastists were centered in Diyarbakr and published a daily paper called *Ileri Yurt* (Advanced Country). Eastism has been called "a transitory period in the rebirth of the Kurdish national movement," and it was persecuted from late 1959, but it did demonstrate that Kurdish ethnicity had not been lost, even if its discourse had changed and its nature had been altered.

In May 1960 there was a military coup, and the democratically elected government of Adnan Menderes was ousted by a more Kemalist and therefore less ethnically tolerant regime. The new government, the Committee of the National Front, made decrees "Turkicizing" the names of Kurdish towns and also Turkicizing Kurds, especially children: boarding schools were established, and Turkish-language radio stations broadcasted to Kurdistan. By late 1960 Kurds in Iraq were battling authorities there, and the leader of the Turkish junta gave this warning to Turkey's Kurds: "If the mountain Turks do not keep quiet, the army will not hesitate to bomb their towns and villages into the ground. There will be such a bloodbath that they and their country will be washed away" (qtd. in Kendal 1993b, 65).

The return of civilian government in 1961, despite certain legal liberalizations, did little to ease restrictions on Kurds. New political parties, especially leftist ones, sympathized with the Kurds and even referred to the Kurds, and publications by and about Kurds appeared, but they were all opposed by the government and shut down whenever possible. The short-lived journals *Barish Dunyasi* (World of Peace, 1962) and *Yeni Akis* (New Current, 1966) were both banned after a few issues, the latter for using the term *Kurdish people.* A minor improvement was that people were no longer executed "for having claimed that the Kurds existed" as they would have been a few decades earlier. But still it was impermissible to write or say anything about the Kurds *as* Kurds, about their culture or history. In 1966 Mehmet Emin Bozarslan's alphabet book for Kurdish children was banned. And, in perhaps the best-known episode of ethnic censorship, Ismail Besikci, who was not a Kurd himself, published in 1969 a study entitled *The Order of Eastern Anatolia: Socio-Economic and Ethnic Foundations,* in which he discussed Kurdish social conditions, and as a result he was discredited professionally and imprisoned on the charge of making "Communist and Kurdish propaganda." He would be jailed repeatedly (1971–74, 1979–81) for subsequent publications. And the leftist Workers' Party of Turkey was outlawed for declaring in its 1971 congress that "there is a Kurdish people in the East of Turkey . . . [who have been subjected] to a policy of assimilation and intimidation which has often become a bloody repression" (qtd. in Entessar 1992, 89–90).

Typically, the two nemeses of Kurdish nationalism figured into the Turkish situation at this point. One was the external factor, in this case the struggles and successes of Kurds in Iraq. Kurdish nationalist rhetoric was seeping into Turkey from Mullah Mustafa Barzani's movement in Iraq, which was a threat in itself. Then, in 1970, the Iraqi Kurds and the Iraqi government reached an agreement that, although never fully implemented, was the closest thing to a victory Kurds have enjoyed before or since. Kurds in Turkey formed a Kurdish Democratic Party (KDP), which was closely linked to Mullah Mustafa Barzani's KDP-Iraq, which itself was based on the KDP-Iran. Yet, due to this success and this connection and the second Turkish military coup in 1971, conditions turned bleak for Turkish Kurds again. Kurdish organizations were smashed, many Kurds were arrested, and Turkish soldiers were deployed to Kurdistan to root out Kurdish separatists.

The second factor was internal: Turkish Kurds evidenced the same divisiveness and tendency to turn on themselves as Kurds elsewhere. To the already-existing KDP were added, in several cases from internal schism and departure of members, a number of new rival Kurdish parties, including the Socialist Party of Turkish Kurdistan, the Revolutionary Democratic Cultural Associations, the Partisans of the National Liberation of Kurdistan (also known as KUK)—whose followers were a younger and more militant breakaway faction of the KDP—and a congeries of smaller groups like Rizgari (Revolution), Ala Rizgari (Flag of Revolution), and Tekasim (Struggle). These groups not only represented different positions on the ideological spectrum, but they also sapped one another's strength and sometimes broke into open conflict with one another. Yet they shared two characteristics in common: a broader base of organization than previous Kurdish activities and an increasingly radical agenda.

The clearest example of this radicalization, and one that had mixed results in terms of both Turks and Kurds, was the Partia Karkari Kurdistan (PKK), or Workers' Party of Kurdistan, which commenced its activities in 1975. It began as a group of students at the University of Ankara, led by Abdullah Ocalan, nicknamed "Apo" (uncle). Ideologically, it mixed Marxism-Leninism with Kurdish nationalism. In 1977 it issued its theoretical treatise on the Kurdish situation, *Kurdistan Devriminin Yolu* (Path of the Kurdish Revolution). In this document the PKK describes Kurdistan as a "classic colonial entity, where Kurdish feudal landlords and 'comprador bourgeoisie' collaborated with the ruling classes in the colonial countries." It also criticizes Kurdish elites for assimilating to Turkish and abandoning their Kurdish culture and brethren. The party's diagnosis for the plight of the Kurdish people is a two-step process: first, a national phase, which would establish an independent Kurdistan, not just within Turkey but across state borders integrating all Kurdish territories; and, second, a "democratic" phase, "to clear away the contradictions in society left over from the Middle Ages . . . [including] feudal and comprador exploitation, tribalism, religious sectarianism, and the slave-like dependence of women." This radical social program went far beyond any mere attainment of national recognition and rights while also adding an internal class-based schism.

Thus, most of the PKK's activities in its early years were intraethnic, aiming at enemies of the party's views and policies—collaborators with the Turkish government, tribes on friendly terms with the government, right-wing parties, rival left-wing parties, and especially the traditional Kurdish elite. It became infamous for its attacks and predations on Kurdish villages, such that the Turkish government actually promoted and armed "village guard" brigades to resist the organization. So, a disastrous pattern developed in which PKK militants abused even their Kurdish brethren by demanding food, shelter, and aid from local people, taking hostages, committing rape, and executing those who did not cooperate with them. This excessive behavior alienated many Kurds from the PKK and led people to support more moderate parties, like the Motherland Party and the government of Turgut Ozal, which came to power in late 1983.

The government's response to Kurdish militancy in the 1980s was to encourage economic development of the East (to remove some of their grievances and integrate them more fully into the Turkish system) and to use force if necessary to pacify Kurdish resistance. The years 1986 to 1988 were particularly violent ones, as the PKK raided villages and killed villagers. Then, in a series of dramatic steps, Ozal made unprecedented concessions to the Kurds, first accepting that Turkey is a multiracial, multiethnic state whose people "come from many different origins as the remnants of an empire" and subsequently that "one out of six Turks is a Kurd" (qtd. in Entessar 1992, 100). In 1991 the law banning Kurdish language altogether was repealed but only so as to decriminalize spoken and sung Kurdish: written Kurdish was still outlawed, as was political or educational use or broadcast.

Kurdish nationalism was not thereby fulfilled or tranquilized. A *serhildan* (uprising) in Mardin province between the "army" of the PKK (the People's Liberation Army of Kurdistan) and the Turkish army presaged the renewed activity of the PKK starting in 1991. In response, the Turkish authorities began to execute Kurdish activists in public. Clearly, Kurdish nationalism is far from finished in Turkey, but it is also far from unified, as Kurdish parties and partisans stand against one another and against Kurdish people and as other Kurds conduct more or less disjoint struggles of their own across Turkey's borders.

Kurds in Iran

The second largest population of Kurds resides in Iran, between four and seven million by various counts. Either way, they compose 10–15 percent of the Iranian population. Iranian Kurdistan lies over 50,000 square miles of mountainous terrain, although the province called Kurdistan, or "Kordestan," is only one area in which Kurds live. Conversely, some 15 percent of the population of Kurdistan is not Kurdish. Like Kurdish regions in Turkey, Iranian Kurdistan is underdeveloped even compared to the rest of Iran, with lower income, higher illiteracy, and a dearth of economic opportunities or social service. it is also worth recalling that, while Iran is and has traditionally been a Shi'ite society, most Kurdish Muslims (some 75 percent) are Sunnis.

Due to the effective manipulation of Kurdish identity and loyalty, and the tribal nature of Kurdish society, any recognizable nationalism within Iran was a late development, coming only at the end of the nineteenth century. At the same time, Kurdish autonomy—what little there was—eroded as the state grew more powerful and confident; the last autonomous principality, Ardelan, fell in 1865. Iranian Kurdistan was affected, however, by the first great Kurdish nationalist revolt, the Sheikh Ubayd Allah rebel-

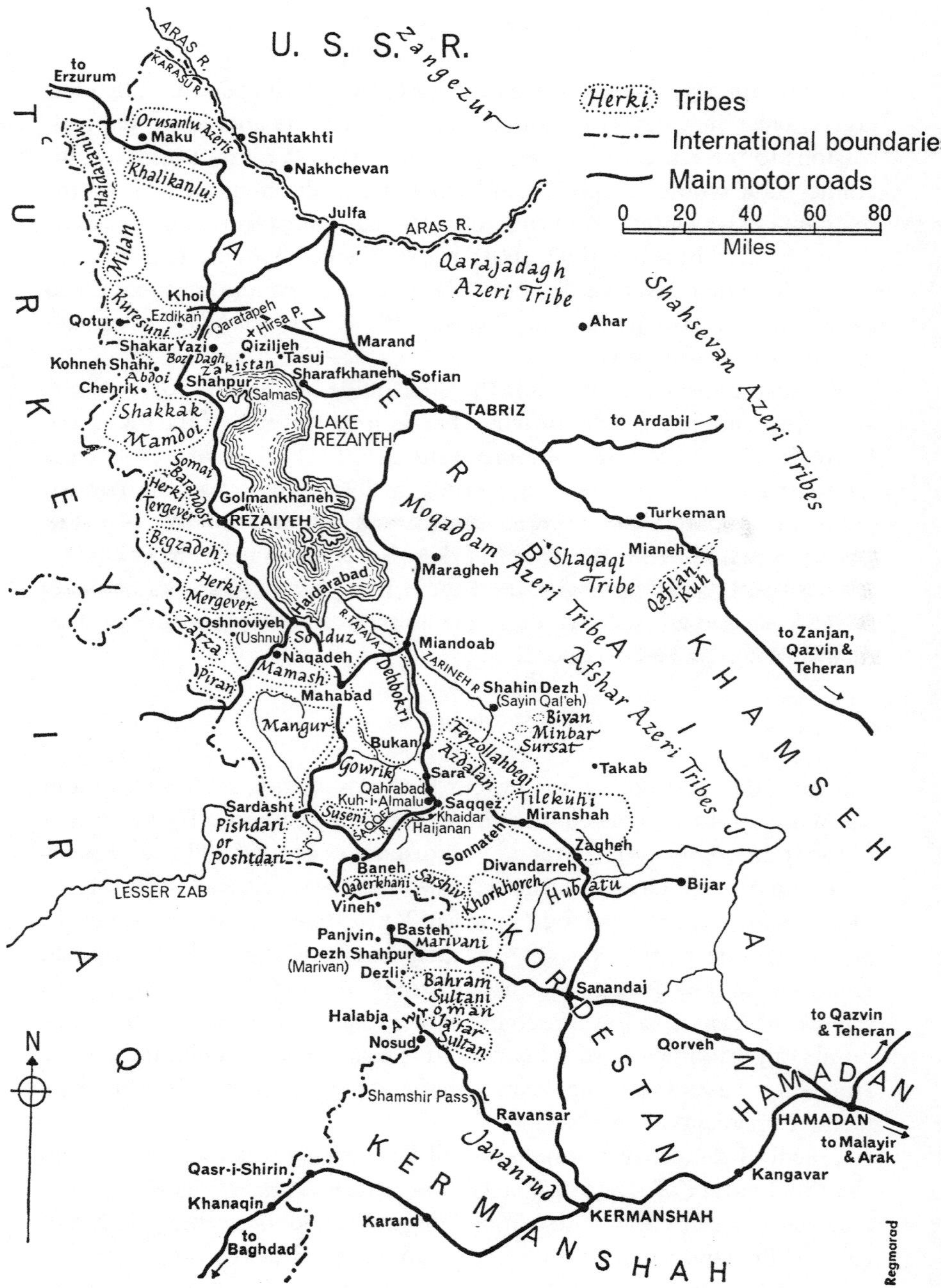

Kurdish Areas in Iran. (Reprinted from *The Kurds: An Historical and Political Study,* by Hassan Arfa [London: Oxford University Press, 1966], p. 49, by permission of Oxford University Press.)

lion, when the *sheikh,* in his pan-Kurdish cause briefly united Ottoman and Persian Kurdistan in 1880. After Ubayd Allah there were a few isolated incidents, but these were as often intertribal as antigovernmental. But the upheavals of World War I and the Kurdish nationalist activities in the form of uprisings in Turkey and Iraq and fed by the (defunct) Treaty of Sevres lit flames in Iranian Kurdistan as well.

The greatest of the early post–World War I movements was propelled by Ismail Agha Simqu (or Simko). Simqu, leader of a faction of the Shikak tribe, rose up in 1918, and by 1920 he held nominal power over much of Iranian Kurdistan, having warred against rival tribes. He spoke the language of Kurdish independence, but his view of that goal was the perennially narrow Kurdish one of "the establishment of his personal despotic rule over the other Kurdish tribes . . . and, with their help, the seizing and exploitation of large sections of non-Kurdish regions to the west and northwest" (Arfa 1966, 58). The weakness of this vision of Kurdish independence became evident in the decisive battle with the Iranian army in 1922, when Simqu's ten thousand men evaporated into a mere one thousand Shikak tribesmen. Also, international politics, which had led Turkey to aid Simqu, led it to withdraw that aid, so that the rebellion was defeated and he fled to Turkey. He was to rise up periodically until 1929, when he was killed by Iranian troops. McDowall concludes that he was never a nationalist in the modern sense but remained to the end "a tribal chief *par excellence,* exploiting the advantages of a tribal culture to mobilize supporters and suppress rivals," and failing for the same reason (1996, 221).

The next important moment, and the only "success" in Kurdish nationalism in Iran, was the establishment of the Mahabad Republic. From 1941 the country was occupied, in the south by Britain and the United States, in the north by the Soviet Union. The north included most Kurdish areas, especially the city of Mahabad, with a lively middle class and urban intellectual life. It was also a center of Kurdish nationalist thought before the war, where a group of leading Kurds there formed the Komala. It is significant that Komala's horizons extended beyond the town, beyond the province, beyond the state: in August 1844 Komala members met with representatives of Iraqi and Turkish Kurdish groups and penned an agreement known as *Peman-i Se Senur* (Pact of the Three Borders), a symbolic statement of the cooperative territorial aspirations of the Kurds.

The Komala was reorganized into the Kurdish Democratic Party (KDP), whose demands included local autonomy, education and administration in the Kurdish language, Kurdish officials to serve in Kurdish offices, general economic progress, and political freedom for and solidarity with other Iranian minorities (Ghassemlou 1993, 106). No explicit reference was made to total independence, perhaps for tactical reasons. In fact, from the very start the precise legal status of this "republic" was vague; its two names—*Dawlati Jumhouri Kurdistan* (State of the Kurdish Republic), the official designation, and *Houkoumati Milli Kurdistan* (National Government of Kurdistan)—left it unclear whether this new entity was indeed a sovereign state or an autonomous region within the state of Iran.

In the end, of course, it was of little import. International machinations and internal divisions doomed the young "state," just like every similar attempt before and since. In May 1946 the Soviet army pulled out of northern Iran, and the Iranian army moved against Mahabad. Without the promised external support the republic had little chance of survival. In addition, many tribal leaders, who benefited from the relationship with the Iranian state, remained loyal to it; others who depended on markets in Iran like that for tobacco opposed the secession from Iran on economic grounds. And many, as mentioned, simply resisted any central government, be it Kurdish or Iranian. Finally, the nationalist movement was obstructed by religious differences among Kurds, never commanding any strong support from the Shi'ite minority.

The demise of the Mahabad republic meant the end of active Kurdish nationalism in Iran for about a generation; although Mahabad remained a powerful symbol of Kurdish identity and political possibility, the theater of Kurdish nationalism shifted away from Iran, and things continued comparatively quietly as tribes dispersed back to their previous territories and the shah's government pursued its policy of pacifying and disarming them. Small irritants and incidents emerged periodically, such as the provincial election of 1952 that the KDP won, but that was nullified by military intervention. There were uprisings that year as well, but they were as much intra-Kurdish and antifeudal as anti-Iranian; this situation led to the interesting consequence of an alliance between government and feudal Kurdish notables against Kurdish peasants and their rebelliousness. With the exception of the revolt of the Javanioudi tribe in the mountains of Kermanshah in 1956, no major Kurdish activity took place until the Islamic Revolution in Iran in 1978.

This "peaceful" period was due in large part to the suppression and manipulation of the Kurds, not only in Iran but in neighboring Iraq. Domestically, Iran's anti-ethnic policies included the exclusive use of Persian in official and administrative affairs, in all publishing, and in all education (however, some limited television and radio in Kurdish was permitted). Ethnic political parties were circumscribed, and Kurdistan became more heavily militarized than any other area of Iran. It is important to see, however, that most of this activity was not uniquely anti-Kurd but was part of the general modus operandi of the shah's government. First and foremost, the shah employed authoritarian practices throughout Iran in an increasing centralization of power. Second, and critical to understanding the ethnic issue in Iran, the Kurds are not the only significant ethnic minority in the state; in fact, they are not even the largest ethnic minority (Azeris are number 1, at nearly ten million). In addition, there are Baluchis, Arabs, and other smaller tribes and groups. Altogether, over half of Iran's population is ethnic (i.e., non-Persian), which make ethnicity and nationalism a more poignant concern in Iran than in some other states where Kurds live.

The opportunity to manipulate Kurdish nationalism, and particularly to deflect it from Iran, arose when Mullah Mustafa Barzani resumed his activities in Iraq in 1961. Iranian Kurds furnished what aid they could to their Iraqi cousins, but after 1966 the Iranian government seized upon this chance to kill two Kurdish birds with one stone. The shah began to supply substantial aid to Barzani's efforts, on the condition that the Iraqi Kurds use their influence to restrain the actions of the Iranian Kurds. This Barzani did, partly out of need and partly out of commitment that the Iraqi cause had a greater likelihood of success than the Iranian cause and therefore could be sacrificed to the former. Hence, Barzani issued a statement to the Iranian Kurds to the effect that, because Iraqi Kurds depended on the shah's support, any Kurdish resistance against the shah's regime was a betrayal of the Kurdish revolution (Entessar 1992, 28). This policy bore several fruits: Iraqi Kurdish militancy kept the Ba'ath regime in Iraq preoccupied and destabilized; Mullah Mustafa Barzani's cooperation with the shah led to the arrest or execution of over forty KDP-Iran members by Barzani's own forces; and, ultimately, a wedge was driven between Kurds in the two states.

Into the 1970s the Iraqi Kurds continued to look upon the shah as one of their best friends and allies, while the Iranian Kurds considered him their main opponent and enemy. The relationship played a part in the clash between Iraq and Iran in 1974–75 over the Shatt-al-Arab waterway, in which Iran used its Iraqi Kurdish allies to harass Iraq. When Iran got what it wanted—that is, an advantageous position in regard to the waterway—it abandoned the Kurds and left them to the mercy of the Iraqi regime and army. Yet the key moment of recent Iranian Kurdish nationalism is the Islamic Revolution in Iran in 1978–79. Kurds had supported the revolution, and, when the shah's regime did collapse, they were left with a degree of autonomy in the north. The Kurds expected a recognition of their autonomy from the new religious government, and on March 24, 1979, the two sides reached an agreement on limited autonomy that included bilingualism in schools, administration in Kurdistan by Kurdish officials, and Kurdish input on a new constitution for Iran. And the leader of the KDP-Iran, Abdul Rahman Ghassemlou (or Qasimlu), assured the new government that "no political force in Iranian Kurdistan wants to secede from Iran. Our demands are framed within the context of the Iranian state" (qtd. in Entessar 1992, 34).

For various and typical reasons, however, the agreement fell apart. The Kurds could not agree on and clearly specify what sort of autonomy they desired or where precisely the boundaries of Kurdistan should be drawn. Some more radical elements among the Kurds opposed any negotiation with a central government. Religious differences, of course, divided the Kurds, many Sunni Kurds afraid of a Shi'ite theocratic state. And "class" differences reemerged, as Kurdish landlords and peasants clashed over land. Most significantly, though, the sort of ethnic autonomy sought by the Kurds (and potentially by all ethnic groups in the state) was anathema to the centralized state envisioned by Ayatollah Khomeini and the new regime. As Khomeini himself said:

> Sometimes the word minorities is used to refer to people such as the Kurds, Lurs, Turks, Persians, Baluchis, and such. These people should not be called minorities, because this term assumes that there is a difference between these brothers. In Islam, such a difference has no place at all. There is no difference between Muslims who speak different languages, for instance, the Arabs or the Persians. It is very probable that such problems have been created by those who do not wish the Muslim countries to be united. . . . They create the issues of nationalism, of pan-Arabism, pan-Turkism, and such isms, which are contrary to Islamic doctrines. Their plan is to destroy Islam and the Islamic philosophy. (Qtd. in Entessar 1992, 29–30)

Accordingly, the final constitution creates a state every bit as centralized as the shah's previous state had been, only Islamic in nature. Even worse, in an August 1979 *fatwa* the Ayatollah Khomeini referred to them as "the atheist people of Kurdistan" (qtd. in Chaliand 1994, 78) while launching a holy war against them. The Ayatollah's *pasderan* (Revolutionary Guards) were deployed to Kurdistan. In the melee interethnic fighting also broke out between Kurds, Azeris, and Turkomans.

This instability presented an ideal opportunity to turn back Islamic fundamentalism, to redress old grievances (like the Shatt-al-Arab dispute), and to deliver a blow to a traditional rival, so on September 22, 1980, Iraq invaded Iran. As usual—an enemy of my enemy being my friend the KDP-Iran sought the friendship and support of the invading Iraqis. Furthermore, this led, as mentioned, to the ironic situation of Iranian Kurds backing Iraq and Iraqi Kurds backing Iran, each Kurdish group hoping that the other state would aid in its struggles with its own local state oppressors. Instead, a series of blows to Iranian Kurds deflected their nationalist hopes. First, Iran turned the tide of the war, recapturing areas of Iranian Kurdistan and counterattacking into Iraq. Second, intra-Kurd conflicts broke out between the KDP-Iran and another Komala, a new committee with an urban, leftist following. Third, in 1988 the war ended, releasing both states to concentrate on their internal (i.e., ethnic) problems. And, fourth, in July 1989 the leader of the KDP-Iran, Ghassemlou, and two associates were assassinated by Iranian security agents posing as negotiators in Vienna.

Kurds in Iraq

The Kurds of Iraq are a small portion of the total Kurdish population, estimated at around three million; however, these estimates are old and subject, as all Kurdish population figures are, to some error due to war and migration. Based on this estimate, Kurds account for up to 28 percent of the population of Iraq, making it something of a "binational" state. Iraqi Kurdistan covers approximately 29,000 square miles, or 17 percent of Iraq's area, suggesting a high-population density (101 per sq. mi. in Kurdistan vs. 65 per sq. mi. in Iraq as a whole). Yet, despite their small size, "the history of modern Kurdish nationalism is dominated by the struggle of the Kurds of Iraq, who have had an influence on the Kurdish movement much greater than their numerical position within the Kurdish nation would suggest" (Bulloch and Morris 1992, 5). This predominance is evident in the number and significance of uprisings that have taken place within Iraqi territory.

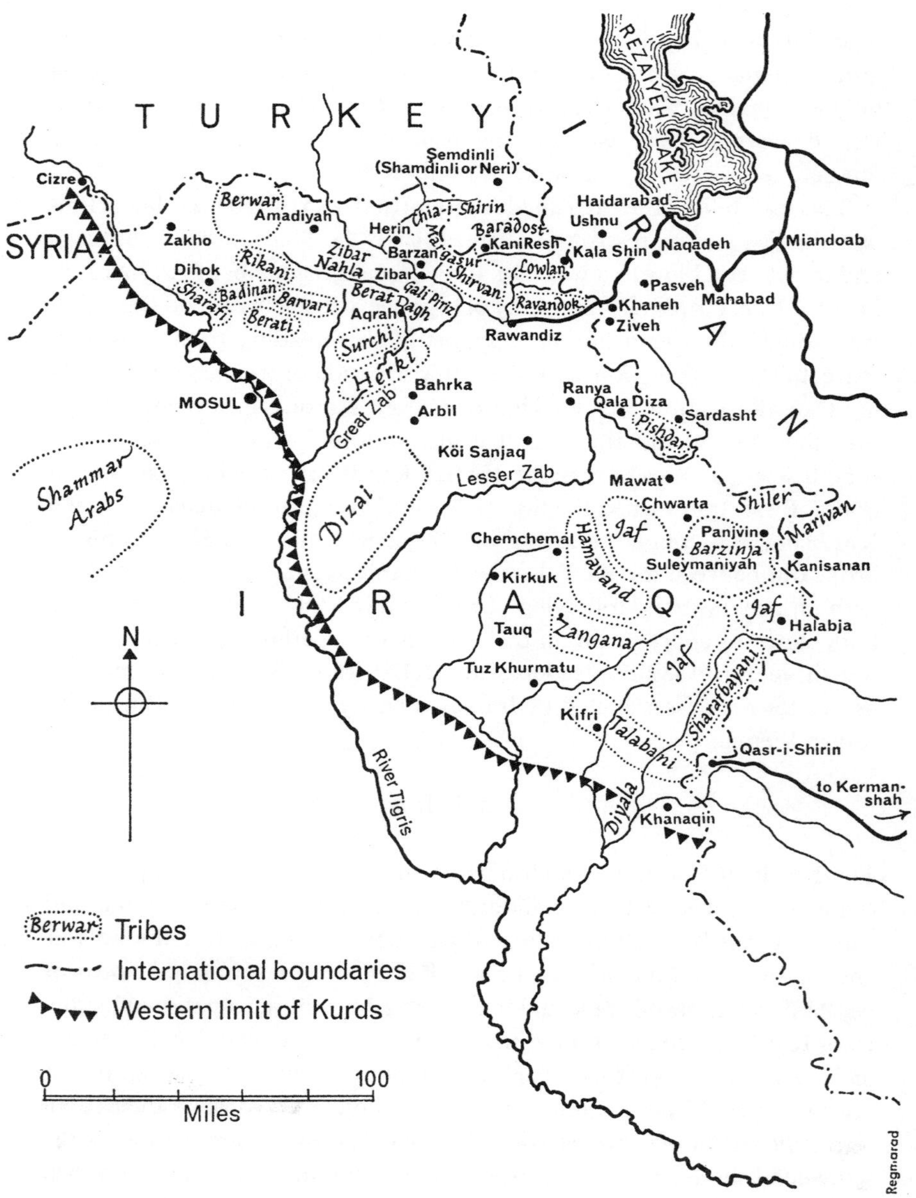

Kurdish Areas in Iraq. (Reprinted from *The Kurds: An Historical and Political Study,* by Hassan Arfa [London: Oxford University Press, 1966], p. 109, by permission of Oxford University Press.)

The reasons for this centrality of Iraqi Kurds in the Kurdish movement are various. They may include the late penetration of Ottoman power, so that Kurdish traditional elites enjoyed a longer period of relative freedom. They certainly include the events in the aftermath of World War I, the intervention of Britain and the creation of the new client state of Iraq. Possibly the fact that Iraq has been more accommodating to Kurdish culture and identity (at times—after all, for a period following the 1958 revolution the state was actually named the Arab and Kurdish Republic). In fact, it has been suggested that Turkey makes war against the Kurds because they are Kurds, while Iraq makes war on them because they are rebels against the state; without its own nationalist ideology Iraq is not torn by the same ethnic virulence. We might add that Iran wars on them because they are minorities. It is not at all insignificant that Iraqi Kurdistan sits on resources of oil, which could make a state there economically viable while at the same time making the region even more critical to any Iraqi regime as well as to the rest of the world. And, doubtless, the strategic location of Iraq, and the never-ending international activities there and in the Middle East in general (from struggles with Iran and Israel to the Cold War and Desert Storm), have given the Kurds endless opportunities to approach foreign powers to plead their case and to play these foreign powers against one another in their own cause—or, more often, to be played by those foreign powers in the interests of those powers.

We have discussed already how Iraq came to exist as a state and how southern Kurdistan came to be part of Iraq (rather than part of Turkey or an independent state) and some of the early Kurdish revolts. More central to Kurdish ethnohistory in Iraq is the Barzani rebellion (beginning in 1931) and the Barzani tribe in general. Three generations before Mullah Mustafa Barzani and his brother, Sheikh Ahmad, a Kurdish clan settled in an area known as *Bar Zan* (migration place) and took their tribal name, Barzani, after their territory, as is common in Kurdish culture. Already by the late nineteenth century Barzan had a reputation as a "utopian community." It was a place "where land was held in common as collective property and where dispossessed refugees from elsewhere, whether Christians or Muslims, were always welcome. This contributed to its becoming a centre of Kurdish nationalism, as activists from various parts of Kurdistan temporarily settled under the protection of the *sheikhs*" (Van Bruinessen 1992, 251). McDowall calls it "since time immemorial an area of lawlessness and tribal warfare, barely touched by any government ever" (1992b, 84).

In such a place a powerful *Naqshbandi* order developed, with its leader of the early twentieth century, Sheikh Ahmad. The *sheikh* sent Barzani men to assist in the Mount Ararat revolt in Turkey. In 1931–32 Iraq and the British Royal Air Force (RAF) crushed Sheikh Ahmad and his followers, who had also resisted the introduction of taxation and police and the settlement of Assyrian Christians in their homeland. They ended up in exile in Suleymaniah, until Sheikh Ahmad's brother, Mullah Mustafa Barzani, escaped in 1943, returned to Barzan to gather his forces, and commenced antigovernment (ostensibly "pan-Kurdish") operations. These operations attracted the support of the Hiwa (Hope) Party and the consternation of Iraqi authority, the latter of which defeated him and drove him out of Iraq (again with RAF assistance) and into Iran, where he joined temporarily with the nascent Mahabad republic. He helped found the KDP-Iraq on the model of the KDP in Iran, but with the fall of Mahabad he fled into the USSR, where he remained until 1958.

The year 1958 was a watershed year for Iraqi Kurds. That year a military coup, the "Free Officers," under Abdul Karim Qasim (or Ghassem), toppled the Iraqi monarchy and established a republic. The new regime seemed much more open to Kurdish concerns than the previous one; for example, the Provisional Constitution of July 27, 1958, stated that: "Iraqi society is based on complete cooperation between all its citizens, on respect for their rights and liberties. Arabs and Kurds are associates in this nation; the constitution guarantees their national rights within the Iraqi whole" (qtd. in Vanly 1993, 150). In line with this decree the KDP-Iraq was legalized, several new Kurdish journals were authorized, and Mullah Mustafa Barzani was welcomed back by the country from his refuge in the Soviet Union. Barzani immediately declared his support for Qasim.

This honeymoon did not last long, for a variety of issues soon divided them. One was pan-Arabism: the United Arab Republic, formed in February 1958, seemed likely to expand to include Iraq, and this sort of Arab nationalism was to the Kurds distinctly inimical to their own nationalistic interests. Another was Qasim's growing military dictatorship, which could brook no autonomy movements and no rival political parties within Iraq. Barzani retreated to Barzan, where he engaged in intertribal conflict, both with Turkoman tribes in the Kirkuk area and with old Kurdish tribal rivals like the Zibaris, the Bardosts, the Surchis, and the Herkis. Consequently, Iraqi land and air forces launched an attack on Barzani's Kurds in 1961 that would last until 1963. By this time Barzani's forces, known as *peshmerga* (those who face death), were a substantial and dedicated fighting corps, numbering up to twenty thousand (later to reach fifty thousand by 1975). They gave the Iraqi army a good fight but not exactly a nationalist fight; in fact, Adamson, who interviewed Barzani during the days of the revolt, reports that the ostensible leader of the "Kurds"

> claims that he has no interest in the Kurds outside Iraq, for he is no great idealist and his loyalties are to the Barzanis and his family. He was living in Iraq. They were living in Turkey, Persia, Syria, and Russia. What did he mean to them or they to him? He had no interest whatsoever in them. How had they helped him or the Iraqi Kurds in their struggle? (1965, 148)

Such sentiments, if they are genuine, indicate the depth of Kurdish parochialism: loyalties extend no further than the family and clan and maybe the "local" (i.e., state-bounded) group. If a group can ask itself, "What are they, my co-culturalists or co-nationalists, to me?" then that group has not achieved national consciousness and mobilization; as a group, as a nation, is does not exist. At any rate, at the same time other types of schisms appeared within the party such as Ahmad's efforts to ally it with Arab nationalists. And, of course, neighbor states were conspiring in the affair, in this case to the benefit of the Kurds, both Turkey and Iran passively aiding them with open borders while Iran actively supported them.

The inconclusive conflict led to a cease-fire in January 1963, followed by a series of changes of government (including two coups) and on-and-off ethnic clashes over the next few years, evincing not only a fundamental political volatility but a specific pattern. As distinguished by Van Bruinessen, "Iraqi governments would first attempt to appease the Kurds, then be drawn into a war against them and be overthrown by a coup d'etat" that would bring another government into power to experience the cycle anew (1992, 28). Renewed vigorous fighting from 1966 and a second Ba'athist coup in 1968 (the first being in 1963) finally brought the two sides to serious negotiations, culminating in the "March Agreement" on March 11, 1970. The agreement, the most successful diplomatic achievement in the history of Kurdish activism, provided an impressive array of guarantees and rights to Iraqi Kurds, including language rights (Kurdish as an official language of Kurdistan); political, educational, and cultural rights; and economic, land, and refugee rights. In the area of politics it was specified that one Iraqi vice president would be a Kurd and that communal representation would assure the Kurdish people a proportionate share of legislative power. It was less than full sovereignty but far better than anything Kurds accomplished before or since.

The implementation of the agreement even began well, but, as always seems to happen, events began to conspire to alienate the two sides. War might have broken out in 1973 if not for the Arab-Israeli War, and then the Iraq-Iran War in 1974–75. These clashes represented the high point (until 1990) of foreign dabbling in Kurdish business, as Israel, Iran, and the United States all fomented Kurdish action of one sort or another. Meanwhile, during the four years in which the March Agreement was supposed to be completely realized, the Iraqi policy of Arabization of Kurdish regions continued: Arab settlers were transferred into Kurdish majority areas, and Kurdish villagers were transferred out to "cluster villages," ostensibly to provide better housing and services to them but no doubt also to disperse them and to put them within easy surveillance. Then, in 1974, the government unilaterally amended the earlier agreement with the so-called Autonomy Law, which was officially the fulfillment of the 1970 agreement but was in fact a significant curtailment of that earlier pact. Rather than accept it, especially with promises of greater aid from its foreign allies, Barzani chose to fight on and did well until the fateful Algiers Agreement between Iraq and Iran, which ended their war on the condition that Iranian support of Barzani end. It did, and Barzani, appreciating the futility of further resistance, ordered his *peshmergas* to stop fighting on March 23, 1975. He retreated to Iran and then went to the United States, dying in Washington, DC, in 1979.

With the defeat of Barzani the Kurdish movement was momentarily interrupted, many tribal leaders doing the usual opportunistic thing of submitting to the government until the next time. The government also continued its assimilationist policies, including deportations and local economic development to bind Kurdistan to the center; with some improvement of rural conditions tribal animosity and nationalist fervor diminished, bringing about a transformation of the Kurdish movement from a tribal-based one under traditional and often religious leadership of *mullahs* and *sheikhs* into a more modern urban-based party movement. One such party was the Komala, a small urban-based Marxist-oriented group. In 1976 the KDP was reformed (as the KDP-Provisional Leadership) under two new Barzanis, Idris and Masud. And, finally, among the major parties the Patriotic Union of Kurdistan (PUK) was organized with Jalal Talabani as head; this party was explicitly composed of elements opposed to Mullah Mustafa Barzani's direction and became the KDP's main rival.

This rivalry, which was to have real consequences for the Iraqi Kurds, is deeper than mere political opportunism or even ideology. It has roots in several aspects of Kurdish culture. First, the Talabani and the Barzani are different tribes, and so traditionally the rise of the one has meant a threat to the other. Second, as distinct tribes, each party drew upon its own base of support—the Barzani party from among the Kurmanji-speaking population and the Talabani party from among the Sorani-speakers—and "as long as they consented to a regional division of authority, serious problems could be avoided" (Van Bruinessen 1992, 28). But the schism was evident as early as the 1960s, when Talabani was still a member of the KDP leadership; at that time the Iraqi government sought out and subsidized Talabani (and other Kurdish representatives) as competition for Barzani and the more militant elements of the KDP-Iraq. For this collaboration Talabani and his faction earned the epithet *jash,* or "little donkeys," pejoratively reminding fellow Kurds that they would let anyone ride them, including the Iraqi enemy. The schism within the KDP and between the Talabanis and Barzanis only intensified in the power vacuum of the mid-1970s, and the new PUK continued to go its own way and attempt to broker its own deals into the 1980s. By 1978 violent conflicts broke out between *peshmergas* of the two parties, squandering valuable energies that could otherwise have been turned to nationalist use.

Kurdish affairs in Iraq were to be affected again by external factors when, in 1980, war broke out between Iraq and Iran. There certainly is a history of each government dabbling in the Kurdish affairs of the other, and once the war began both sides again pursued the same tactics. Iraq attempted to use the KDP-Iran against Iran, while Iran sought the cooperation of the KDP-Iraq and the PUK in its efforts against Iraq. Kurds again failed to heed their common cause and instead allowed their local interests rather than their national interests to dictate their behavior; further, the Kurds allowed those local interests to be hijacked by foreign and entirely self-interested parties.

In fact, it was this parochial Kurdish interest that led the PUK in 1983 to negotiate a cease-fire with Iraqi president Saddam Hussein. The PUK's military efforts had been preoccupying up to fifty thousand Iraqi soldiers needed in the war against Iran, so both the PUK and the Iraqi regime saw some advantage in a break in hostilities and the appearance of a rapprochement of some kind. The PUK advanced a series of demands, many of them nationalistic in nature, which Baghdad either accepted or agreed to consider. This alliance of convenience did not last any longer than all of the others; as the negotiation process disintegrated, Iraqi measures against the Kurds resumed, and, most important, Iraq managed to cultivate new and better allies of convenience—in the form of the United States, Turkey, the Soviet Union, and France—in its bid to be the agent to resist and maybe even topple the Islamic regime in Iran. Hussein did not need Kurdish cooperation anymore. Iraqi/Kurd violence increased with the general escalation of the war. In one Amnesty International report just one of the many punitive attacks by Iraq against the Suleymaniye areas in 1985 resulted in over two hundred killings, three hundred incidents of torture, and eight live burials (Bulloch and Morris 1992, 158).

By spring 1987 the PUK controlled most of the Suleymaniye and Arbil regions, while the KDP dominated major portions of Dahuk and Mosul provinces. Not long after, the two parties actually reconciled and subsequently merged to form the Iraqi Kurdistan Front, but not before Iraq savagely attacked the Kurdish village of Halabja with poison gas on March 16, 1988. Five thousand people died in what was far from an isolated incident: before the date of the Halabja raid there are reports of chemical attacks on twenty-one separate days. Hussein had also installed Ali Hasan al-Majid (later to be known as the "butcher of Kuwait"), as chief of the Bureau of Northern Affairs. Referring to areas only partially under government control, he is reported to have said: "It is the duty of military forces to kill any human being or animal that exists in these areas, which are considered totally forbidden" (qtd. in Bulloch and Morris 1992, 159). Under his authority four thousand villages were destroyed and a half-million people displaced.

This disaster was followed by the conclusion of peace once again between Iraq and Iran on August 20, 1988, depriving Kurds of their Iranian allies and freeing Iraq's entire army to pursue them. Five days after the Iraq-Iran cease-fire began, sixty thousand troops launched a major offensive against the Kurds, in which 478 villages were destroyed and one hundred thousand people put to flight (McDowall 1992b, 65). As a finale to this campaign, whole towns and villages were relocated to "so-called victory cities, in fact virtual concentration camps for those who had been evicted from their land" (Bulloch and Morris 1992, 8). And so things may have remained at least for a time, despite the attention of the world that had been drawn to the Kurds by the Halabja attack, if not for the advent of yet another foreign influence upon Kurdish activity, this time the Persian Gulf War. After that war, with Iraq's army defeated, Iraqi Kurds began to rise up with the encouragement, if not aid, of the United States and its Coalition allies. The "intifadah" began as a popular movement in the village of Ranya on March 4, 1991, leaving the Iraqi Kurdistan Front in the rear trying to catch up to the mass uprising. Iraq responded with air and land assaults, driving two million Kurds out of Iraq, a half-million into Turkey, one and a half million into Iran. In a final act of self-destructive divisiveness an agreement negotiated between the KDP and the Iraqi government in June 1991 was denounced by the PUK, which set about trying to draw Turkey into the Kurdish problem in Iraq. Subsequently, Iraqi Kurds engaged in clashes with Turkish PKK Kurds in October 1992 operating within Iraq.

Conclusion

To appreciate fully the scope, and the limitations, of Kurdish ethnicity—that is, of Kurdish ethnic consciousness and ethnic mobilization—it must be remembered that, in addition to the large Kurdish populations in Turkey, Iran, and Iraq, there are also significant numbers of the nation living in enclaves in other neighboring states and in an international diaspora. Some three-quarters of a million live in several regions in Syria, constituting 8 percent of Syria's total population; this group has had on-and-off contacts with Iraqi Kurds over the years. Kurds have played a not insubstantial role in Syrian life, including leading roles in the 1949 military coup. As everywhere, Kurdish fortunes in the state have depended partly on outside forces and developments, such as the union with Egypt to form the UAR in 1958; this event "triggered the first round of oppressive behavior towards the Kurds" as well as exacerbating ethnic tensions in Iraq (McDowall 1992b, 122). A smaller but considerable number of Kurds inhabit trans-Caucasian areas of the former Soviet Union, perhaps three hundred thousand in all, with the majority within Azerbaijan and Armenia (Azeris and Armenians, unfortunately, both having a burden of history with the Kurds). Finally, some half-million Kurds live in Western Europe, over four hundred thousand in Germany alone. The French socialist government even helped establish the Kurdish Institute in Paris, and expatriate Kurds, such as the members of Khoybun, have been a factor in Kurdish nationalism.

These Kurdish elements have not been the leading elements, however, in defining and moving the Kurdish nation. The leading dynamics, as we have seen, have been the traditional elites, with their essentially tribal and feudal cultures and their essentially personal or local interests, and external international forces, with their interests and strategies that temporarily involve and even sometimes serve the Kurds but ultimately abandon them in pursuit of some other or larger gain. It is critically important that, as Van Bruinessen argues: "In virtually all Kurdish parties and organizations, leading roles were played by Kurds from the traditional leading stratum—aghas, sheikhs, and their relatives and close associates" (1992, 38). This is a crucial fact first because, in the absence of more modern political organization, traditional tribal elites could only call upon a fairly limited constituency, always faced the jealousy and competition of rival elites, and tended to fail to attract more modern or nontribal elements of the Kurdish nation such as the intelligentsia, urban dwellers, and working classes, to their cause. This personalized, pragmatic, military style of ethnicity has meant that a movement often does not outlive its leader by much and that any movement is generally assured of generating limited interest and mobilization and, in fact, even opposing "intranational" movements.

This is the internal bane of Kurdish nationalism and ethnicity; it is also, consequentially, the complication if not refutation of a simple traditionalistic, or primordial, view of their nationalism and ethnicity. I have argued that the "givens" of Kurdish culture are at least as much responsible for the obstruction of national consciousness and mobilization as they are for the realization of those national goals. Tribal divisions and elite rivalries may have been traditional in Kurdish society, even equilibrating in a certain sense, but they are certainly not the raw material of a modern Kurdish nationalism and ethnic identity and have actually positively impeded the development of that nationalism and identity. In other words, what is traditional or even traditionally "functional" may not be the same as, or functional, for modern ethnicity. Let us not forget, also, that some aspects of what we tend to consider traditional Kurdish culture are in fact historical, even recent historical, constructions.

The effects of international factors have been clear and repeated in Kurdish ethnic conflict too, and few major powers of the last century have not left their marks on the Kurds in some way or another. The Kurdish movement(s) ebb(s) and flow(s) with the vicissitudes of international interest, and the Kurdish movement(s)—and even Kurdish identity itself—are a by-product of the interaction of traditional Kurdish culture (and cultural diversity), state policies and practices by governments under which they find themselves, and great power geopolitical struggles. Accordingly, we find that, for instance, in Turkey, where official attitudes have been the least compromising to Kurdish ethnicity and rights, the Kurds "have developed a more uncompromising posture vis-à-vis the Turkish state than Kurds in Iran and Iraq" (Entessar 1992, 9). Where there have been rays of hope for Kurdish autonomy, as in Iraq, Kurdish leaders and parties have been at least willing to consider negotiation and coexistence within the state framework. The Kurdish case shows also that a nation can be the source of much of its own frustration.

There is perhaps no better way to end this chapter than by a particularly ironic observation by another nationalist, Nehru, on the Kurdish situation in Turkey. The general point is no doubt valid for a good many cases of ethnic conflict, however, and shows the essential irony of ethnicity as a world political force: "The Turks, who had only recently been fighting for their own freedom, crushed the Kurds, who sought theirs. It is strange how a defensive nationalism develops into an aggressive one, and a fight for freedom becomes one for dominion over others" (qtd. in Bulloch and Morris 1992, 178–79).

Chapter 5

Rwanda and Burundi: When Two Tribes Go to War?

In the past our proper name was Bantu. We are Bantu. "Hutu" is no tribe, no nothing. Muhutu *is a* [*Tutsi*] *word which means "servant." . . . It is a name that the Tutsi gave us.*

—Hutu refugee in Tanzania

Do not forget that genocide is unknown to our history and culture, and even the word is inexistant [*sic*] *in our language. How can it be differently? Tribalism was unknown before the arrival of the whites. Before colonialisation, our society had reached a degree of cohesion and national unity that many European countries lacked. If you have any doubts, question your ethnologists and historians.*

—Government of Burundi, 1972

In the summer of 1994 television screens across America and the world conveyed images from Rwanda of violence and cruelty: victims macheted across the head and face, villagers burned alive in huts and churches, bodies lying by the side of the road or floating in congested rivers. *This* was genocide as most people know it. The groups involved became household names for a time. Hutu and Tutsi—surely this was also the prototype in the average mind of "tribal" conflict, a primordial clash between distinct societies that had been at each others' throats from time immemorial, whose differing cultures made them natural enemies; how else to account for the ferocity of their response? The evidence seems conclusive: these two groups with clearly distinguishable and named identities and even distinctive "racial" characteristics had come to blows repeatedly since 1959 in *two different states,* Rwanda and Burundi, where they coexist.

Yet a closer examination of the case throws all of these conclusions and the suppositions upon which they are based into question. What precisely are Hutu and Tutsi? Even more so, why are we in the West so ready to perceive them as tribes and to perceive their struggle as a tribal struggle? One very seldom, except metaphorically, hears the Bosnian Serbs and Muslims or the Quebec francophones and anglophones described as tribes. This illustrates an important tendency, not only within anthropology but within our culture at large, to see non-Western, non-"modern" especially African, people as tribal—or maybe, better yet, to see non-Western people *as* nonmodern and therefore as tribal. The main antagonist groups have also been characterized as ethnic groups, races, castes, and other types of collectivities. Which is most true or accurate, or are they all true in some fashion? Have they really been at war, or even at odds, perpetually from some indefinite past? If not, why now? And, finally, why should there be different courses of events in the two states, Rwanda and Burundi, if the same two groups and the same primordial conflict exist in both?

This chapter does not seek so much to answer these questions as to explore the sociocultural intricacies illustrated by them. We will see, for instance, that the exact status of the categorical designations "Hutu" and "Tutsi" is unclear and has shifted over the past century or so (the period for which we have historical and ethnographic documentation). Indeed, this is the whole point of the present discussion: that what appears to be the most concrete instance of ethnic or traditional phenomenon can in actuality be a complex, fluid, contextualized matrix of indeterminate factors and forces. In fact, not only is the *conflict* not "primordial," but the very *identities* that support the conflict are not primordial. Yet, when certain cultural and social elements were put in reaction with new forces and interests (such as colonialism, Christian missionization, representative democracy, and "progressivism" / social justice) and stirred by specific critical decisions and events, a precipitate of ethnicity, ethnic stratification, and ultimately ethnic conflict was formed. As Malkki ably argues and demonstrates, history—or "historicity"—and even ethnicity or "nationness . . . are produced and elaborated as a result of exigencies of everyday practice" (1995, 241).

In this chapter it will be necessary and advantageous to consider not just Rwanda but also its neighbor and colonial coterritory, Burundi. Although such was not the original intent when I conceived of the chapter, which was to analyze the ethnic conflict in Rwanda alone, it became abundantly clear that the two must be discussed in relation—first, because the two share a precolonial and colonial history and have continued to influence each other in contemporary times politically and socially (not least, refugees from the one have often become significant forces and ethnic irritants within the other) and, second, because the two share the same pluralistic character as mixed Hutu-Tutsi states, so that any differences between them in terms of ethnic relations and ethnic conflict are of significance to us. In short, Rwanda and Burundi serve somewhat the same purpose for us as Kurds in Iraq, Kurds in Iran, and Kurds in Turkey did in the previous chapter—a kind of natural laboratory of ethnicity, an opportunity to observe similar traditional, cultural, and demographic preconditions refracting through varying circumstances and producing varying ethnic "effects." While it is slightly more difficult to deal with Rwanda *and* Burundi in one chapter than to deal with Rwanda alone, it is well worth the effort and gives us unexpected insights into the diversity and circumstantiality of ethnicity and ethnic conflict.

The "Tribes" and Their Markers and Relations

Rwanda and Burundi are small states, the former some 10,170 square miles, the latter about 10,745 square miles. Both are also densely populated; Rwanda prior to the most recent massacres had a population around 8.1 million, with a density of over 796 per square mile, while Burundi is home to some 6 million, with a density of 558. Understandably, these estimates are uncertain and subject to error due to the recent killings and refugee migrations.

In terms of ethnicity the first thing we must take into consideration is that there are *three* basic ethnic or social groups presently in both countries. These groups are the Hutu, who constitute the vast majority in both populations (up to 85 percent); the Tutsi, who are a much smaller yet generally dominant group (around 15 percent); and the Twa, a tiny minority at 1 percent. Collectively, these three groups are known as "Banyarwanda," eastern Africa's largest tribe or ethnic group, depending upon how you construe such terms. This proposition raises two interesting points. First, if, at the higher level of integration the Banyarwanda are one tribe or ethnic group, then how should we conceptualize the lower level of Hutu, Tutsi, and Twa? All three, for instance, speak the same language, Kinyarwanda or Kirundi (the latter in Burundi). Second, the Ban-

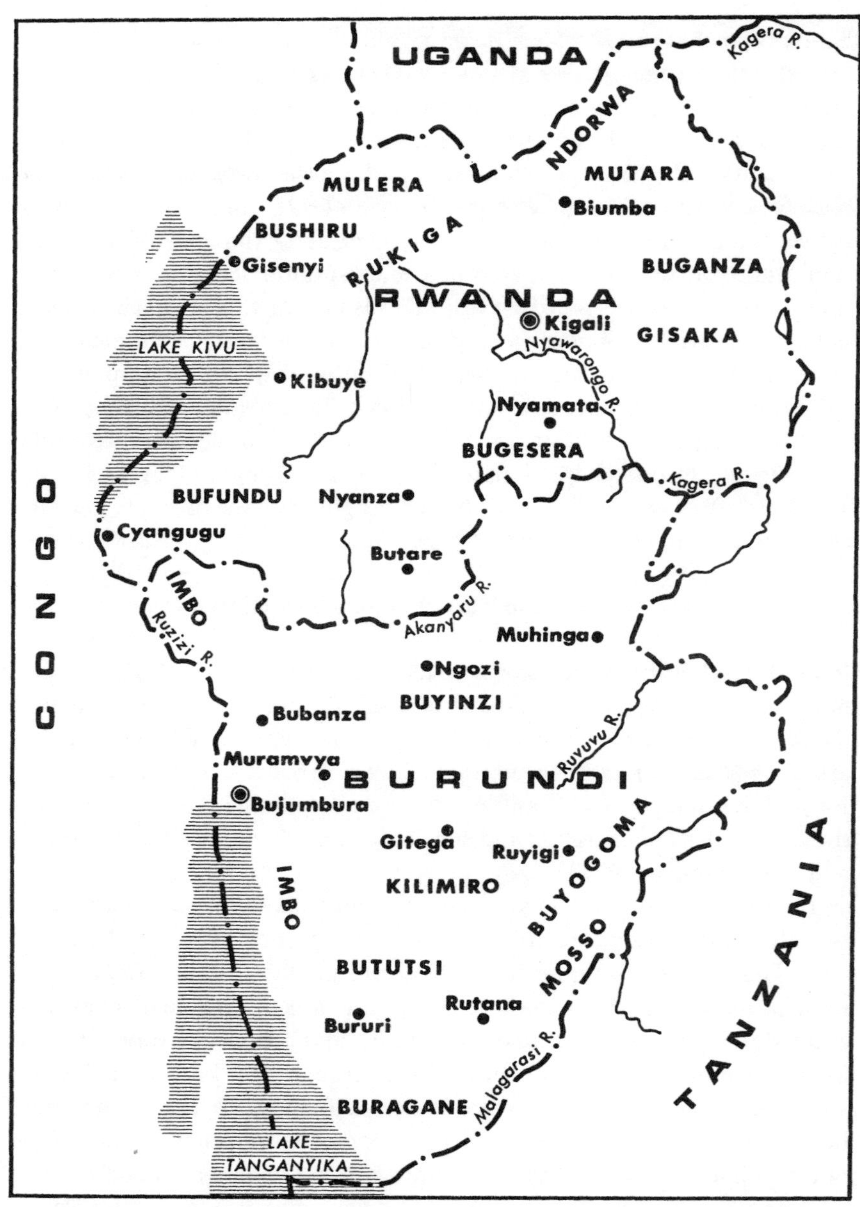

Rwanda and Burundi. (From *Rwanda and Burundi,* René Lemarchand. Copyright © 1970 by René Lemarchand. Reproduced with permission of Greenwood Publishing Group, Inc., Westport, CT.)

yarwanda are not limited to the territory of Rwanda and Burundi but are found also in Zaire, Tanzania, and Uganda; in fact, they are the sixth largest ethnic group in Uganda.

In addition, Rwanda or Burundi each has named collectivities and social identities unique to itself and not found in the other. For instance, in Burundi the *ganwa* are an important social collectivity; as we will see, they have been a key factor in Burundi society, and their own ethnic status has been subject to controversy. In fact, Lemarchand argues that, while "the main line of cleavage in Rwanda was between Hutu and Tutsi, in Burundi the crucially important distinction was between the *ganwa,* on the one hand, and the Hutu and the Tutsi on the other" (1970, 35). In Rwanda a regional differentiation exists, with the indigenous population of the north calling itself neither Hutu nor Tutsi but, rather, Kiga or Bakiga and claiming to be a distinct and autonomous culture. Furthermore, there is intra-Tutsi differentiation between Hima-Tutsi and Banyaruguru-Tutsi. Finally, lineage and clan identities contribute both to intragroup differentiation and intergroup cohesion: Tutsi, Hutu, and Twa all share the same set of clan names.

Yet the three Banyarwanda groups have been and are often distinguished historically, racially, economically, and symbolically. By all accounts the earliest inhabitants of this area of East Africa were the Twa, hunters and gatherers. Hutu peoples arrived sometime later, with a new subsistence technology, horticulture. Most recently, pastoral peoples migrated into or conquered (depending on the particular version of the events) Hutu/Twa regions and eventually established themselves as the culturally, economically, and usually politically dominant segment of a mixed society. But this "Tutsi" penetration into and hegemony over Hutu/Twa society was less than total; in some areas, such as northern Rwanda, it never advanced very far at all, and, even in some regions where domination was relatively developed by the time of the arrival of Europeans, it had only been achieved shortly before, during the reign of King Rwabugiri of Rwanda in the mid-nineteenth century. Therefore, the Hutu-Tutsi relation is certainly not timeless or primordial, having at most a several hundred year history and in some places considerably less.

The nature of this relationship is also open to discussion. Hutu and Tutsi are often, perhaps generally, taken to be racial categories, with specific physical characteristics attributed to each category. The racial traits (or at least stereotypes) of these groups are expressed in colonial documents from 1925, which describe the three races. Twa are portrayed as members "of a worn out and quickly disappearing race. . . . he is small, muscular, and very hairy; particularly on the chest. With a monkey-like face and a huge nose, he is quite similar to the apes whom he chases in the forest." Hutu, the documents claim, "display very typical Bantu features. . . . They are generally short and thick-set with a big head, a jovial expression, a wide nose and enormous lips." The Tutsi, finally, "has nothing of the negro, apart from his colour. He is usually very tall, 1.80 m. at least, often 1.90 m. or more. He is very thin. . . . His features are very fine: a high brow, thin nose and fine lips framing beautiful shining teeth. Batutsi women are usually lighter-skinned than their husbands, very slender and pretty in their youth, although they tend to thicken with age" (qtd. in Prunier 1995, 6). Maquet, after discussing the "socially accepted descriptions" of the three races, goes on to mention that some objective physical measurements do not coincide with the stereotypes. It is worth noting that, according to Ress (1988), most Burundians claim that they cannot distinguish an individual as Hutu or Tutsi dependably on appearance alone.

Along with physical stereotypes Maquet also gives us personality stereotypes for each group. In his account, which he admits is based on interviews with Tutsi exclusively, the Twa are seen as "gluttonous, loyal to their Tutsi masters, lazy, courageous when hunting, without any restraint." The Hutu are believed to be "hardworking, not very clever, extrovert, irascible, unmannerly, obedient," while the Tutsi are characterized as "intelligent (in the sense of astute in political intrigues), capable of command, refined, courageous, and cruel" (Maquet 1961, 164). The 1925 reports cited earlier continue to laud the Tutsi: "Gifted with a vivacious intelligence, the Tutsi displays a refinement of feelings which is rare among primitive peoples. He is a natural-born leader, capable of extreme self-control and of calculated good-will." This stereotype system applies predominantly to Rwanda; it is important to realize, as we will discuss, that the racial stratification system of Rwanda was far more advanced and rigid than in Burundi, where "society was relatively free of racial tensions" (Lemarchand 1970, 24). In fact, as a number of scholars of Rwanda and Burundi have argued, the fact and intensity of racial ideology can be linked to political and social factors other than race in the two cases.

The domestic racial perspective was furthered by certain European observers, who saw not only unlike but unequal races in the Hutu and the Tutsi. As references to the "fine," "beautiful," and "vivacious" Tutsi suggest, the racial judgments of Europeans were based on more than physical characteristics but also on "aesthetic impressions," as Destexhe persuasively argues: "Individuals were categorised as Hutu or Tutsi according to their degree of beauty, their pride, their intelligence and political organisation. The colonisers established a distinction between those who did not correspond to the stereotype of a negro (the Tutsi) and those who did (the Hutu)" (1995, 38). Thus, racial categories and assignments reflected not only Europeans' racial aesthetics but also their racism: the less-Negroid population was deemed "more Caucasian" and therefore superior. A missionary, François Menard, went so far as to characterize the Tutsi as "European under a black skin"; the German resident of Rwanda, Richard Kandt, appreciated the Tutsi for "the sublimity of their speech, the tasteful and unobtrusive way of their dress, their noble portraits." On the other hand, the Hutu were described by the duke of Mecklenburg as "ungainly figures . . . who patiently bow themselves in abject bondage to the later arrived yet ruling race, the Tutsi" (qtd. in Ress 1988, 73).

Contemporary anthropologists contributed to this view, playing out the conventional wisdom that African civilization was some product of Asian, even Caucasian, even biblical, culture—in particular an offshoot of Old Testament kingdoms like Kush and Sheba that could be traced back to the person of Ham, a son of Noah who was cursed for seeing his father naked. Accordingly, the anthropologist Charles Seligman offered the term *Hamite* to denote those "pastoral Caucasians" from central Asia who interacted with "the two more primitive African stocks, the Negro and the Bushman" to produce African civilization but who were "better armed as well as quicker witted than the dark, agricultural Africans" (1930, 158). This interpretation appealed to the racial preconceptions and conceits of the day and served a function for colonial administrators who looked for a group through which to rule an African society like Rwanda or Burundi. In this search "Hamites were seen to be 'born rulers' and were granted, at least in theory, a right to a history and future almost as noble as their European 'cousins'" (Linden 1977, 2).

Perhaps the most significant distinction between the three groups traditionally was economic or occupational. Generally speaking, though not strictly, the Tutsi were pastoralists, the Hutu agriculturists, and the Twa hunters as well as ironworkers and, according to Maquet, "singers, dancers, and buffoons." As in many such traditionally "plural" societies, the groups were thereby stratified or ranked, with the Tutsi being the "aristocracy," the Hutu lower, and Twa lowest and considered sometimes "half jokingly . . . to be more akin to monkeys than to human beings" (1961, 10). This ranking had some of the qualities of a "caste system," especially in

Rwanda, and some writers refer to the groups as castes. In Rwanda the Tutsi particularly tried to maintain an ideology of their superiority over the others, as reflected in their mythology and their behavior. In one myth the first king of Rwanda assigned his three sons, Gatutsi, Gahutu, and Gatwa, to guard pots of milk overnight. Only Gatutsi faithfully did so, Gahutu falling asleep and spilling his and Gatwa drinking his; their conduct led to their ultimate social destinies: the ennoblement of the Tutsi, the enserfment of the Hutu, and the banishment of the Twa (Segal 1964, 5).

Maquet, one of the main advocates of the caste interpretation of Rwandan society, points to other evidence of the closed stratification of the three groups. Besides the hierarchy of the castes and the "hereditary occupation" of each, he mentions the tendency toward endogamy of each group. Intercaste marriage was not ordinary, he indicates, although it was not prohibited, at least between Hutu and Tutsi (between Twa and the others, he suggests, there were prohibitions); in fact, his Hutu informants claimed it was common, although the Tutsi called it rare. Interestingly, in regard to "hypergamy" for Hutu women, it seems that neither the women nor the men were generally very proud of the arrangement. Ultimately, Rwandan society was based upon and integrated by what he famously called the "premise of inequality," in which the Tutsi have generated, and the Hutu and Twa have accepted, the belief that "people born in different castes are unequal in inborn endowment, physical as well as psychological, and have consequently fundamentally different rights" (1961, 165).

These generalizations about caste status and behavior, however, including and perhaps especially the economic one (the relation of groups to cattle ownership), must, like all generalizations, be tempered by the complexities of empirical reality. Maquet writes that birth was the "usual way in which one became a Tutsi, a Hutu, or a Twa." Yet it was not the *only* way, and even Maquet admits that descent does not lead to a racial distinction between the three groups. In a particularly contingent and subjective definition he proposes that "a Tutsi, a Hutu, or a Twa is a person who regarded himself, and was regarded by all those who knew him, as a Tutsi, a Hutu, or a Twa" (135). Again, the fastest way to this mutual regard was birth, but the social system also allowed for change in "birth" status. In fact, to a certain extent, Hutu and Tutsi were *achieved* statuses almost as much as they were *ascribed* ones. In a circumstance closely resembling the account in Haaland (1969), it was possible for an individual or family of one category, through economic success or failure, to change category and become the other. If a Hutu acquired enough wealth to own a herd of cattle and adopted the ways of a Tutsi, he could transform his social identity into Tutsi by the process of *kwihutura,* or "shedding of Hutuness," and *become* a Tutsi. Furthermore, the social distance between Hutu and Tutsi was not always as great as it seemed; not all Tutsi owned the same number of cattle, or necessarily any cattle, and not all Hutu were without cattle. Despite the ideology of Tutsi nobility, not all Tutsis were nobles, and some were poor. Especially in Burundi, but also to an extent in Rwanda, the social variations within the Tutsi category were as great as or greater than those between categories. And, finally, the Hutu were never traditionally stripped of political status and opportunity entirely, a substantial number (if not a proportionate number) of Hutu occupying chiefly or other offices. Consequentially, in modern times we will find that it is often Tutsi who deny the existence of ethnicity at all in Rwandan or Burundian society; the political rationale for this attitude should be abundantly clear.

A description of the traditional ethnic relations in Rwanda and Burundi, especially of the subtle and cross-cutting ethnically "atomizing" forces in those societies, would be incomplete without some mention of what are often called the "feudal" qualities of the societies. In precolonial days, and even into the colonial period, Rwandan and Burundian societies were highly decentralized (Burundi even more so than Rwanda) due to two different structural components of social organization: the system of chiefdoms and the clientage system. These relationships bound individuals and kin groups to one another and to the power structure in various, often contradictory, and ethnically nonexclusive ways. The exact nature and operation of these social institutions also gave Burundi a different political and ethnic quality than Rwanda, which affected its colonial period and even its modern situation.

Before the nineteenth century, kinship provided the basic integration of society, which was decentralized. The feudal system, with the "structures of Tutsi domination" that it established, is of more recent introduction and is a consequence of the expansion of central state power as a superimposition on this original social order. The lowest level of political organization was the "hill" (*mosozi*). Each hill had a hill chief, who was head of what Gravel calls a "nuclear feudal cluster," which was "the smallest socio-political group of the hierarchy" of Rwandan society. These chieftainships were not exclusively Tutsi. One of the main effects of this administrative structure was to diminish the role and power of kinship leaders and institutions.

After the hill level was the district, which subsumed a number of hills and their chiefs and placed them under a dual district chiefdom, one a "land chief" (*munyabutaka*) and the other a "cattle chief" (*munyamukenke*). Their duties were primarily fiscal—to collect prestations and dues and to funnel that wealth on to the higher levels of administration, which culminated at the king, or *mwami.* The *mwami,* at least in Rwanda, had theoretically unlimited powers, was the titular owner of all land, cattle, and other wealth in the state, and had semidivine status. The power and status of the *mwami* in Burundi was conditioned by a system of hereditary princes (called *ganwa*) that impeded centralization of the state and elevation of the king.

In addition to, and partly as a response to, this administrative structure, a system of clientage also developed in Rwanda. Clientage took a great variety of forms, but the common thread of these relationships was a person or kin group of lower wealth or prestige who "offered his services to and asked protection from a person whose status was higher and whose wealth was greater" (Maquet 1961, 129). The lower-status party was known as *mugaragu,* or "client," and the higher-status party as *shebuja,* or "lord" or "patron."

Clientage is one of the most studied aspects of Rwandan society and is typically considered to be one of its most traditional aspects—and the traditional, or premodern, form of Tutsi hegemony.[1] We must be cautious, however, about such assertions. For one thing, according to Newbury, at least in parts of Rwanda clientage before the nineteenth century involved only a small segment of the population and, even more significantly, did not always involve the very lowest strata in society. Rather, she argues, until comparatively recently "economic and political security could usually be obtained by means other than clientship" such as lineage ownership of land, marriage transfers of wealth, or friendship exchanges of cattle or other property (1988, 81). In fact, in her analysis the expansion of the clientage system, and the degradation and exploitation of the *mugaragu* role vis-à-vis the *shebuja* role, was a consequence of growing insecurity following the insinuation of effective state power into more areas of the kingdom and more parts of people's lives, undermining kin-based security systems.

Furthermore, at the early stage of clientage evolution only a few types

1. In Burundi clientage was considerably less developed and less central to social organization. Some forms, like *buhake, muheto,* and *gikingi,* did not exist, while a less binding and more flexible *bugabire* contract had little political importance in precolonial times.

of client relations existed. These included principally direct clientship to the king, land clientship, and *muheto* clientship. The first of these is self-evident; it entailed providing gifts and services to the king and often sending individuals to the king's court to "pay court" for part of the year. The status and benefits gained thereby could far outweigh the burdens; in fact, one benefit was the opportunity to bypass more local authorities such as the hill chief. In regard to land clientship, recall that in the distant past land was ordinarily held by a lineage, by the institution known as *bukonde,* whereby a lineage cleared and occupied its own land, often over generations. *Bukonde* did not necessarily have any relation to clientship, but when immigration and settlement increased, especially under the auspices of an ascending central authority, the newcomers would possibly seek land rights from *bukonde* lineages and become *bagereerwa* land clients. This relationship required a rent-in-kind and perhaps part-time labor for the patron but was informal and often ended in the absorption of the outsiders into the lineage. The other main form of land clientship was *gikingi,* in which the king or other official granted land for use by a cattle-owning lineage. This relationship may have begun as a reward for chiefs or other loyal servants; the *gikingi* holder then exercised total control over his fief and could in turn open his tract to occupants, who became his clients.

Muheto clientship is the last and most interesting of these forms. This institution linked a lineage, not an individual, to a *muheto* ("social army" or, literally, "bow") chief. This practice evolved originally, Newbury suggests, as a kind of military service (as the name indicates) but eventually developed into an economic relationship. The patron-chief collected gifts and prestations of local manufacture, often luxury goods, and especially a cow if the client lineage owned cattle. That cattle were a primary offering *from* client *to* patron has two implications: first, it distinguishes *muheto* from the later institution of *buhake,* in which cattle transfer proceeded in the opposite direction; second, it means that client lineages tended necessarily to possess some wealth (in order to own cattle in the first place) and therefore not to be the lowest elements of society (i.e., Tutsi or sometimes wealthier Hutu). In other words, *muheto* clientship was not intended for the poorest and least-secure groups in society and certainly not for Hutu exclusively. Instead, being a *muheto* client, at least early on, conveyed a certain amount of status and prestige; for the patron-chief it was a way to enlist and integrate the upper strata of his region (Newbury 1988, 76–77).

The Evolution of Ethnic Stratification

As is perhaps clear from the discussion so far, Hutu and Tutsi have been distinct groups or, better yet, distinct categories, for some time. Yet they have not been closed categories, and they have not been entirely descent based or what we conceive as ethnic categories for that whole period. Numerous students of Rwanda and Burundi question whether Hutu and Tutsi were initially ethnic and tribal groups: Watson maintains that "'Tutsi' refers to a 'noble,' as 'Hutu' refers to a 'commoner' and not to different tribes" (1991, 21). And what is more, the "class" distinction between Hutu and Tutsi up to the nineteenth century is not a hard nor a wide one: there were upper and lower Tutsi and upper and lower Hutu. Not all Tutsi were nobles, and not all Hutu were peasants. Finally, clientage, the relationship that supposedly implied subordination, did not degrade the client to the extent we generally envision and largely overlooked the Hutu population. This begins to change, however, by the nineteenth century, when political developments, essentially external to ethnicity, crystallize incipient ethnic identities and expand the gulf between them. Here is where Newbury directs us to search for "the processes of class formation that underlay perceived ethnic stratification" (1988, 16).

It is at the point of state evolution and the centralization of royal (i.e., Tutsi) power that Rwanda and Burundi part company, for this process is much more successful and gets much further advanced in the former than in the latter. Let us, then, consider Rwanda first. The decisive moment of state integration in Rwanda is the reign of Mwami Kigeri Rwabugiri from 1860–95. Before his time, because of the social fragmentation inherent in the kinship system and the local (hill chief) political system, the kingdom was largely uncentralized, and court power had penetrated very unevenly throughout the realm. Yet, as Newbury expresses it, Rwabugiri "strove to break through traditional restraints and augment the prerogatives of the throne" (40), and this he did by means of military conquest and the extension and intensification of relations of stratification, including clientage.

Rwabugiri's administrative integration replaced, and came at the expense of, the earlier, less formal, and less hierarchical integration emanating from the kinship and client systems. The innovations came in two areas. First, a more bureaucratic political structure was established: the kingdom was divided into provinces, each with an appointed provincial chief, who in turn appointed hill chiefs. The entire system was a great device to collect and channel wealth to the center. Necessarily, new chiefs were introduced by the court, usually though not always Tutsi. In addition, lineages within each province were called upon to provide men for service in the royal army, injecting a regional component into Rwanda's military. Rwabugiri's second innovation, however, was potentially even more significant for the shift in ethnic relations in Rwanda; this other innovation was the extension of previous forms of clientship to new constituencies (especially less powerful and prestigious individuals and lineages) and the introduction of novel clientage relations. For instance, *muheto* relationships increased to include cattle-owning lineages that had never partaken in the institution before, both Tutsi and Hutu. Also, the practice was extended to non-cattle-owning lineages, which could obviously not fulfill the traditional cow prestation requirement; such groups offered other good instead and were, revealingly, referred to as "Hutu" by patrons, whether or not they were "ethnically" Hutu.

In addition, new institutions such as *bureetwa* and *buhake* were established. The former was a distinctly low-status form of clientage, for those who had not the wealth to offer material prestations; rather, the *bureetwa* client brewed beer and provided manual labor for a patron such as a hill chief. This burden fell disproportionately—and increasingly, after colonialism—upon the Hutu population and represented a widening of the status gap between client and patron, accompanied by an escalating exploitation of the client. Such clientage lost most or all of its prestige.

Buhake is a more complicated case and has received more attention in the literature. It has been referred to as "cattle clientage," but this does not distinguish it from our earlier *muheto.* The key differences between the two practices are that *buhake* bound an individual and not a lineage to a patron and that it involved the transfer of cattle in exactly the opposite direction than *muheto*—that is, from patron to client. The implications of these differences are important. In the first place, they tended to isolate the individual from his kin group and maximize the potential of clientage from the patron's point of view: the greatest possible pool of clients was generated as well as the most vulnerable. In the second place, the terms of the clientship shifted distinctly in favor of the patron: ostensibly, early *buhake* contracts may have incorporated a certain degree of equality and reciprocity, "based more upon a positive attempt by a client to maximize his power position than upon fear of refraining" (Newbury 1988, 90). But, as the institution evolved and grew, its terms changed.

In later *buhake* relations the client enjoyed usufruct rights over a patron's cow but exposed himself to a variety of less than prestigious obligations and dangers. Maquet lists these obligations, which included personal service for the patron, labor, presents, and, especially for Hutu clients, working in the patron's gardens or guarding his compound at night. Furthermore, the contract did not expire at the death of its founders but was inherited by their descendants. The principal danger in the relationship came from the client's dependence on the cattle that remained property of the patron. The patron could reclaim the cattle and, in fact, also might confiscate cattle that were the personal property of the client originating from other sources. This situation was possible because of the growing power and prestige differential between client and patron; a client needed some personal wealth to enter a *muheto* bond but precious little to make a *buhake* one. Therefore, as in the case of *bureetwa,* clientage was opened to lower strata of society than before, and the burdens and dishonor of clientship increased with the vulnerability of the clients. As Newbury concludes, "When extended to the less powerful, institutions which initially displayed integrative elements evolved into forms . . . which were essentially exploitative" (1988, 90).

In Rwanda, then, with the reforms begun by Rwabugiri and continued and expanded by his successors (and by European colonizers), *Tutsi* and *Hutu* "became not only economic but also political labels; 'ethnicity,' such as it was, came to assume a political importance, determining a person's life chances and relations with the authorities" (Newbury 1988, 52). Precisely the same thing cannot be said, however, about Burundi, where political evolution, and therefore ethnogenesis, were taking a different course. In Burundi the centralization of power in the *mwami* never advanced as far as in Rwanda, meaning that social distinctions premised on the elevation of Tutsi status never rigidified as they did in Rwanda. Hence, as indicated earlier, Hutu and Tutsi were slow to emerge as the key, indeed the sole, social identities in society, and, even when they did (probably not until the middle of the twentieth century), they had a significantly different vector in Burundian society than in Rwandan.

Lemarchand invokes the concept of a "system of structural instability" to characterize Burundian society and politics, a system in which various groups and interests share power and status in ways that create perpetual opportunities for intrigue and conflict and preclude any one group or interest from triumphing permanently but also precludes actions that would resolve the fundamental instabilities in favor of a decisive monopoly of power. One of the prime examples of this system is the tradition of royal succession, with four dynastic names—Ntare,

Mwezi, Mutaga, and Mwambutsa—each representing a different lineage: Batare, Bezi, Bataga, and Bambutsa, respectively. Under Mwami Ntare Rugamba (r. 1795–1852), however, a practice was instituted of appointing royal sons as administrators of provinces, especially newly acquired provinces. These princes, or *ganwa,* became hereditary officials or chiefs, eventually competing with one another and with the crown for power. The implications of this system were several and significant. First, as mentioned, Burundian society and politics were more loosely integrated than Rwandan; there were more centers of power. Second, competition within Burundian society was more dynastic than ethnic; this created a struggle between descent groups that overshadowed any struggle between ethnic groups. Third, because of their precarious political positions, both *mwami* and *ganwa* "had to adopt a far more conciliatory attitude towards the 'lower orders'" (Lemarchand 1970, 24), a situation rendered unnecessary in Rwanda by its relative monarchical absolutism. Finally, the *ganwa* eventually became identified as a separate status category, if not an ethnic group. In other words, because society was not solidary on the basis of ethnicity, it could not be exclusivistic on the basis of ethnicity either. Thus, ethnic competition and ethnic conflict could take a number of forms other than Hutu versus Tutsi, and in fact the intra-Tutsi and the *ganwa*-Tutsi aspects were much more determinant for a long time, even through the colonial period and arguably into and after independence.

Thus, as I have tried to show so far, social distinctions in Rwanda and Burundi are not as neat and simple as we might think. We can see that the precise denotations of the ethnic titles are not identical or even completely clear and, even more, that they have changed over time due mainly to shifts in the political system and in the political advantages that a Tutsi group could gather unto itself. In Rwanda, where the Tutsi group or rank or status (or what have you) succeeded in centralizing and monopolizing authority and prestige, *Tutsi* became a meaningful ethnic designation of superiority and *Hutu* a meaningful one of inferiority or degradation; in Burundi, where Tutsi status was refracted by intra-Tutsi differences and Tutsi-*ganwa* competition, *Tutsi* and *Hutu* failed to coalesce as *the* salient group designators, at least until much later in history. To complete the story, however, we must consider how subsequent developments, in particular colonialism and national independence, in combination with the traditional social preconditions described so far, led to the present system of bipolar, stratified, and violently competitive ethnic relations.

Colonialism and Ethnicity

It is a truism to say that colonialism produced major changes in traditional societies. Yet the changes that colonialism wreaks on a society are not always the same nor unidirectional, and Rwanda and Burundi were affected somewhat differently, given the nature of their "precontact" culture and the direction and state of their cultural evolution at the time of contact; in some ways this evolution was altered, while in other ways it was perpetuated and advanced. More than anything else it should be kept in mind that traditional societies were not without their own history before Europeans came but that those societies were changing and evolving on their own and that in many cases changes that are typically attributed to colonialism may in fact have been under way prior to it. In other words, the traditional culture that Europeans encountered—or constructed—upon their contact with non-European societies was not very ancient (it may have been of fairly recent vintage) and was not always in an "equilibrium state," if there is such a thing. The very notion that non-Western societies were primordial and ahistorical, as we have long since learned, is a specious one.

The early days of concentrated colonialism in Africa, after 1890, found Rwanda and Burundi in the midst of social and political turmoil. Britain and Germany had originally partitioned East Africa in 1890, each seeing Rwanda and Burundi as keys to their geopolitical strategy for Africa. The region was still largely uncharted, however, only a few explorers (like Burton and Speke in 1858) and missionaries (from 1879) having penetrated it. The Germans successfully pressed their claim for the territories and held them, as the joint colony of Ruanda-Urundi, until World War I. The German "explorations of possession" after 1892, particularly in Burundi, found "a situation bordering on chaos" (Lemarchand 1970, 49). A drought (1889–91) had just broken but was followed by an epidemic of smallpox that killed up to one-third of the population; other plagues and pestilences also troubled the people and animals of the area. Politically, things were at the point of virtual civil war. Mwami Mwezi Gisabo, who had ruled since 1852, was old and had been suffering challenges to his authority for twenty years, mainly from *ganwa* of the Batare line (the descendants of his predecessor, Ntare Rugamba) who resisted his efforts to establish Bezi hegemony. Walking in on the middle of this struggle, it was natural, Ress maintains, for the Germans "to conclude that these Tutsi people were predominant" (1988, 70). Meanwhile, in Rwanda the strict centralization of power was shaken when Rwabugiri died, in 1895. This momentous event was followed within months by the arrival of a European force and, the next year, by a violent clash between the Bega and Banyiginya clans for power, which was to continue throughout the colonial period.

Out of all this confusion both the Germans and the Ruanda-Urundians had to make some sense. Based on what Weinstein and Schrire call the European "habit of ethnicity or tribalism," the colonial administration looked to assign each individual to one of a set of distinctive and exclusive group (tribal) identities and to determine and isolate the "ascribed social values to each tribe" (1976, 8), much as was noted by Leach during his fieldwork in Burma. The obvious available candidates for such a categorization were "Hutu" and "Tutsi," and, as we have seen, Western prejudices and preconceptions, mixed with the political climate at the moment of their arrival, led them not only to identify but to identify *with* the Tutsi as the rightful ruling race. As an illustration of this favor—a "natural" ethnocentric reaction—the administration desired to bring missionary education to the Tutsi chiefs to make them into both Christians and qualified operatives in the colonial system. This, however, entailed a reversal of earlier trends, in which most of the Christian converts were Hutu. Western education for Tutsi chiefs, and especially discrimination against Hutu in education, could only serve to widen the gulf, and inflame the resentment, between the two groups.

From the perspective of the court and the chiefs, European power and institutions presented simultaneously a threat and an opportunity—and, ironically, the same threat and opportunity that Rwabugiri's rise had presented. The threat was a loss of autonomy, but the opportunity was novel and better means to control and exploit the people who depended on them for leadership and patronage. Europeans became, without their explicit knowledge, new super-patrons, and a clever and enterprising individual, especially one with some access to power and education, was able "to manipulate the situation in his personal advantage. Forwarding his own ambitions, he gained power that he then used in a way that his European patrons would have condemned, in principal, at least" (Newbury 1988, 56). Interestingly, but understandably, this phenomenon had the opposite effect in the two different parts of the colony: in Burundi it tended to increase fragmentation (as chiefs and ganwa struggled for leverage against the *mwami*), while in Rwanda it tended to increase centralization (by taking advantage of the already-existing political infrastructure and further consolidating power in the hands of chiefs and patrons, which was not only no threat to the *mwami* but was actually part of his apparatus of state).

As a result of World War I, Ruanda-Urundi fell into the hands of Belgium, which received a League of Nations mandate in 1923. It was during this phase of colonialism that the most sweeping and profound social transformations occurred in the colony, transformations that, especially in Rwanda, served to solidify ethnic categories and intensify ethnic stratification. Even so, a number of these changes worked through or upon the preexisting (but not at all primordial) institutions of chieftaincy and clientage. These reforms, starting in the 1920s, pursued two goals: economic production and administrative efficiency. Both of these goals could be most easily reached initially through the chiefs, who already had "administrative," and in many cases also patronage, authority over the local people. Particularly after a famine in the 1920s, the Belgian administration devised a variety of programs and policies that increased the labor and revenue demands on the Ruanda-Urundian people, and these demands were to be met through the auspices of the chiefs. Thus, at least for a time, the system of indirect rule and the "modernization" of the society and economy not only did not weaken traditional authorities and relations but actually strengthened them, auguring "a substantial increase in the demands that chiefs were required to (and were able to) make on the population at large" (Newbury 1988, 151).

That indirect rule was a devil's bargain, for the chiefs in the short run and for Rwandan and Burundian ethnic relations in the long run, was not immediately apparent. Nevertheless, the reforms that followed one upon another had contradictory and generally inflammatory effects on the societies. Reorganization of the political structure, progressive dissolution of clientage relations, and introduction of new forms of economic exploitation fell upon these societies in rapid succession. One of the first actions to "streamline" the chief system and to eliminate overlapping powers and obligations came in 1926, when some chieftaincies were abolished and others merged into larger single units. *Muheto* chiefs were eliminated altogether and the *muheto* form of clientage abolished; new policies also dispensed with *gikingi* land tenure. And the total number of chiefs was reduced; for example, in Kigali province the 119 chiefs and 324 subchiefs were eventually pared down to 5 chiefs and 72 subchiefs (Linden 1977, 187).

The impact on the chiefs and their subjects/clients was complicated while tending in one observable direction. Admittedly, many chiefs lost their positions in the reform, but the position of chief itself was strengthened in the consolidation. For one thing, the curtailment of *gikingi* landholding meant that chiefs or subchiefs could legally appropriate such lands for themselves. The dissolution of *muheto* bonds (a comparatively high-status form of clientage) left many lineages without the benefits, such as they were, of the relationship. Thus, many people—individuals now, not lineages—were driven to seek clientship on less favorable terms such as *buhake*. And, overall, the "vast interlocking network of relationships" (especially in Rwanda) of various kinds of chiefs to one another and of various kinds of patrons and clients—relationships that could be set off against one another to mitigate the power of any one of them—was stripped away, exposing individuals (without the protection or comfort of their corporate groups any longer) to increased insecurity and exploitation.

As would be expected, these effects were acutely felt by the Hutu segment of the population, most noticeably in Rwanda. This fact is clearly evinced by the aborted attempt to install some Hutu chiefs in the 1926 reforms; in response to warnings from the local Catholic bishop regarding the deleterious results of removing Tutsi from their traditional hegemony, the decision was reversed; Hutu chiefs were dismissed and replaced with Tutsi, and in fact in some areas Tutsi were seated in traditionally Hutu chieftaincies such as in the north of Rwanda. The outcome—the growing monopoly of positions of importance by Tutsi and the enhancement of the power of those positions—was that, while not all Tutsis were chiefs, very nearly all chiefs were Tutsis, so that *Tutsi* was evolving to become synonymous with power and high status (which could be used more freely and harshly than ever now that many traditional constraints on the prerogatives of chiefs and patrons had been removed) and *Hutu* to become synonymous with subordination and exclusion (Newbury 1988, 179).

A final and critical element in the ascendancy of the Tutsi was their conversion to Christianity throughout the 1920s, culminating with the deposition of the conservative king Musinga (who had resisted many efforts by the Belgians at reform, especially when it would erode the powers and privileges of the crown) and the elevation of his son Rudahigwa, a "Christian" king, to the throne in 1931. "The conversion of the Tutsi was a corporate recognition that the source of power within the State had shifted away from the *mwami,*" writes Linden in his study of the Catholic Church in Rwanda (1977, 173). But, even more so for our purposes, it marked the undermining of the Hutu-dominated and Hutu-oriented church and the final alignment of the Tutsi ethnic group with the new fountains of power and prestige in society.

As mentioned, Hutus had been among the first, and until the 1920s the majority, of converts and occupants of church positions such as mission students and catechists. This would turn out to be consequential in two ways, particularly in terms of the new skills and the new dignity and self-confidence that participation in the church would bring and in terms of the "ethnic ceiling" that they would encounter outside the church—and within it after the Tutsi conversion—in regard to their social opportunities that would enhance their sense of identity as a discriminated Hutu class. The colonial administration, however, sought to embrace the Tutsi as functionaries and clerks in their administration, and the best way to accomplish this end was to entice the Tutsi into the missions. As Lemarchand states, the École des Frères de la Charité, or, more commonly, the Groupe Scolaire, was opened in 1929 in Astrida (giving its graduates the nickname "Astridians") specifically "to recruit students from among the sons of Tutsi chiefs and to tailor the curriculum to the functions and skills expected of a chief" (1970, 74). This institution, he maintains, was to be a key to the supremacy of the Tutsi in the late colonial era.

The arrival of substantial numbers of Tutsi to mission schools, and the administration's plans for them, had a markedly negative effect on the Hutu. This increasingly distinct and disadvantaged status served to segregate them from their Tutsi schoolmates or to exclude them from educational opportunities altogether; of course, as in all other regards ethnic, this situation was worse in Rwanda than in Burundi, the former building upon its preconditions of Tutsi domination to achieve ever higher levels of exclusivity and to reinforce and bear witness to "their sense of collective superiority vis-à-vis the Hutu" (Lemarchand 1970, 75). The Hutu, on the other hand, found some nascent ethnic definition in these conditions: a small but educated Hutu elite had been produced along with and before the Tutsi intelligentsia, an elite who could and would express their aspirations and perceive the social reality of the ethnic ceiling that blocked these aspirations, as the new crop of Tutsi chiefs and clerks emerged to monopolize the limited economic and political opportunities for "natives" in the administration. Not unlike Sri Lanka, this ethnic ceiling and the palpable obstacles to social mobility and the realization of the promises of Western and Christian culture and education contributed to the coalescence of a sense of group (what we would call ethnic) identity and to an embitterment of the identity.

Throughout the 1930s and 1940s the rationalization of Ruanda-Urundian economics and social organization continued, with new and more harsh exactions added to already-existing ones and with changes to the nature of chieftaincy and clientage that stripped away the feudal characteristics of these institutions and bureaucratized and "capitalized" or commoditized them. In addition to the remaining "feudal" bonds (*bureetwa* and *buhake*) as well as the new taxes and corvee labor (known as *kazi*), colonialist enterprise began to demand labor for its own projects, most notably coffee planting and anti-erosion programs (especially after 1937), mining and manufacturing, and of course the war effort. The chiefs were expected to organize the recruitment of this labor, and in the early years of this system the chiefs would often keep the wages earned thereby for themselves. The most onerous chores, including *bureetwa,* were typically assigned to the lowest-status persons, and this tended to mean Hutu.

Wage labor was certainly a new and extra burden for locals who were expected to provide it while also meeting their obligations for clientship, taxes, *kazi* labor, and forced cultivation. This exploitation caused considerable resentment toward the chiefs as the most visible agents of the economic system; chiefs and patrons who, under feudal arrangements, were supposed to protect their clients and moderate their demands imposed upon them, were taking advantage of them most acutely. Yet, as Newbury points out, wage labor for Belgian interests was also an avenue of escape from feudal and political obligations to chiefs and patrons. In fact, the colonial administration offered incentives to wage laborers in the form of exemption from *kazi,* tax breaks, and the substitution of *bureetwa* services with cash payments. That the chiefs appreciated this threat to their prerogatives is evidenced by their attempts to obstruct labor recruitment by making life more difficult for their subjects who tried to work in the wage-labor market. Wage labor was no panacea for exploited villagers, but it was one more way in which traditional and feudal society was undermined.

Finally, the chiefs themselves were bureaucratized, becoming salaried functionaries of the colonial administration. The process of cash replacing traditional exchange media can be further observed in the 1949 substitution of *bureetwa* clientage with a mandatory cash payment (although some chiefs continued to compel their patrons to provide the services for years afterward) and eventually, in 1954, the abolition of *buhake.* If the intention of these reforms, however, was to emancipate villagers from dependence, even feudal dependence, they were not entirely and immediately successful. Many chiefs were happy enough to see traditional clientage end, because they had identified new sources of prestige (such as education, Christianity, and administrative service) and wealth (such as salaries and cash exactions) and because it freed them from the reciprocal obligations of the customary relationships. On the other hand, former clients were not decisively liberated because they still had to pay the chiefs (as agents of the administration) various sorts of fees and, even if, for example, they escaped a clientage bond like *buhake* and acquired propriety rights to their own cattle, they often had no place to pasture the animals and so were compelled to "reinfeudate" themselves as land clients to patrons who were lower in prestige than their former patrons, thus depressing their own status. The changing forms, without any real change in the terms, of relations between powerful and weak, higher-status and lower-status, only served to make "the Hutu peasants more conscious than ever of their continued dependence on the ruling oligarchy" (Lemarchand 1970, 132). In fact, if anything, it laid bare the mechanisms of exploitation in a way previously unknown and highlighted, and partially *created,* the growing status-gap between the Hutu and the Tutsi groups.

In conclusion, the colonial period, rather than simply erasing or reversing the traditional culture and relations of Rwandan and Burundian societies, acted upon the preexisting structures, some of them of fairly recent invention themselves, in complex ways to alter and yet perpetuate certain aspects of that structure. The terms of power—in which precisely power comes from and what precisely it demands—changed, but the essential nature of power, and even more so its *holders,* did not change much at all; for instance, abolishing feudal institutions like *muheto, bureetwa,* and *buhake* did not take the power, prestige, or wealth away from the chiefs. Quite the contrary, colonialism and modernization (in the sense of "rationalization" of the economy and its underlying social relations) placed new tools of domination and exploitation in their hands that (though not unambivalently) enhanced their power and prestige. As Lemarchand has stated, the effect of this process was to extend "'the premise of inequality' to an entirely new field of human endeavor" (1970, 134) and to widen the gap of inequality—and of identity differentiation—between the strata of society. In Burundi this did not have immediate or critical consequences for Hutu-Tutsi relations (both Hutu and Tutsi being subordinated to the *ganwa*). In Rwanda, with not only the predominance of Tutsi chiefs but with the removal of many indigenous Hutu chiefs, this issue was liable to emerge more clearly as a Hutu versus Tutsi problem, an extrapolation and aggravation of a traditional tendency in the society. Thus, protest and political mobilization, when it came, was more likely to be ethnic in the conventional sense and more anti-*mwami* (who was after all a Tutsi and the head of the Tutsi regime) in Rwanda than in Burundi, where politics was cast in more dynastic terms—one *ganwa* line against another, involving and seeking little mass mobilization—and pro-*mwami* (as the one, though weak, force of unification in society) and only later, and for different reasons, in familiar ethnic terms.

Independence and Ethnic Mobilization

In the early 1950s, as independence for Ruanda-Urundi became more imminent, activities within the colony began to become more political, with the formation of political parties and the jockeying for position in the new government that would follow. It was clear from early on, to the consternation of some international observers, that the colony would not remain united but that instead it would split into two polities as it had been before colonization. Therefore, from now on we must carefully and clearly distinguish between developments in Rwanda and those in Burundi, for they diverge, although they also cross and interact in the most palpable ways at various moments, as when one state harbors ethnic refugees from the other and becomes the staging point for operations against the original state or when ethnic violence in one state raises the fear of violence in the other. At any rate, as independence beckoned, all the changes wrought by colonialism, together with what Lemarchand has called the "rehabilitation of traditional statuses" made possible or thinkable by the removal of foreign power, bore their poisonous fruit first in Rwanda, then in Burundi, then repeatedly back and forth in the two states to the present day.

In Rwanda, by the 1950s an incipient new class showed signs of emergence, a class of *évolués* of both Tutsi and Hutu origin, united more by their shared educational background with each other than by cultural or ethnic commonalities with "their own kind"; this situation again mirrors that in Sri Lanka and many other former colonies. This group was relatively isolated from the rural experience of growing, and growingly ethnic, stratification, yet it was not immune to it; as discussed earlier, Hutu had been underrepresented in this new elite group and had met with limited opportunity to enjoy their elite status. It was, however, events outside their own activity or control that were to split and mobilize this "class" along ethnic lines initially.

One of these events was a change of attitude in the Catholic Church. After World War II a number of socially conscious young missionaries, often of working-class or even ethnic origin themselves (e.g., Belgian Walloons), took up residence in Ruanda-Urundi and brought more progressive views, including social justice and majority rule. As early as 1948, there is a perceptible division within the church, the Tutsi clergy finding common cause with Tutsi chiefs against Hutu clergy and some Hutu-sympathetic "White Fathers." These differences were to undermine the potential new biethnic or nonethnic *évolué* class (to leave it "stillborn," in Linden's words) and fortify ethnic categorization. A second such event was a dramatic reversal of position by the administration. Up to this time, taking advantage of the preponderance of Tutsi authorities and justified by their own theories of race and racial superiority, the administration had allied itself conspicuously with the Tutsi, committing itself to "'respect and reinforce' the power of 'indigenous authorities' (by which was meant Tuutsi [*sic*])" (Newbury 1988, 155). Motivated by democratic principles, among other things, the Belgians found oppression of 85 percent of the population by 15 percent (or less than 15 percent, since not all Tutsi held office or even high status) increasingly intolerable and became sympathetic and then supportive of Hutu demands. This support was to be decisive in the political evolution (read: ethnic evolution) of independent Rwanda in the early years.

In 1953 a new system of electoral colleges at the subchiefdom level was introduced, which would be important bodies as they would choose from among their ranks the members of subchiefdom councils, which would in turn select higher-level councils, etc.; in other words, they would serve as the base of the entire political structure. (Subchiefs, chiefs, and the administration still chose the members of the electoral college; it was not determined by popular vote.) Many Hutu were chosen to serve at the base level: Webster reports that Hutu held a 58 percent majority of electoral college seats (still not equal to their proportion of the population but substantial) and a large minority (over 47 percent) of subchiefdom council seats. At higher levels, however, this percentage dropped to only nine (1966, 256). His explanation is that Tutsi were still perceived as higher in status and prestige and better able to get things done politically and that in face-to-face interaction on the lower councils the Hutu were intimidated into voting for Tutsi candidates for higher councils; others see the entire electoral process as flawed and manipulated in favor of the Tutsi. Furthermore, in 1956 the Vice Governor-General proposed to add four new members to his council to represent Hutu (a weak version of communal representation), but the *mwami* refused to accept the proposal.

Simultaneously, educational opportunities for Hutu opened, as, for example, the Groupe Scolaire began to welcome Hutu students: their numbers increased from virtually zero before 1955 to almost one-third by 1959. A vibrant Hutu counterelite was thus in creation, the threat of which helped to unify the disparate elements within the Tutsi category (chiefs, clergy, average citizens, etc.). And, as independence appeared to approach ever closer, this Hutu group intensified its political activity, attempting to effect what changes it could now lest independence find and enshrine a Tutsi-dominated system. One of the main tasks of this counterelite became to "awaken" Hutu identity, to forge a solidary bond between Hutu *évolués*, petit bourgeois, and rural peasants on the basis of Hutu ethnicity. In other words, the critical movement was to foster a cross-class ethnic identity, as opposed to a cross-ethnic class identity such as the nascent Hutu-Tutsi "elite class" noted earlier. As Lemarchand puts it, with the decision to shift their constituency away from the shared Hutu-Tutsi elite to the interclass Hutu ethnic group, "the Hutu counter-elite were able to use the solidaristic ties of clientship to build up a political clientele of their own, and, later, to manipulate this following for revolutionary ends" (1970, 118).

The Hutu leadership had, and took advantage of, infrastructural resources to accomplish this mobilization. Probably the most significant of these was the Catholic Church itself, its schools, its presses, and its contacts outside of Rwanda. Journals like L'Ami, Kinyamateka, Soma, and *Temps Nouveaux d'Afrique* became key instruments of Hutu expression and activism. They also made use of publications and organizations within Belgium to make their cause and their views known and to win sympathy in the mother country, the one that held ultimate power over politics in their land. Finally, party organization within Rwanda was called for, and one of the first incarnations of Hutu political will was the Cooperative Travail, Fidelité, Progres (TRAFIRO), formed in December 1956 with the guidance and assistance of the Catholic Church, which was to serve as the center from which Hutu ethnic and political activity grew.

At that moment the Tutsi monopoly on political power was nearly complete, with the group holding all 43 chiefdoms, 549 of 559 subchiefdoms, and 82 percent of all official posts. As of late 1956–early 1957, the Superior Council of Rwanda contained less than 6 percent Hutu yet was generally expected to become the government of Rwanda upon independence. In February 1957, shortly before a United Nations mission arrived to review progress toward independence, the council issued a "Statement of Views" expounding its perceptions and wishes for Rwandese in Rwandan affairs, more training for Rwandese elites, and the elimination of discrimination between Rwandese and Europeans; no mention was made of Hutu-Tutsi problems or discrimination. In fact, according to some reports, the council actually sought to strike the terms *Hutu* and *Tutsi* from official papers. This would be entirely understandable, since it is clearly in the dominant minority's interest to minimize or ignore group distinctions so that their minority status is not used as a weapon against them to question their legitimacy; also, in the Hutu response they explicitly objected to just such an action by the government.

This response, which was something of a trumpet call to the Hutu people and the first real public political challenge to Tutsi hegemony, was called the "Manifesto of the Bahutu," issued in March 1957 and signed by nine Hutu intellectuals. The manifesto, subtitled "A Note on the Social Aspects of the Indigenous Racial Problem in Rwanda," states that the social and ethnic problem in Rwanda "lies in the political monopoly of one race, the Tutsi race, which, given the present structural framework, becomes a social and economic monopoly." It does not advocate ethnic confrontation and conflict but sees the potential for it in the prevailing circumstances: "From this to a state of 'cold' civil war and xenophobia, there is only one step." To prevent the escalation of competition into conflict, it calls for more attention to the social inequalities between Hutu and Tutsi (and analyzes the cultural/ethic tension between them in terms of the political, economic, and social differences between them, i.e. did not assert ethnicity, at least not combative ethnicity, as a primordiality), for specific policies to address poverty and oppression of Hutu, and for cooperation within an integrated Rwandan society; the Tutsi-dominated leadership should see to "the integral and collective promotion of the Hutu," and the Belgian authorities should take "more positive and unambiguous measures to achieve the political and economic emancipation of the Hutu" (qtd. in Lemarchand 1970, 149–52). The authors maintain that they offer their criticisms and remedies "not at all as revolutionaries" but as co-nationalists with the other components of the Rwandan state. Hutu ethnonationalism as such is not evident in their words, but the resources and rhetoric for such an ethnonationalism can be extrapolated from them; Lemarchand writes, for example, that the issues and language of the manifesto became a "staple news item in the local press" and a major subject of popular discussion among the rural Hutu.

Action followed words, in the particular form of political mobilization. One of the signers of the manifesto, Gregoire Kayibanda, in June 1957 founded a party called Mouvement Social Muhutu (MSM). Kayibanda was one of the Hutu *evolues* who had written in the Catholic presses of the need for the elites and the rural masses to recognize their common cause and act in unison; he was also to become instrumental in the Hutu movement and eventually to become the prime minister of Rwanda. Yet, like all aspiring political movements, the Hutu movement was not entirely unified. For one thing the communication and organizational links between the elites and the peasants were less than perfect. For another, other would-be leaders offered themselves and their visions of Rwandan society to the population. Among them were Joseph Gitera, who founded the Association pour la Promotion Sociale de la Masse (APROSOMA) in October 1957, and Aloys Munyangaju, later president of that party. APROSOMA was a more radical and populist organization than MSM; Newbury goes so far as to call it "vindictive and messianic." MSM was more firmly anti-Tutsi, yet it was Gitera's party that agitated conservative Tutsi more, perhaps as an assault on their class status and privileges rather than on their cultural identity. At any rate, the stage was set for a Tutsi counterresponse and the ultimate breakdown of ethnic relations in Rwanda.

In ethnic response to the rising Hutu sentiment, the more conservative Tutsi chiefs, as is often possible at moments of high rhetoric and political uncertainty, began to ascend over the progressive and moderate segments of the ethnic group. A statement issued by a contingent of Tutsi courtiers expressed their position all too clearly:

> the relations between we (Batutsi) and they (Bahutu) have always until the present been based on servitude. There is, therefore, between we and they no foundation for brotherhood. . . . Since it was our kings who conquered the Bahutu country and killed their petty little kings and thus subjugated the Bahutu, how can they now pretend to be our brothers? (qtd. in Webster 1966, 43)

Whether or not this statement reflected a consensus among Tutsi is irrelevant, since it reflected the attitudes of the most vocal and influential set of Tutsi, and, even more to the point, it was the position which the Hutu leadership saw and reacted to.

Yet, by struggling against the ethnic issue in Rwanda, the Tutsi leadership and the *mwami* helped to underline it as *the* issue in Rwanda. Hutu elites, seeing slight and diminishing potential for serious reform under the existing system, and with independence now very near, were radicalized. Furthermore, the choice of "frame" for the debate by the Tutsi elite—history, the kingdom and the *mwami,* the symbols of state—gave the Hutu a target for their protests and their identity formation. This target was construed as larger than the Tutsi chiefs, more profound than the Tutsi ethnic group; it was the taken to be the very "historical symbols of Tutsi supremacy," including the *mwami*ship, the entire monarchy, and the Karinga drum, an instrument literally adorned with the severed genitals of vanquished Hutu kings and a particularly offensive object to them. The Hutu movement, which might have settled in 1957 for political reform, by 1959 aimed at nothing less than revolution and the overthrow of the monarchy. The Tutsi were helping to make their worst dreams come true.

It is no small fact that on July 25, 1959, Mwami Mutara III died. Conservative Tutsi notables rushed to name the half-brother of Mutara (and son of Musinga), Jean-Baptiste Ndahindurwa, as successor. The Belgian authorities were not pleased with this procedure but, finding it a fait accompli, ratified it. The new *mwami,* given the reign name Kigeri V, at age twenty-one, was not the force to hold a fragmenting Rwanda together, so on August 15, 1959, a "national party," the Union Nationale Rwandaise (UNAR) was founded that was more like an instrument of Tutsi interest: mostly Tutsi in membership, it was pro-monarchy and anti-Belgian, and it rejected the notion of any inherent division or disharmony between Tutsi, Hutu, and Twa, arguing instead that the ethnic tensions of the day were to be blamed on the evil policies and practices of the colonial administration. Another smaller and more moderate party, the Rassemblement Democratique Rwandais (RADER), was also formed with a platform of reforms including a constitutional monarchy and expanded democratization.

In counterresponse to the Tutsi mobilization evident in this string of events, Kayibanda reorganized his MSM on October 19, 1959, into a political party, the Parti du Mouvement de l'Emanicipation Hutu (PARMEHUTU), with enhanced integration and enhanced militancy. The Tutsi authorities viewed this development with alarm, publishing a note that described the Hutu party as "supported by the government and the priests" and exhorted the Rwandan people: "Children of Rwanda! Subjects of Kigeri, rise up! Let us unite our strengths! Do not let the blood of Rwanda be spilled in vain. There are not Tutsi, Hutu, Twa. We are all brothers! We are all descendants of Kinyarwanda!" (qtd. in Lemarchand 1970, 161). An interesting contradiction of spirit, indeed, compared to the statement by the Tutsi chiefs made previously.

At any rate, the stage was set for conflict with the players named and positioned and the themes (racial and historical) well announced. The violence began in earnest on November 1, 1959, with the attack on a Hutu subchief (and member of PARMEHUTU), Dominique Mbanyumutwa, by Tutsi associated with UNAR. In retaliation a group of Hutu attacked some Tutsi notables, particularly a vocally anti-PARMEHUTU subchief named Nkusi. The spark of violence quickly erupted into a flame that burned across Rwanda for days. Although Hutu activities followed detectable patterns, scholars generally agree that they were not premeditated or centrally orchestrated; Hutu, in small gangs, would usually loot and burn Tutsi homes but not take Tutsi lives.

The Belgian authorities at first did nothing, in fact denying the *mwami*'s request, on November 6, to order in his army to restore order. The *mwami* deployed *muheto* and militia forces anyway, however, and a Tutsi counterattack of considerably greater force, structure, and political focus ensued. Hutu political leaders were targeted and arrested or killed. In the mayhem at least two hundred people, maybe more, were killed, and thousands became refugees, many leaving Rwanda for haven in Burundi, Uganda, Tanzania, or Zaire. Beyond that the violence, which Lemarchand calls a "jacquerie" (peasants' revolt) rather than a revolution, changed the terms of ethnic relations and ethnic expectations in Rwanda. For the Hutu a nagging question—should the Hutu movement focus on only representatives and leaders of the Tutsi political system or on the entire Tutsi community cum Tutsi?—was answered resoundingly with the latter, and any kind of pluralistic society seemed only, and increasingly, remotely possible. For the Tutsi the fears of Hutu majoritarianism had been realized (and only put down by force), so they could clearly see what their future in a Hutu-dominated Rwanda might be. Finally, the switch in sympathy and alliance of the Belgian administration was sealed: after the incidents of November 1959, three times as many Tutsi were arrested as Hutu, and many Tutsi chiefs (up to 350) were unseated and replaced with Hutu candidates (often members of PARMEHUTU or APROSOMA) or, occasionally, RADER members. By the beginning of 1960 Hutus occupied almost half (22 out of 45) of Rwanda's chiefdoms and over half (297 out of 531) of the subchiefdoms.

These developments were followed all too rapidly by a Belgian administrative decision to reorganize Rwanda by abolishing the 554 chiefdoms and subchiefdoms and consolidating these units into communes, of which there would be 229. Accordingly, elections were necessary to choose the heads of these communes (titled "burgomasters") and the councillors who would serve with them; the elections were set for July 1960. The campaign itself turned into something of a Hutu-Tutsi struggle as well as a referendum on the monarchy, and various outbreaks of fighting occurred during the process. In opposition to continued Tutsi minority rule, PARMEHUTU, APROSOMA, and RADER united in a Common Front, and in the end the Hutu parties, and PARMEHUTU in particular, won a commanding victory. PARMEHUTU was by far the most successful single party; of the major parties UNAR performed the worst.

With PARMEHUTU in such a strong position, old alliances, even intraethnic ones, were precarious, and not much time passed before the "minority" parties (minority in the sense of having fewer members in the government, not necessarily of representing a minority of the population nor a minority ethnic group) realigned to become a joint "opposition" to the dominant party. This was attributable not only to mere expediencies of electoral politics but also to the conduct of the PARMEHUTU incumbents, which left them open to criticism. Lemarchand argues that the new burgomasters committed many excesses because their formal powers were not clearly defined but, even more, that a new incarnation of clientage was engendered with the burgomasters as the latter-day patrons who, like their predecessors, abused their privileges, especially against their Tutsi constituency. The opposition, not without some justification, complained that PARMEHUTU was "deliberately attempting to crush all other parties through corruption and intimidation" and that this new "kind of feudalism is worse than the old one" (Lemarchand 1970, 189). Could it be that privilege—whether founded on ethnicity or numerical majority—leads necessarily to arrogance and exclusivism?

Be that as it may, in answer to its critics, the entire body of elected burgomasters and councillors met on January 28, 1961, in the town of Gitarama and abolished the monarchy and all of its symbols, especially the accursed drum. The body then declared itself the government (the constituent assembly) of Rwanda and designated Dominique Mbanyumutwa as president and Gregoire Kayibanda as prime minister. These actions were confirmed by a popular referendum in September 1961, when some 80 percent of the vote favored the dissolution of the monarchy and PARMEHUTU gained 35 of the 44 seats in the new Legislative Assembly.

That this revolution could not have been successful without the complicity of Belgian authorities is evinced by their behavior in the face of it and by the conclusions of outside observers. As Lemarchand notes, once the revolution was under way (as early as 1959), any attempts "by Tutsi incumbents to repress the insurgents were immediately nipped in the bud by the administration" by, for example, refusing to call out the armed forces, arresting Tutsi counterinsurgents, and removing Tutsi officeholders from their positions. The administration stood by as PARMEHUTU and the Hutu in general rose to grasp the structures of power, and it is reasonable to assume that the Gitarama gathering had every expectation that the government would accept, if not hail, a Hutu-dominated republican system. United Nations observers also reported their impression that the Belgians not only knew in advance of the planned coup but actually participated in it. Such encouragement made the actions of the ethnic protagonists more likely.

The United Nations Commission for Ruanda-Urundi, in its March 1961 report, was nevertheless critical of the political course in Rwanda and in fact prophesied further trouble ahead: "A racial dictatorship of one party has been set up in Rwanda, and the developments of the last eighteen months have consisted in the transition from one type of oppressive regime to another. Extremism is rewarded and there is a danger that the [Tutsi] minority may find itself defenseless in the face of abuses" (qtd. in Lemarchand 1970, 194–95). Indeed, attacks on Tutsis were part of the revolution and continued after its successful conclusion. Many of their attacks were planned and executed with official, even military, precision; others were more spontaneous and isolated ethnic incidents. And others yet were not ethnic in the strictest sense but more "personal," in the form of settling old scores between clients and patrons or between traditional enemies or rivals of one sort or another. The outcome of this period of conflict and violence was an extremely large, and extremely volatile, Tutsi exile community; by some accounts 120,000 to 130,000 Tutsis fled from Rwanda into neighboring states by 1963, constituting anywhere from 40 percent to 70 percent of Rwanda's total Tutsi population. These refugees not only became a critical factor in subsequent Rwandan history, organizing and returning to take up the ethnic struggle again, but were also to be significant elements in the internal politics of their host states, whether Burundi (where militant refugee Rwandan Tutsis would help shape Tutsi-Hutu ethnic relations and political decisions in that state), Uganda, or others.

Whatever else is true, ethnicity had certainly developed quickly and served definitively to tip the levers of power away from one group and toward another. Precisely because of the completeness and rigidity of Tutsi domination of state, the Hutu response and Hutu demands were forceful, and ethnic conflict, when it came, was heated and intense. Also, because Tutsi were identified so thoroughly with the state and especially with the monarchy, the Hutu movement logically took the form of an anti-monarchist movement as well. Finally, because at least some Tutsi apologists had defended the status quo on historical grounds—arguing that their Tutsi ancestors had conquered the place and therefore they were entitled to rule it today—Hutu responses were bound to invoke their own interpretation of the past, one that had long been available but not until recently exploited politically. For the Hutu, and especially for PARMEHUTU, the Tutsi could be cast as foreigners, as "colonialists of the Ethiopian race" who had no more right to be in Rwanda than the Europeans and who, like the latter, should return to their home and leave Rwanda to its "natural" and original inhabitants (conveniently forgetting the historical precedence of the Twa people). Opening the issue of history and traditional intercommunal relations allowed for a new construction of nationhood as equivalent to Hutu-hood, such that Rwanda could be envisaged as the rightful state of the Hutu nation exclusively.

Burundi around Independence

Colonialism encountered a considerably different and more fragmented society in Burundi than in Rwanda, especially between the two predominant dynastic lines, the Bezi and the Batare. Ironically, colonialism in Burundi strengthened the *ganwa* position over the *mwami,* perpetuating or enhancing social decentralization, whereas in Rwanda it had strengthened the *mwami* and the centralized state; yet, in both cases, this is comprehensible as a continuation of traditional social vectors. Also, some of the same factors came to affect Burundian society as Rwandan: particularly after Belgian rule began, a consolidation of the political structure commenced, and the new more exploitative economic relations were introduced. In regard to the former process the 133 chiefdoms extant in 1929 were reduced to 46 in 1933 and 35 in 1945, naturally increasing the power and prestige of the remaining *ganwa* chiefs in the process. The benefits of this political evolution, however, were not evenly distributed; in particular, there was a clear pattern of Bezi *ganwa* gains and Batare *ganwa* losses. As regards the latter process, such economic practices as taxes, *kazi* labor, forced cultivation, and wage labor were added to the traditional obligations of peasants and clients; still, it must be remembered that clientage was never as widespread nor as burdensome traditionally here as in Rwanda.

Even in the early period of colonialism the forces that would crystallize and mobilize ethnic identities by generating or exacerbating ethnic segregation and grievances were already evident and at work. In precolonial Burundi social rank and prestige depended more upon kinship affiliations and connections to the king or a princely house; Hutu-Tutsi distinctions provided at best a secondary source of social status. As illustration, a missionary, Bernard Zuure, wrote in 1931 that Hutu and Tutsi differences were "so minimal that one can speak of a common culture" (qtd. in Lemarchand 1994, 43). Interestingly, "regular" (non-*ganwa*) Tutsi also lost ground, though not as precipitously as Hutu—thirty chiefs in 1929 to ten in 1945. Also, Hutu were disadvantaged in education, underrepresented at such institutions as the schools for chiefs. Finally, as in Rwanda, with the growing power of the remaining chiefs under Belgian authority, life for commoners became more insecure, driving them often to seek protection in some (now more exploitative and low-status) clientage relationship, aggravating the distance between classes. In particular, the term *Hutu* began to take on more officially pejorative meanings, increasingly associated with inferiority and servitude, although the opposing category was still less "Tutsi" than "ganwa." It was not uncommon, at this stage in ethnic evolution, for a patron to refer to his Tutsi clients as "Hutu," and the *mwami* might refer to the very Tutsi or *ganwa* chiefs (his clients) as his "Hutu."

The period after World War II saw the rise of new elites, especially educated young Bezi chiefs. Yet, as in earlier points in Burundian history, the hegemony of the one group was never thorough, in this case because of internal schisms within the Bezi side (which even led some to join forces with Batare against their intragroup rivals, in the kind of fraternal dissension that we encountered over and over again in our analysis of the Kurds) and because of the decade (1944–54) of administrative favoritism toward the Batare faction as opposed to the Bezi. Even so, as late as 1959, Bezi continued to head almost one-half of the chiefdoms in Burundi, and, more significantly, dynastic rivalry continued to be the central political dynamic in the society. The terms and sources of the struggle changed under the impact of colonial modernizations, but the nature and pivotal position of the contestation endured—and obstructed the formation of more strictly ethnic constituencies and conflicts.

The key development of the late pre-independence period is the politicization or "popularization" (in the sense of involvement and mobilization of the masses) of this traditional, nonethnic intra-*ganwa* competition. This politicization was formalized in 1957 with the creation of a political party known as Parti de l'Unité et du Progrès National (UPRONA) by Chief Leopold Bihumugani (also known as Biha). The leaders of UPRONA were Bezi, and the provocation that led to political mobilization was a perception of administrative policies and proposed changes that would have diminished some of the authority of the *mwami* and thus of the Bezi chiefs, who were of course tied to the existing political system and had established strategic ties with the crown. It was no great help that Batare leaders welcomed the proposed reforms, either. One of the most interesting features of the new party, beyond its "clan" rather than ethnic base, was its promonarchy platform; in fact, the indigenous name for the party, *Abadasigana,* is a traditional term for "the group of individuals who formed the personal retinue of a *mwami.*" That the head of UPRONA after 1958 was Prince Louis Rwagasore, eldest son of Mwami Mwambuta, and a *ganwa* representative of the Bezi, further highlights the political-dynastic connection. That UPRONA was not an ethnic party but a party of "national unity" led by, and serving the interests of, a traditional elite, is clear from the fact that it sought to appeal to the entire Urundian nation across ethnic/caste lines and that it included both Hutu and Tutsi in its leadership; Rwagasore himself was noted for his Hutu sympathies and even for certain Hutu-like physical traits.

Naturally enough, the Batare section also entered party politics with its own organization, Parti Democrate Chrétien (PDC), founded by Joseph Biroli and Joseph Ntitendereza. Biroli, like Rwagasore, had been educated in Europe and was one of the modern elite chiefs. Yet the PDC offered a more "progressive" platform (including various social issues) and membership (a large proportion of Astridians) and was less inclined to urge for immediate independence. All these features made the Belgian authorities well inclined toward PDC and less so toward UPRONA. In fact, it has been argued that the administration positively thwarted UPRONA, as when Rwagasore was under arrest during the communal elections of November 1960; not surprisingly, PDC dominated the results, carrying 942 of 2876 total seats, compared to UPRONA's 545.

Events were converging on Burundi, however, that would have fateful consequences not only for the state but for ethnic relations within it. First, remember that, beginning in November 1959 and continuing for several years, ethnic violence in Rwanda had sent a stream of Tutsi refugees into Burundi-Tutsis filled with ethnic animosity and designs on taking their ethnic fight back to Rwanda at their earliest opportunity. This agitated ethnic refugee population had a chilling effect within Burundi, causing fear in its own Tutsi population; having observed what happened in its neighbor, the Burundian Tutsi "reasoned that if this was the way that Hutu behaved once they obtained power, then this is what would happen in Burundi if the Hutu were to become dominant" (Weinstein and Schrire 1976, 15). Further, the *mwami* and the Bezi nobility feared the loss of the monarchy in a republican revolution like Rwanda's. Hence, the monarchists (such as UPRONA) did what they could to secure the monarchy, including expressing openness to a constitutional monarchy and reaching out to Hutu and Tutsi alike in gestures of national unity; the *mwami* himself became more active in politics, ostensibly acting as an impartial third party, or an "umpire," but increasingly imposing his will on the course of politics and therefore infringing upon what had been until then (and traditionally) a comparatively "acephalous" political arena for chiefs and *ganwa* princes.

The *mwami*'s interventions in political life offended Batare as well as Bezi, Tutsi as well as Hutu. Also, in his attempt to balance all the various interests within the kingdom, he offered concessions to Hutu demands but in the process drew criticism from his Tutsi subjects. The goal was to achieve independence without a republican or ethnic revolution. He succeeded but at great cost. With independence set for 1962, parliamentary elections were called for September 1961. UPRONA played the national unity and pro-monarchy cards to attract voters and came away with an 80 percent landslide and 58 of 64 seats in the Legislative Assembly. This triumph was not to be enjoyed for long, however, as UPRONA's Rwagasore was assassinated on October 31, 1961, in a plot that eventually led to the execution of the PDC's Biroli and Ntitendereza as well as three others. In one tragic moment both major parties were deprived of their leadership.

So independence came to a Burundian monarchical state in early 1962, but not before the "Gitarama coup" and its republican and majoritarian revolution back in Rwanda. With this model in sight, and the intra-*ganwa* rivalry temporarily decapitated (from the loss of its leadership), the ethnic dimension in Burundian life began to rise in volume and pitch. We must not overestimate its power or appeal at this early date; as Lemarchand notes, in 1962 "political divisions were not always consistent with ethnic cleavages" and "neither the Hutu nor the Tutsi were totally and permanently 'in' or 'out' of government" (1970, 353). Again, it was the *mwami* playing the key intermediary role, balancing Hutu against Tutsi interests, for example, over the next few years alternating Hutu and Tutsi prime ministers. But the controlled balance never worked very well, considering the *mwami*'s constant meddling (from the elected government's point of view) in political affairs, and democratic (or at least majoritarian) ideology and its role model in Rwanda.

On the first count Burundi's prime minister resigned in June 1963, complaining of the *mwami*'s tampering with the government; he was replaced by a Hutu, Pierre Ngendadumwe, who also did not last long. Between 1963 and 1965 five different governments were appointed, each balancing Hutu and Tutsi evenly (but not proportionately), and the very instability in parliamentary politics strengthened the *mwami*'s hand in the state. The ethnic juggling act, with the *mwami* as the master juggler, satisfied no one, understandably. The *mwami*'s policies simply suspended, temporarily, the political competition that was inevitably on the way. Thus, on the second count dissatisfied Hutu, especially elites with some knowledge of or tie to Rwanda and PARMEHUTU, began to demand more. Yet the very importation of PARMEHUTU's ethos into the Burundian context called for a somewhat inappropriate appraisal of Burundian society and ethnic affairs—or, more to the point, an interpretation of Burundian society as hinged on ethnic identities and rivalries, as in Rwanda. In a sort of self-fulfilling prophecy, PARMEHUTU-inspired Burundian Hutus "imputed to the Tutsi of Burundi motives which they (the Tutsi) at first did not possess but to which they eventually gave a substance of truth" (Lemarchand 1970, 344). The "false definition" of Burundian society as an ethnic oppression structure of the Rwandan type led to Hutu militancy and to Tutsi and *ganwa* extremism in reaction, thus making the definitions seem to fit. Even more, the definition of society as fundamentally and exclusively composed of two distinct and incompatibly groups even functioned to *create* that ethnic reality—to simplify all the social complexity (Tutsi, Hutu, Twa, Hima Tutsi, Banyaruguru Tutsi, *ganwa,* commoners, rich Hutu, poor Hutu, etc.)—into just two traditional and irreconcilable ethnic groups.

The process of ethnogenesis was also facilitated by racial and historical arguments: Hutu leaders invoked a ("fictitious") past in which a self-conscious Hutu nation had been oppressed and systematically deprived of its land, wealth, and autonomy by the foreign invading "Tutsi tribe," while Tutsi leaders claimed "that ethnic differences do not exist, except in the form of imported 'tribal ideologies,'" largely an effect of colonialism. The veracity of either claim is ultimately beside the point; the important thing is that, to a great extent, they worked . It was the *mwami*'s continued pattern of behavior that put the flame to the fuse of this ethnic bomb. In 1965 yet another legislative election was held, in which Hutu candidates won 23 out of 33 seats. The *mwami* refused to accept the assembly's choice for prime minister (a Hutu), however, and instead appointed his own *ganwa* man; he also attempted to extend his influence in the organs of state. As a result, on October 18, 1965, a group of Hutu army officers mounted a coup against the king that was unsuccessful but brought a heavy-handed response from the government. The prophecy was being fulfilled.

Naturally, one prime component of the response was the arrest and execution of thirty-four members of the coup. Yet retribution went much farther: Hutus were virtually purged from the ranks of the army, Hutu politicians and officials were arrested and some shot, and mutual acts of terrorism were conducted in the countryside, with the army rounding up and killing innocent Hutus. Estimates of the casualties run between twenty-five hundred and five thousand. Shortly thereafter, on November 2, the *mwami* departed to Europe, never to return. Leaving virtually no effective government behind him, the *mwami* named his heir, Prince Charles Ndizeye, to look after the country in his absence. The nineteen-year-old prince was no king, however, so a military regency ruled for him until they discovered that they could rule without him. In November 1966, with Prince Charles (now crowned as Mwami Ntare III) out of the country on business, what Lemarchand calls the "praetorians"—the new, military, largely Tutsi elite of young army officers and police forces—deposed him and took control of the state. The leader of this group was the king's prime minister, Capt. Michel Micombero; his ostensible rationale for the action was the army's "obligation to discharge a 'sacred trust,' that of 'defending the independence and liberty of the people' against the devious manoeuverings of a regime ensconced in 'corruption and nepotism'" (Lemarchand 1970, 440).

The initial coup was followed up by a republican one by the end of the month. The monarchy was abolished, and an increasingly authoritarian (though structurally weak and Tutsi-dominated) state grew in its place, which Micombero steered until his own deposition in 1972. For the moment, however, the significance of these events is the virtual preemption of the ethnic question in early post-independence Burundian politics—a question that was perhaps not well conceived anyhow—and a return to a kind of dynastic, or intra-Tutsi, politics; the old *ganwa* elite had been displaced and replaced with a new (but still Tutsi) elite, mostly young and educated, mostly Hima Tutsi, and mostly from the southwest region of Bururi, the area of Micombero's birth and of many of his officers. For the next period in Burundian society interethnic conflict will be much less central than intraethnic, as Tutsi of two different regional factions, Bururi and Muramvya, vie for supremacy. The Hutu will be largely ignored and then caught between these quarreling groups.

The Cycle of Ethnic Conflict in Rwanda and Burundi

In Rwanda, where the Hutu-Tutsi distinction was more determinative of status and power, the battle over ethnicity came earlier and more decisively than in Burundi. Hutu effectively grasped the levers of power and sent Tutsi fleeing in large numbers into neighboring states, including Burundi. A group chased into refugee status, however, is not a group vanquished, as history would prove; rather, in their havens Rwandan Tutsis organized into bands known as *inyenzi* (cockroaches) to plan and execute raids and eventual invasion and counterrevolution in their abandoned homeland. As early as November 1963, an abortive invasion was conducted, but a second, better-coordinated attack followed a month later; on December 21, 1963, *inyenzi* forces from Burundi, Uganda, Tanzania, and the Congo began a penetration of Rwanda, and, though not all the plans materialized, enough fighters crossed into the state to evoke an armed response from the Rwandan army, led by Belgian officers. In civilian response to the threat Hutus rose up and killed ten to fifteen thousand Tutsi, including twenty Tutsi notables who were named "on a list of prospective future ministers in a Tutsi-led government that had been found on the body of one of the attackers" (Watson 1991, 5). All of the incursions were foiled and met with harsh Hutu countermeasures. Each episode merely upped the level of ethnic animosity and thirst for vengeance, preparing the way for even greater violence.

In neighboring Burundi conflict and violence followed its own course, which was predictably less thoroughly ethnic than in Rwanda. After seizing power in 1966, the military junta of Micombero had rigidified, becoming protective of its position and privilege, seeking to suppress opposition, whether from Hutu or Tutsi. In fact, once again "rank" status outweighed ethnic status in Burundi: the army, like the *ganwa* before it, appeared and acted like a separate distinct rank, or caste, and, "like the *ganwa,* most of the officers refuse[d] to openly identify themselves as Hutu or Tutsi" (Lemarchand 1970, 461). Rather than crystallizing as a Hutu versus Tutsi struggle, Burundian politics and society took the form of power elite versus everyone else. Thus, the rivalries were as much, or more, intra-Tutsi than interethnic.

One particularly virulent form of this intraethnic confrontation was the regional rivalry between the Bururi (a southern and Hima area) and the Muramvya (a central and Waruguru area) factions. The Bururi was especially antimonarchy and anti-Hutu, seeing the two as a dual threat (Hutu, as populists, being feared as desiring to restore the ethnically aware and sensitive monarchy). An alleged Hutu plot was uncovered in late 1969, leading to the elimination of Hutu leaders and the purge of the army of Hutu elements. With this accomplishment secured, the internal Tutsi factions turned on one another, the Bururi linking the Muramvya to the monarchy and the Hutu. It is more or less true that the Muramvya group contained Tutsi who had enjoyed high status during the monarchy and might be inclined to support it. By 1970 Micombero was convinced that the Muramvya were a threat to him and to the republic, and he began to move against them.

Burundian government actions against the Muramvyans—arrests, show trials, beatings, and death sentences—brought the Tutsi to the brink of intraethnic civil war and raised the specter of a Hutu rebellion while the ruling caste was so internally divided. Tensions were exacerbated by the return of Mwami Ntare from exile on March 30, 1972; although guaranteed safe passage by Micombero, he was arrested immediately, some government advisors recommending his execution. At least some observers attribute this decision to ethnopolitical motives—"to provoke a Hutu rebellion and force the hand of the Muramvya faction" (Weinstein and Schrire 1976, 301). Whether or not this was the intention, something like it was the outcome after Micombero dissolved his cabinet on April 29.

Within hours violence flared in three disparate regions of Burundi, suggesting some degree of coordination. That April 29 was a Saturday, a traditional market day, when large populations would be out and about, was felicitous, allowing for less conspicuous massing of men and arms.

Thomas Melady, U.S. ambassador to Burundi at the time, reports that some four to five thousand Hutus were involved in the outset of the violence (we might call it rioting), and apparently their main objectives were army and police installations and the government radio station. Once the shooting started, "cars were being stopped . . . and people were being dragged out from their cars and killed" (1974, 4). Whatever organization there may have been initially degenerated, as the rebellion turned into "a mass chaos of settling scores between individuals." According to Ambassador Melady, the official interpretation of these events was "that Burundian (Hutu) armed rebels allied with Zairian exiles (Mulelists) attacked southern Burundi, Gitega, and Bujumbura on April 29–30; that about 50,000 people were killed and that they were mostly Tutsi. . . . the goal of the invading force was to establish a Hutu-dominated republic and to liquidate the Tutsis" (1974, 11). Yet he contends that the actual victims numbered more around one to two thousand. One of these victims, however, was the *mwami,* who was apparently assassinated while under arrest by an official of the government named Shibura on the very night of the outbreak of fighting. Government fears that the *mwami's* presence would incite Hutu and Muramvyan Tutsi to join forces in support of the monarchy no doubt contributed to this action.

The same fears—not only ethnic fears but more strictly political ones—led to the characteristically disproportionate government reaction to the unrest. In parts of the country Hutus were indiscriminately massacred. In other parts the purge was more systematic: "intellectuals," which includes teachers, students, or any Hutu with any education, were singled out. There are indications that Tutsi students actually helped prepare lists of their Hutu classmates for the process. One of the more curious and tragic aspects was the international response, especially within Africa. There was widespread support for the Burundian government, the Organization of African Unity accepting Burundian claims that "the situation in Burundi was primarily the result of outside aggression sponsored by neocolonial forces. The delegation also claimed that tribalism was not a factor in the Burundi crisis and that Burundi had achieved a 'tribal homogeneity unparalleled in Africa'" (Melady 1974, 25–26). In defense of the ruling junta, Tanzania sent ammunition, and Zaire actually deployed paratroopers.

Before it was all over, in 1972, anywhere from 80,000 to 150,000 people had been killed, mostly Hutu, and another 60,000 had left the country. More critically, however, the central contradiction in the country had shifted from the intra-Tutsi dynastic, or regional, one to the ethnic one. Even rural folks now became conscious of the salience of Hutu or Tutsi identity, and many Burundian Tutsi now saw the Hutu as *the* enemy and the total eradication of Hutu leaders—and maybe of the Hutu people—as the only solution, the "final solution," to Burundi's problems. In a twisted evolution of ethnic relations "the killing of Hutu seemed to have become part of the civic duty expected of every Tutsi citizen" (Lemarchand 1994, 98).

Surely, the utter defeat and the resultant fright of the Hutu led to over a decade of unchallenged Tutsi hegemony in Burundi. The decimation of Hutu elites, the complete monopoly of power and prestige by the Tutsi elites, the thorough reduction of Hutu to a subordinate class, even the confiscation of Hutu property—all these strengthened Tutsi control for almost a generation and gave Burundi, finally, an ethnically oriented and stratified society like Rwanda had had for many generations. Not that peace or unity came to the Tutsi: a coup on November 1, 1976, replaced Micombero with Lt. Col. Jean-Baptiste Bagaza. Efforts to "integrate" (euphemistically expressed) Burundian society—the revival of UPRONA as a mass party, the nationalization of secondary schools, the suppression of the Catholic Church, new programs of villagization and mandatory identity cards, not to mention systematic local terror—failed to bring about stability or unity.

Instead, the army revolted again in late 1987, installing Maj. Pierre Buyoya. The appearance of lessened oppression of Hutus raised that group's hopes for the first time in fifteen years while scaring conservative Tutsis. Outside Burundi, Hutu refugees had meanwhile organized a Hutu Peoples Liberation Party (PALIPEHUTU). An excerpt from one of its pamphlets reads: "whether it's Micombero, Bagaza, or Buyoya, they all come from the same hill and they are all Bahima [Tutsi]. . . . It's this detestable race which has stolen from a huge number of Hutu since Burundi's independence, and now all Tutsi are getting together to exterminate the Hutu" (qtd. in Ress 1988, 97). This kind of inflammatory rhetoric, on both sides, helped to push circumstances past the crisis point, and on August 14, 1988, violence broke out again, this time in northern Burundi, an area particularly aggravated by government attempts to control local agriculture by blocking the transport of its coffee crop across the border to Rwanda (where prices were better for farmers). Within a week one-fifteenth of the population of the region involved was killed. The initial killing was primitive hand-to-hand combat; a great many of the victims were "slashed in the same fashion with a machete blow on the side of the head or a slice on top of the skull, just above the ear. . . . there were virtually no body wounds" (Ress 1988, 105). And the brutal, genocidal ethos—the routinization of killing—already evinced by Tutsi perpetrators was visible among the Hutu, who referred to death as their *gukora* (work) and *gutema* (cutting down) Tutsis as their mission.

Estimates of Tutsi casualties vary between two and five thousand. The usual Tutsi reprisals yielded considerably more Hutu victims (up to fifteen thousand), employing heavy weapons and massacring Hutus at will. Subsequently, in late 1988 Buyoya assembled a new government with a Hutu as prime minister and a cabinet evenly divided between Hutu and Tutsi. He promised to turn more power over to the Hutu, but not a proportional share of power, not 85 percent; rather, Buyoya argued in a speech that it is "an insult to democracy to confuse the demographic majority with the political majority" (qtd. in Ress 1988, 114). This is an argument that ethnic minorities holding the reins of power have made again and again in various national contexts.

Into the 1990s: Resurgence of Ethnic Conflict

Rwanda and Burundi entered the 1990s with internal tensions at a high point, both ethnic and otherwise. In both states one-party or military governments ruled—Hutu in Rwanda, Tutsi in Burundi—but it was not the ethnic composition alone of the governments that offended citizens' sensitivities but also their authoritarian nature. Thus, resistance was directed at least as much at the dominant power elite as at the "opposing ethnic group," except that it just so happened that in Rwanda the dominant power elite was more thoroughly identified with the an ethnic group.

As so often in the past, Rwanda set the pace for the twin societies. Rwanda had been relatively quiet for a generation, with the Hutu-controlled junta (most recently headed by Juvenal Habyarimana) securely ensconced in power. Yet danger to the regime lurked in two corners: Tutsi exiles residing in states bordering Rwanda and extremist Hutu in and out of the government. As mentioned, a large community of Rwandan Tutsi inhabited such states as Tanzania, Zaire, Burundi, and Uganda and played significant roles in the affairs, political and ethnic, of each. But the connection between Uganda and the refugee Tutsi was singularly important, both for Uganda and subsequently for Rwanda. One particular Tutsi, Paul Kagame, had become the head of military intelligence in the

Ugandan government of the late 1980s and had been instrumental in organizing an expatriate resistance there called the Rwandanese Patriotic Front (RPF), with its military wing, the Rwandanese Patriotic Army (RPA). From its bases in Uganda it invaded Rwanda on October 1, 1990, with a force of some seven thousand men to pick up the ethnic gauntlet of the previous generation.

The ensuing fighting settled into a three-year but inconclusive war, which encouraged Habyarimana and Kagame to pursue negotiations; these talks yielded an agreement in August 1993 known as the Arusha Accord (after the city in Tanzania, made famous by Julius Nyerere's earlier declaration there in 1967) to put an end to the conflict. The accord called for the disarming of the RPA or its integration into the Rwandan national army, the establishment of a transitional and multiparty government, and the deployment of a 2,500-man United Nations peacekeeping force (to be named the UN Assistance Mission to Rwanda, or UNAMIR) to oversee the transition. There were, however, many Hutu, inside and outside the government, who welcomed no such concessions to their former Tutsi lords (so they felt), and this sentiment was perhaps stronger inside the military junta than outside it. In particular, a faction from the Gisenyi region and affiliated with Habyarimana's wife had gathered considerable power and benefit during their twenty-one-year reign as well as effectively organizing such contingents as the presidential guard (a two thousand–man force) and various *interahamwe* (those who attack as one) militias. These groups saw nothing to their advantage in a "democratic," multiethnic government; in fact, the jealous guarding of their perquisites would have pitted them against any challenger, Tutsi or Hutu.

In the meantime, in Burundi conflict had continued to take the form of internecine Tutsi struggle. An attempted coup failed in early 1989, organized by Tutsi officers opposed to Buyoya's government on the basis of ideology *and* kinship. Understandably, antigovernment Tutsi and antigovernment Hutu had a certain amount in common, as they had in the days of the Bururi-Muramvya schism, although those common interests were limited and led to a temporary alliance. Radical actions taken by Hutu activists severely strained this spirit, however. As early as mid-1990, in a mirror image of events in Rwanda to follow, bands of Hutu exiles in Tanzania attacked military targets in southern Burundi with primitive weapons (sticks and machetes) as well as guns. When RPA Tutsis invaded Rwanda, Hutu sympathies on the Burundian side of the border were energized, and PALIPEHUTU found more vigorous support; some of this support actually came from the Rwandan government, eager for an ally against their Tutsi enemies.

All of this agitation led to a Hutu uprising in Burundi in November 1991, which Lemarchand characterizes as "a series of carefully coordinated attacks . . . by small groups of Hutu activists . . . against military and police installations" in three provinces (1994, 155); notice again that Hutu targets did not include or emphasize civilians. In typical fashion the official response was much fiercer than the initial threat, one pair of observers commenting: "The search for culprits rapidly deteriorated into a manhunt, resulting in the blind massacre of Hutu for no other reason than they happened to be Hutu" (qtd. in Lemarchand 1994, 157). Approximately three thousand Hutu died. In addition, the government rooted out the Bagaza faction, whose members were suspected of either supporting the uprising or of hoping to benefit from it, perhaps even to lead an uprising of their own when the regime was weakened.

In this climate Buyoya chose to call the first free election in Burundi's history in mid-1993; maybe he believed his power so perfect, or his policies so popular, that he would surely win. Yet, by this time, a rival political party had emerged from its underground birth in 1983 to become a legitimate challenger for rule. This party, the Front des Democrates du Burundi (FRODEBU), stood for multiparty democracy, power sharing, and reform. Its leader was Melchior Ndadaye, a Hutu, and his victory (with 65 percent of the vote) and his party's (with 65 out of 81 seats in the National Assembly) gave Burundi a new look for the future—an uncertain future but a potentially bright one. Instead, Tutsi soldiers attempted a coup only days after the election, and on October 21, 1993, Ndadaye was assassinated. In reaction, rioting and violence left between 50,000 and 100,000 dead, and the army remained rebellious for the next several years.

And so, with both Rwandan and Burundian society highly sensitized to the ethnic issue, their histories converged tragically on April 4, 1994, when a plane carrying Rwandan President Habyarimana and new Burundian President Cyprien Ntaryamira was shot out of the sky over Kigali, the capital city of Rwanda. Naturally enough, the RPF was immediately blamed, but it denied responsibility. Yet the fear and confusion surrounding the event were sufficient to mobilize a ferocious anti-Tutsi movement; according to reports, in the wake of the assassinations the government radio station called on Rwandans to "kill the Tutsis." Armed gangs of Hutu, often soldiers, were prepared with lists of ethnic and political targets to do just that. The rest is all too well-known. Perhaps a half-million Rwandans, mostly Tutsis, were butchered in the most savage and public manner. Yet even this was not a strictly ethnic outburst; leaders and members of rival or moderate Hutu parties were also selected, and in fact one of the architects of the killings was himself a Tutsi. Thus, unarmed civilians were macheted, burned in their homes, or killed en masse in sanctuaries like churches; in fact, in the carnage virtually the entire Rwandan Catholic clergy, much of it Tutsi, was exterminated. All of us watched in horror as bodies piled up on roadways or floated down streams. Even the acting prime minister, Agatha Uwilingiyimana, was hunted down and shot, along with her Belgian United Nations escort.

Finally, the RPF reemerged to defend the Tutsi and, in their words, the Rwandan nation. So successful were they that the Hutu soldiery was quickly defeated and the Hutu ethnic group sent into retreat. Around two million refugees were created as Hutus, frightened by rumors of Tutsi vengeance or intimidated by threats of Hutu instigators, fled for their lives into the usual neighbor states. The new Tutsi-led government tried to assure that Rwanda was now safe for citizens, Tutsi and Hutu, to return: a new "government of national unity" was established, containing only about one-third RPF members in the cabinet and a considerable number of Hutus. The government also criticized Tutsis returning from exile who attempted to expropriate land from demoralized (or absent) Hutu. The new prime minister, Faustin Twagiramungu, summed up the attitude of the new regime: "We all have to be Rwandans; that's the ideal. We can't say that because I'm in the majority that the minority must disappear." Minority governments have made these kinds of soothing noises in the past; time will tell what the newly reinstalled Tutsi or the newly disempowered Hutu will do.

Significantly, Burundi did not implode like Rwanda upon the death of its leader. Perhaps the threat was less imminent; perhaps assassination of leaders has become too commonplace there. Or perhaps the army's secure control of the state made such conflict redundant. This is not to say that society was free of tension; no, limited confrontations in the vicinity of the capital, as well as in some rural areas, belied a level of anxiety and animosity that could explode into war and a degree of agitation by Rwandan *interahamwe* and other dispossessed Hutu who fled Rwanda but not ethnic strife, taking it with them where they go. But at least in the short term after the Rwanda debacle, Burundi did not follow it into ethnic meltdown.

Conclusion

That Burundi did not spiral into genocide in 1994 the way Rwanda did highlights one of the central points of this chapter—that even neighboring societies with the same apparent ethnic groups, a shared provocation, and entangled populations and fates do not necessarily follow the same ethnic course. Rather, the specific ways in which ethnic groups relate to one another in the traditional context, the specific ways in which they relate to the stratification system, the specific ways in which they relate to colonialism and to the subsequent introduction of electoral politics—all of these factors help to determine the observed antagonisms (or lack thereof), grievances, and conflicts between them; in fact, these factors play a role in the very ways in which groups of whatever distinction consolidate into *ethnic* groups in the first place.

In both Rwanda and Burundi, Hutu and Tutsi (and Twa and *ganwa* and Hima and others) were not originally or primordially ethnic groups but, rather, some other type of group; this other type of group has been labeled caste, category, status group, rank, and the like. What is abundantly clear, however, is that these groups stood in different relations to one another (by the late nineteenth century; the following characterization may not hold as completely before that time) and to the power structure in the two polities. In Rwanda the identification between the Tutsi group and political power and privilege was considerably stronger than in Burundi, where both Tutsi and Hutu groups were subordinate to a special class of nobility that came very close to evolving into distinct ethnic group in its own right. Both societies were, in addition, monarchical states, but the monarchy had different political characteristics and different ethnic consequences.

That colonialism exacerbated some of the social contradictions in these societies is clear. Modernized administration and economic practices added to the burdens of the laboring classes of the population and aggrandized the roles of chief and patron (temporarily but consequentially) vis-à-vis those classes, augmenting the differences between them. What is fascinating, however, is the "persistence over time of . . . norms which even today continue to reflect the specific characteristics of their traditional cultures" in both societies (Lemarchand 1970, 465). The growing perception by Rwandans that Hutu and Tutsi ethnicity was at the center of their society, together with the fact that ethnic positions were increasingly rigid and that ethnic demands were increasingly shrill, made an ethnic revolution more likely there than in Burundi, where distinctions between Hutu and Tutsi "were never sharp enough initially to produce as violent and drastic transformation" (493). Even so, the obvious injustice of a 15 percent minority ruling an 85 percent majority in Burundi, plus the "demonstration effect" of ethnic conflict in Rwanda after 1959 and the significant influx of Rwandan refugees to Burundi, acted as a catalyst to precipitate ethnicity and ethnic conflict there as well. Yet conflict in Burundi, which has been more frequent than in Rwanda, has rarely been as purely ethnic. This is not to suggest that ethnic tension is absent there; Hutu have lived with the knowledge that they are a disadvantaged and even terrorized group, while Tutsi have lived with the fear that a vengeful revolution like Rwanda's may take their power along with their lives. In fact, this fear, even paranoia, helps explain the extreme reactions to generally limited Hutu insurgencies in the past. But in the end ethnicity is *the* dynamic in Rwandan society, whereas it is only one (but a major one) dynamic in Burundian society.

In conclusion, then, ethnicity has become a crucial characteristic and dividing line in both societies but not equally nor in the same ways; even more significantly, the social complexity that existed or exists has been gradually simplified into two exclusive ethnic categories (Lemarchand 1994, 14). The ethnic fallacy was perpetuated in the press during the latest round of conflict in Rwanda, with constant references to the "tribal conflict" and the "centuries of hatred between the Tutsi tribe and the Hutu tribe" and eyefuls of sensationally horrific slaughter, the intensity and irrationality of which could only derive from some archaic age and emotion. We can now see, however, that ethnicity and ethnic conflict, even of this magnitude, is not primordial but is in fact recent—a product of economic and political contradictions and competitions introduced in the nineteenth and twentieth centuries; of interpretive processes acting on a past so as to reconstruct out of history a pattern of abuses and usurpations designed to reduce one group under absolute despotism; of actions and decisions by individuals, communities, or parties to indulge in or self-consciously "play" ethnic politics to arouse—or even invent—a constituency. In effect, we might say that the "premise of inequality" that supposedly structured Rwandan society (in particular, in comparison to Burundian) has been replaced by or evolved into a "premise of ethnicity"—a discourse or ideology of the "national order of things" (Malkki 1995, 5)—with all the attendant struggles, epistemological and political, typical thereof.

Chapter 6

Bosnia: Of Myths and Maps

Five nations,
Four languages,
Three religions,
Two alphabets,
But only one desire—independence.

—Yugoslavian folk saying

Why should I be a minority in your state when you can be a minority in mine?

—Vladimir Gligorov

The struggle over the political and ethnic fate of the fragmented and failed state of Yugoslavia, particularly in its constituent republic Bosnia, has given the world new images and terms of intercultural hatred and cruelty, like the infamous *ethnic cleansing.* The persistence of the fighting has offended both American humanitarian sensibilities and faith in our international peacekeeping institutions such as NATO and the United Nations, and it raises a variety of fears, from the resumption of Cold War hostilities between the United States and Russia and the spread of the conflict into neighboring former Yugoslavian republics and beyond through one of the most ethnically diverse regions on the planet to the memory of how and why World War I began.

The war is often likened to a "tribal conflict" between two or three ancient enemies who have hated one another for centuries and who have been thrown together artificially in a republic (and then, unwisely, an independent state) and asked to live together in a fashion inimical to their primordial natures. Lately, however, some voices have been rising to question this perception of the Bosnian situation, this assumption "that what has happened in that country is the product—natural, spontaneous, and at the same time necessary—of forces lying within Bosnia's own internal history." Rather, new and growing opinion of the Bosnian case is that this construction of the conflict is a myth, not only false but politically motivated, "carefully propagated by those who caused the conflict, who wanted the world to believe that what they and their gunmen were doing was done not by them but by impersonal and inevitable historical forces beyond anyone's control" (Malcolm 1994, xix). In other words, while there are cultural differences and potential differences between segments of the Bosnian and Yugoslavian population, Woodward wisely reminds us that the political consequences depend less on the differences themselves or the collectivities that participate in them and more on the individuals and groups who seek to organize discontent based on those differences (1995, 88).

In this chapter we will examine and expose the myths and misconceptions behind the Bosnian question and, more centrally, consider how history and culture are employed in various kinds of political arguments to contest such things as rights to land, sovereignty, and the very possibilities of ethnic coexistence. At the bottom of the beliefs and preconceptions are that Bosnia is an artificial and recent political invention with no particular appeal to any of the parties concerned, while the parties themselves are distinct and ancient nations that have never succeeded in coexisting, except during the period when the totalizing and ethnicity-negating ideology of communism imposed an artificial but uneasy truce upon those parties. In this light the problem is essentially a "geographical" one—which groups belong where and which land is the real and natural homeland of which groups and should be incorporated into which post-Yugoslavian state—and therefore the answer is essentially a geographical one: divide the land correctly and the problem is solved. In other words, the Bosnian conflict presumes to prove that discrete and primordial nations makeup the landscape of Bosnia and that these nations can survive, physically and/or culturally, and enjoy their singularity and solidarity only as monoethnic communities.

Under attack, and therefore at stake, is not only the Bosnian Muslim ethnic group (a problematic notion itself, as we will see) but also the very conception and existence of a culturally plural society in the Balkans; as one source puts it, the object of "cleansing" is more than the Bosnian Muslims but actually "the unique and dangerous cosmopolitanism" of Bosnia, especially its cities, "which clearly had no place in the new 'pure' nation-states emerging from the ruins of Yugoslavia" (Ali and Lifschultz 1993, xiii). In other words, what is being contested is "two visions of society and democracy," one pluralistic, the other exclusivistic.

We must, then, comprehend the developments in Bosnia from this larger perspective. In this chapter we will proceed by first investigating the identity status of the corporate actors in the Bosnian scenario and the wider Yugoslavian context. Next, we will analyze how culture became nationalism in the nineteenth century, at least for some of the ethnic groups in the picture; that is, ethnogenesis and nationalism were uneven processes for the various cultural groups in the Balkans. As always, both internal and external/international forces will be seen to impinge on this ethnogenesis. We will then observe how actions and decisions taken within the present century have determined the subsequent course of ethnic relations in both integrative and disintegrative ways. The current conflict will subsequently emerge not simply as a revival of historical hostilities but also as a response to circumstances such as constitutional crisis, economic failure, and territorial competition. We will see, rather, that understanding the case in terms of "historical ethnic animosities and a return to the pre-communist past are ways of dismissing from consideration what collapsed and why. They are a way of saying there is nothing to understand" (Woodward 1995, 21).

Bosnia and Bosnians

What exactly is Bosnia, and what are Bosnians? It is important to remember at the outset that the present case includes at least three main protagonists: the Muslims, the Serbs, and the Croats. The Serbs and the Croats each, with the demise of Yugoslavia, have a "pseudo"-nation-state, pseudo because each state, Serbia and Croatia, also contains a number of ethnic minorities, while it does not contain the entire nation of its eponymous group; there are Serbs in Croatia and (to a lesser extent) Croats in Serbia. And there are both in Bosnia. Hence, for our purposes, and to clarify usages in the media, we will take *Serbian, Croatian,* and *Bosnian* to mean residents of the respective states, regardless of their ethnicity, and *Serb, Croat,* and *Muslim* will refer to ethnicity, regardless of state of residence. It should be noted that there is no such ethnicity as Bosnian.

The political term *Bosnia* refers to an area almost at the geographic center of the former Yugoslavia. It derives from the name of the river, the

Bosna, that flows through the region. As such, Bosna or Bosnia has had a distinct "territorial-historical" (Woodward 1995, 37) identity for centuries, although it has not usually been sovereign, being incorporated into various states at various moments in history—most recently the Ottoman Empire, then the Austro-Hungarian (Habsburg) Empire, and lately Yugoslavia. Yet in most of these multinational polities Bosnia has been retained as an administrative unit, recognizing its political identity. In fact, Donia and Fine maintain that Bosnia "has had more durable and widely recognized borders through the centuries than either Serbia or Croatia" (1994, 7).

Serbs, Croats, and "Bosnians" alike are members of a family of peoples called Slavs; this they share with numerous other nationalities in Central and Eastern Europe, including the Bulgars of Bulgaria, the Poles of Poland, and most notably the Russians. In distinction from their Slavic cousins, the Serbs, Croats, and Bosnians are sometimes classified—and sometimes, especially at the formation of the state of Yugoslavia, classify themselves—as southern, or *yugo,* Slavs. All three speak roughly the same language, Serbo-Croatian or Croatio-Serbian, although it comes in several dialects; for historical reasons, however, the one language is written in two different scripts, Latin by the Croats, Cyrillic by the Serbs, largely as an effect of their relative proximity to two medieval centers of Christendom.

Therefore, in at least two important senses, racially and linguistically, the peoples of the central Balkans could be construed as one group. In what sense are they more than one? And are they *really* more than one? As our entire presentation so far, from the earliest chapters, should suggest, the first question is complex and subtle, and the second question is ultimately meaningless. They are more than one group if they think and act as if they are; however, such thought and action, as definite as it may be at the moment, is no proof that is has always been thus. On the other hand, there are concrete ways in which the three groups differ, and these concrete differences serve as the raw material from which ethnicity is made. The most significant difference to note is religious. Croats are predominantly Roman Catholic, Serbs largely Eastern Orthodox. And, consequentially, there is within Bosnia a considerable Muslim population. This has led to something of a misconception in the world community regarding precisely who the Bosnians are and who is fighting whom in Bosnia. It is *not* correct to say that all Bosnians are Muslims; Bosnians include Muslims as well as Christians of both churches. Even more, Serb and Croat are easily conceived as national or ethnic terms, but Muslim is (or was) a confessional, not national, identity. We, and they, are conflating two very different levels of social organization into one. As we will see, it is not until late in the socialist period of Yugoslavian history that *Muslim* becomes a national term in the region.

We must reject out of court any "primordial" argument about Muslim identity in Bosnia, since Islam did not arrive there until the fourteenth century at the earliest. Arguably, some Turkish Muslims migrated to Bosnia as a result of the expansion of the empire, but this would account for a minute proportion of the Bosnian Muslim population. Instead, the Bosnian Muslim community emerged as the outcome of conversions of indigenous Bosnians to Islam for various reasons (to be explored in subsequent pages). In other words, the Bosnian Muslims are by and large racially or ethnically (other than by confession) *the same as* the other Bosnians who did not convert to Islam. A number of Croat and Serb nationalists, based on this historical fact, come to the interesting conclusion that the Bosnian Muslims are not *really* Bosnian Muslims but are *really* Croats or Serbs; naturally, the Croats tend to argue that they are Croats, while the Serbs argue that they are Serbs. A contradictory aspect of this interpretation is that, if they are in actuality kinsmen, it seems irrational to kill them.

One way to approach the question of ethnic identities and relations is ethnographically. Lockwood (1975) provides us with a look at Bosnian village life in the 1970s. In his study he points out that there are certain distinctive markers that set apart the groups that, sometimes but not always, share a social space. The people of the village of Skoplje Polje themselves distinguish between what they term *nacija,* or "nations"—what we might call nationality or ethnicity—which Lockwood characterizes as more or less endogamous groups that act as closed social networks with unique cultures or subcultures. "Members of each consider themselves, and are considered by others, as a distinct and unique variety of mankind. . . . members of each of these social groups are perceived as possessing certain God-given qualities regarded (albeit wrongly) as unchanging and unchangeable" (22–23).

Differences of *nacija* are particularly tied for them to language and religion, and especially the latter; Lockwood maintains that each confessional group is viewed as a *nacija* and that the term is "often used to refer specifically to religion, but always in the context of ethnicity associated with it." Accordingly, each religious *nacija* bears its objective marks of ethnicity. Most conspicuous are differences in dress, cuisine, and language. All three domains are marked by small and subtle variations in a basic style—for example, color of the sash worn with the traditional men's costume (red for Christian, green for Muslim) or style and color of headgear for both sexes (e.g., maroon fez or beret for Muslim men, black cap for Catholic/Croat men, and soft-billed cap or "overseas cap" for Orthodox/Serb men). In terms of language it is most interesting that "Eastern" (Turkish, Arabic, or Persian) words are naturally most plentiful among village Muslims but that many have been absorbed into standard Serbo-Croatian; language differences are not so complete, and Serbo-Croatian is not so pure.

This relatively neat picture of ethnic distinctiveness is complicated, however, by two additional factors: the presence of other ethnic groups besides the three we have referred to so far and a proliferation of identities including the extension of the concept of *nacija* to groups other than what we normally think of as ethnic groups. Lockwood encounters Gypsies, Albanians, and Cincars (descendants of a group called Vlachs) and finds references to a former Jewish community in his village; this reminds us that Serbs, Croats, and "Muslims" are not the only distinct peoples within Bosnia or the Balkans in general. Even more, he finds that further distinctions are made that are ethnic in character although not based on the major ethnic markers that tend to concern us. Villagers distinguish on the basis of locality and region and entertain characterizations and stereotypes for such social distinctions. Level of assimilation and acculturation also figures into their estimations of a person's identity. Finally, there is a sort of "class" distinction made within the Muslim community between the "peasants" (*balije*) and the "descendants of aristocracy" (*begovi*) who "comprise a separate social grouping that shares certain characteristics with ethnic groups." The *begovi* are, according to his report, an endogamous group with a distinct culture and a separate layer in the social stratification system, often occupied in the professions. Most significantly, the local people consider them and refer to them as a *nacija.*

Obviously, then, the identities of and boundaries between groups are anything but simple and clear-cut and may not entirely conform to our own ordinary notion of ethnicity in the region. The most profound lesson in this exercise is that, while the actual objective differences between individuals and groups may appear minor, what is really significant is how people in the society experience and use those differences in their social interactions and valuations. In other words, the essential factor is the "social distance" between groups that may cohabit the same territory and even interact in certain socially constrained ways. Indeed, Lockwood's main focus is on market behavior in this diverse social setting, and his ultimate conclusion is that, despite regular contact and a lack of any great amount of spatial or economic differentiation, the groups still maintain their basic social distance; therefore, even though an individual may share market space and mode of production with people from other *nacija,* those contacts "are likely to be superficial and his knowledge and understanding of different ethnic groups remain minimal. Thus, in spite of habitual contact with members of other groups, ingroup feelings and ethnocentrism remain high. Despite repeated exposure to foreign ideas and ways, there is remarkably little transference and each subculture remains intact" (210). That is, the amount of objective cultural difference and of objective physical separation or interaction between groups is, in the end, less decisive than the subjective and symbolic uses to which those differences are put.

Ancient and Medieval Slavic States

According to most historical accounts, the Slavs arrived in the Balkans in the sixth and seventh centuries C.E. Before that time records refer to earlier inhabitants of the region known as Illyrians; they appear in contemporary Roman documents that mention these people, and at least one Roman emperor, Septimius Severus (ca. 193 C.E.), was purportedly an Illyrian. Next to arrive were the Goths (third century), who have been claimed at pivotal moments in Balkan history to be the ancestors of the Croats and Bosnians.[1] The Slavs were the subsequent settlers in an already diverse land. They apparently arrived as a confederation of different tribes known as Slaveni; in particular, the Croats and Serbs established themselves in the region after 620. A number of pieces of evidence have led observers to conclude that the two groups were probably of Iranian origin. For one thing the population pattern decipherable from earlier migrations such as the Huns suggests a vector back to central Asia and the Iranian plateau. Further, the very names of the two groups and of their early leaders seem Iranian in derivation: *Croat,* for example, is not a Slavic word but is believed to be based on the Iranian *Choroatos* (rendered *Hrvat* in Serbo-Croatian). This interpretation has been exploited in various ways for various purposes in the cause of nationalism: some Croat nationalists accept

1. A 1942 memorandum to Nazi Germany maintained: "By race and blood we are not Slavs; we are of Gothic origin. We Bosnians came south to the Balkans in the third century as a Germanic tribe" (qtd. in Malcolm 1994, 5). The political motivation of such a statement should be clear.

Iranian descent for themselves but reject it for the Serbs, creating a supposed racial distinction between the two peoples, while pan-Slavic nationalists deny the Iranian connection altogether.

The Croats and Serbs each established medieval kingdoms in the Balkans early in their history. Each was, typically for the period, less an ethnic state than a collection of traditional regions or provinces brought together by dynastic conquest. The Croatian kingdom grew out from its root in Istria (northwestern Croatia today) during the rule of King Tomislav (910–28) to include both coastal areas like Dalmatia (with the important cities of Split and Dubrovnik) and inland areas like Slavonia and parts of modern Bosnia (especially the western part, Hercegovina). In fact, the site of Tomislav's coronation is located in present-day Bosnia and is an important element of the Croatian claim on at least parts of the region today. Serb leaders, too, created an independent kingdom by the twelfth century, quite distant from modern Serbia. The kingdom of Stefan Nemanja rose along the Adriatic, roughly in present-day Montenegro, and expanded westward. Stefan Uros II Milutin (1282–1321) conquered the areas south to Macedonia and east to the Danube, but it was Stefan Dusan (1331–55) who ruled over the greatest Serbian kingdom. In fact, in 1346 he took the grandiose title "czar of the Serbs and Greeks" at his seat in Skopje, the modern capital of Macedonia. With the decline of medieval Serbia after Dusan's death, Serbs gradually migrated east into the contemporary region of Serbia. Both of these small fledgling states, and many others besides, found themselves situated between the two great regional powers of the day, Rome (in the revived form of the Holy Roman Empire) and Byzantium. Periodically, one or the other of these empires would erupt into the scene and establish suzerainty over some part of it.

The earliest-known reference to Bosnia, in a 958 Byzantine document, seems to recognize the regional integrity of the unit, calling it "Bosona." Bosnia, however, was repeatedly overrun and occupied, in part or in whole, by foreign powers, from the Byzantines to the Bulgarians to the Hungarians. Yet, throughout these and subsequent conquests and exchanges of territory, little real outside authority penetrated the remote and mountainous Bosnian countryside, rendering it something of a no-man's-land between its larger squabbling neighbors. This situation supported the growth of an independent Bosnian kingdom but somewhat later in history than those of the Serbs and Croats. The nominal authority of the Hungarian king was openly questioned with the emergence of Ban Kulin (*ban* being a Croatian term for "ruler") in the upper Bosna river val-

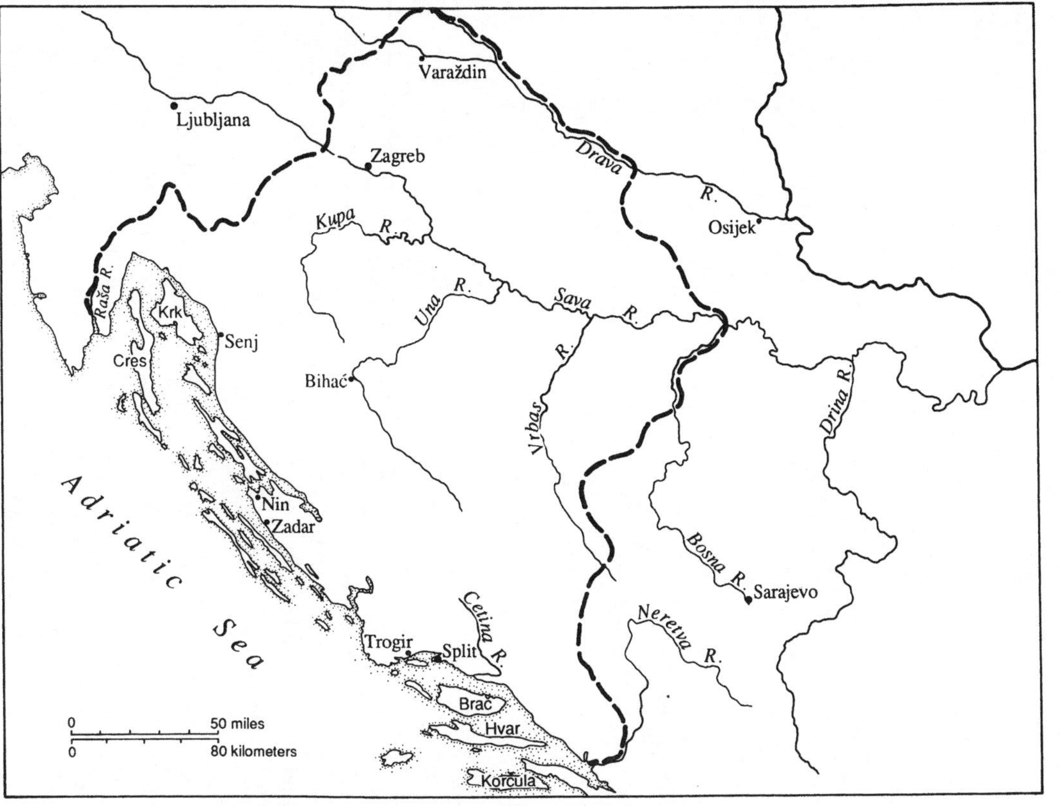

Croatian lands in the tenth century. (Reprinted from *South Slav Nationalisms—Textbooks and Yugoslav Union before 1914,* by Charles Jelavich [Columbus: Ohio State University Press, 1990], p. 2, by permission of Ohio State University Press.)

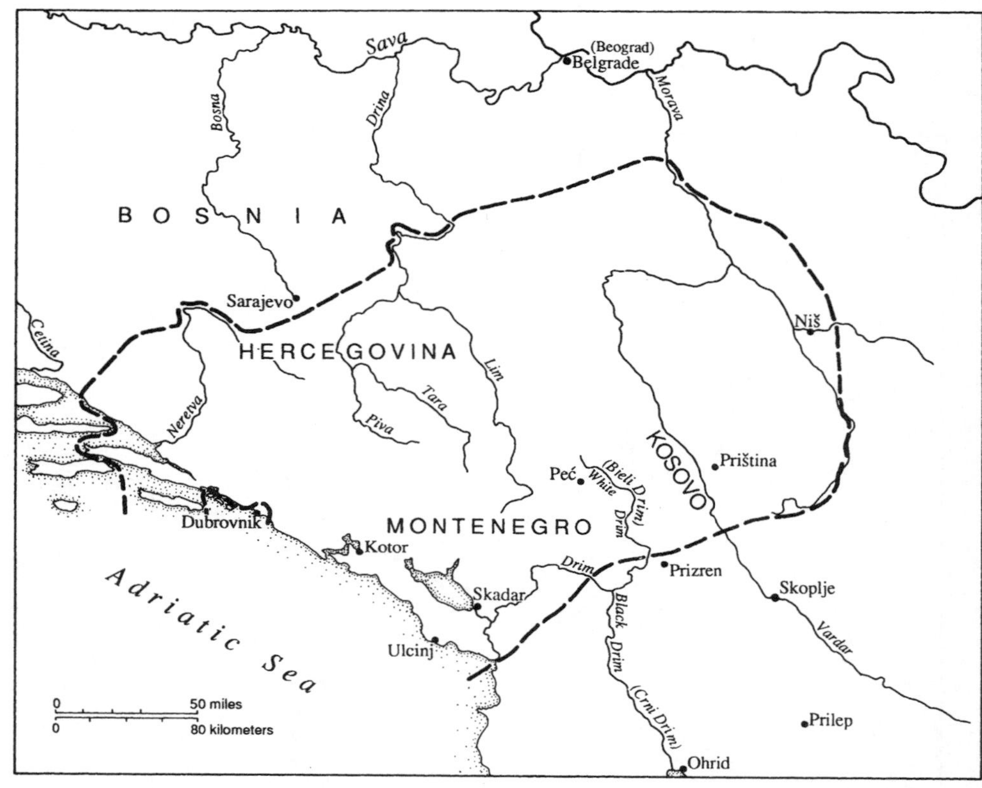

Serbian (Nemanja) lands in the twelfth century. (Reprinted from *South Slav Nationalisms—Textbooks and Yugoslav Union before 1914,* by Charles Jelavich [Columbus: Ohio State University Press, 1990], p. 4, by permission of Ohio State University Press.)

ley in 1180. The Bosnian state strengthened and grew under Ban Stjepan Kotromanic, who ruled from 1322 to 1353, who furthered Bosnian freedom from Serb and Croat forces and extended its own power into the region of Hum, or what is known today as Hercegovina. His successor, Stjepan Tvrtko (r. 1353–91), completed the expansion of Bosnia, incorporating southern and western areas (including parts of the Dalmatian coast)—in fact, reaching roughly the borders of modern Bosnia, except for the stretch of land in the northwest around Bihac. Indeed, he went so far in 1390 as to declare himself "king of Bosnia, Croatia, and Dalmatia."

Religious identities also began to be settled early yet separately from political ones. Christianity arrived in the Balkans in the ninth century

Bosnian kingdom in the fourteenth century. (Reprinted from *South Slav Nationalisms—Textbooks and Yugoslav Union before 1914,* by Charles Jelavich [Columbus: Ohio State University Press, 1990], p. 188, by permission of Ohio State University Press.)

from both the east and the west; understandably, Roman Catholicism had its best successes in the western Balkans, especially Croatia and Dalmatia, while Orthodox Christianity won most converts in the east, predominantly Serbia and Macedonia. Bosnia, the remote middle ground of east and west, was also the meeting point of these two traditions. The import of this fact is that neither faith developed a firm foothold in the territory. Well into the eleventh century there was no strongly organized church in Bosnia and few resident priests of either denomination. Of the two, Catholicism was evidently the more influential, but its teachings were imperfectly known and its central authority weak. Two results followed from these conditions: first, Bosnian religion remained somewhat more open and syncretistic (some would even say heretical) as well as superficial and, second, this attitude toward faith together with the political implications and uses of Christianity at the time led to a schism in Bosnia that to this day continues to distort perceptions of who Bosnians are and what they believe.

Effectively cut off from the structure of the Roman church for many years, an autonomous Bosnian Church was established. This Bosnian Church has traditionally, and often pejoratively, been labeled "Bogomil" after a heretical movement emanating from Bulgaria after the tenth century. Bogomil Christianity was Manichaean, with strong unorthodox views on dualism. The Bogomil theory was, of course, not the only possible explanation for the independent church; theories that it was an offshoot of the Orthodox Church or of the Catholic Church were and are advanced, especially by partisans of the respective religions. But the Bogomil theory held court longest and has only recently become widely discredited. Its particular power rested on its apparent ability to answer two other riddles about Bosnian culture: the meaning of the numerous stone monuments (known as *stecci*) spread across the countryside; and the reason for large-scale conversion to Islam during the Ottoman period. To examine the first riddle, it was conjectured that the *stecci,* numbering some fifty-eight thousand in modern surveys, were gravestones for Bogomil burials. It has since been noticed, however, that Catholic and Orthodox believers also commissioned such stones and that Bogomil-like motifs are often merely pre-Christian or unconventional Christian rather than truly Bogomil. There are other and more subtle, including doctrinal and practical, reasons to reject the Bogomil theory, but they need not detain us here.[2]

We should note at this point the political efficacy of embracing such a view as the Bogomil theory of Bosnian religion. One effect is the "alienation" or stigmatization of the medieval Bosnians and their distinct culture. If the unique culture of the Bosnians, expressed in *stecci* and other artifacts, can be stigmatized as a product of heresy, it can be discredited and the integral identity of the medieval Bosnians questioned or rejected; parties who are interested to thwart claims of a genuine and worthwhile Bosnian culture and identity might enjoy such a theory. Another effect is the degradation of the future converts to Islam in Bosnia: if they can be shown to have been "inferior" Christians to begin with, it is easier to understand their readiness to entertain the (at least in some of the literature, as displayed earlier) despised religion, and it is easier to condemn them for it than to redeem them for it. Either way, the Bogomil theory is a

2. For more information, see Malcolm 1994, 29–42.

useful weapon with which to beat the ancestral Bosnians and, by proxy, the contemporary Bosnians.

At any rate the significance of the Bosnian Church in its time was at best limited. The Bosnian ruler Stjepan Kotromanic restored an organized Catholic presence in his kingdom when he accepted a Franciscan mission in the 1340s to combat the "heresy" of the Bosnian Church. By 1347 Kotromanic himself had converted to Catholicism, and nearly all subsequent rulers were Catholic, at least nominally, giving them more kinship with Croatia than Serbia. The Bosnian Church survived another century, even through the early Ottoman period, until all of its members died or converted to one of the other religions in the vicinity—many but not all to Islam.

Ottoman Conquest and Islamicization in Bosnia

The Ottoman Turks brought Islam to southeastern Europe during their territorial expansion in the early fourteenth and fifteenth centuries. The conquest of the Balkans is, in fact, a key moment in Balkan, especially Serb, nationalism (at least in its present-day rhetorical construction). The crucial confrontation between Turks and Slavs was the famous and often-evoked Battle of Kosovo Polje (Field of Blackbirds) in 1389. Bosnian king Tvrtko sent Bosnian soldiers to fight along with other Slavs in a predominantly Serb army; although both sides apparently suffered heavy losses, and both were able to emerge from the battle claiming victory, the Serbs in particular remember this episode as a bitter defeat, in which their Prince Lazar was killed.[3] By 1392 all of Serbia was under their control, but Sarajevo did not fall until 1451, and parts of northern Bosnia remained out of Ottoman jurisdiction until as late as 1527. The Ottomans and their rival neighbors the Hungarians traded large sections of territory back and forth during several decades of struggle during this period.

The facts of the conquest of the Balkans throw into question part of the conventional wisdom about Islamicization in Bosnia—that it was a rapid and wholesale process. Rather, scholarly opinion at present favors a slow and relatively "shallow" conversion process. Early Ottoman census figures in Bosnia seem to support this view. In 1468 there were only 332 households registered as Muslim, compared to 37,125 as Christian; in 1485

3. Lazar was not at the time actually the king of Serbia, although modern-day Serbs seem to remember him as such. Instead, the main claimants to the Serbian throne were in fact the Bosnian king Tvrtko and another nobleman named Marko.

Christian households still outnumbered Muslim 30,552 to 4,134 (showing also a significant net loss of population in the region). Even in the 1520s a majority of Bosnians were still listed as Christian, and the urban population was generally more Islamicized than the rural population (Malcolm 1994, 52–53). Furthermore, there were other factors at play within Bosnia that affected the religious composition of the realm. One such factor was the overall depopulation referred to earlier; another was regional population transfer, with many Christians leaving Bosnia for Serbia or Croatia and many Muslim Slavs or non-Slavs migrating or being relocated to Bosnia and nearby areas. Most notably, the Serb departure from the Kosovo region led the Turks to transfer large numbers of Albanian Muslims into the vicinity, which is, of course, a matter of great concern and nationalistic outrage to many Serbs today—that their beloved and historical "heartland" has an Albanian majority.

If the conversion of Bosnians to Islam was less dramatic than is often supposed, it seems also to have been less deep or total. In fact, at least one source on Bosnian history maintains that "*acceptance* is a better word than *conversion* to describe what happened" (Donia and Fine 1994, 44). This stems, goes the argument, from the fact that before Islam arrived Bosnian Christianity was "peculiarly weak and fragmented." Further, Bosnians in this period converted not only to Islam but also to Orthodox Christianity with a concomitant decline in the Catholic and Bosnian Churches, although there were also cases of conversion *from* Islam and Orthodoxy *to* Catholicism. This refutes another aspect of the conventional wisdom about Bosnian religion—that Islamicization was the defining religious dynamic of medieval Bosnia and that it was predominantly or exclusively members of the Bosnian Church who became Islamicized. In reality this conversion process was multidirectional; converts came from multiple sources.

In the end, however, we cannot overestimate the impact that the Ottoman period had upon the ethnic situation in Bosnia and the Balkans. First and foremost, except for the very earliest stage of Turkish authority, Bosnia was acknowledged once again as an integral domain, an administrative unit within the empire. Beyond that it is important to remember that the Ottomans did not organize their empire into ethnic or national groups but into religious communities or millets. As a result, religion became a, if not the, primary organizing and identifying principle in Bosnia and Turkish Europe, and strong forces existed to encourage assimilation, if not conversion, to Ottoman/Muslim culture. First, Ottoman millet policy provided for greater tax and other burdens on non-Muslims and various legal privileges for Muslims. Bosnian Muslims enjoyed disproportionate, but not exclusive, benefits under this arrangement, such as access to feudal estates and titles like *agha* and *beg.* In addition, the taking of slaves from among conquered peoples, who could achieve freedom upon conversion, and the growth of a significant Muslim urban culture contributed to the spread of Islam among the local citizenry. Conversion to Islam could also be interpreted as a political statement of the times, a confirmation of preference for Ottoman rule over Hungarian.

Also, Turkish rule left a considerable mark on the non-Muslim elements of society. The millet system reinforced the distinction between the two major Christian churches and resulted in an official preference for the Orthodox over the Catholic. Part of the reason was no doubt the identification of Catholicism with the Ottomans' main competition in Central Europe, the Austrian empire. Thus, the Orthodox community actually thrived and grew during the early Ottoman period, while Catholics was constantly under pressure, many fleeing north to friendlier places. Interestingly, Ottoman rule helped to install non-Muslims in portions of Bosnia, which provides a basis for territorial claims today. Although, as mentioned, many non-Muslims departed from Bosnia under Ottoman rule, other non-Muslims were welcomed into Bosnia, particularly to depopulated sections such as northern Bosnia and what would become known as the "Krajina" (for "frontier" or "military border"). Consequently, the ethnic distribution of the region was reshaped, and areas that had previously been predominantly one group or another changed hands or became mixed. The effect in Kosovo, as mentioned, is immensely important in today's context.

Slavic Nationalism(s) in the Nineteenth Century

The nineteenth century was the century of nationalism in much of Europe, and nowhere more so than in the Balkans. The peoples of the Balkans found themselves in the middle, literally, of a shifting international context. The Ottoman Empire was in sharp decline, presenting opportunities for local expressions of self-determination. At the same time, new foreign powers were ascending, in particular the Austrian, or Habsburg, empire to the north and Russia to the west. Already, well before the nineteenth century (1683–99) Austria had driven the Turks out of much of southeast Europe and captured Hungary for itself and adventured as far as Serbia (which necessarily entailed crossing Bosnia). As a result, Muslims from more northern lands sought refuge in Bosnia, increasing the Muslim population there and intensifying social problems as well. By the eighteenth century at the latest Bosnia and the Balkans were becoming restless, with local tax revolts breaking out in various sites.

Interestingly enough, Austria's initial push into Bosnia was met by serious resistance from concerted Muslim and Christian forces, again suggesting less division than unity between the two when it came to outside threats to local political and economic interests. Austria eventually succeeded in penetrating deep into Bosnia and Serbia but withdrew in 1791 in exchange for Ottoman recognition of their status as "protector" of the Christians within Turkish territory. The opening years of the nineteenth century saw the first serious uprising in Serbia, which eventually led to Ottoman acceptance of limited autonomy for the province. This development should not be misinterpreted, however, as entirely a modern-style ethnic movement; rather, it seems to have commenced with an intra-Muslim protest to reforms by local Muslim (Janissary) notables against distant central Ottoman power, much like many of the contemporary activities among the Kurds, not at all ethnic but purely political. A secondary uprising broke out among the Serbian Christians, but it too was more anti-Ottoman than anti-Muslim, although Malcolm reports of forced baptisms of Slavic as well as Turkish Muslims.

Thus, despite the fact that these early nineteenth century events were not ethnic in the modern sense and that the ethnic groups as we know them today had not yet coalesced with the distinct identities they currently possess, we can see in the activities some of the foundations of both the groups and the bases of their conflicts. For instance, that the majority of the toiling class in Serbia was Christian and the central authorities Muslim helped to emphasize that social difference. That many Serbian Muslims fled to Bosnia further helped to identify Bosnia with the "Turk" enemy. And that, in 1815, Serbia was granted its own assembly and elected prince helped to define the outlines and fan the flames of Serbian nationalism for the future, which in turn would largely determine the course of interethnic relations in the region. Finally, that Serbian Orthodox Christianity came to be perceived by the Ottomans as part and parcel of Serbian resistance and resulted in the shift of official state preference away Orthodoxy and toward Catholicism can be implicated in the differentiation and opposition of Orthodox and Catholic identities upon which, as we will see, "Serb" and "Croat" ethnic identities were originally premised.

Bosnia, too, was restive in this period, but this early discontent was no more ethnic, in fact far less, than in Serbia. A significant portion of the population had converted over the centuries, and many enjoyed the perquisites thereof, including roles in the Janissary corps and offices like the *kapetanije* (captaincies), the military administrative positions in the Bosnian frontier. After the corps was eliminated in the 1827 Ottomans reforms, Husein Kapetan in 1830 led a three-year insurgency against the state that was supported by most of Bosnia's *kapetans.* At the same time, the economic conditions in Bosnia were deteriorating, with the entire economy and infrastructure relatively backward and rent and other exactions on the peasants escalating. Landlords used the disorder after war and reform to attempt to exploit their inferiors more utterly. Although this burden may have seemed to fall disproportionately on the Christian population (the vast majority of landowners with serfs being Muslim, well into the twentieth century), it weighed heavily upon the Muslim peasants too. In essence the real dynamic of stratification and inequality was not Muslim-Christian but gentry-peasant, but the latter could and would be translated into the former. At first, of course, whenever possible the local nobility strove to divert popular unrest against central authorities, but, as central authority weakened and withdrew, as it did through the middle of the century, the conflict became focused as a matter of the lower classes of society against the local aristocracy, which was, consequentially, largely Muslim. Thus, as the century progressed and class distinctions began to translate into religious—and religious into communal—distinctions, relations between Muslims and Christians in Bosnia hardened.

This ethnogenesis process entailed a new equation of religious with national identities and boundaries. Specifically, in distinction to *Muslim, Orthodox* was coming to be coterminous with *Serb* and *Catholic* with *Croat.* This process was less one of discovery than of creation of identity, as is evidenced in such stories as that of Teofil Petranovic, an Orthodox teacher in Sarajevo in the 1860s who assembled a team to go among Orthodox villagers and convince them to abandon the self-referent *hriscani* (the local word for *Orthodox*) and henceforth refer to themselves as "Serbs." Naturally enough, the cultural markers that distinguished the three religious communities, which had little or no valence in and of themselves, began to take on political and ethnic significance and to serve as boundary conditions for the emerging new national identities.

Thus, it was with the Serbs and Croats that ethnogenesis first took hold among the south Slavs and this partly because both groups had members not only in multicultural Bosnia but also spread out across the two major regional empires. Nationalism commences, then, as a sort of reunification and irredentism movement, to bring together the diasporic national community (while at the same time creating or inventing that community). One famous example of this is the document known as *Nacertanije* (Outline) written by the Serb political theorist Ilija Garasanin in 1844. The essay expresses the belief that it is necessary to "ensure national survival by a mission to unite Serbs in scattered parts of the Habsburg and Ottoman empires"; it also foresees the crucial role of "other neighboring peoples" in realizing this goal (qtd. in Dragnich 1992, 7). It is possible to anticipate in these attitudes the doctrine that is often referred to as "Greater Serbia," which is also regularly blamed for much of what has transpired in the present Bosnian and general Balkan war.

Serb and Croat nationalisms presented alternative, and in some ways opposing, interpretations of ethnic identity and national destiny, not only for themselves (which alone would have pitted them against each other in contested areas) but also for all southern Slavs. Croat nationalists like Ante Starcevic and Josip Frank advanced the argument that "Croat" was not only a distinct identity in the Balkan region of the empire but *the* distinct identity in the region. According to Starcevic, all southern Slavs were Croats, including the Serbs, who did not rate a distinct name or a distinct culture; he considered the very name "Serb" to have ignoble, even slave, derivations (as *Slavo-Serb*), and he rejected the validity of the Cyrillic alphabet. His follower Josip Frank was a virulent anti-Serb, opposing any alliance or unity between the two groups and organizing persecution of Serbs within Croatian territory. For its part Serb nationalism also had its extreme and exclusivistic side. The best-known early Serb nationalist was Vuk Karadzic (coincidentally sharing a surname with the leader of Bosnian Serbs in the current conflict), who in 1849 published a treatise entitled "Serbs All and Everywhere," in which he professes that Serb identity and culture is the primary and genuine southern Slavic one and that Croats are really Serbs.

This clash of nationalistic claims is apparent, for example, in the school curricula and textbooks of the time. Jelavich (1990) finds that these claims were sometimes competitive, sometimes contradictory. Serb books tended to take not only Serbia but also Montenegro, Macedonia, Bosnia and Hercegovina, at least part of Dalmatia, and sometimes part or all of Albania and Croatia itself as "Serb lands"; naturally, all yugo-Slavs were portrayed as Serb. Croat books obviously taught that Croatia, Slavonia, Dalmatia, and Istria were distinctly Croat territory and that Serbia, Montenegro, and Macedonia were foreign lands; they also often claimed Bosnia-Hercegovina. Both sets of literature looked back nationalistically at their histories—to the first settlement of the Slavs to the medieval kingdoms to the Christian conversion—although the Serb texts tended to be more ethnonationalist, while the Croat ones were more pan-Slavic. Even here the differences between the traditionally exclusivistic Serb and inclusivistic Croat positions were perceptible.[4]

The claims and counterclaims of the two groups over national and cultural primacy would be interesting and important enough in their own right and would be and no doubt have been a necessary and sufficient condition for subsequent ethnic conflict in the Balkans, especially but not exclusively in territory that they cohabit or contest historically. Even more to the point, however, is the relation of these claims to the third group, the Bosnian Muslims. Both nationalisms inevitably embraced the Muslims as well: Croats defined Muslims as Croats, Serbs defined Muslims as Serbs. For their own part the majority of Bosnian Muslims not only asserted their own unique identity but asserted it on different grounds than their fellow Slavs, "as confessional, leaving the issue of their national identity an open question well into the socialist era" (Donia and Fine 1994, 110).

In other words, while they regarded themselves as a *distinct* group, they did not regard themselves as a *national* group; they were followers of a faith, not members of an ethnic group. Interestingly, and significantly, although most Bosnian Muslims declined the invitation to identify and to affiliate as Croat or Serb, some accepted, and when they did, they more often chose Croat. Finally, and perhaps most interestingly and tellingly, since it also accords with early Bosnian behavior in regard to religion, Donia and Fine write that "Muslims changed from one national identity to another with about the same ease that an American might change political parties" (1994, 111). Ethnicity in Bosnia, in this formative stage, was a remarkably fluid proposition, but this would end as social boundaries firmed and grievances acquired more substance and depth through time.

A turning point in Balkan nationalism came in the 1870s, as the independence movement in Serbia gained momentum and peasant-landlord (which rhetorically and more often than not empirically meant Christian-Muslim) tensions in Bosnia grew. Bosnian peasant uprisings, initially in response to intensified exactions such as taxes and conscription, in their

4. For more, see Jelavich 1990.

early phase involved Christians and Muslims alike; however, aggravating factors like the controversy over the construction of an Orthodox cathedral in Sarajevo cast a religious hue on the situation. It is in this period, beginning around 1871, that Josef Koetschet, the Swiss physician who became an advisor to Bosnian governors and helped to revitalize Bosnian Muslim culture by building Muslim schools in Sarajevo and printing school textbooks and a journal entitled *Bosna,* comments that "we first began to see a picture of religious hatred" (qtd. in Malcolm 1994, 130). In 1876 Serbia, which had enjoyed a degree of political autonomy within the Ottoman Empire since the second decade of the nineteenth century, together with Montenegro declared independence from the empire. Russian assistance led to the creation of the state of Serbia in 1878.

Meanwhile, the expansion of Austria-Hungary caused dismay to the Bosnian Muslims, who viewed the development as merely the exchange of one foreign ruler—and this one not Muslim—for another. Accordingly, Bosnian Muslims put up fierce resistance to Austrian occupation, necessitating the commitment of seventy to eighty thousand Austrian troops to the cause. And the Bosnian Christians, who at first welcomed Austria as liberators, soon found themselves disappointed when the new administration did little to reform the social and economic relations in the province: Muslim landlords were largely left in place, and the burdens on peasants were not substantially altered. Instead, ethnic relations were complicated by the introduction of almost one hundred thousand Austrian and Hungarian settlers into Bosnia over the next three decades.

Interestingly, as a preventative to further Serb and Croat nationalism in their new possession, the initial policy of the Habsburg Empire in Bosnia was to encourage Bosnian identity and nationhood. *Bosnjastvo* (Bosnianism) was promoted through support for investigation and preservation of Bosnia's unique customs and history, even if these things were somewhat idealized, if not invented; it was around this time that the theory of Bogomil culture in Bosnia and the symbolic interpretation of the funereal *stecci* was disseminated—at the time to demonstrate Bosnia's uniqueness, subsequently to demonstrate Bosnia's inferiority. Simultaneously, Austrian authorities sought to deflect any tendency toward political activism in Bosnia by strengthening (yet harnessing) religious identities and institutions of all three denominations. This was to prove less successful and somewhat counterproductive—not eliminating politicization of identity and its concomitant demands but, rather, splitting it along religious lines and providing the Bosnian (or, essentially, Muslim) nation with the symbols of nationhood, like the *stecci,* which it needed to justify itself.

It was only now that a modern Bosnian-Muslim nationalism begins to emerge, partly as a response to the reasons cited earlier and partly as a response to the social and political challenges presented by Austrian rule. One vehicle for this process was the journal *Bosnjak* (The Bosnian) begun in 1891 by Mehmed-beg Kapetanovic, which expressed the view that Bosnians were neither Serbs nor Croats but a distinct, though related, people and that both Croat and Serb claims to some sort of central or primordial status vis-à-vis the southern Slavs were fallacious. It remarked, for example:

> Whereas the Croats argue that the Orthodox are our greatest enemies and that Serbdom is the same as Orthodoxy, the Serbs wear themselves out calling our attention to some bogus history, by which they have Serbianized the whole world. We shall never deny that we belong to the South Slav family; but we shall remain Bosnians, like our forefathers, and nothing else. (Qtd. in Malcolm 1994, 148)

On a more practical level Muslim leaders also took advantage of traditional and not-so-traditional institutions to organize Bosnian Muslim activity and identity. Among the traditional institutions available were, of course, Muslim schools and *waqf* organizations. Muslim leaders, especially around Mostar, also pressed the government with relatively modern methods such as petitions and political delegations for more freedom to manage Muslim educational, charitable, and cultural institutions. Although such activities were opposed by the Austrian authorities, some concessions were won by Muslim activists, such as the establishment of an office of leadership over all Bosnian Muslims independent of central Muslim/Ottoman power, *the Reis-ul-ulema* (head of the *ulema* [religious community]). This comparatively "modern" office was joined by other, distinctly modern developments in Bosnian ethnogenesis, including the shift of nationalistic energy away from the religious sphere and toward the political-economic. This shift was marked by the rise of the (mainly Muslim) landowning class as the vanguard of national activity; as Donia and Fine maintain, the turn-of-the-century Muslim autonomy movement "established the precedent that religious concerns of the community . . . were superseded by the secular interests of the Muslims' political leaders" (1994, 108). The formalization of this new political reality was the inauguration of the first Muslim political party in December 1906, the Muslim National Organization; the mission of the party, however, was still premodern, or pre-ethnic—not to mobilize and liberate the Bosnian Muslim people but "to protect the archaic privileges of the Muslim landlords against the demands of Christian peasants for agrarian reform."

The ethnopolitical activity among the Bosnian Muslims was matched by activity among the Serbs and Croats, which was further influenced by the agitation of these ethnic groups outside Bosnia. A Serb newspaper called *Srpska Rijec* (Serbian World) was followed in 1907 by a Serb political party, the Serbian National Organization (SNO), which, like its Muslim counterpart, drew most of its support from and found most of its interests with the upper classes; understandably, SNO political leaders did not insist on agrarian reform that would have improved the conditions of Christian peasants and in fact were able to enter into an alliance with Muslim landowners. Croat nationalism had, if anything, an even smaller social base in its early life, emanating principally from the small intelligentsia and middle class and from the Franciscan order. Representing the two distinct interests of these segments of Croat society, two political parties took shape, one secular in outlook (the Croatian National Union, founded in February 1908) and one clearly Catholic in orientation (the Croatian Catholic Association, founded in January 1910). Like the SNO, the Croatian parties, particularly the former, sought and occasionally made alliances with the Muslim contingent.

It must be stressed that, while there was some tension and some grievance between the three emerging ethnic groups, there was no generalized ethnic hatred and no distinct ethnic conflict between them. Observers at the time, such as the Englishman H. E. Thomson, marveled at just this fact; in writing of the Christians in Bosnia, he stated:

> It is strange that they should bear so little hatred to their former oppressors, and the explanation lies probably in the fact that they are all of the same race. Whatever the reason may be it full bears out the contention of all who have studied the country in Turkish times, that . . . the deplorable condition of the people was due to agrarian rather than to religious causes, and that if these causes could be removed, the ill-feeling engendered by them would gradually die out. (1897, 180–81)

Although it appears that the removal of economic/agrarian grievances was not sufficient to prevent political mobilization and eventually conflict and war along ethnoreligious lines, it is interesting and important to note that such conflict, and the animosity upon which it is premised, has not been an ancient and continuous aspect of Balkan life. Rather, paralleling the solidification of particularistic ethnic politics in Bosnia and the Balkans as a whole were other more ethnically inclusive philosophies as well.

Pan-Slavic Nationalisms

"Monoethnic" nationalisms were not, however, the only "cultural" ideologies in the air. Pan-Slavic ideologies and movements took as their subject not any one ethnic group but the entirety of the southern Slavic family. One of these southern Slav movements aimed at less than full national sovereignty but, instead, for a level of recognition for the Slavs who found themselves within the Austria-Hungary Empire. Based on the fact that the Hungarians had won a sort of autonomy within the Austrian empire in 1848, leading to the so-called Dual Monarchy and the name Austria-Hungary, this Slavic doctrine, known as Trialism, sought a similar status for the Habsburg Slavs, a kind of "third" nationality with explicit rights and privileges within the empire. Although this notion appealed most strongly to Croats, as the largest and oldest south Slav group of the empire, it attracted others as well, as evidenced by the formation of the Serbo-Croat Coalition in 1905. The emperor viewed such developments with suspicion, however, particularly as the imperial intention was now clearly not only to limit the rights of Balkan nationalities but, even more, to annex Bosnia and Hercegovina—and Serbia, if possible—permanently to the empire.

Another still more inclusive and more important national ideal of the age envisioned all southern Slavs, within whatever state at the moment, as one nation. This movement became known as "Yugoslavism" and can be traced to the early-nineteenth-century concept of "Illyrianism," which ensued from the nationalistic concepts of the French Revolution as it impacted upon the Balkans. Both Illyrianism and Yugoslavism enjoyed most support from, and arose from, Croats. Illyrianism and Yugoslavism were explicit attempts to imagine a broader and more inclusive identity based on shared rather than differentiated cultural and historical premises—"belief in the ethnic, linguistic, and cultural unity of the South Slavs, support for their unification, and/or the belief that the South Slavs are or should become one nation" (Djilas 1991, 15).

Illyrianism as practiced by Ljudevit Gaj in the 1830s focused on language, in particular on organizing a common South Slav literary language. At the time, three main dialects of Serbo-Croatian were spoken in various parts of the realm—stokavian, cakavian, and kajkavian; Croats alone spoke the latter two, while Croats and Serbs shared the former. Thus, the early Illyrianists promoted stokavian as the national language of yugo-Slavs, despite the fact that many, including many of the Illyrianists themselves, did not speak it at all or as their first language. Accordingly, they used such devices as reading circles, "didactic poetry," and literary journals like *Danica ilirska* (Illyrian Morning Star) to further interest and familiarity in the language.

Yugoslavism proper came a few decades later under the leadership of Bishop Josip Strossmajer and Franjo Racki. Also a pan-Slavic "superethnic" movement, it was based on a "*nad-plemenska* (supratribal) national consciousness" in which the Serbs and Croats were considered "tribes" of one common Yugoslav nation. Strossmajer in particular poured considerable energy and wealth into the promotion—no, the realization—of this idea, supporting schools, books and journals, cultural research and exhibits, and other kinds of Yugoslav experiences. One important element of this movement, lacking in the Illyrian movement, was a political party, the National Party, which even succeeded in gaining agreement to a future "allied state" (Banac 1984, 91).

Both pan-Slavic ideologies, though no more or less valid than any other attempt at national mobilization, were especially problematic in relation to Serbia. First, it never penetrated very deeply into the Croat population, remaining rather an elite and academic affair. Most Serbs were less than enthusiastic about Illyrianism, partly because they already spoke stokavian—which many considered their *ethno*national language—and partly because they rejected the Westernizing and Catholicizing potential of it. In fact, it went against the Serbs' own well-advanced national cultural movement, which had assembled a body of Serb literature, history, and traditions and which itself proclaimed a rival pan-Slavism in the form of "Serbism." As Teodor Pavlovic wrote: "We feel that we can never accept the terms Illyrian, Illyrian language, Illyrian people, where it concerns the historical appellation, language, and nationality of those people of our lineage. . . . Why, these people are by descent, name, and language all true Serbs, who call themselves Bosnians, Montenegrins, Slavonians, Dalmatians, and so on, by their home regions" (qtd. in Banac 1984, 79). Serb scholars like Vuk Karadzic were already deeply involved in their own Serb cultural/linguistic projects, and of course politically Serbia was by mid-century engrossed in its own nation-state genesis. Pan-Slavisms were either a distraction or an aspect of building sovereign Serbia. Finally, needless to say, at the same time supranational entities of the older type—

namely, multinational empires like Austria-Hungary and the Ottoman Empire—opposed pan-Slavism (as well as more nationalistic Slavic movements) as threats to their own integrity and sovereignty, which of course they were.

War and the Creation of Yugoslavia

Nevertheless, Yugoslavism came by the turn of the century to look like the best bet for national recognition and perhaps even statehood. And it was generally appreciated that such a state could not survive, and probably not come into existence, without the support of Serbia and Serbs; they were, after all, the largest and most powerful group and the only one with a state already. Serbia justifiably had its own national interests to consider, which could potentially be advanced within a larger South Slav field; simultaneously, other Slavic groups could look upon Serbia as the Piedmont or the Prussia of Yugoslavs. That Serbia should play such a role is hardly unreasonable, but, by playing this role, the Serbs and the other peoples of Yugoslavia, particularly the Croats as well as the Slovenes, could and conceivably did approach and practice Yugoslavism with very different interpretations and expectations.

Ultimately, events external to the ethnic groups and movements themselves—particularly sweeping international events like war, which cleared away the rubbish of older political structures—played a key role in Balkans political evolution and ethnogenesis. For the Balkans, and especially Bosnia, these events began with the 1908 Austrian annexation of Bosnia and Hercegovina. For its part Serbia began to take its own defense and interests more seriously, for example, raising additional revenue for war. New Serbian nationalist groups like Narodna Odbrana (National Defense), Ujedjenje ili Smrt (Unification or Death), and Crna Ruka (Black Hand) became active. And, perhaps most prophetically, Serbian leaders pressed their territorial claims, especially the one for "sufficient Bosnian or Hercegovinian territory that a connection would be established with Montenegro" (Banac 1984, 66). Meanwhile, Yugoslavism also gained momentum with the formation of "the Croat-Serb or Serb-Croat or Yugoslav Progressive Youth Movement" among college students and led by the Bosnian author Ivo Andric, and of Mlada Bosna (Young Bosnia), both in 1910.

History tells how the heightened nationalism(s) of the Slavs gave rise to a series of wars in the Balkans between 1912 and 1914 and ultimately sparked World War I; there is no need to repeat that familiar story here. Let it suffice to say that both Serbian nationalism and Yugoslavism gained during those years and that these gains were not entirely or necessarily at odds. The growing support and conviction for a Yugoslav state, presupposing a Yugoslav national identity, is evident in this passage from a declaration by Slovenian Yugoslavs in 1913:

> As it is a fact that we Slovenes, Croats and Serbs, constitute a compact linguistic and ethnic group with similar economic conditions, and so indissolubly linked by common fate on a common territory that no one of the three can aspire to a separate future, and in consideration of the fact that among the Slovenes, Croats, and Serbs, the Jugoslav thought is even today strongly developed, we have extended our national sentiments beyond our frontier to the Croats and Serbs. . . . By this we all become members of one united Jugo-slav nation. (Qtd. in Cohen 1993, 10)

In fact, the assassination of Austrian archduke Franz Ferdinand in Sarajevo on June 28, 1914 (the anniversary of the Battle of Kosovo), the spark which ignited World War I, can be traced to Yugoslavism, as the assassin Gavrilo Princip and his gang were affiliated with Mlada Bosna. As a consequence, the brewing hostilities and competitions in Europe boiled over into World War I.

During the war Yugoslavism took a major step through the formation of the Yugoslav Committee, an extragovernmental exile organization (based in Rome and London) composed of leaders of the various major South Slav groups. Pasic sent Serbian representatives to the committee, and there were Slovene members as well, but the committee was dominated by Croats; among its Croat members were Franjo Supilo, Hink Hinkovic, Ivan Mestrovic, and the chairman, Ante Trumbic. The Yugoslav Committee, being not only largely Croat but also explicitly pan-Slavic, naturally rejected Greater Serbianism and advocated instead a kind of "ethnic federalism" in any future Yugoslavia, which put them at cross-purposes with ethnic nationalists, Serb and otherwise. At the same time, a diluted form of pan-Slavism more akin to the old Trialist doctrine was offered in May 1917 by the leader of the Slovenians in the Austrian government, Monsignor Korosec. In this plan, known as the May Declaration, unification of "all the lands in the Monarchy inhabited by Slovenes, Croats, and Serbs" was envisioned, and many in all of these groups, as well as many Bosnians, supported it as the best deal so far. Others, however, saw it as incomplete or as an abandonment of specifically national goals. Either way, it came to nothing, as Austria failed to act on it until it was too late.

The real instrument of South Slav political integration, though, was the July 1917 Corfu Declaration prepared by the Yugoslav Committee, in which the various groups present, together with the Serbian government, agreed to unite in a "constitutional, democratic, and parliamentary monarchy with the [Serbian] Karadjordjevic dynasty at the head" (qtd. in Cohen 1993, 26). This was the breakthrough that was to lead not only to the demand for a single unified Yugoslav state but also to the recognition and acceptance of that state by the architects of the postwar peace. Yet two stumbling blocks stood in the way of genuine Yugoslavism and an enduring state built upon it: incompatible expectations regarding how the state would be governed and the fact that Yugoslav identity was more a goal, a "remote vision," than a reality—an identity that needed to be carefully constructed before it could be handed the reigns of a state and which faced many obstacles, old and new, to that construction.

So it came to be that a Yugoslav state was added to the map of Europe. On October 29, in an attempt to deliver the Allies a fait accompli (something the Kurds might have done but failed to do), the Croatian parliament, which until then had still been subordinate to the Austrian empire, seceded from the latter and declared its allegiance to a state of Slovenes, Croats, and Serbs. Finally, on December 1, 1918, Prince Alexander, of the Serbian Karadjordjevic dynasty, formally announced the creation of the "Kingdom of Serbs, Croats, and Slovenes." The state was *not* originally named Yugoslavia but was, rather, an explicitly multiethnic, though ideally monoracial and mononational, entity.

Further, in addition to the three named ethnic groups in the new state, other nations, protonations, and nationalities or minorities, Slav and non-Slav, joined or were swept into it; the former included Vojvodina, Montenegro, and Bosnia, while the latter case included Hungarians, Albanians, and others. To be precise, the "tripartite" kingdom was roughly 42 percent Serb and Montenegrin (a lively debate exists about whether these are one ethnic group or two), 23 percent Croat, 8 percent Slovene, 5 percent Macedonian, 5 percent Bosnian Muslim, and 4 percent Albanian; confessionally, the population was about 47 percent Orthodox, 39 percent Catholic, and 11 percent Muslim. This ethnic, religious, and cultural diversity alone would be enough to make coexistence and political cooper-

Kingdom of Serbs, Croats, and Slovenes, 1918–29. (From *Bosnia and Hercegovina,* by Robert Donia and John Fine, p. 123. Copyright © 1994 by Columbia University Press. Reprinted with permission of the publisher.)

ation highly problematic, but more crucial were differences in political orientation and interpretation between the major groups. Having borne a state, the practical question of what sort of state it should be was inescapable. The Corfu Declaration had been relatively, and probably intentionally, vague on the mechanisms and structures of the eventual Yugoslav state. The Croats in particular, in drafting the declaration, had pushed for more ethnonational autonomy, suggesting, for example, that the future constitution require ratification by a majority of each ethnic group; Croats and Slovenes both would repeat this kind of preference throughout the Yugoslav period. Serbs, on the other hand, tended to negate ethnicity and to support the notion of a simple majority of Yugoslavs of whatever ethnicity to make political decisions, since it was they who stood to gain the most in a system that downplayed particularistic identities in favor of an ostensibly majoritarian ideology.

In any event a basic ideological disagreement lay at the heart of the new Yugoslav state. Croats and Slovenes wanted, and came away from Corfu believing they had gotten, a federal or even confederal state, with strong recognition and protection of ethnonational rights and prerogatives. Serbs, however, wanted and expected a strong centralized unitary state, based in Belgrade and largely organized along Serb lines. Whether or not this was part of some Greater Serbia plot or merely a difference in style or perspective is really immaterial, for it is not unreasonable to pursue national (by which we mean, in this case, state) integration in such instances of cultural pluralism. Either way, however, it led to disappointments and frustrations that were to have a highly corrosive effect on ethnic and social relations in the state. Accordingly, when the so-called Vivodan constitution was written on June 28, 1921 (again, the Kosovo anniversary), the centralized unitary model won the day, and a Serb-dominated polity was inaugurated. The state supposedly consisted of the "three-named Serbo-Croatian-Slovenian people," but most of the instruments of power were held by the Serbs. Besides the monarchy itself, the office of prime minister was filled exclusively by Serbs, who in turn often issued appointed local officials.

It should go without saying that there were great political differences in the kingdom, inside and outside Bosnia. By and large Bosnians had supported the constitution, guaranteeing as it did the territorial-administrative integrity of Bosnia-Hercegovina. Within the new state, however, many Muslims felt the need for a new Muslim political organization, and a number of parties were formed, including the Muslim Organization, the Yugoslav Muslim Democracy Party, and the Muslim Union. But the most important, and the only party to gain more than a fraction of a percentage point in the first Yugoslav assembly elections, was the Yugoslav Muslim Organization (YMO), established in February 1919 in Sarajevo. A party of urban middle-class as well as traditional elite landowning Muslims, it was split initially over its position on federalism versus centralism. One faction, led by the first president of the YMO, Ibrahim Maglajlic, supported the centralized Serb-style state that the kingdom was becoming; the other wing, headed by the man who came to dominate the party, Mehmed Spaho, sought to maintain an independent Bosnian presence and identity within the Yugoslav state and found itself, therefore, naturally in concert with Croatian and Slovenian opinion on the structure of the state. Thus, once again, history placed the Bosnian Muslims in the camp of the Croats, in opposition to the Serbs.

On the other hand, social issues, especially agrarian ones, continued to be sore spots in Bosnia, and reform, as can be discerned from the support base and program of the YMO, was slow in arriving. Early in 1919 King Alexander had committed himself to the abolition of serfdom (which was still in effect at that remarkably late date), the redistribution of rural property, and the compensation of large landowners who were to lose their estates. The YMO did what it could to delay and soften the appropriate legislation: serfdom was not fully ended until 1931, and the party managed to arrange handsome remuneration for the landlords. Not a little of the unrest that would turn ethnic actually originated here in economic and "class" contradictions, with the (mostly Christian, hence Serb or Croat) peasantry perceiving the (mostly Muslim) landlords as obstacles and enemies of their liberation and equality; in truth, Muslim peasants fared no better than Christian peasants, but, as often happens, the lines of mobilization and identity formation would follow ethnic rather than class contours.

At any rate, in an effort to literally efface ethnonationalism, instead of recognizing the ethnonational territories of Croatia, Serbia, and Slovenia, the state was divided into thirty-three *oblasts,* or provinces, within which, interestingly and because of the work of Spaho, only Bosnia was still recognizable as a unit. These kinds of policies only fueled the suspicions of ethnonationalists and enabled even more extreme positions. For example, the Croatian Peasant Party, founded by the brothers Stjepan and Ante Radic, maintained a Croat nationalist stand based on the "authentic" identity and traditions of rural Croatia. Similarly, Stojan Protic's Serbian Popular Radical Party represented the extremists of Serb nationalism; in fact, Protic has been quoted as saying in regard to the "Bosnian problem": "Leave that to us. We have the solution for Bosnia. . . . When our army crosses the Drina, we will give the Turks [local Muslims] twenty-four hours, or even forty-eight hours, of time to return to their ancestral religion. Those who do not wish to do so are to be cut down, as we did in Serbia earlier" (qtd. in Cigar 1995, 17). Qualifying his remarks, he explained that the Muslims would not necessarily all be killed, but "there can no longer be any Turks [Muslims] in Bosnia. They can flee across the Sava [River, into Croatia], or wherever."

The Rise and Fall and Rise and Fall of Yugoslavia

The troubles of Yugoslavia was destined to become the tragedy of Yugoslavia. The proximal manifestation of this tragedy was the assassination of Stjepan Radic, who had become a member of parliament, on June 20, 1928. But the more pervasive one was the ongoing and increasing tension between the federalists (and separatists)—which means roughly for our purposes the Croats—and the centralists (and, after a fashion, supremacists)—which means roughly for our purposes the Serbs. Bosnians, especially Bosnian Muslims, tried in various ways to adapt to the situation: by founding their own ethnic organizations and parties, by welcoming Yugoslavism as an end to divisiveness, by attempting to play the middle position between the Serb and Croat factions in the government (thus making themselves a desirable political ally in the parliament to be courted by one side or the other), and by identifying with the lesser of the two evils from the Bosnian point of view (i.e., the Croats). In fact, all the Bosnian Muslim members of parliament in 1924 identified themselves as Croats except Spaho, who insisted on his Yugoslav identity; even so, the contentious nature of Bosnian identity is illustrated by the fact that, while Spaho called himself Yugoslav, his two brothers called themselves Croat and Serb, respectively—clearly no biological or descent distinction.

Be that as it may, King Alexander became convinced that stronger Yugoslav medicine was needed to suave the wounds of the fledgling state and nation: on January 6, 1929, he dismissed the National Assembly, nullified the constitution, and declared a dictatorship with himself as head of state. One of his first decrees was to change the name of the Kingdom of Serbs, Croats, and Slovenes to the "Kingdom of Yugoslavia." For internal political boundaries he crafted nine *banovinas* that intentionally eschewed traditional names and boundaries. In a certain sense, it appears that Serbia and Bosnia suffered more than Croatia and Slovenia (and also Macedonia) from this scheme, as the latter three are still partially visible on the new map, yet the borders were drawn such that Serbs constituted a majority in six of the nine units.

Finally, in an effort to instill the new Yugoslav identity King Alexander banned political parties and traditional symbols and manifestations of ethnic identity, such as flags and songs of ethnic, regional, or religious character. Only the Yugoslav flag was to be flown, and only gestures of Yugoslav nationality were to be made. As his hand-chosen premier, Gen. Petar Zivkovic, explained: "The old traditions and separate flags of the

Serbs, Croats, and Slovenes belong to the past. The true Yugoslav acknowledges the national tricolor only and does not know any racial or religious differences among the nation's inhabitants" (qtd. in Cohen 1993, 16). As might be predicted, this situation was more alarming to the Serbs than to the Croats and Bosnian Muslims. For their part many Croats welcomed the suspension of the Vivodan Constitution as a first step toward greater autonomy, or at least a diminution in Serb hegemony; as we will see, however, not all Croats were satisfied. The Bosnian Muslims in general also supported the king's actions. Reorganization of the kingdom, while it cost the Muslims the territorial integrity of Bosnia, also gave them a religious benefit: all Muslims in the state of Yugoslavia were placed under a single *Reis-ul-ulema* (based in Belgrade), thus achieving a greater Muslim integration than at any time since the departure of the Ottoman Empire.

The sense that Alexander's actions were temporary, however, was dashed when a new constitution was published in 1931, making Yugoslavia a hereditary monarchy and defining the political structure of the state, which was euphemistically deemed "guided democracy." Serb, Croat, Slovene and Muslim "ethnicists" alike were upset by this development; in particular, a radical Croat fringe continued to agitate for greater Croatian autonomy or even separation. Among the new generation of Croat leadership were Ante Pavelic and Vladko Macek. Macek rose to the head of the Croatian Peasant Party, which continued to be a force in Yugoslavian politics after Radic's death, and from within the party Macek pursued a course of action to expand if not liberate Croatia. In November 1932 he and the party issued the so-called resolution demanding an end to the autocracy and to Serb domination of the state. Slovenian and Bosnian leaders (including Spaho) made similar assertions and were arrested for it, along with Macek Subsequently, Slovenian and Bosnian resistance to the monarchy abated; the Slovene People's Party retracted the earlier forceful statement and issued a new one, maintaining that their demands "for a reorganization of the state should not be interpreted as an attack on the existing Yugoslav state and denying any connection with the Slovene federalists or Italian fascists" (Dragnich 1992, 76).

Macek's rhetoric was more inflammatory and more widely disseminated. To the international press he commented that Yugoslavia was "like a sick man with an incurable disease who certainly will die. That death will liberate Croatia" (qtd. in Dragnich 1992, 75). But his was not the most extreme position: Ante Pavelic and another contingent of Croats organized the Ustasha (Insurrectionists), a Croat ultranationalist group that favored

Banovine of Yugoslavia, 1929, and Banovina of Croatia, 1939. (Reprinted from *The Contested Country,* by Aleksa Djilas [Cambridge, Mass.: Harvard University Press, 1991], p. 130, by permission of Harvard University Press. Adapted from *A Short History of the Yugoslav Peoples,* by Fred Singleton [New York: Cambridge University Press, 1985], 159, by permission of Cambridge University Press.)

total independence for Croatia through the destruction of Yugoslavia. Most immediately, a Ustasha team (in cooperation, according to Cohen, with the Internal Macedonian Revolutionary Organization), assassinated King Alexander during a visit to France on October 9, 1934.

Yugoslavia was not destroyed by this action; rather, the short-term effect was a lessening of central, monarchical control and a certain openness to popular political organization. Macek was released from prison, some political parties were allowed to form, and a new (but relatively weak) government was established. But this left Croat nationalists unfulfilled, and Croat-Serb tensions remained the defining dynamic in the state. In the medium term the Croat ultranationalists got some measure of what they sought: Yugoslavian federalism and Croatian autonomy. In

1939 a change of government placed Dragisa[5] Cvetkovic in the prime ministership, and he succeeded in concluding an agreement with Macek for power sharing between Yugoslavia and Croatia. The Cvetkovic-Macek *Sporazum* (Agreement) of August 20, 1939, redefined Croatia's territory and its prerogatives within the multinational state. Croatia was restored as an administrative unit (*banovina*) with something of its traditional boundaries through the addition of parts of Slavonia, Dalmatia, and Bosnia-Hercegovina to its territory. Within its territory Croats gained considerable power over their own affairs, except those with international ramifications (foreign policy, war, and international trade).

On several counts this arrangement did not bode well, however. Bosnia (or the *banovinas* into which Bosnia had been divided in 1929) lost in the deal; in fact, the crown rejected a plan—a remarkably familiar plan—by Cvetkovic and Macek essentially to divide Yugoslavia into Serb, Croat, and Slovene spheres of influence and to "permit" Bosnia to decide whether to join Croatia or Serbia. It seems that, then and now, Serbs and Croats alike could be all too ready to ignore or sacrifice Bosnian territorial integrity and cultural identity to their own ethnopolitical interests. At any rate, the rearrangement also left an ethnic mixture within Croatia that could not help but be a future issue for the ethnic groups of Yugoslavia: roughly one-fourth of the population of the new *banovina* of Croatia would be Serb, not Croat, and a large number of Muslims were subsumed as well. Other smaller ethnic minorities were not seriously considered in the proposal. And, ultimately, we will never know the potential success or failure of the agreement, since it was followed closely by the outbreak of World War II and the fall of the first Yugoslavia.

World War II not only destroyed the kingdom of Yugoslavia, but it also left a bitter aftertaste of ethnic vengeance. After Yugoslavia fell, on April 17, 1941, the state was disassembled, but the Ustasha was permitted to create an "Independent State of Croatia" (known by the initials NDH) with Ante Pavelic as head of state. The NDH state was considerably expanded territorially, including most of Bosnia and Hercegovina. Yet the treatment by the Ustasha state of its ethnic minorities, especially but not exclusively its Serbs, became the defining aspect of the state and one of the principal grievances between Serbs and Croats even today.

The Ustasha state has often been compared unfavorably to Nazi Germany; according to Dragnich, "ranking German officials in Croatia

5. According to Cohen, the first name was Dragljub.

became horrified by the nature and extent of the killing, and came to believe that Pavelic wanted to kill all Serbs" (1992, 103). In fact, Pavelic is reputed to have expressed a "one-third, one-third, one-third" policy in regard to Croatian Serbs, to the effect that one-third would be killed, one-third would be pushed out of Croatia, and one-third would be converted to Catholicism. Whatever the policy underlying Ustasha actions, estimates of Serb casualties at their hands run between five hundred thousand and one million out of a total Croatian Serb population of something less than two million. In haunting reminiscence of 1990s atrocities, whole villages or enclaves were depopulated or destroyed. In addition, Jews and Gypsies were targeted for discrimination and elimination. Although there is considerable disagreement on the numbers, it is possible that 90 percent or more of the thirty thousand Jews in Croatia were killed, most sent off to German concentration camps to perish there.

Bosnian Muslims occupied a more anomalous position vis-à-vis the new NDH state. Many joined the various opposition parties and organizations, and an unknown number died, more as political enemies than ethnic ones. At the same time, many Bosnians chose, as they had at various moments in history, to identify as Croats, which they were invited and encouraged to do by Croat nationalist ideology (Bosnian Muslims being conceived as errant Croats). And, at the extreme, some Muslims participated in the Croat government and war effort: a special Muslim division within the military structure was created to contribute to anti-Serb activity, and members of the YMO were coaxed into collaboration with the Ustasha party. In other words, Bosnian Muslims participated on both sides of the war and found themselves allied in some instances with Croats and in other instances with Serbs.

In opposition to the Ustasha stood two principal organizations, both of which operated within Bosnia and in fact had distinct ties to Bosnia. One was the remnants of Yugoslavia's political leaders and royalty, under the leadership of Colonel Draza Mihailovic, who found himself in Bosnia at the outbreak of the war. He and his group, predominantly Serbs, moved their operations east into Serbia with the aim of liberating Yugoslavia in its previous Serbian-royalist form. This group became known as the Yugoslav Army in the Homeland, or the Homeland Army, or colloquially as "Chetniks." The name Chetnik comes from the legendary Serb bandits who fought for the Serb cause against the Ottoman Empire; the latter-day Chetniks went so far in identifying with their heroes that they "reverted to peasant garb and grew long hair and beards, cultivating the appearance of primitive Serbian brigands" (Donia and Fine 1994, 143). Although they received the recognition of the Yugoslavian government-in-exile, their practices and policies, not surprisingly, earned them support mainly from Serbs. There is even evidence of a Greater Serbia strain to Chetnik politics, such as the documents written by Stevan Moljevic that called upon Serbs "to create and organize a homogeneous Serbia, which must include all the ethnic territory inhabited by Serbs" to be followed by "the cleansing (*ciscenje*) of the land of all non-Serb elements. The thing to do would be to send the offenders on their way: Croats to Croatia, and Muslims to Turkey or Albania" (qtd. in Malcolm 1994, 178–79). While such statements may not have characterized all Chetniks nor Chetnik official policy, they were a force in the movement and in how outsiders viewed the movement.

The other key opposition group was the "Partisans," or Communists, which also emerged and operated out of the hills of Bosnia. A Communist Party had existed in Yugoslavia before the war, led since 1937 by Josip Broz, more commonly known as Tito. The Communist resistance differed from the Chetnik in that it had a definite theory or ideology behind it, one that had appeal (though not total appeal) beyond any one ethnic group. This ideology was quite naturally a derivative of socialist, particularly Soviet, praxis and emphasized the centrality of economics and the social relations of production in the constitution of a new universal culture; Tito's slogan "Bratstvo i jedinstvo" (Brotherhood and unity) meant more than the old Yugoslavism, as can be gathered from these words by the Slovenian Communist Edward Kardelj:

> The growth of universal culture depends on the consciousness of a universal community, or the common interests of all peoples of all languages. And that consciousness will develop parallel with the development of the means of production with the new forms of the social division of labor, with the progress of socialist societal relations. . . . In that sense we are also speaking of the amalgamation of nations in a universal community. (Qtd. in Cohen 1993, 22)

Thus, as for Lenin at the same stage of Communist society building in Russia, Yugoslav socialism necessarily included a nationality policy. The administrative structure of a future Communist Yugoslavia would incorporate national units or republics, as the Soviet Union incorporated its various "socialist republics" along (more or less) national or ethnic lines.

Only by respecting national groups and cultures could the party claim to liberate them, as Tito himself stated:

> The term National Liberation Struggle would be a mere phrase and even a deception if it were not invested with both an all-Yugoslav and national meaning for each people individually. . . . The liberation and emancipation of the Croatians, Slovenes, Serbs, Macedonians, Albanians, Moslems, etc. . . . Therein also lies the essence of the National Liberation War. (Qtd. in Cohen 1993, 23)

Practically speaking, this translated into a proposal for a "federal" state based on national republics or provinces. Two factors cannot be overlooked, however, in assessing this proposal. One is the unquestioned but unstated "leading position" granted to the Communist Party; it would be, like the USSR, a federal state with a strongly monopolistic central government. The other is the lack of specificity concerning precisely how these national units would be demarcated or how they would integrate politically, especially given the previous troubled attempt at Yugoslavism. This imprecision, though, was at least in part strategic, since naming any exact territorial boundaries would only set off the "inter-national" debate and competition again and sap the strength of the movement, and since, in the end, the party did not really believe in ethnicity or nationality. Milovan Djilas, a contemporary and ally of Tito, observed in retrospect:

> We proceeded from the view that national minorities and national ambitions would weaken with the development of socialism, and that they are chiefly a product of capitalist development. . . . Consequently the borders inside our country didn't play a big role. . . . We felt that Yugoslavia would be unified, solid, that one needed to respect languages, cultural differences, and all specificities which, exist, but that they are not essential, and that they can't undermine the whole and the vitality of the country. (Qtd. in Cohen 1993, 24)

As usual, though, for the Bosnian Muslims the implications of this perspective were particularly ambiguous. In the process of recognizing and respecting national rights and identities, would they be defined as a national group? And for all Yugoslav peoples the question of the boundaries of these national units loomed large. In 1936 Kardelj had expressed doubt regarding the national status of Muslims: "We cannot speak of the

Muslims as a nation, but . . . as a special ethnic group" (qtd. in Malcolm 1994, 181). Accordingly, the plan was to create five national units within postwar Yugoslavia, one for each of the five nations of Yugoslavia, which were considered to be Serbs, Croats, and Slovenes, as well as Montenegrins and Macedonians; Bosnia would persist as a separate administrative entity but not as a national republic.

The Second (and Final?) Yugoslavia

The immediate future of Yugoslavia was essentially settled with the arrival of the Soviet army in Belgrade on October 20, 1944. In power now, and having learned their politics from the Soviet Union, the Partisans under Tito proceeded to install their Soviet-style Communist/federalist state in Yugoslavia. In 1945 a Democratic Federative Yugoslavia was declared, with Communists securely in control. In January 1946 a constitution was issued, closely following the USSR's and enshrining the two basic principles of Tito's and general Communist government: the rights of national constituent groups and the leading role of the Communist Party. True to wartime promises, the constitution created six republics, five of them national (Serbia, Croatia, Slovenia, Montenegro, and Macedonia) and the sixth Bosnia-Hercegovina, as well as two "autonomous regions" (Vojvodina and Kosovo) that were associated with Serbia.

Even so, a number of issues were left unsettled, or were even created, in this political division. For one, while the republic names conformed to national conceits, the republic borders did not conform to demographic realities; in fact, it would have been, and remains today, nearly impossible to do so, since the "nations" of Yugoslavia live among one another, either in pluralistic communities or national/ethnic enclaves. For the Serbs this meant that a large percentage of the nation was left outside the national republic, the greatest part of the expatriate community (one and a half million) living in Bosnia but many also in Croatia. Other potential slights to the Serbs were the expansion of Croatia's territory, including some mostly Serb regions (which had just suffered the brutality of the Croat Ustasha) and the partitioning off of what were widely felt to be Serb lands, such as Vojvodina, Kosovo, and even Montenegro. Vojvodina, too, was majority Serb, although its status as a part of Serbia proper was dubious; with a large Hungarian minority Hungary also had claims to it. And the insult in segregating Kosovo from Serbia should be obvious. Never mind that over the ensuing centuries population shifts had left a vast majority of Albani-

Federation of Yugoslavia, 1945–91. (From *Broken Bonds,* by Lenard J. Cohen. Copyright © 1995 by WestviewPress. Reprinted by permission of WestviewPress.)

ans (some 70 percent then and more now, non-Slavs and predominantly Muslims) in this cradle of Serb nationhood and that Tito had even considered turning the province over to Albania.

This mention of Kosovo and its Albanian population raises another issue for socialist Yugoslavia: the presence of various nonnational groups within the nationally conceived republics and state. As noted, the major nations were recognized as *narods* in the vernacular, but other so-called national minorities, or nationalities, such as Hungarians, Romanians, Albanians, and even Bosnian Muslims lived as ethnic groups without national rights in the republics. Bosnia-Hercegovina, the perennially multinational heartland of Yugoslavia, was given republic status but not a national identity, rather, being left divided between Muslims, Serbs, and

Croats, none with a majority. And, as was common practice in the Soviet Union, Tito regularly posted members of one nationality to offices in other national republics, especially Serbs to positions in Croatia.

The question of Bosnian Muslim national identity did not go away. Indeed, Tito and the Communists hoped and believed that a new supranational identity would develop, one that was more than the old (and unhappy) marriage of distinct ethnonations in royal Yugoslavia but which was an organic unity, a true merger and *emergence* brought about by shared economic interests and progress and by socialist institutions. In a way Bosnia was held out as a model for such a process, its multicultural heritage and its openness to Yugoslavism as opposed to ethnonational identity being known and appreciated. And it is true that in the 1940s and 1950s, and before and since, Bosnians were more inclined to self-identify as Yugoslavs than as any particular yugo-Slav nationality. One caveat, of course, is that "Muslim" was not an available legal category with which to identify at that time; in the early days of the socialist state it was still felt that Muslim identity would fade as the faithful "decided on their national identity," that is, decided whether they were Serbs or Croats. Yet the persistence of a distinct "Bosnian Muslim" identity is evidenced in the 1948 census, in which—given the option to identify as "Muslim Serb," "Muslim Croat," or "Muslim, nationally undeclared or undetermined"—around 90 percent of Muslims eschewed national titles. In 1953, given the choice of "Serb," "Croat," and "Yugoslav, undetermined," roughly the same percentage of Muslims, though few Serbs and Croats, chose the latter. Arguably, the real meaning of these statistics was not so much that Muslims were committed Yugoslavists but that they were stating their distinctness from either of the official national groups, a distinctness that could become the ground for a new nationality.

And so it was to be. In 1961 the census introduced a new category, "Ethnic Muslim," to which 972,954 Bosnians subscribed. In 1964 Muslims were declared a *narod* on par with Yugoslavia's five others—but the only one without a national republic. Finally, in 1968 came the fulfillment of the ethnogenesis of the Bosnian Muslims: the Bosnian Central Committee declared that it "has been shown, and present socialist practice confirms, that the Muslims are a distinct nation" (qtd. in Malcolm 1994, 199). Accordingly, the 1971 census offered "Muslim, in the sense of a nation" as one of the official ethnic categories. Even so, Malcolm makes the interesting observation that this drive for national recognition was not so much an indigenous Muslim one as a top-down effort of the Communist regime to secularize religious identity and render it comparable to other national identities. And it must be remembered that simultaneously opposite forces were operating in Yugoslavia, as they always had—forces that sought to claim Bosnian Muslims as either Serbs or Croats and perhaps to annex the appropriate territories to either Serbia or Croatia. The "ethnic partition" of Bosnia was even then a suggestion.

Meanwhile, other types of grievances, economic and political, were rising to drive wedges between the nations of Yugoslavia. One source of grievance was the development policy pursued by the Yugoslav Communist Party (YCP), in particular industrialization decisions and the uses of the federal budget. The problem was that, constituted as national units, the republics were inclined to perceive contributions to and distribution of state resources in national terms, as a form of national competition. Thus, differences in cost or benefit of economic development between the various republics were apt to be taken as a national cause and to arouse ethnonational rather than merely political fervor.

Like a typical Marxist state of the time, Yugoslavia pursued a course of industrialization coupled with agrarian reform. The first Five-Year Plan, in 1947, targeted such underdeveloped regions as Bosnia, Macedonia, and Montenegro for major investment; on the other hand, Slovenia and Croatia were already the most industrialized. Agrarian reform also affected Bosnia powerfully: landholdings were limited to 35 hectares per individual owner, resulting in the expropriation and redistribution of over 1.5 million hectares. The traditional Bosnian Muslim landlord class was finally undermined, although certain social vestiges of the class persisted past its demise as a class. Needless to say, some Bosnian Muslims opposed the Communist Party over such issues, but the difference was economics based, not ethnic based. Despite these actions, Bosnia continued to languish economically compared to the more advanced parts of the state; in 1961 a large portion of the republic was recognized as underdeveloped. These conditions yielded the highest rate of emigration, mostly Serb to Serbia, which helped tip the demographic scale toward the Muslims in the way that could only alarm the remaining Bosnian Serbs.

At the same time that Bosnia and the other underdeveloped republics and provinces trailed behind the rest of Yugoslavia economically, the more developed republics found their own grievances. As producers of a disproportionate share of gross domestic product, Slovenia and Croatia in particular came to resent the collection and allocation of state revenue, which amounted to, in their mind, the extraction of their wealth to subsidize other republics—or, since the republics were nationally constituted, other *nations.* Serbia, too, although considerably behind the former two, was aggrieved that, as the largest and leading nation in the state, it did not receive a greater share of the wealth. The debates and recriminations over the federal budget were, therefore, a source of real divisiveness.

Besides the economic ones, there were political and cultural issues rising up to challenge Yugoslavian unity. Under Tito's ideology of "self-management" (as opposed to orthodox/Stalinist Marxist centralism and statism) local and republic enterprises had a certain degree of freedom in their own affairs; republics also had their own Communist Party organizations. Giving republics more voice and rights *as* republics, however, was tantamount to enshrining the national or ethnic question in politics. By the 1960s national and cultural concerns were beginning to show, especially, of course, in Croatia. For example, Croats complained about the predominance of Serbian words in the Serbo-Croat language, about representation in politics and the media, and about control of institutions like banks. In 1971 the Croat literary society Matica Hrvatska published statistics to support these arguments, showing that Croats were underrepresented in the League of Yugoslavian Communists (LCY) and in such positions as judgeships and media (i.e., television and radio) directorships. Events led in mid-December 1971 to rioting in the streets of Zagreb and to the suppression of Croatian nationalism by federal authorities.

Old-fashioned ethnonationalism having reared its head and republican competition coming to be framed in nationalistic terms, Serb nationalism was bound to reemerge as well. Croat agitation and demands stirred the Serbs, who were already aggrieved. Kosovo naturally was an acute issue; the Serb percentage of the population was declining and the Albanian majority was becoming restless about the dominance of the Serb minority in the province, culminating in anti-Serb riots in 1968. As a consequence, Serbian Communist Dobrica Cosic uttered these prophetic words in the same year: "One could witness even among the Serbian people a reignition of the old historic goal and national idea—the unification of the Serbian people into a single state" (qtd. in Malcolm 1994, 205). Serbs also claimed their rights to a larger chunk of Yugoslavia's federal budget and a stronger voice in federal affairs, since the state was after all centered in and based upon their republic. And, finally, "Serb culture" in the form of Orthodox Christianity and the historical legacy of the Chetnik fighters was reawakening, all of this in large part a sort of "defensive nationalism" in response to Croat nationalism.

Predictably, these two external (and not-so-external) forces had their implications for Bosnia too. Serb writers such as Josip Potkozorac continued to argue that all the population of Bosnia was really Serb. Serb nationalists within the League of Yugoslavian Communists such as Cosic opposed the granting of *narod* (nation) status to the Bosnian Muslims. And, ultimately, Serb and Croat nationalists "started to talk openly of carving pieces of 'ethnic' territory off Bosnia and incorporating them in Croatian and Serbia respectively." It was unnecessary to justify their position with evidence of any actual oppression or disadvantage for their groups; "purely statistical oppression on the one hand and bogus ethnic history on the other, were sufficient" (Malcolm 1994, 204).

Ethnic pluralism was given official recognition, and ethnonationalism was given a boost, by the 1974 constitution. The constitution created a collective federal presidency made up of nine members, one from each of the republics and provinces, plus Tito himself. Ostensibly intended to represent and balance all the republican and national interests in the state, it instead established an unwieldy and competitive political structure within which, as "authority devolved to the republican level, each of the republics started behaving like a ministate" (Donia and Fine 1994, 191). Such an arrangement could conceivably have worked in a context in which the constituencies shared some degree of fellowship and common identity; instead, only Tito's personality was able to hold it together. When he died in 1980, there was no glue to adhere the nations and moderate their exclusivist demands. Further, the constitutional requirements that the head of the federal presidency rotate annually among the republican representatives and that virtual unanimity exist before any important decision could be taken came close to paralyzing the government of Yugoslavia.

The End of Yugoslavia, or the End of Yugoslavism

> *By their oppression the Communists created this longing among people to express their religious or national identity. Perhaps in four or five years we shall have passed through the minefield to the horizon of civil society. For now, unfortunately, our party* must *be sectional. The parties that try to represent everyone are small and weak. There is a real risk of civil war here; our main aim as a party is to keep Bosnia-Hercegovina together.*
>
> —Aliya Izetbegovic

The death of Tito left more than a political vacuum, which, together with an undeniable economic crisis, laid the foundations for factional competition. Since the late 1970s Yugoslavia's former showcase economy had been in decline, income dropping by the mid-1980s to the mid-1960s' level. Factories, built in the early Communist days, were obsolete, and unemployment rose; simultaneously, a burdensome national debt of $33 billion accumulated by 1988, which fueled inflation to the rate of 250 percent that year. These conditions could only aggravate the already-existing competition for limited state resources, a competition that now had no charismatic umpire.

The economic crisis and the political vacuum opened a window to republic-level politics and politicians, and at the republic level the appeal of ethnicity was that much greater. As early as 1981, Kosovo was showing signs of wear in its multiethnic population: the Albanian majority protested against the power and privilege of the Serb minority, while the Serbs "claimed that they were being subjected to 'genocide' and 'terror' by Albanian nationalists" who, presumably, wanted ultimately to separate Kosovo not only from Serbia but perhaps from Yugoslavia (Cohen 1993, 46). Serb and Croat nationalisms found a free arena for their claims and counterclaims.

Inevitably, as always, this would implicate Bosnia, where Islam, and even more so Islamic nationalism, were perceived as a threat to its own nationalistic aspirations. Virulently anti-Muslim writing appeared, such as Vuk Draskovic's 1982 novel *Noz* (The Knife), offering up juicy stereotypes of Muslims. Especially in view of the Islamic Revolution in Iran in 1978–79 and the rise of Islamic fundamentalism in many quarters, there came to be a (convenient) view that there was a worldwide Islamic conspiracy afoot, which was a threat to Yugoslavia (if not to the Serbs and Croats directly) and to which the Bosnian Muslims subscribed. Never mind that the Bosnian Muslims were renowned for the mildness of their religious convictions. In the minds of nationalistic opportunists Muslims were Muslims, all a danger to and deviance from Serb or Croat or Yugoslavian or even Western culture.

In 1983 Bosnian "Islamic nationalism" went on trial in Sarajevo, when thirteen Muslims faced charges of "conspiring to transform Bosnia into an Islamistan" (Donia and Fine 1994, 200). Among the defendants, who incidentally were all found guilty, was Aliya Izetbegovic, who would eventually become (and continues as of 1997 to be) the president of independent Bosnia-Hercegovina. Izetbegovic, a lawyer, was convicted largely on the evidence of his writings, including a document published in 1970 called *Islamic Declaration* and later works entitled *Islam Between East and West* and *Problems of the Islamic Renaissance.* Izetbegovic and his codefendants were condemned as fundamentalists and separatist nationalists, as pan-Islamists and anti-Westerners. In a sort of "compulsory nationalism"—that is, one that is ascribed to and forced upon one community or population by another—Bosnia's Muslims were lumped together by other radical nationalists, especially Serb, not only with Bosnia's more right-wing voices but with international Islam and even with "Eastern" culture or "primitive society." Accordingly, writes Serb intellectual Dragos Kalajic, they do not belong to "the European family of nations"; instead, they are, culturally and genetically, the product of another, less savory people—of the five centuries of Ottoman rule during which, "in satisfying their sexual impulses . . . the Ottoman armies and administrators—drawn from the Near Eastern and North African bazaars—created a distinct semi-Arab ethnic group" (qtd. in Cigar 1995, 26).

This view enabled dedicated anti-Muslim ethnonationalists to perceive Bosnia's Muslims as not only inferior but also threatening. They could be attributed with negative characteristics such as a "propensity to theft, a lack of ethics, laziness, authoritarianism, a 'neo-primitive lust for power,'" and, in Kalajic's words, an incapacity to understand "the essence of one of the basic traits of the European, namely the institution of the uniqueness of personal freedom which is fundamentally about any collectivity" (qtd. in Cigar 1995, 26–27). The threat from the Bosnian Muslims was equated with the much-misunderstood concept of "jihad," or holy war. To nationalistically minded non-Muslims, the Bosnian Muslims were on a jihad, despite the fact that the latter had not lifted a hand in anger at the former; this interpretation called for a fairly loose construction of the concept, however, as in Darko Tanaskovic's description of an "economic, diplomatic, and especially a demographic *jihad*"—one fought with the weapons of "high birthrate, the building of mosques, and pressure on non-Muslims" to leave designated areas where Muslims will settle and "then step up the birthrate in order to achieve numerical superiority gradually" (qtd. in Cigar 1995, 28).

As such, the Bosnian Muslims were construed to pose a threat not only to their neighbor nations but to Europe, to Christianity, and to Western civilization itself. In the widest interpretation this struggle could be extrapolated beyond (and thus disconnected from) local Muslim versus Serb or Croat groups and call for, in Kalajic's words, "the general mobilization of

European energies, and a supranational, suprareligious, supraideological union of Europeans" (qtd. in Cigar 1995, 26). Serbs were singularly scandalized by the fact that the Croats could defend the Bosnian Muslims instead of joining "the Serb Christians in defending shared Christian principles. Rather, they have sought to join the unjoinable, the cross—which is the most hated symbol for the Muslims—and the crescent . . . it is absurd for some Christians to cooperate with the Muslims against the Christians," according to the editor of *Pravoslavlje,* a journal of the Serbian Orthodox Church (69).

Still, as ubiquitous as these messages were in Serb society, they lacked the endorsement of mainstream institutions and the weight and machinery of state until about 1986, the year that saw the drafting of the "Memorandum" of the Serbian Academy of Arts and Sciences and the rise of Slobodan Milosevic to federal leadership. The memorandum (prepared by a committee, not the entire membership, and never endorsed by the whole) picked up and developed the Greater Serbia ideology on the basis of a kind of Serb primordial identity. The drafters of the memorandum perceived dangers to the Serb nation in the alleged assimilationist and nationalist policies in other republics, which threatened to identify, for example, Serbs in Croatia as Croats or Serbs in Bosnia as Bosnians. In these republics, they insisted, the "cultural currents of the Serbian people are alienated, encroached upon, or are declared valueless, neglected or crumbling, its language repressed, and the Cyrillic script gradually is disappearing" (qtd. in Cigar 1995, 76). Hence, the need to recognize and integrate ethnic Serbs across republic frontiers was urged: blaming Tito and the federalists for the fact that the Serb nation "did not get its own state like other peoples," the rectification of this national insult must be "the establishment of the full national integrity of the Serbian people, regardless of which republic or province it inhabits" (23).

One of the main, though by no means the only, objections of the Serb nationalists was the detachment of Kosovo from Serbia, and this became one of the key issues in the rise of Milosevic. He became head of the Serbian Communist Party in 1986 and, in the absence of any other integrating political agenda in the post-Tito era, raised Serbian national interests, initially economic interests, within the federal state, as the focal political issue of the day. Interestingly, however, some observers judge him to be a man "without any real nationalist motivation" (Glenny 1994, 34), whose main ambition was merely a strong and centralized Yugoslavia, with a strong Serbian component and with himself in command. Early in his regime he took control of the media like television and the journals *Politika* and *NIN,* and his use of demonstrations and protests in the streets was new and highly effective in the uncertain context of post-Tito Yugoslavia. Yet, at least in part, the appeal to ethnic issues and sentiments, not only in Serbia but in certain other republics as well, was a means to mobilize, and to a degree to *invent,* a constituency for leaders and would-be leaders such as Milosevic. To this end he and the authors of the memorandum served one another's interests, the memorandum raising concerns that the government could address and rally people around and Milosevic giving the ultranationalist intellectuals behind the memorandum the legitimacy and political voice that they sought.

Serbia's first nationalist accomplishments were close to home: in 1988 Milosevic forced the leadership in Vojvodina and Kosovo out of office and inserted his own officials, and in March 1989 the Serbian republican constitution was rewritten to integrate those two detached provinces into Serbia proper. Then, in the ultimate symbolic gesture Milosevic and a large number of pilgrims and politicians converged on Kosovo on June 28, 1989, for the six hundredth anniversary of the Battle of Kosovo, which had inflamed Serb memory (and memory of the animosity toward "the Turk") for six centuries. In the nationalist display that day Milosevic cited that, all these years later, and on the same ground, "we are again engaged in battles and quarrels. They are not armed battles, but this cannot be excluded yet" (qtd. in Glenny 1994, 35). According to one source, the ceremony included

> crowds, flanked by Orthodox priests and a paramilitary phalanx, holding aloft two sets of icons: reproductions of the golden Byzantine kind, and modern kind, portraits of Slobodan Milosevic. Emerging from a helicopter, he took the podium from dancing maidens in traditional folk costume, and transported the crowd to heights of frenzied adoration with a simple message: never again would Islam subjugate the Serbs. (Vulliamy 1994, 51)

Such displays were not, however, limited to the hallowed ground of Kosovo, nor did they go unnoticed in the other republics. Predictably, much of this activity was aimed at Bosnia. For example, at around the same time, a troupe of Serbs traveled around Bosnia with what they alleged were the remains of Prince Lazar, the Serb leader and martyr of the Battle of Kosovo; the party also proclaimed to the Muslims that "we will do our utmost to crush their race and descendants so completely that history will not even remember them" (qtd. in Cigar 1995, 35). Government-controlled television broadcast such slogans as "For the Good Life: Partition and Separation" into Bosnia, and marches and rallies (organized and orchestrated by Milosevic) offered up their own slogans like "Oh Muslims, you black crows, Tito is no longer around to protect you!" "We love you Slobodan because you hate the Muslims!" and "I'll be first, who'll be second, to drink some Turkish blood?" (34). Bosnian Muslims were linked with and equated to the Ustasha from World War II, and a revived threat was seen from them. And, as the television commercial mentioned earlier indicates, suggestions to divide Bosnia into Serb (and probably Croat) enclaves appeared again: the nationalist Draskovic actually produced his own map showing where Serbia's new borders would be and which formerly Muslim territories would be enclosed.

Meanwhile, alarm in other republics was growing, and old nationalisms that had poisoned Yugoslavia in the past were reforming. Some of the alarm and the demands engendered by it were more or less strictly political: in the face of increasing Serbian centralism of Yugoslavian politics, Croatia and Slovenia in particular lobbied for a more federal system, as they had during the eras of royal and Titoist Yugoslavia. Each also had its own elements of ultranationalism and separatism as well. By the end of 1989 Milosevic controlled four of the votes of the federal presidency (Serbia, Vojvodina, Kosovo, and Montenegro), effectively allowing him to block or override the remaining republics. This alone stirred anti-Serbian and antigovernment feelings; at the same time, the old economic grievances, that Croatia and Slovenia were contributing more than their share to the federal budget, lingered. Slovenia by itself was providing 25 percent of federal funds while amounting to only 8 percent of the population. Also, as the northernmost and therefore most "Europeanized" of the republics, considerable criticism of the Milosevic regime and of the Yugoslav army cropped up in the Slovenian press. Their protection, they reckoned, lay in the 1974 constitutional structure, virtually requiring unanimity in federal decision making; this way no majority of Serb-controlled votes could railroad the other republics. As early as June 1989, Slovenian Party leaders warned that they would not accept majority rule on the federal presidency and hinted that such a system might result in their withdrawal from the federation. Serbia condemned this attitude as not only anti-Yugoslavian but anti-Serbian; it responded by severing all business links with Slovenia in December 1989.

Rumblings of discontent could also be heard in Croatia and in Kosovo. In the latter, anti-Serb activity by the local Albanian (Muslim) majority had increased in 1989 and early 1990, and Serb crackdowns on the populace were denounced by the other nationalities. In Croatia, with its long history of nationalism and autonomy seeking, old grievances and demands were resurfacing in the climate of ethnic competition and national self-assertiveness that had developed in Yugoslavia. In the same month of Slovenia's action Croatia, too, expressed its desire for multiparty politics and more republican power sharing; simultaneously, in what Cohen calls "a classic case of Croatian and Serbian nationalism feeding upon one another," a kind of ethnopolitical mobilization occurred in the former as the main opposition to the bankrupt Communist structure there. A political party, Hrvatska Demokratska Zajednica (HDZ, or Croatian Democratic Union), emerged under the leadership of Franjo Tudjman, a former Partisan and Croat nationalist. Tudjman, who had recently been easily reelected (November 1995), stood on a platform of confederation based on Croatian "identity and sovereignty"; according to Tudjman, Croats had suffered under the Communist regime (curiously, as we have seen, Serbs expressed the same feeling), and it was necessary now to "restore Croatian legitimacy."

In early 1990 multiparty elections were called for Slovenia and Croatia; however, as Woodward points out, the impetus for these elections did not come from the ordinary citizens but from elites, including "politicians seeking more political power over their territories and opposition intellectuals seeking more political influence over the course of events" (1995, 117). In Slovenia a coalition of Center-Right parties known as the Democratic United Opposition of Slovenia (DEMOS) defeated the reconstituted Communist Party in the legislative election but lost in the presidential one. In Croatia the HDZ won a landslide victory in all contests and catapulted Tudjman to the presidency. By late 1990 the two republics had presented a draft confederal agreement that would essentially end the Yugoslavian federation and replace it with an alliance of sovereign states. Naturally, the Yugoslavian government and those calling themselves Yugoslavs opposed this move, as did Serbs and Montenegrins; the most strident opposition came from those Serbs who lived outside Serbia proper, the 25 percent of the nation residing mainly in Croatia and Bosnia-Hercegovina. Fatefully, but perhaps inevitably, Slovenia and Croatia, following a predetermined plan, declared their independence from Yugoslavia on June 25, 1991. In less than a day Yugoslavian (federal) forces were sent into Slovenia.

The war in Slovenia was brief (troops were withdrawn by July 19), partly because of the preparedness of Slovenia's own forces and partly because the stakes for the federal (and Serb-dominated) army were not very high: few Serbs live in Slovenia. The stakes in Croatia are considerably higher. Milosevic had long since condemned Croatian separatism, stating that Croatia might secede but not with the Serb-populated territories that it contained, in particular the Krajina and Knin. Some six hundred thousand "ethnic Serbs" lived within the borders of Croatia at the outset of conflict, and, in response to the 1990 elections in the republic-cum-state, these Serbs had organized their own political party, the Serbian Democratic Party (SDS), which was by most accounts a local phenomenon but probably had the blessing of Serbs in Serbia and was supplied with arms by Gen. Ratko Mladic of the Yugoslavian army, a Bosnian Serb and radical nationalist. Krajina Serb leaders began to refer to the area as the "Serb Autonomous Region of the Krajina" as early as January 1991 and organized a referendum on the future of the Krajina in May: only Serbs were allowed to vote, and 99 percent voted for secession from Croatia and integration with Serbia. When Croatia as a whole voted to secede from Yugoslavia, a war ensued between the Croats and the Yugoslavian army, plus militias of the local secessionist Serbs, which took over ten thousand lives and resulted in thirty thousand other casualties. A truce in early 1992 suspended the hostility in Croatia but allowed for its transfer to Bosnia.

Conclusion: The Battle for Bosnia

> *Before this summer ends we will have driven the Turkish army out of the city, just as they drove us from the field of Kossovo* [sic] *in 1389. That was the beginning of Turkish domination of our lands. This will be the end of it, after all these cruel centuries. We Serbs are saving Europe.*
>
> —Serb soldier

As in all cases of ethnic conflict, the proximal causes are both internal and external. For Bosnia the proximal external cause was the tug-of-war between Croatia and Serbia, between Tudjman and Milosevic, over their "conationals" and the territory they inhabited. Unfortunately for Bosnia, both sets of conationals were represented in large numbers in that republic, and, as the rhetoric heated up (and succeeded, as the epigraph proves) and the political lines were drawn on the dissolving Yugoslavia (literally and figuratively), they began to get agitated as well. Bosnia's Muslims were the first to adopt a sectional party, the Stranka Demokratske Akcije (Party of Democratic Action, or SDA), which alleged to recognize Serb and Croat rights in the republic but claimed Muslims as the "autochthonous Bosnian nation" (Pavkovic 1991, 113). In the multiparty election wave that swept across Yugoslavia, Aliya Izetbegovic, leader of the SDA, became president of Bosnia-Hercegovina. This alarmed the Bosnian Serbs, some of whom formed their own version of the SDS led by Radovan Karadzic. And, when Slovenia and Croatia made their declarations of independence, Bosnia-Hercegovina began to contemplate doing the same. Significantly, but not unusually, Muslims and Croats found themselves allied in the cause of Bosnian sovereignty, which Serbs adamantly opposed.

Karadzic and the Bosnian Serb leadership declared their own "Serbian Autonomous Region of Hercegovina" in September 1991 and established its outlines militarily with the help of the Yugoslavian army (which was by now basically the Serbian army) and paramilitary groups like Vojislav Seselj's Chetniks and the unit known as the "Tigers" of Zeljko Raznjatovic (also known as "Arkan"). In the fragmenting context of multinational Bosnia, Bosnian Croats also organized their own party, the Croatian Democratic Alliance, which designated its own sphere of interest and influence in western Hercegovina (especially around the city of Mostar), or "Herceg-Bosna" as they refer to it. Bosnian Muslims were left holding the government of a dissipating republic and appearing to participate in its dissipation. In February 1992 Karadzic, Izetbegovic, and Mate Boban of the Bosnian Croats met in Lisbon and agreed in principle to the ethnic "cantonization" of Bosnia; Izetbegovic soon backed out of the agreement, but the notion of the division of Bosnia into ethnic enclaves or cantons was now on the table. Immediately, however, Bosnia held its own referendum on its relation to Yugoslavia, and over 99 percent of the votes (with Bosnian Serbs, however, boycotting the referendum) were cast in favor of independence. On March 1, the day the referendum results were announced, fighting broke out.

The details of the war in Bosnia, which dwarfed the wars in Slovenia and Croatia, are well enough known and documented elsewhere. Two final things call for our attention, however. One is that virtually all plans and proposals to bring the fighting to an end have entailed some degree of ethnic partition, whether it be the Vance-Owen plan or some other. Fortunes have shifted for the various combatants, as have alliances (at times Croats have fought alongside Bosnian Muslims, at other times against them), but the suggestion that Bosnia return to its prewar multiethnic and multicultural society has been seldom raised or entertained. As Karadzic himself has stated: "There is no return to a united Bosnia-Hercegovina. The time has come for the Serbian people to organize itself as a totality, without regard to the administrative [existing] borders" (qtd. in Cigar 1995, 39–40). If this requires taking over half of Bosnia's land for less than one-third of its population, in order to create a "corridor" connecting disparate Serb regions, then so be it.

This, then, raises the second and concluding observation about the war in Bosnia, which is that it is, in the estimation of a number of its students, more than a war of one nation against another nation and certainly more than a continuation of some old, even ancient, inter-national feud; to believe the latter is, in the words of Malcolm, "to read from the script prepared by Karadzic and Milosevic." To be fair, it is also the script of many an ethnonationalist in the broken wreckage of the former Yugoslavia, and its like can be distinguished in many presumably primordial ethnic contexts. It is a deception, however, because "it disguises a consequence for a cause and mystifies the conflict as an orgiastic free-for-all, far removed from political calculation" (Thompson 1993, 174). Rather, Pavkovic ultimately sees the struggle as one for control of territory that each nationalism claims for its own nation. The particular savagery of the fighting Woodward explains as the result of the essentially local battles in the context of the collapse of modern civil institutions, such that there was a "natural tendency to rely on older (pre-state) mechanisms of solidarity and insurance adapted to survival—family, kinship, ethnicity" (Woodward 1995, 237), which became a sort of self-fulfilling prophecy.

Yet beyond that—or perhaps because of that—the war in Bosnia, with its atrocities and its ethnic cleansing, is a war against a culture and against a multicultural ideal. Karadzic has declared that in a Bosnian war the Muslims would "disappear from the face of the earth." He continues: "They are . . . threatened not only in the physical sense, and I did not think that they might disappear only physically; rather, this is also the beginning of the end of their existence as a nation" (qtd. in Cigar 1995, 37). Accordingly, the war for Bosnia has included a war against Muslim culture and history in Bosnia, against the memory and symbols of such a culture and history. The attack has been taken to mosques, for example, between eight hundred and a thousand of which were damaged or destroyed, and to the famous medieval bridge in Mostar, shelled to death deliberately and unnecessarily. Cemeteries, with their "Bogomil" stones, schools and their libraries, and old towns and neighborhoods have been targeted. And, most lamentably, major resources and collections of medieval and Ottoman history and culture such as the National and University Library and the Library of the Institute for Oriental Studies (both in Sarajevo) and the National Library in Mostar have been destroyed; the Institute for Oriental Studies alone housed invaluable documents of historical, artistic, and political interest—all proof that a vibrant Muslim society once reigned there.

Ultimately, if the war in Bosnia is more than a war against an ethnic group but a war against memory, it is also a war against possibility, the possibility of ethnic coexistence and even supra-ethnic integration. That Bosnians always ranked above other "Yugoslavians" in the rate of self-identification *as* Yugoslavians (as opposed to one ethnic category or another) is no small or coincidental fact. Neither is the fact that the Bosnian army and government contained Muslims along with Croats and Serbs up to the early 1990s. Bosnians, *as* Bosnians, rather than Muslims or Croats or Serbs—that is, those who believe in a distinct and historically real Bosnian identity—do not fight to advance this or that ethnic cause but "to preserve a culturally diverse society in which Muslims, Serbs, and Croats have lived, if not in complete harmony, at least peacefully. They are also defending the idea of a democratic republic founded on universal rights rather than those based on ethnicity" (Thompson, qtd. in Harrison 1993, 181). This "cosmopolitan," pluralistic, noncommunal ideal is anathema to the ethnonationalism—Serb, Croat, or Muslim—of post-Yugoslavian politics, which sees "new 'pure' nation-states emerging from the ruins of Yugoslavia." In the end, then, the story of Bosnia is not just a story of ethnic groups against one another but also of ethnicity against another, less exclusivistic, and less intolerant view of the world.

Chapter 7

Quebec: Masters in Our Own House

Je me souviens [*I remember*].
—Quebec provincial motto

If the cases presented in the previous chapters have proven anything, it is that not all ethnicity is the same. It follows that not all ethnic conflict is the same. Ethnic conflict need not even be deadly to be recognized as conflictual. Conflict may also be political, polemic, or a number of other forms, alternately or simultaneously. This fact is one reason for including a chapter on Quebec in a book about ethnic conflict. There are other reasons as well. Quebec is to Canada as Bosnia or Croatia or Slovenia is to Yugoslavia—a separatist polity claiming cultural distinctness and (therefore) political sovereignty that may yet fracture the federation. As recently as the autumn of 1995, Quebec was voting on a referendum of secession from Canada, which was defeated as all similar recent referenda there have been. And, lest it be forgotten, Quebec has been the scene of authentic ethnic violence and terrorism, especially during the volatile 1970s and the so-called October crisis, during which the federal government had to pacify resistance in the province. It is sanguine to remind ourselves that such events are possible in a nearby and civil society like Canada. No society, no state, is entirely beyond the call of ethnicity.

As the epigraph says, Quebec remembers. What Quebec, or at least the ethnic entrepreneurs or the ethnically conscious of francophone Quebec, remembers in particular is a history of injustices and "humiliations" that have been likened to slavery or colonialism and which have led one activist to describe the Quebecois as the "white niggers of America." Thus, the ethnically conscious of Quebec hold up their history and their culture (or, better yet, the history of slights and assaults, yet survival, of their culture) as the banner of their identity and the source of their claims *for* and *on* a state. Quebec ethnic nationalism, which will be defined much more extensively in subsequent pages, takes the specific form of political separatism, as the only means by which to ensure the survival and progress of the ethnic nation. Yet, at the same time as Quebec remembers, Quebec, like all ethnicities and all social collectivities, also forgets and interprets and invents.

The present chapter will undertake to illuminate how culture and history have been mobilized, used, sometimes discovered, and occasionally created to defend and then to advance an ostensible nation. We will see that this nationalism, this conflict, and even the nation to which it addresses itself have shifted over the years and can be linked quite conspicuously to the economic and political circumstances in which the nation finds itself. In particular, processes of modernization, industrialization, and urbanization play a major role in the activation and escalation of ethnicity, ethnic demands, and ethnic conflict. One of the greater ironies we will encounter is that, as the francophone nation became in some ways *socially* more like the larger society around it, it became *ethnically* more self-aware and mobilized. Ultimately, as in the other cases we have explored, Quebec nationalism will emerge not as a mere reflex of history and culture, as a primordial movement of history and culture but also as "an analysis [of that history and culture] that is a *melange* of fact and frustration" (Scott and Oliver 1964, 4). In other words, it will reveal itself to us as made, not born.

Two Majorities, Two Solitudes

Canada, Quebec, Quebecois, French-Canadian—these names seem to designate real, concrete, and enduring social entities, but, like most if not all social designators, they are in fact slippery and mutable. The proper terms to use, and their exact designations, have shifted over the years as the definitions and goals of identification and nationalism have changed. Canada is, of course, the name of a state, a state that came into being as such only about two hundred years ago; *Canadian* here will refer to any citizen of that state, regardless of his or her ethnicity. Two main languages are spoken in Canada—English and French. *French-Canadian* (which seems to be little used these days as an ethnic term) or *francophone* will refer to the French-speaking minority, regardless of where they reside in Canada. It is unusual, or at least it has been until recently, to hear the term

English-Canadian (it would be akin to *European-American*); however, *anglophone* is a regularly employed term to distinguish this language community from the francophone one, and I will use it here. In fact, for the early "French Canadians" *Canadien* (in French) was employed to mean only themselves, in distinction to *les anglais,* who were not real Canadians. One occasionally also hears the term *allophone,* which means all those people who speak neither English nor French as their mother tongue, of whom there has been an increasing number this century, complicating the ethnic picture in Canada.

At any rate Quebec is one of the ten provinces of Canada and one of the two original provinces (along with Ontario). Quebec, like most of Canada, contains both anglophones and francophones, but it holds far more Canadian francophones, more French Canadians, than all of the other provinces put together. In recent decades, as *French-Canadian* has fallen out of use, *Quebecois* has emerged as a more powerful and evocative term, also indicating a shift in the source and aim of francophone ethnonationalism. *Quebecois* will here be used, as it is used in contemporary Canadian political and social discourse, to designate the francophone population of Quebec. On the other hand, *Quebecer* will refer to any resident of Quebec, regardless of his or her primary language. Naturally, like all ethnic category names, these terms are not neutral but have political and polemic valences.

For its two hundred years Canada has been a predominantly English-speaking society with close political and social ties to England and, from 1867 until the 1980s, a constitution approved by the English Parliament. Over three-quarters of the population is anglophone, and English has been the primary language of administration and commerce throughout the state. During the same two hundred years Canada has alternately recognized and refused to recognize "Quebec" as a distinct thing in its midst (although I believe history shows that more often than not, and certainly for the last century or more, it has recognized rather than refused to recognize the "fact"). The fact is the well-known "French fact," that in Canada there is not only a "French" or French-speaking minority but a francophone group or nation with certain characteristics of a complete and intact society. A critical aspect of this "intactness" is that the francophone minority has been and continues to be concentrated in Quebec, although it is represented in all regions of Canada, especially New Brunswick, where it constituted 34.5 percent of the population in 1991. All told, less than one-quarter (23.8 percent) of Canadians identified themselves as francophone in 1991; at the same time, however, that 84.5 percent of francophone Canadians live in Quebec gives the community an overall compactness and territorial focus that has allowed it to remain—or to become—a nation in a certain sense. Even more, their concentration in Quebec makes it possible to claim, with some truth, that they are not merely a minority but also a *majority*—a majority in their own land. Thus, René Levesque, Quebec nationalist and one-time premier of the province, could argue "that in fact there are *two majorities,* two 'complete societies' quite distinct from each other trying to get along within a common framework" of the Canadian state (1968, 20).

In addition, francophone Canadians can justify their parity with anglophone Canadians in another way—by claiming to be one of the "two founding races" of Canada, not mere passive sojourners in the state but active and equal originators of that state. Since the seventeenth century both England and France were exploring and colonizing northern North America. By 1750 some fifty thousand French colonists occupied "Nouvelle France" (roughly but not exclusively what we would call Quebec today) while English colonists settled on the east coast (Newfoundland, appropriately enough, was the initial contact site in Canada for explorer John Cabot), in "Upper Canada" (the area of Toronto and Ottawa today), and of course in the thirteen colonies that would become the United States of America. Before they were Quebecois, the "Canadiens," or francophone, settlers were legendary fur traders and ruralites. They were not necessarily a unified group: in a class (and politically motivated) analysis of early colonial society, Vallieres maintains that the true *Canadiens,* the *Habitants* as they were known, were distinguished from the French elite who dominated the economy, "the French of France." Still, *Habitants* and French of France alike were set apart and socially distant from the English settlers who surrounded them, making for what Hugh MacLennan calls in the title of his famous Canadian novel the "two solitudes." Until 1759 there was no Canada in the modern sense, and English and French Canadians could not seriously be construed as one nation. For many ethnonationalists this is still the case.

Between 1756 and 1763 England and France were engaged in a great military struggle across the extent of their colonial holdings, especially North America and India. Canada the state was born from the conflict, in the triumph of the English over the French (marked by the fall of Quebec City in 1759) and the cession of French Canada to England by King Louis XV in the Treaty of Paris that formally ended the war in 1763. From the francophone perspective the event was equally though oppositely cataclysmic; it was "la Conquête," leaving them abandoned and orphaned by their mother country to the mercies of their English masters. The Conquest is usually perceived as the first and greatest of all insults, threats, and humiliations of the French-Canadian nation. In fact, the 1759 conquest was not the first assault against French settlers by English ones. In 1755 English and American (who were, after all, still legally "English" at the time) soldiers had forcibly evicted the French "Acadians" from their homeland in eastern Canada (Nova Scotia to be precise), a group that was truly lost to history, except for their dispersed descendants in New Brunswick and in Louisiana (the "Cajuns") and for Longfellow's epic poem "Evangeline."

The immediate and understandable posture of the new Canadian (i.e., English) regime was assimilationist, despite the fact that the English constituted a small minority at the time, probably less than ten thousand in total. Even so, the new unified colony's essential dualism was recognized in the adoption of a two-party system, one party for each "race." Thus, the English Party and the French Party were formed to represent the interests of the disparate communities, and French law was even integrated into the colony's administration in the form of a dual court system, the lower court based on French principles and the higher court based on English ones. Soon, however, dualism was extended and the French fact recognized even more explicitly in the Quebec Act of 1775, which restored French civil law to its place in the colony as well as accepting the rights and privileges of the French-Canadian elites, namely the Catholic Church and its priests and the landowning "seigneurial" class. In his class analysis of Quebec's history Vallieres sees in this arrangement a linking of elites across ethnic lines, establishing cooperation and preserving interests that were *interethnic* but *intraclass.* If this is the proper reading of history, then ethnic identities and interests had definitely not emerged as determinative at that stage of social development.

During the American Revolution, which sent Loyalists in the new United States scurrying out of the country and across the border into English Canada, some fifty thousand "Englishmen" emigrated, primarily to Nova Scotia and Quebec, tipping the demographic balance for the first time in favor of the English in Canada. This demographic shift led in 1791 to the Constitutional Act that partitioned the colony into two parts: Upper Canada (later to become Ontario), an English-speaking region, and Lower Canada (Quebec), a generally French-speaking one. This action

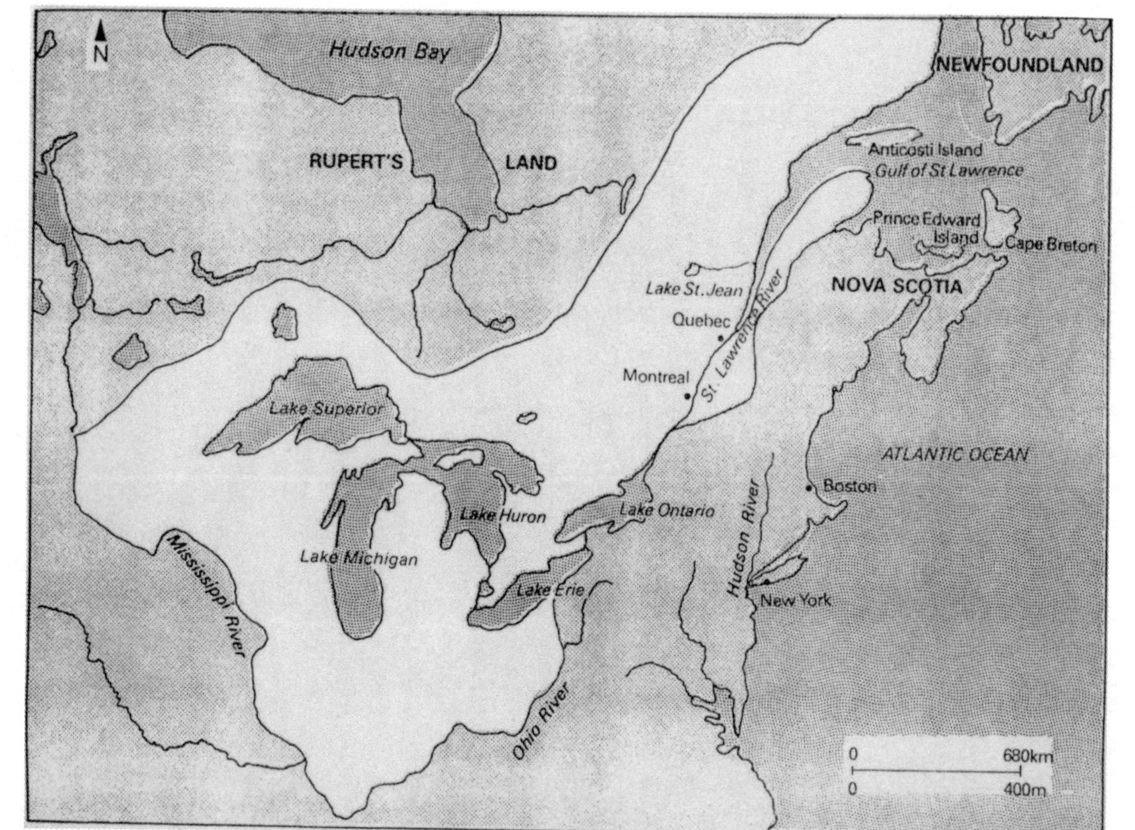

Quebec Boundaries, 1774. (From *Historical Maps on File,* map 6.026. Maps copyright © 1984 by Martin Greenwald Associates. Reprinted by permission of Facts on File, Inc.)

may be interpreted as perpetuating and protecting francophone culture and community within its own ethnolinguistic preserve, or as the first step in carving out a greater place for anglophone culture and community. Both interpretations have some justification, and both effects resulted. "The Loyalist emigres from America had, in effect, impelled the first act of separatism in Canada" (Lamont 1994, 56).

Despite the fact that the anglophones and francophones lived in their two solitudes, divided by the gulf of language and by their respective urbanism and ruralism, they were not immune from each other's presence. Tensions lingered and grew as English immigration and industrialization increased in the early nineteenth century, bringing anglophone society even into the francophone stronghold and traditional home, Montreal. Anglophone business interests sought to expand their influence and to further anglicize Canadian, including Quebec, culture. The change was evident to Alexis de Tocqueville, renowned chronicler of the early American condition, who wrote in 1831 of Lower Canada:

> The bulk of the population and the immense majority, everywhere, is French. But it is easy to see that the French are the vanquished people. The rich classes belong for the most part to the English race. . . . The clergy and much of the enlightened classes are French; they have come to feel strongly about their subordinate position. The French newspapers that I read maintain a constant and lively opposition to *les anglais.* . . . I cannot believe that they will ever fuse together, or that there can be an indissoluble union between them. (Qtd. in Johnson 1994, 11)

By the early 1830s the English-Canadian business class, in both parts of Canada, was pressing for the reunification of the Canadas. Quebec's National Assembly was disbanded, its army officers dismissed, and its newspaper closed. In 1834 Louis-Joseph Papineau and John Nielson, founders of the Parti Canadien, issued ninety-two resolutions protesting the English plans for Canada. When England responded unfavorably, a short-lived but memorable rebellion broke out. Papineau and his *Patriotes* first organized a boycott of English goods then orchestrated an armed insurrection centered in Montreal but extending into the countryside. The *Patriotes'* uprising was put down by force, and Papineau fled to the United States, but a new grievance and a new bitter memory had been made for the francophones. Even so, if Vallieres is correct in his assessment of the rebellion, it was still not an ethnic movement of the modern sort but, rather, a narrow class or almost personal action; the *Patriote* leaders "had only sought to bring pressure on the English in order to obtain for themselves, for their class—and not for the Habitants—a new division of power which would bring them certain additional revenues and a greater share in the economic advantages of the system" (1971, 27). In this case the *Patriote* movement would more closely resemble the premodern uprisings of the Kurds, for example, than the modern nationalist-separatist movement in Quebec. Subsequently, the Act of Union in 1841 rejoined Upper and Lower Canada into a single Canada with a single (English-derived) government and an anglophone majority of about 625,000, as opposed to 500,000 francophones.

By 1860 happenings inside and outside Canada were leading it in new directions. Partly to secure Canada's permanent independence from the United States and partly to integrate and rationalize its territorial holdings in North America, England in 1867 concluded an agreement to establish a constitution for an expanded Canadian confederation still under the protection of the mother country, known by the uninspiring name "British North America Act" (or BNA Act). Specifically, the BNA Act resplit Canada into two provinces, Ontario and Quebec; in addition, two new provinces, Nova Scotia and New Brunswick, entered the confederation. It established a central, English-style government that actually protected French-Canadian interests in two ways: first, Quebec and Ontario received equal numbers of seats in the upper legislative house, even though the former was less populous than the latter; and, second, federal legislative and judicial activities were to be conducted in English and French. In effect, the French fact was recognized as a Canadian fact, concentrated in but not limited to Quebec. The powers of the federal and provincial governments were detailed in a way that need not concern us here, except to say three things: (1) the provinces retained clear and considerable powers vis-à-vis the federal government, making for a degree of provincial autonomy that is perhaps foreign in the United States (creating in essence a "confederation" rather than a U.S.-style "federation"); (2) "residual powers" not allocated to either level of government explicitly were granted to the central government (exactly the opposite as in the United States); and (3) no amendment process was included, on the assumption that amendments would be approved by London.

In regard to culture, language rights were not enshrined so much as religious rights (which in the present case are not completely separable), which also follows the crucial line along which "identity" or ethnicity at

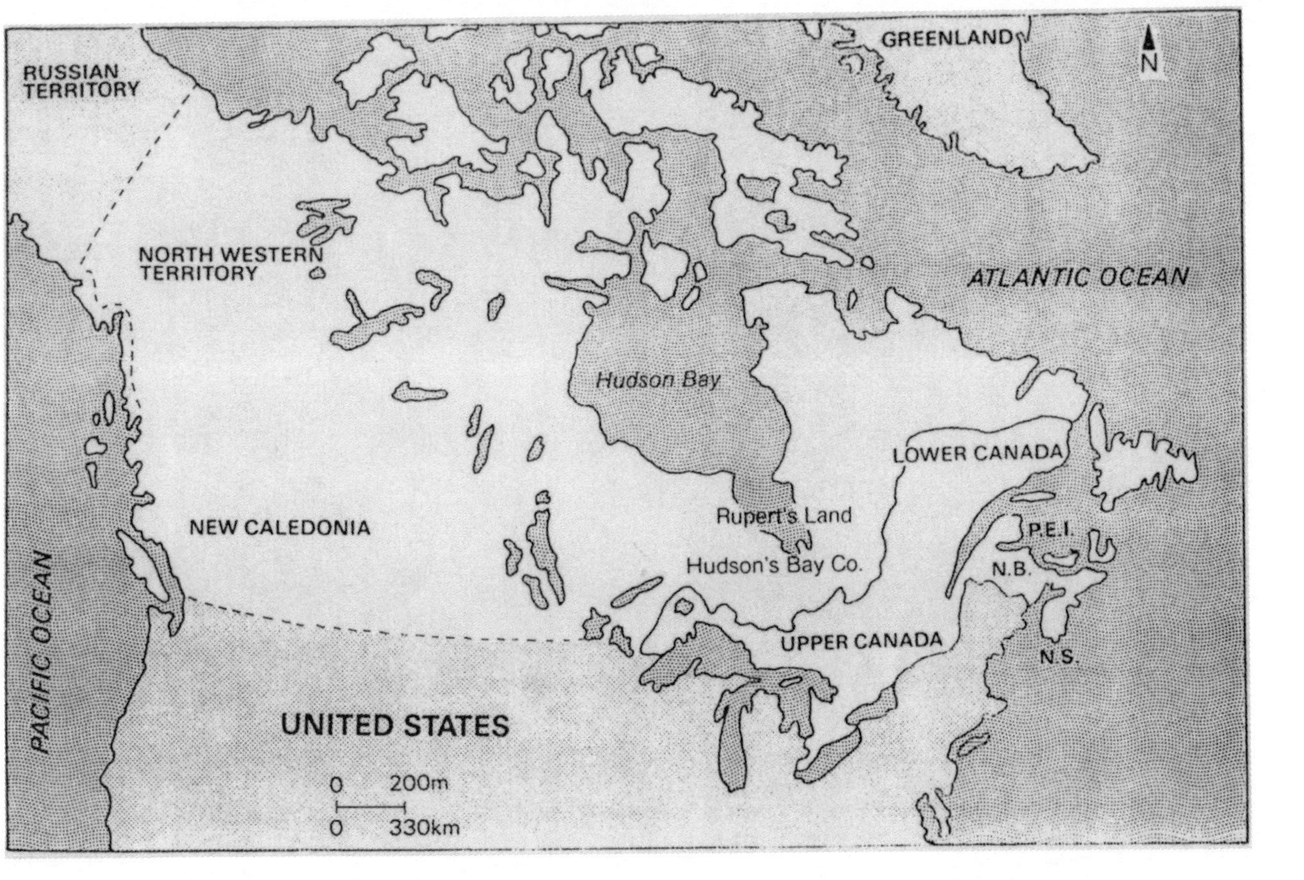

Quebec and the Canadian Federation, 1849. (From *Historical Maps on File,* map 6.032. Maps copyright © 1984 by Martin Greenwald Associates. Reprinted by permission of Facts on File, Inc.)

that time was defined. The francophones were basically Catholic, the anglophones basically Protestant. Section 93 of the BNA Act guarantees "any Right or Privilege with respect to Denominational Schools which any Class of Persons have by Law in the Province at the Union." This provision would serve to protect Protestants in Quebec as much as (or more than) Catholics in the rest of Canada, as events would prove in the near future: since education was constitutionally now a provincial matter, anglophone/Protestant majority provinces could, and would, legislate their own desires in regard to religious schools—and to language training and language of instruction as well.

As the new Canadian confederation expanded to include western provinces like Manitoba and Saskatchewan, where much smaller minorities of francophones typically resided, ethnic issues arose and even escalated there; in fact, history shows that some of the early battles (figuratively and literally) in Canada over culture and cultural politics took place not in Quebec but, rather, in Ontario and the West, where French Canadians and metis (mixed French and Indian) were the vast majority in mid-century but were a small minority by the end of the century due to anglophone migration from the east. These provinces, especially Manitoba, exercised their provincial prerogatives over education often to the disadvantage of the francophones. In 1885 the province of Ontario made a law requiring French schools to offer English as a subject; in 1890 this law was extended to require that those schools offer the same curriculum as English-language schools, using English-language textbooks. Also in 1890 Manitoba dispensed with bilingual administration and services and ended government funding for separate schools. The following year, in the Northwest Territory, French was abolished in government and in most schools.

Yet the assault on French and on the French Canadians took a more palpable form for many francophones in the so-called Riel rebellion, which also occurred in the west. When Manitoba (then known as the Red River Colony) was first annexed by Canada in 1869, many of the area's French and metis opposed the move. Louis Riel organized a resistance, captured the town of Fort Garry (present-day Winnipeg), and declared an independent republic. Canadian troops moved against the breakaway republic, and Riel fled Canada for the United States and became a U.S. citizen but was encouraged to return and resume his rebellion in 1884. Instead, after a mismatched confrontation, Riel was apprehended, tried by an anglophone Protestant jury, and hanged in November 1885. French

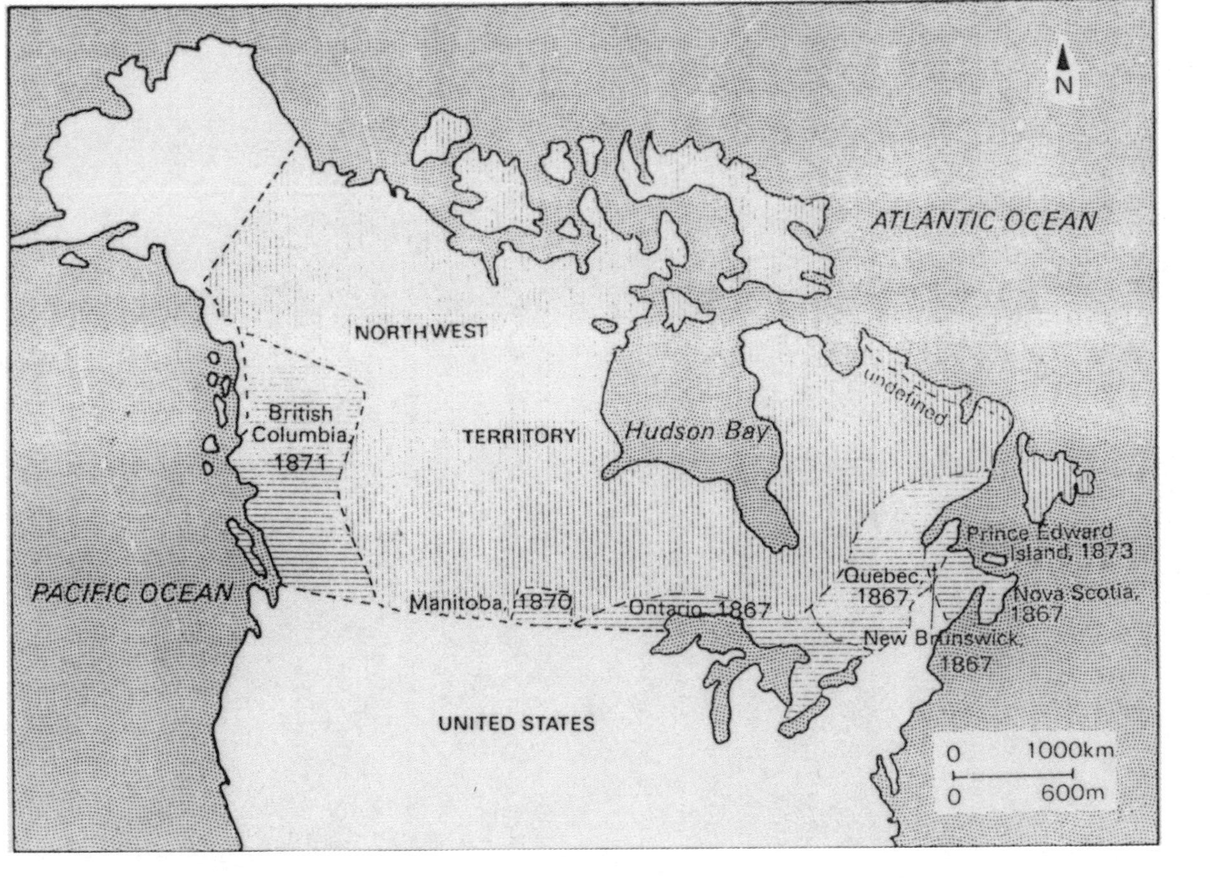

Canadian Federation, 1873. (From *Historical Maps on File,* map 6.034. Maps copyright © 1984 by Martin Greenwald Associates. Reprinted by permission of Facts on File, Inc.)

Canadians now had a potential national hero, a "symbol of French-Canadian resistance to assimilation and domination" and could now extrapolate that English Canadians would use any means including murder to prevent any realization of the former's political or social aspirations, while English Canadians could brand the French Canadians as traitors and murders who were unfit to share Canada with the former. The *Toronto News* went so far as to publish the opinion that Riel should be executed by strangulation with the French flag, "the only service which that rag can render to this country" (qtd. in Quinn 1979, 22).

Canadian Identity?

One remarkable thing that emerges from a study of Canada is its self-image as suffering from a fairly pervasive and profound "identity crisis." This is not entirely startling, since all states, and especially all new states, must deal with the problem of national (here taken as state) identity and integration. Modern states want to and try to foster an identity, which is at least in part a construction and a fiction. From Canadians, however, one gets the sense that a convincing national identity and culture has never been constructed and that they are now it. Canadians joke about their lack of identity, or perhaps better yet their uncertainty about the validity of their identity: "Canadians are the only people in the world who continually pull themselves up by the roots to see if they are still growing," goes a Canadian saying. Margaret Atwood has expressed that "Canadians are forever taking the national pulse like doctors at a sickbed: the aim is not to see whether the patient will live well but simply whether he will live at all" and that "it is not at all clear that Canadians ever did fully 'establish this fact of our own existence" (qtd. in Bell and Tepperman 1992, 62–63). William Kilbourn simply says: "The Canadian identity—the phrase is both a chimera and an oxymoron" (qtd. in Stark 1992, 135).

Why this extensive and explicit problem of identity? Most obviously, it is because of the two unreconciled identities within the state, the "two solitudes." Contrary to what some francophone nationalists might argue, Canada has always been aware of its internal dualism, in a way that, for instance, the United States has not been until very recently. The partition of Canada into two linguistic provinces, the Act of Union, the BNA Act—all of these and more are premised on the recognition of a basic dualism in society. The prime minister at the time of 1890, Sir Wilfrid Laurier, saw this dualism so clearly that he concluded: "We have come to a period in the history of this young country when premature dissolution seems to be at hand" (qtd. in Lamont 1994, 52).

Yet why have the two solitudes persisted? Why have they not merged into one, whether assimilated into the majority English/Protestant/anglophone identity or blended into a new, third, Canadian identity? We will try to answer this question with reference to the social organization and ethnopolitical mobilization of the francophone community in the next section, but for now it is important to emphasize the particular lack of seminal, inspirational events and personalities in the state-national history of Canada that could serve as the rallying point for a pan-Canadian identity. Canada's constitution (the BNA Act) was, as far as most Canadians are concerned, handed to them rather than made by them, and its entire history has been, instead of the glorious (if fictional) journey that is the United States, a series of small steps and mild accomplishments. It is the grand, salutary triumphs and tragedies that forge a state-nation out of its constituent nations and make its identity. "Bereft of heroes, epic victories or tragic defeats, the legendary links in a unifying history, Canadians still pine to define their national soul"; the lack of these character-building moments "has delayed and obscured Canadians' attainment of a staunch identity, an integrating vision of nationhood" (Lamont 1994, 44–45). Therefore, Bell and Tepperman conclude, "In failing to create her own symbols of identity Canada failed to bridge the chasm between francophone and anglophone cultures" (1992, 72). Revealingly, Nicol and Whalley see the solution as the reinterpretation of Canada's history, "a judicious revision of certain events to give them the heroic aura presently minus" (1966, vii–viii).

Not that Canada has been bereft of national fiction. English Canada, in its ethnocentric self-certainty, generally defined *itself* and its culture as Canada, with the French fact a quaint and distinguishing element of its uniqueness from other English societies. Although dualism and bilingualism were recognized and even protected, assimilation was expected and desired, or, better yet, the French minority was basically ignored (much as the United States ignored its minorities until it became impossible to do so). Pierre Trudeau, a French-Canadian but hardly an ethnonationalist, remarked that "the Anglo-Canadians built themselves an illusion [of a British nation-state in Canada] by fencing off the French Canadians in their Quebec ghetto. . . . Outside Quebec they fought, with staggering ferocity, against anything that might intrude upon that illusion: the use of French on stamps, cheques, in the civil service, the railroads, and the whole works" (1968, 164). In other words, there was a master fiction in operation in Canada, one that maintained that Canada was politically, culturally, and linguistically English. It just didn't convince everyone.

What we find, then, is not a singly unified and unifying vision of Canada among Canadians but two (or more) differing and competing visions. We can think of these two visions in a variety of ways. One dimension of the competition is between the individual and the collectivity, while another is between the centralized/federal and the local/provincial level of government; interestingly, but not entirely surprisingly, these two dimensions overlap in important ways. In the centralized/federal vision of society there is one Canada, in which all individuals participate equally *as* individuals; it may be a unilingual and unicultural society or a bi- or multilingual and bi- or multicultural society, but it is a single society. Federalists like Trudeau, to whom I will return, echo this sentiment in their theoretical statements: members of such a liberal society

> enjoy certain fundamental inalienable rights and cannot be deprived of them by any collectivity (state or government) or on behalf of any collectivity (nation, ethnic group, religious group or other). . . . [O]nly the individual is the possessor of rights. A collectivity can exercise only those rights it has received by delegation from its members. (Qtd. in Lenihan, Robertson, and Tasse 1994, 36)

The collectivist vision, on the other hand, tends to be a local/provincial vision, since the collectivity, being a minority—and in the case of the French Canadians cum Quebecois, a fairly concentrated one—in the state as a whole, requires some lower-level recognition and autonomy; they are a subsociety and look to a substate for their leadership and protection. The nationalist Levesque explains it clearly in his theoretical writing:

> French Canadians are more than a collection of individuals; they form a national community with its own culture and history, and today they prefer to call themselves a nation. . . . [Therefore, in Quebec] French-Canadians form a political society with its own powers and institutions and, above all, a state whose machinery and direction they control. (1968, 89–90)

As we will see subsequently, Quebecois, once francophone nationalism becomes reformulated on the basis of that identity, regard Quebec more than Canada as their national state.

Thus, the anglophones, or English Canadians, and the francophones, or French Canadians or Quebecois, not only derive their traditions and symbols from different sources in the past, but they also orient themselves toward different levels of "politics" in the present and for the future. Anglophone allegiance and identity, by and large, are aimed at and tied to the federal state; it is the product and guarantor of the English traditions that "made" Canada in the political sense. Resnick, something of an English-Canadian nationalist, argues that "English Canada has forged an identity based upon strong identification with the institutions of the federal state" (1990, 19). It is toward the federal level that they look for resolution of social problems, and the collapse or fragmentation of the federation would be a more profound loss for them than for the French Canadians. The latter, as francophone nationalism has evolved and modernized, have increasingly looked upon the federal government as the instrument of anglophone cultural and linguistic domination and assimilation and therefore upon the provincial government of Quebec in particular as the vehicle of their national aspirations.

Another important aspect of Canada's identity crisis seems to be its relationship to its giant American neighbor. The sheer social and cultural gravity of the United States has always been a concern for Canadian nationalists, who fear, if not the actual annexation of their country into the United States (which appears much less likely today than at some points in the past, although there has been speculation that a balkanized Canada might lead the Maritime provinces, separated from the rest of Canada by a sovereign Quebec, to join the American union), then the cultural subjugation of their country to the vast "culture machine" that is the United States. Resnick again writes that "English Canada, throughout its history, has experienced simultaneous attraction to and fear of the United States. Yet the desire not to be overwhelmed has been persistent and it fuels national sentiment today" (1990, 19). Thus, despite the fact that Canada and America share language and historical heritage, an awful lot of Canada's activity has been an attempt to distinguish itself from the latter and to prevent "further loss of identity through [the United States'] invasive culture and the inexorable pull of trade currents toward some unwanted, homogenizing continentalism" (Lamont 1994, 24).

The report of the Association of Universities and Colleges of Canada, published in 1978 under the title *To Know Ourselves,* concluded that "there is no developed country in the world with comparable resources that devotes as little attention to the support of its own culture and of education relating to itself" (qtd. in Bell and Tepperman 1992, 63). To attempt to remedy this situation, the Canadian government in recent decades has created or funded institutions to proliferate its own culture and self-education. As long ago as 1913, the Canadian National Gallery was established with a mind, according to the minutes of the meetings of the board of trustees, "to instil [*sic*] national pride, to encourage a sense of national identity, and to create appropriate values in this heterogeneous new and cultural diverse country." In 1936 the Canadian Broadcasting Corporation was created with a similar mission: to bring Canadian programming (radio and television) to Canada, to free it from foreign (mostly United States) influence and dependence, and to serve as "the cornerstone, not only of the Canadian broadcasting system, but of Canada itself." Other institutions like the National Film Board, the Canada Council (to support artists and arts organizations), and the National Arts Centre followed, all with the aim to promote and even to produce a Canadian identity and consciousness—as the first head of the NFB, John Grierson, put it, to be "the eyes of Canada . . . through [which to] see Canada and see it whole—its people and its purposes" (Handler 1988, 74).

Quebecois Culture and Identity

Meanwhile, the reaction of francophones was not always sympathetic to these actions by government. National cultural institutions could be and often were interpreted as assimilationist, both in the sense that a single national culture was being packaged and sold to Canadians of different cultural backgrounds and that this national culture tended to present and represent English language and culture interests more than French ones. Just as Canada as a whole felt and feels a need to protect and preserve its culture from embracing, assimilating foreign intrusion, so French Canada came to feel a need to protect and preserve its culture from embracing, assimilating federal intrusion. In response, francophones, mainly but not exclusively in Quebec, have mobilized to perpetuate, collect, and in some cases even invent their unique culture. We will return to this matter in some detail in the discussion of the evolution of francophone/Quebecois nationalism in the next section, but some comments are due at this point.

As early as the mid-nineteenth century, a few French-Canadian scholars were in search of "authentic" French-Canadian culture, and they began to "find" it in the same place where Norwegian nationalist-minded scholars did, as mentioned previously in this study, and where nationalists tend to—in the folk society. In 1863 and 1865, for example, Hubert LaRue and Ernest Gagnon published studies of French-Canadian folk songs from the real folk of the francophone nation, the rural population. This discovery, however, like many such scholarly researches on folk culture, incorporated two anthropological fallacies: first, taking a temporally local cultural product as a timeless bit of tradition and, second, taking a geographically local cultural product as a socially general tradition of all French Canadians. Furthermore, as we observe in retrospect again and again (and observe often enough in our own day), such scholarship was not necessarily ideologically or politically neutral: Handler maintains that, "according to folklorists, a return to folk sources was precisely what was needed to stimulate national culture. Their larger purpose was to encourage the French-Canadian intelligentsia to seek inspiration in the folk culture of Canada rather than in French high culture" (1988, 74). In effect (to take some poetic license with a term of political consequence in the late twentieth century in Canada) what was transpiring was a "patriation" of French-Canadian culture away from the mother country of France and to the new and real homeland of the distinct and authentic people. In the process "that a folk tradition has been created for urban Quebecois who are no longer folks seems unquestionable"; that "folk society" as such was created out of patches and scraps of living tradition, memory, and hopeful wishing is another way of looking at this search (Handler 1988, 79).

It is provocative to think of the role of professional anthropology in all this. A "movement" of popularizing French-Canadian folk culture began in the early twentieth century under the leadership of Marius Barbeau, who studied under R. R. Marett at Oxford and then worked for Edward Sapir in the Victoria Memorial Museum. Yet, as North American anthropology was still in its museum-and-curiosity phase at this point, Barbeau's collection of French materials did not come alive until he met Franz Boas, who encouraged him to think seriously about early colonial French-Canadian culture. Barbeau himself later credited that the folk culture movement born thereby "was brought about by Dr. Franz Boas in 1914 when, at an annual meeting of the Anthropological Association in New York, he invited the author of this article to collect French Canadian folktales and publish them in the *Journal of American Folklore.* This urge released new initiatives within Canada . . . that have been highly productive ever since" (qtd. in Handler 1988, 72). Barbeau and his colleagues went on to collect folk data and to disseminate it via "folklore shows" to the public, urban-ites, and educated francophones. Clearly, anthropology must and should want to look at its own part in such "applied" uses of its methods and findings.

At any rate what began (more or less earnestly) as scholarship quickly became or gave substance to politics and law. For example, in 1922 Quebec passed the Historic or Artistic Monuments Act to identify, inventory, and preserve French-Canadian artifacts and features. The act enshrined the concept of "cultural property," which belonged to the French-Canadian nation as a whole and which survived from or represented the original style and genius of that people. This opus of archaeological, anthropological, and historical material constituted the nation's patrimony, or *patrimoine,* its collective heritage and the physical store of its identity. Fairly naturally, the more ancient, the more authentic: initially, the *patrimoine* particularly consisted of French-colonial remnants, although this was to change as it and the notion of cultural property expanded.

In 1956 Quebec's Royal Commission of Inquiry on Constitutional Problems (also known as the Tremblay Commission) presented its report. While I will return to the report and the entire political and cultural struggle it symbolized between Ottawa and Quebec City, it is necessary to appreciate the explicitness with which culture and cultural concerns energized the entire argument. Quebec's demands on or against the central government turned on cultural claims and on a fairly self-consciously anthropological sense of culture. Notably, the second volume of the Tremblay Commission's report begins with a section called "The Problem of Culture" and attempts to formulate a definition of culture that would buttress Quebec's claims not only to special status but to represent the French-Canadian/francophone/Quebecois nation. In this section culture is defined "as an organic collection of knowledge, of means of expression and of values" that are part of or instantiations of a universal Culture; on the other hand, Culture manifests itself in particular national culture: "Every national culture is a[n] . . . interpretation of a philosophy either universal or tending towards universality. What there is of *national,* and consequently of difference in it, is not the thought but its form; on one side the expression and, primarily, the language; on the other side . . . usages, customs, traditions, etc." (Government of Quebec 1956, 15). Thus, although "Culture" is universal, it is accessible to actual human beings only in the form of national culture, characterized as "the totality of the rational and spiritual values forming the collective patrimony of a determined human group." Before moving on, let us consider two final things in the commission's attitudes: first, the invocation and lionization of the *patrimoine;* and, second, although we could not see it in the discussion so far, the subordination of culture in the anthropological sense to religion. This latter highlights a critical aspect of French-Canadian identity and of its changing forms of nationalism.

To conclude these remarks on the formalization and institutionalization of French-Canadian culture in the face of and in distinction to a generalized but largely anglicized national, Canadian culture, it is worth mentioning such institutions as the Ministère des Affaires Culturelles (MAC), established after the 1960 provincial election, and the Institut National de la Civilisation, created in 1967. The ministry, a provincial government department, was designed to promote the French fact in Canada through such devices as an arts council, a historic monuments council (already in place since 1922), an urban planning office, a language office, and an extraprovincial francophone office. The institute, a short-lived thing, was intended as a research facility and museum for studying "the civilization of Quebec" by means of all social scientific disciplines from "ethnography (including demography, classic and peasant popular art, popular traditions, etc.) to Quebecois Amerindian ethnology and archeology."

Despite the fact that some francophone leaders have been active in institutionalizing their culture, it remains that "the francophone nation" has an identity crisis of its own, or at least some unresolved identity issues, if students of that culture are correct. For one thing, the precise contents of that culture have yet to be specified; at the same time, the aspects of the culture that are central to its political identity and ethnopolitical mobilization have changed over the years (principally from religion to language). Currently, the French language is the most often referred-to element of the culture, yet it is a double-edged sword: speaking French makes the Canadian francophones different from other Canadians but similar to Frenchmen and other international francophones. Are the French Canadians, then, part of larger "French" nation, or are they a nation unto themselves? And are all francophone Canadians the nation or only those in Quebec? Another key aspect of the culture is Catholicism, but this fails to distinguish them from the international Catholic community and also is a less decisive phenomenon than language in current identity formulations. The society was at one time primarily agrarian and rural but no more. In fact, as we will see next, there is a basic (though largely decided, for the moment) question about whether the francophone nation is distributed throughout Canada or is coterminous with Quebec.

But the identity problems of French Canada go deeper and resemble in microcosm those of Canada as a whole. Nicol and Whalley in their study of Canadian identity suggest that "Canada is history's foster child. Despite the comfortable circumstances of her homeland, she cannot shake off the suspicion that she does not know her real parents" (1966, viii). The same can be said of French Canada as a subset of Canada. Handler notes that francophone nationalism posits something like a collective individuality that was born with French colonization but ripped from its mother's lap, or perhaps orphaned by her, with the Conquest; such an image "allows nationalists to psychologize history—that is, to discuss the history of the nation as if it were the history of a person" (1988, 42). If this is so, it is an arrested childhood, one that shows up in the symbology of the national personality, such as its literature.

On this subject Dufault (1991) finds that the themes and patterns in francophone literature indicate certain internal struggles regarding the historical and social position of francophones vis-à-vis the larger Canadian society. Childhood itself is a major theme: according to Chatillon, images of childhood recur "with a continuity, a persistence that can rightly qualify as obsessional" (qtd. in Dufault 1991, 13; my trans.). In fact, one of the more common genres of French-Canadian literature is the fictionalized autobiography, in which the protagonist starts out in his or her childhood, usually idyllically remembered, and then matures into a decidedly darker and more threatening world. The most frequent expression of affect in these stories is loss and alienation as the characters leave their childhood behind. Even more, it is not simply the innocence of childhood that is left behind but regularly also the familiar rural, village way of life: in many of the novels the tale begins in the bosom of the French-Canadian folk community and takes the characters, as they grow up, to the city, where they have many strange and unsettling experiences in contact with urban culture and *les anglais.* From Philippe Aubert de Gaspe's *Memoires* (1866) to Hugh MacLennan's *Two Solitudes* (1945) and beyond, this pattern is evident.

Childhood is certainly a common enough symbol of innocence and of self-discovery, but in French-Canadian literature it seems to serve two special purposes. One is the idealization of traditional, agrarian French culture; childhood (authentic culture) is looked back upon as beautiful and perfect, especially in contrast to the adult, urban experiences that the characters later have. The second purpose of the child image is the representation of the collective, national, experience of the community. As I have said, it is commonplace to hear the francophone nation likened to a child and, even more, to a child who has not completed and has not been allowed to complete its normal maturation process. This situation is attributed to the historical fact that it was "orphaned," stunted in its growth, by the defeat at the hands of the English and the withdrawal of France in the eighteenth century. "The Conquest cut too early the umbilical cord that tied us to the mother country" (Bouthilette, qtd. in Dufault 1991, 14; my trans.). The result, according to some francophone interpreters, has been the permanent scarring of the "national psyche." Bouthillete asserts that "profoundly debilitating feelings of loss and alienation have pervaded the collective consciousness since 'la Conquête'" (qtd. in Dufault 1991, 14; my trans.). In the political realm Vallières stresses that the defeat of the *Patriotes* rebellion in 1837–38 "caused such a national inferiority complex, such an ideological withdrawal," that the nation is only now, by great force of will, recovering from it. Truly, history has become psychology, and psychology has become history.

Evolution of Nationalism in French Canada

It is unquestioned that there has been a "French" presence, a French fact, in Canada since its founding as a unified English colony in 1759 and subsequently as a constitutional state in 1867. History suggests clearly that the francophone and anglophone communities of Canada were engaged with each other from the start: the society's duality was recognized, francophones joined anglophones in governmental institutions, and francophone groups and organizations existed to combat assimilation and to promote French-Canadian culture and language. This should not be construed, however, as modern nationalism. Rather, despite a certain amount of formal contact between the "two majorities," they remained "two solitudes" partly by choice and design, not in direct competition or confrontation *as* ethnic groups. Vallieres described the French response to English domination and potential anglicization as a "'tactical' withdrawal" by a subject people aimed at preserving their identity and culture by shielding themselves and it from the forces of English Canada as much as possible. Essentially, this entailed a kind of self-segregation, literally a geographic separation, of the French Canadians into their rural, traditional villages, mainly in Quebec, leaving the towns and the most of the rest of Canada to the English.

The goal of this stand was cultural survival, called "la survivance." *La survivance* as a national policy, if we can call it that, has been described as "defensive, inward-looking and conservative." It sought to preserve the community and culture by "avoiding contamination by urban, English [society] and maintaining . . . purity in the homogeneous environments of rural and small-town Quebec. *La survivance* was not a strategy of linguistic promotion or confrontation with the English" (Levine 1990, 33). In other words, French Canadians did not strive at that point to transform Canada into a French society nor to separate Quebec from Canada as a sovereign state nor even to give French a parity with English in Canada's politics and economy. In fact, it seems that language was not even the chief focus of this traditional culture but, rather, religion was.

Understandably, then, the chief agent of *la survivance* was the religious organization and elite, the Catholic Church. Hence, nationalism was less critical to survival than orthodoxy and the persistence of true belief, giving *la survivance* its conservative character. As I noted in the discussion of the definition of culture in the Tremblay Commission report, spiritual values were still seen to be central, even predominant, in French-Canadian culture: it is religion, the report states, that gives culture "its general inspiration and directive thought; while religion borrows from culture such and such means of integration within . . . daily life" (1956, 6). In the case of French-Canadian culture it derives its uniqueness from "its Christian inspiration and its French genius." In 1919 Henri Bourassa could still give a speech in which he asked, "Are we more French than Catholic?" and answered himself with the credo that "man belongs to God before he belongs to himself; he must serve the Church before serving his fatherland." He continues that "the only universal and complete society [is] the Church" and that the French language is closely tied to and deeply steeped in the faith—that it "encourages, among those who speak and write it, Catholic ideas, Catholic mores, Catholic traditions, and Catholic culture" (1919, 11).

Thus, French-Canadian society through the nineteenth century and into the twentieth was a Church-dominated and priest-dominated society. In the "power vacuum" created by the Conquest and the withdrawal, elimination, or co-optation of French-Canadian secular elites, the church expanded to fill the available space, numerically and structurally. The number of priests per capita in Quebec grew during the nineteenth and early twentieth centuries to one for ever 504 Catholics by 1951, the highest rate of any Western society (Bell and Tepperman 1992, 96). This is partly based on the high status of the priesthood and the relatively open recruitment from among French-Canadian families but also on the lack of economic development in the society, which left few opportunities for young Catholic men other than the priesthood. Beyond sheer numbers, however, the pervasiveness of the church in the life of the community was considerable. Handler reckons that 50 percent of these priests were engaged in "religious work" per se, while the other 50 percent performed what we might call "social work" in the form of education, health care, charity, and other such crucial social services that were not yet (but would soon become, portentously) prerogatives of the government. These social offices gave them great access to and control over cultural production and cultural reproduction in the forms of school curricula and reading material, movies and other types of entertainment, and even labor unions. In their view foreign influences (namely, English-Protestant Canada) were contaminating, and the secular state, the materialistic industrial economy, and the liberal city were corrupting, all of which should be avoided by their French-Canadian flock.

Therefore, early French-Canadian opposition to English Canada and its state and economy was not exactly ethnic in the modern sense. *La survivance* created and defended group boundaries, which modern ethnicity does as well, but the latter "uses" those boundaries to bump up against rival ethnic groups and challenge them for land, wealth, power, or other resources, not to flee from those rivals and, in effect, abandon the rivalry. In other words, the mobilization of French-Canadian identity, which took the form of a sort of nonmobilization, was not rooted exclusively or even particularly in cultural difference with *les anglais* but in the defensive posture of the Catholic Church, "which distrusted [the] state as a rival power and as a child of the Revolution, liable to be dominated by anti-clericals, Protestants, or even socialists" (Trudeau 1968, 109). And it was anything but a spontaneous expression of a nation's will but, rather, a managed, though perhaps thoroughly sincere, exercise by a dominant but traditional elite.

Try as it may, however, to hold back the forces of modernity, the church could not keep the modern society out of French Canada nor the French Canadians out of the modern society. Perhaps the greatest single factor in this change in the early present century was World War I, which thrust Canada into world affairs and francophones into the broiling and shifting urban, industrial society of Canada. This change, which was as much demographic as cultural, took francophones out of the village in large numbers and therefore out of the hands of their priests; in the process the will to survive was gradually replaced by a will to compete, to progress, and, maybe more important than anything else, to see themselves and their culture in the wider horizons that had been opened up to them—at first, a place beside English but eventually, at least in their "home," the place formerly occupied by English.

Urbanization was probably the most important single factor in the evolution, the modernization, of French-Canadian ethnicity. Statistics show that in the middle of the nineteenth century Quebec was less than 15 percent urban, while Canada as a whole was around 13 percent urban; by World War I those figures approached 45 percent and 42 percent, respectively. By the 1930s both the province and the state were over half-urban, and the trend continued in the following decades. The effects on francophones were dramatic. They were distinctly "not at home" in the wider anglicized society, even in the old French city of Montreal. They were increasingly occupied in secular, materialist activities like industry, and they found themselves in competition, generally on the lower side of the competition—with anglophones. *La survivance* had kept them alive culturally, but it had kept them back economically.

Above all else, as an immediate effect, urbanization and modernization created new types of French Canadians, particularly a middle class and intelligentsia. These types were in a better position in terms of education and organization to take up the cause of the new French Canadians, but theirs was a transitional and mixed nationalism, a blend of modern and traditional ideas that preserved much of the religious flavor of francophone nationhood. The transitional phase lasted from the early twentieth century until about the 1960s, when what Quebecois call *la grande noirceur* (the great darkness) lifted and ethnonationalists began to realize the centrality of the state in their cultural struggles; until that time ethnicity retains much of its premodern, especially religious, character, while it is alloyed with certain aspects of modern, even anthropological, thinking.

The "modern" francophone movement can be traced to the turn of the century and to such new, urban institutions as the Catholic French-language newspapers like *L'Action Sociale* (Quebec City, 1907), *Le Devoir* (Montreal, 1910), and *Le Droit* (Ottawa, 1913) and the religious and linguistic associations like Société du Parler Français, Association Catholique de la Jeunesse Canadienne-Français, and Ligue Nationaliste. These institutions all served consciously cultural-political purposes, although varying ones, from promoting language to promoting the faith. The single most influential group, however, which produced the most influential individuals, ideologies, and cultural products, was L'Action Française, a post–World War I progeny of these earlier organizations. L'Action Française is noteworthy not so much for its mass appeal and mass impact (which were lacking) as for its formulation of an ethnonational discourse and imagery, its (albeit tentative and incomplete) embrace of the forces and effects of modernization, and its overt "political" action, if we take that term in its widest sense.

Let us consider the messages and the metaphors first. Perhaps the most significant figure in L'Action Française was Abbe Lionel Groulx, who coined the term *maîtres chez nous* (masters of our own house). As Groulx put it: "We have to choose whether to become once again the masters of our own house or whether to resign ourselves forever to the destiny of a serf people" (qtd. in Simeon and Robertson 1990, 42; my trans.). For Groulx and his coreligionists (for he was, after all, like many of the members of this and other early nationalist groups, an official of the church) this "people" was at once more and less than the modern ethnic group, and the symbols and metaphors deployed to typify it are reminiscent of nineteenth century (both popular and scholarly) thought yet also of much contemporary opinion in regard to ethnicity. In particular, Groulx's vision of French-Canadian ethnicity was racial and organic.

Groulx and L'Action Française inherited the tradition in French-Canadian historical writing—and the convention of the era—of construing what we would today call ethnic groups or nations as races. This can be traced back at least to François-Xavier Garneau's *Histoire du Canada* (1845). Garneau's history pitted the two races of Canada, English and French, against each other in a grand conflict; it made that conflict the central and defining fact of Canadian history. Even more, though, it attempted to show that French Canada had a history—and a future. It was, like all nationalistic histories, a salutary and cautionary tale; the nation's identity rested in its glorious past and in the traditions handed down from that past: "Let the *Canadiens* be faithful to themselves; let them be wise and persevering, may they not be carried away by the sparkle of social or political novelties. . . . A part of our strength comes from our traditions; let us not leave them or change them, except gradually" (qtd. in Johnson 1994, 37–38).

In Groulx's thinking this moral history was combined with the organic racial theories of the time to produce "a peculiarly biological view of ethnicity. For him, 'races,' in the sense of nationalities, pass on from generation to generation a common soul of the nation" (Johnson 1994, 41). We can find this sentiment reflected right up to recent decades, in the very political literature of Quebecois nationalism; René Levesque evokes it again when he says of the national personality, or soul: "This is a physical fact. To be unable to live as ourselves, as we should live, in our own language and according to our own ways, would be like living without an arm or a leg—or perhaps a heart." Identity emerges from culture, and culture emerges from collective personality, the national soul: "Any one who does not feel it, at least occasionally, is not—is no longer—one of us" (1968, 15).

Two things follow from this view. First, while culture (in the form of language, customs, etc.) is the critical expression of this national soul, it is not the essence of that soul. At this stage the national culture is only a particular and local manifestation of a more ineffable essence. More central to this essence than language for these early nationalists is spirit, which gives to the French-Canadian nation its special mission in North America, if not the world. Louis-Adolphe Paquet, a contemporary of Groulx, expresses this in the extreme:

> We are not merely a civilized race, we are the pioneers of civilization; we are not merely a religious people, we are the very messengers of the idea of religion. Our calling is not so much to handle capital as to weigh ideas; it is not so much to light the fires of factories as to make the light of religion and intellect shine as widely as possible. While our rivals may claim hegemony over industry and finance in a struggle that is no doubt courteous, we would rather compete on questions of doctrine; the laurels we seek are evangelical ones. (Qtd. in Clift 1982, 12–13)

Second, then, a race with such a distinct national soul, and one so steeped in spiritual matters, must be careful not to lose that soul, lest it lose its identity as a collectivity if not its very life. The struggle for survival persists in a deep concern for cultural and spiritual contamination and pollution now that the nation is in direct contact with the crass secular materialists in the new urban environment. Groulx refers to a kind of "moral hygiene" that forbids the mixing of incompatible elements that would corrupt and ultimately confuse the national soul; these include, in its most palpable form, exogamy and miscegenation as well as moral and cultural pollution (picking up secular, materialistic, individualistic habits from *les anglais*) and linguistic assimilation.

Thus, although L'Action Française found itself in, and was a product of, an urbanizing, modernizing social milieu, it remained noticeably ambivalent about these changes. Urbanization presented a "series of dangers to the French Canadian community. All facets of city life, from crowds and mobility to the popularity of the Sunday movie, were interpreted as so many distress signals to the French Canadian family" (Trofimenkoff 1975, 71). Industrialization was suspect as well for its materialism, its secularism, its mixing of the races in the workplace, and its erosion of the primordial agrarian tradition of francophone culture. This is not at all surprising, since we see again and again in the anthropological literature that it is often at the moment of urbanization and modernization that cultural concerns and fears are born, which may take the form of various kinds of revivalist and fundamentalist movements, of which ethnicity is one variation. Traditional church authorities were even more sure of the threat and glorified the former rustic existence of the *Habitants:* "it is there that our race drew its strength, it is there that our survival was assured, there that those virtues which are characteristic of our people and have made it the happiest and the most religious people on the earth, grew and were strengthened" (qtd. in Johnson 1994, 39). The church was also instrumental in many social organizations among the urban migrants, not least of all the unions such as the Union Catholique des Cultivateurs and the Confederation des Travailleurs Catholique du Canada, but not so much to advance social and urban causes as to ensure a Catholic spirit in the activities of these individuals and groups.

Nevertheless, despite the church's admonitions and L'Action Française's ambivalence, the urbanizing and modernizing processes were not to roll back, and in fact the latter engaged in what can only be considered modern, urban ethnic action. For example, it confronted the English establishment with language demands of the most mundane kind, fighting for French translations on product packaging, for correct French vocabulary and grammar in printed media like catalogs, and for telephone operator assistance in French. These demands were sometimes merely for inclusion alongside English, other times for exclusive French usage; banks, for instance, were pressured to adopt French business names and to provide checks and other banking forms solely in French (Trofimenkoff 1975, 50–52). Finally, an *Almanach de la Langue Française* was published annually that included not only the usual fare of calendars of religious events and saints' days but also more modern, politicized material such as "essays, stories, poems, songs, pictures, and even the occasional cartoon, each glorifying the linguistic, social, and religious traditions of French

Canadians" (38). Together with the folkloristic activities of the aforementioned Barbeau, these and other elements made for an increasingly powerful and conspicuous movement and mobilization of French-Canadian culture and an increasingly modern-looking one.

French Canada, therefore, was beginning to come off of the defensive and go on the offensive; this trend was slow and restricted at first, but it would gain momentum throughout the coming decades. And, although some francophones could conceive and advocate a sovereign French-Canadian state by this time, such was not the main thrust of the cultural movement of the period. Such remained the case, despite a heightened national consciousness at least among some elites, from the 1930s even into the 1950s in Quebec, as it passed through its period of *la grand noirceur* under the Union Nationale Party and premier Maurice Duplessis. Under Duplessis's various administrations (he held the premiership from 1936 to 1940 and again from 1944 to 1959), and especially after World War II, nationalism took the primary form of provincial autonomy from federal authority. This fact began to alter the character of francophone nationalism, giving it a more distinctly territorial aspect, identifying it more completely with the province of Quebec than with the pan-Canadian francophone diaspora. Yet it remained short of full modern ethnonationalism. In Quinn's analysis of the Union Nationale he asserts that Duplessis "still idealized the rural way of life and looked upon the farmer as the most stable, industrious, and law-abiding social type, 'the true French Canadian'" (1979, 79). In Duplessis's own words, "In the rural class we find the stable element which can counteract the spirit of disorder which is being found in some urban areas these days" (qtd. in Quinn 1979, 85).

When Duplessis died in 1959, *la grand noirceur* was lifted, and dawn broke to reveal that a revolution was taking place. It is referred to in Canadian society and scholarship as the "Quiet Revolution," and naturally it was not as sudden or as unexpected as the name suggests. I noted earlier that the urbanization of Quebec and of Canada in general progressed without pause from the first part of the century and that a new urban, educated elite and a new urban working class were being prepared thereby. Accordingly, the influence of the church and of traditional authorities, interests, and values was on the wane. Despite the fact that tradition-minded cultural organizations (like L'Action Française) and political parties (like Union Nationale) had not caught up with it, the revolution was already on. The really revolutionary part of the Quiet Revolution was the heightened consciousness of the facts that were evident from looking at the new Quebec and the new Canada and the orientation of provincial government to embrace and especially to participate in such changes, to use the power of government to pursue and promote national interests.

In some ways the Quiet Revolution was like a renaissance, with a surge of cultural activity and productivity in the francophone community; the arts, publishing, and organizations of French Canada proliferated in what Johnson calls "an outbreak of hope. Suddenly everything seemed possible" (1994, 112). The term used at the time and since to characterize the moment was *épanouissement* (blossoming or expanding). Perhaps more basically than anything else, the francophones had finally made the adjustment to modern urban life, which meant ending their cultural isolation. In fact, the new middle class and elites (especially what Fournier has termed the *travailleurs du langage,* i.e., those in occupations that depend on literacy and the control and manipulation of information, like managers, educators, journalists, and other such intelligentsia) now viewed isolation as the sure road to the diminution, marginalization, "folklorization," or ultimate disappearance of their culture; only active engagement in the business of everyday modern life could guarantee that French-Canadian culture would remain a living and progressing entity.

But, ironically, participating in the broader social reality of Quebec and Canada meant accepting many of the norms and values that had seemed so foreign and threatening to the previous generation of nationalists and elites. Entering fully into this wider society, therefore, entailed dramatic change, a certain cultural convergence between Canada's two majorities and thus a direct competition between the two majorities for the benefits of the new society. Most ironically of all, it was this cultural convergence and this direct competition that actually facilitated ethnicity in the fully modern sense among the francophones. The very terms of national identity were undergoing a change: increasing numbers of Quebec francophones, "while retaining the sense of the priority of political community that underpinned all Quebec nationalism, defined that community in more secular, materialist, and individualist terms" (Simeon and Robertson 1990, 156) instead of the former religious/Catholic, spiritual, agrarian/communitarian ones.

The new political leadership was crucial to the *épanouissement* of French Canada, and in fact it was partially the *épanouissement* of the government that made the cultural flowering possible. In 1960 the Union Nationale was replaced in office by the Liberal Party of Jean Lesage. Lesage appreciated the significance and potential of government in social and cultural affairs and used its power to promote national or ethnic interests and to modernize the institutions of the provincial society (or, perhaps we should say, to promote national interests *by* modernizing the institutions of the society). Whereas Duplessis's administration had eschewed interventionism, Lesage's embraced it; as the latter maintained, "the only power at our disposal is that state of Quebec. . . . If we refuse to use our state, we would deprive ourselves of what is perhaps our only means of survival and development in North America" (qtd. in Simeon and Robertson 1990, 179).

This situation was exacerbated by the feeling of a growing number of Quebecois that they were "behind" the anglophones in their own province in terms of economic wealth and power; "catching up," or *rattrapage,* was necessary to correct this injustice. Yet this race, or competition, was quickly construed as a "national liberation struggle" in which anglophones had an unfair advantage and in fact were responsible for the backwardness of francophone society. This interpretation was at least a little disingenuous, for it was its own traditional elites, especially the clergy but also the provincial government as typified by the Union Nationale, which had advocated its withdrawal (a "strategic" withdrawal, perhaps, but a withdrawal all the same) and had therefore blocked and actively resisted the francophone community's development in pace with that of the anglophone community's. The point is not to blame the church and the traditional elites, wholly or in part, for French-Canadian economic backwardness and weakness, although Johnson concludes that *rattrapage* "turned into an operation in which English-speaking Canadians were held responsible for disastrous choices made in the past by Quebec's elites" (Johnson 1994, 32). Instead, the point is to illustrate how a new set of Quebecois elites interpreted their history, always a mixture of remembering and forgetting, to give that history and their present situation meaning and to suggest a course of action.

In the cause of *rattrapage* Lesage set out to modernize—which often meant to secularize—the institutions of Quebec. In the decade of the 1960s provincial government spending per capita increased over 200 percent, and the bureaucracy more than doubled in size. This growth was necessary as the government moved into new fields like education, social services, and even industry. It took over the control of schools, wresting this responsibility away from the church, and invested heavily in higher education. It became active in health care and retirement funding, creating in 1965 the Caisse de Dépot et Placement to manage the province's own pension plan. It established economic enterprises under state auspices, including the 1962 Société Genérale de Financement, which sought to support francophone-owned businesses. Finally, and most notably of all, it nationalized the important utility Hydro-Quebec, which became the symbol and cornerstone of francophone economic independence from English Canada.

The Institutionalization of Nationalism and the Quebecois Nation

> *As they grow more free, more democratic, better educated, and richer, Quebecois necessarily are more clearly conscious of their identity as a group, and have a better understanding of sovereignty as the essential condition for improving their collective life. Social progress nourishes nationalism, until nationalism appears as the indispensable key to social progress.*
>
> —René Levesque

Under the impact of the Quiet Revolution a reevaluation of the nature and extent of francophone nationalism was begun. Until the early or middle part of the twentieth century French Canadians had more or less thought of themselves as French Canadians, as a Canadian minority, that is, one dispersed across Canada, although concentrated particularly in Quebec. They were a nation in the spiritual sense but not in the territorial sense, and that nationhood rested on their shared religious identity more than their shared language, which was merely a vehicle and expression of the religion. Yet, with the "statist" policies of the provincial government of Quebec, it became possible and then common to see the nation in a territorial sense too, as a "majority" in its own land, *chez nous;* the homeland was taken to be Quebec. "Maîtres chez nous" had been a slogan for some decades, as we have seen, but never before had the "home" been so clearly and territorially defined. The nation was no longer a dispersed and rootless minority, but a society within a society, and increasingly Quebec came to be viewed as a state within a state. To symbolize and realize this ambition a conference, called "Les États-Generaux du Canada Français," was summoned in 1967, invoking the French revolutionary spirit to assert the claims of the nation, which were (1) that French Canadians were a nation; (2) that Quebec was the national territory of that nation; and (3) that as a nation the Quebecois were entitled to self-determination. It is not insignificant that, in the same year, French president De Gaulle visited Quebec and stoked nationalist sentiment by reminding them that they were a distinct nation and endorsing their struggle to become masters in their own house, going so far as to cry: "Vive le Quebec! Vive le Quebec libre!" (qtd. in Levesque 1968, 63).

With the rightful home of the nation thus identified, the nature of the nation was altered. The nation was no longer "the French Canadians" or "the francophones" but "the Quebecois." This, as can readily be appreciated, was and is a two-edged sword: concentration in and focus on Quebec gives the nation a defensible claim to majority status in its homeland and raises it above the status of other "minorities" on the Canadian scene, but it also defines out the francophones who do not reside in Quebec. Not being *in* Quebec, they are not *of* Quebec, are not Quebecois, and thus not part of the nation struggled for. In the interest of consolidation of the ethnic claim, a portion of the ethnic group gets left out; even so, demand for rights and recognition as Quebecois is more powerful than as francophones or as French Canadians. The territorial aspect gives the nation a location from which to launch its activities and, even more crucially, a government by which to launch them. In fact, it might be argued with some justification that the state was not the product of the nation, but vice versa: the nation, the Quebecois nation, was produced by the state (the Quebec government) and its political activities.

Quebec separatism follows from this view of the nation and its rights to self-determination—its need to rule itself to preserve and promote its distinct culture and identity. This movement was energized, however, and its radical edge was motivated in practice, by a further interpretation, one borrowed from the discourse of international cultural struggle of the times, that is, the interpretation of colonialism. Beginning around 1960, and partly as a result of anticolonialist struggles going on in the world (especially the francophone world) at the time, some more radical sectors of the Quebecois movement began to perceive Quebec's relationship to the Canadian union as a colonial one. The first important organization to maintain this view was the Rassemblement pour l'Independance Nationale (RIN), a small political party whose 1960 manifesto voiced Quebecois nationalism in the language of anticolonialism: "At the present time when, the world over, peoples emancipate themselves from the colonial yoke and nations demand their full independence, French Canada can no longer accept to remain under the economic and political trusteeship of the outsider" (qtd. in Levesque 1968, 46). This position suggested not only a radicalization, even militancy, in the Quebecois movement but a dramatic social distancing from the rest of Canada: anglophone Canadians were not fellow countrymen but oppressors and foreigners, and Canada was not the homeland but the agency of colonial oppression. The only answer to Quebec's problems was decolonization.

This radicalization and militancy was fully realized in the spring of 1963, when a group known as the Front de Liberation du Quebec (FLQ) emerged. The FLQ took up the language of anticolonialism and socialism and added to it a dash of terrorism; that its name, its ideology, and its methods were modeled after the terrorist Algerian Front de Liberation Nationale (FLN), has not gone unnoticed. The FLQ's manifesto, which appeared in April 1963, contains such statements as these:

> Quebec is a colony!
> We are a colonized people, politically, socially, and economically. Politically, because we do not have any hold on the political instruments necessary for our survival. . . .
> Socially, too, Quebec is a colony. We represent 80 percent of the population, and yet the English language prevails in many fields. French is gradually relegated to the realm of folklore. . . .
> . . . it is no longer enough to want independence, to work within the existing political separatist parties. . . .
> Only a full-fledged revolution can build up the necessary power to achieve the vital changes that will be needed in an independent Quebec.
> . . .
> QUEBEC PATRIOTS, TO ARMS! THE HOUR OF NATIONAL REVOLUTION HAS STRUCK! (Qtd. in Scott and Oliver 1964, 83–87)

Pierre Vallières, the chief theoretician of the FLQ, in his "autobiography" adopts the imagery of the "nigger" to express the condition of Quebecois in their oppressed country: Quebecois, he says, "are aware of their condition as niggers, exploited men, second-class citizens. . . . Were they not *imported,* like the American blacks, to serve as cheap labor in the New World?" (1971, 21). Regardless of the fact that the *Habitants* of colonial Canada were not imported by anybody and that precious little immigration from France took place after the Conquest, this kind of talk is incendiary. Nationalism is a critical ingredient in the struggle against imperialism and colonialism; in this sense Vallières's and the FLQ's theory of liberation is a Leninist theory of national liberation against international capitalism and imperialism. In another book he argues that the class struggle cannot develop in a society that has not recognized itself first as a nation, that a nation cannot be reduced to economics or even culture but can only know itself as a national state.

The birth of the FLQ and the revolution was literally incendiary, being announced with a string of bombings of mailboxes and other such symbols of federal authority but also of other more prominent targets, including the Montreal Stock Exchange, the Board of Trade, and Eaton's Department Store, beginning in the spring of 1963 and continuing until 1970 or so. Occasionally, violent demonstrations occurred, as in June 1968, when Prime Minister Pierre Trudeau's visit to Montreal set off a protest injuring 135 people. The most serious incident, however, and the one that caused the federal government to intervene with the War Measures Act, was the kidnapping in 1970 of Quebec's labor minister, Pierre Laporte, and the British trade commissioner, James Cross. When Laporte was killed at the hands of the FLQ, the federal government stepped in and effectively crushed the organization.

Although these were tense times in Quebec and Canada, we should not overestimate the role of the FLQ nor of the militant fringe of the Quebecois movement. The movement carried on within political channels, settling basically into a routinized constitutional contest between the province of Quebec, now cast as the legitimate national mouthpiece of the Quebecois, and the federal government of Canada. And by the end of the 1960s this nationalism had become "institutionalized" by way of the adoption of the nationalist platform by mainstream political parties, which made Quebec sovereignty a legitimate political issue and made the disintegration of Canada a thinkable proposition. At the same time, and partly as a consequence of Quebec's activism (i.e., to preempt Quebec's separatist aspirations), Canada as a whole reconsidered seriously its cultural problem and recognized itself formally as a bicultural, bilingual society. These steps led Canada to become an institutionally "multicultural" society, in other words, to politicize its society along cultural lines.

Interestingly, while Quebec complained of its disadvantage in comparison to English Canada, the province enjoyed unusual freedom and power apart from the central state; in fact, Dion has argued that the province is already "the most powerful subnational government in all of the OECD countries in terms of its share of resources and its scope of intervention" (1992, 78). Quebec has had its own assembly, its own tax collection system, its own social welfare institutions, and even its own overseas bureaus. On the federal level Quebec has hardly been denied power as well: during the last hundred years a Quebecer has held the office of prime minister roughly half the time. In regard to culture, since the 1791 Constitutional Act (which divided Canada into upper and lower provinces along linguistic lines) and the 1867 BNA Act, Canadian politics has recognized, has almost been premised on, the distinctness of French-Canadian culture and of Quebec as the seat, if not the "national homeland," of that culture. In 1963 Canada revisited the cultural issue via the Royal Commission on Bilingualism and Biculturalism (RCBB), appointed to study the scope and potential solution of the language/culture problem. The RCBB found, among other things, that there was in actuality a significant (35 percent) wage gap between francophones and anglophones in Quebec and that Quebecois were underrrepresented in the ownership and management of business in their province. Yet the commission rejected Quebec's avowed answer to this injustice, which was to transform Quebec into a veritable national homeland and, thereby, a truly French society. Instead, it proposed that the federal government undertake to make francophones "feel at home" anywhere in Canada through language policy to make Canada thoroughly friendly to both of its language majorities and expressly bilingual in regions where both groups reside in large numbers.

So it was that two competing visions of Canadian nationhood and the place of language in that nationhood—and, therefore, the place of Quebec in that nationhood—evolved. The first vision we might call the federal, or bicultural vision, the most conspicuous proponent of which was Pierre Trudeau, former prime minister of Canada and himself a Quebecois. The second vision we might call the territorial, or "Quebec nationalist," one, associated in recent years most closely with René Levesque, founder of the Parti Quebecois (PQ) and former premier of Quebec. Both were not only politicians but articulate theorists and symbols of their culture and nationalism.

Levesque gave the Quebec separatist movement a political legitimacy, and political machinery, it had never enjoyed before, making the movement the top priority of the provincial government. He and the *pequistes* (as followers of the PQ were known) accepted the "collective personality" notion of Quebecois identity when he referred to the "physical" quality of that identity as well as the colonial notion of the relation between the two majorities. Finally, he also concurs in the interpretation that Quebec is not only a distinct society but a national homeland, "this Quebec, the only place where we have the unmistakable feeling that 'here we can be really at home'" (1968, 14). For Levesque the issue was to "secure once and for all . . . the safety of our collective 'personality,'" and the only solution was a political solution—that is, for Quebec as a society to have "the power for unfettered action . . . in fields as varied as those of citizenship, immigration, and employment; the great instruments of 'mass culture'—films, radio, and television; and . . . international relations," not to mention the courts and the economy, including off-shore rights (1968, 21).

Politically, this meant sovereignty. But Levesque's version of Quebec sovereignty foresaw the newly freed state of Quebec in continuing association with Canada, in economics (e.g., in the use of a currency and maybe in some joint planning) and perhaps in foreign policy. Hence, the PQ's slogan was "sovereignty-association." Culturally, this meant the "francization" of Quebec society, in particular the reestablishment of French as the dominant language in society and the establishment of the francophone community as the dominant force in the provincial economy. Not only was French not the language of everyday life, but alarming studies had appeared showing that it was actually declining. The seriousness of the issue can be seen in Quebec's Legislative Bill 85, presented in 1968, which called for recognition of French as the first language of Quebec but for freedom of language rights in education (i.e., that education would be provided in both languages and parents could choose the medium of instruction for their children). The bill was savagely attacked, however, and ultimately withdrawn. In March 1969 language activists held a demonstration at McGill University to protest the English nature of the institution. A riot broke out in Saint-Leonard, a suburb of Montreal, over school language policies there. In October 1969, when Bill 63 reintroduced English-language rights in education, although the bill identified French as the "priority language," required "working knowledge" of French in all students, and established an official Office de la Langue Française, Levesque led the opposition. Clearly, a significant proportion of Quebecois had moved beyond the inclusivist position toward an exclusivist, confrontational, and uncompromising one.

Trudeau, on the other hand, was not deaf to the complaints of the Quebecois, agreeing that anglophone Canadians had often behaved as if they "held special and exclusive rights" in the country's political, economic, and cultural institutions (1968, 5). Yet he also felt strongly that Quebec's, or more broadly francophone Canada's, complaints should and could be addressed within the federal and constitutional structure. This position was based on a number of points. First, he rejected ethnonationalism; second, he considered the cost, economic and otherwise, of Quebec separatism and the fragmentation of Canada to be too high. He countered the claim that Quebec's culture and language were dying with the argument that in fact these phenomena were in no danger—"Their survival is already assured" (30)—and that Quebec already possessed all the means necessary to guarantee it. Finally, he prophesied that the new Quebecois version of francophone nationalism would only lead to a more self-conscious and militant English-Canadian counter-identity; the territorial view of identity, if it claimed Quebec as the national state of the francophones, would surrender the rest of Canada as the national state of the anglophones, despite the fact that both territorial entities contain substantial language minorities. In the end he concluded that the notion of two nations, each with its own territory and state, was "dangerous in theory and groundless in fact" (31).

Biculturalism and bilingualism were the only solution to the identity problem in Canada for Trudeau. Not only would it make francophones at home anywhere in Canada, but it would also raise anglophones' consciousness about the true nature of their society. Most critically of all, it would serve as the cultural glue to integrate the two Canada's into one: it would forge a new, more inclusive Canadian identity and remove the grievances that generated Quebecois nationalism. Accordingly, the federal government followed up with the 1969 Official Languages Act, formally equalizing the status of English and French throughout the country. The government encouraged, with substantial grants of money, the teaching of French everywhere, either as a first or a second language, as well as the activities of French social and cultural organizations inside and outside Quebec. Constitutional conferences were held to take the policy a step further and enshrine it in the very fabric of the polity.

Well meaning as these actions were, they misjudged the aspirations of the nationalists in Quebec, who had already come to reject the suggestion of a bilingual Canada in favor of a unilingual Quebec. Demographically, Quebec, and especially Montreal, had become more unilingually French during the twentieth century, as rural populations moved to the cities and as anglophones migrated out. Even more centrally, nationalists had become more rigid in their demands, and the provincial government had become aggressive in the pursuit of its powers and privileges, both as a national government and merely as a lower-level government vis-à-vis

Ottawa. Especially after the 1970 "October crisis," when the central government intervened against FLQ violence, many extremist nationalists increasingly viewed that government as the opponent of Quebec.

Language became more and more the defining issue and French unilingualism the explicit and uncompromising goal; as a later party document would state, in remarkably Sapir-Whorfian terms: "Our language, the French language, is the basis of our identity and the vehicle of our culture. . . . Our language, which names things and delineates concepts, also constitutes—since that is its first function—a way of thinking, of reflecting, and of understanding the world. We will not renounce this manner of being and speaking" (qtd. in Johnson 1994, 383).

Beyond that, bilingualism was looked upon with suspicion as a perpetuation of English domination within an overwhelmingly English-majority state. In 1971 the Quebec Association of Teachers of French published its so-called Black Paper, in which it went so far as to say, "Bilingualism, in the end, always produces a bastard people" (qtd. in Johnson 1994, 124). According to Fullerton, and reminiscent of the culture wars within the United States' academy, francophone teachers were even telling their students that learning English was dangerous and unpatriotic (1978, 149). Even Quebecois literature and arts reflected this newfound disdain for bilingualism, blaming it for fuzzy thinking and confused identity.

That linguistic nationalism had become institutionalized is evident from the legislative onslaught against Ottawa and Canada that began even before the PQ took power. In 1971 the assembly passed three bills giving Quebec control of communications within its borders. In 1974 came Bill 22, ending the equality of the status of Quebec's two languages; the government was to act upon the principle that French is the official language and to promote French as "the ordinary language of communication." The aim was the francization of Quebec society, as noted in the cultural (*patrimoine*) laws and institutions constructed at around the same time, and was the beginning of putting a publicly French face on that society. Subsidies were provided to enterprises that contributed to the support of French through hiring or corporate practice, and public signs were to be written in French, although English was not proscribed—yet.

When Levesque and the PQ assumed power in 1976, however, the rush toward cultural and real political sovereignty was accelerated. Nine months after taking office, Levesque oversaw the passage of a string of legislation affirming the place of French in Quebec society, including the

"Charte de la Langue Français" and a controversial stipulation that all public writing, such as signs and billboards, must be in French. More important, the Quebec government was getting ready to put its policy of sovereignty-association to the electoral test. A referendum was called for May 20, 1980, in which Quebec citizens were asked to vote not on sovereignty-association directly but on whether the provincial government should be charged to negotiate with Canada on the subject. Yet, even with this moderate language, the referendum went down in defeat, 59.5 percent against, 40.5 percent for. Anglophone Quebecers naturally voted overwhelmingly against the idea, and Quebecois themselves rejected it narrowly, 52 percent to 48 percent. As a result, the PQ was split and at least part of it was further radicalized, dumping the "association" half of its previous sovereignty-association motto, while the federal government was at once heartened and chastened, realizing how close Canada had come to disintegration.

Now, in the cool that was the aftermath of the referendum, was the time to hammer out a more lasting and just solution to Canada's cultural and political identity problems. Meetings were held between the federal government, headed by Trudeau, and the provincial leaders in 1980 and 1981 to settle a variety of issues, the most basic being the "patriation" of the constitution, that is, breaking the constitutional link to England and writing its own document to replace the BNA Act under which it had operated for over the century. Quebec, however, felt—and was—left out of these deliberations. In fact, the day after the Quebec sovereignty referendum Trudeau sent his representative to all the provincial capitals except Quebec City. And, as the document took shape, with its formalization of individual over group rights and of the equality of all Canada's provinces, Levesque and the PQ voiced their objections to it. Most disconcertingly for the Quebecois nationalists, the language rights adopted into the draft constitution would potentially, and eventually, lead to federal blockage of some of Quebec's own language policies. This was particularly galling to Quebecois because some other groups, including native peoples and women, had succeeded in putting some specific protections into the document.

The Constitution Act was enacted on April 17, 1982, without the agreement or signature of Quebec. Neither side considered the matter concluded, but it did seem that the most extreme edge of Quebec nationalism had blunted. It was to rise again, however, when Prime Minister Brian

Mulroney chose to reopen the issue a few years later and create the circumstances for yet one more perceived humiliation of Quebec and its cultural pride—the so-called Meech Lake accord.

Nationalism, Multiculturalism, and Other *Isms*: Meech Lake and Beyond

In 1987 Canada was still without a constitutional agreement that included Quebec. The danger of Quebec separating from Canada had apparently subsided, but in the mind of Trudeau's successor, Mulroney, Canada had already separated from Quebec via the 1982 Constitutional Act, and something was needed to bring the province back into the federal fold. So a conference of premiers was called at the retreat of the prime minister at Meech Lake. To many participants and observers this was to be the "Quebec round" of constitutional talks, taking up unfinished business from five years before but also to be followed by further meetings to discuss other issues, including ones dear to the other provinces.

Quebec's new premier, Robert Bourassa, came to the talks with five very specific demands that would condition the province's acceptance of any new agreement. These demands included three strictly political ones (the right to name the three justices from Quebec who would sit on the Canadian Supreme Court, the right to opt out of certain federal spending programs with full compensation, and the right to veto future constitutional changes), one mixed political/cultural one (greater provincial control over immigration to Quebec) and, most fundamentally, a cultural one that premised all the others (constitutional recognition of Quebec as a "distinct society"). All of these conditions were met in the agreement without much difficulty. Specifically, the section that deals with the distinct society demand provides for the fact that

1. the recognition that the existence of French-speaking Canadians, centred in Quebec but also present elsewhere in Canada, and English-speaking Canadians, concentrated outside Quebec but also present in Quebec, constitutes a fundamental characteristic of Canada and
2. the recognition that Quebec constitutes within Canada a distinct society.

The agreement goes on to state that the government of Quebec is the political instrument "to preserve and promote the distinct identity of Quebec" and that the agreement itself does not "derogate from the powers" of the federal or provincial governments "relating to language." So Quebec had gotten what it wanted—formal acceptance of its cultural distinctness relative to the rest of Canada and the political tools to exercise that distinctness. Well, Quebec almost got them.

The Meech Lake accord stirred the cultural debate in Canada the way nothing ever had before, not just in regard to Quebec and language but across the entire spectrum of multicultural issues. Bourassa looked upon it as the license to promote not only French but the francization of the society actively through legislation, without fear that the federal judiciary would strike down such laws. Jacques Parizeau of the PQ, which was out of power but not out of action, saw the potential: "If we come to power, there is no doubt that I'm going to use it . . . I'm going to use that for everything it's worth. It's remarkable how much one could get through that clause. . . . what a weapon it could be for people who have the sort of—shall we say, political project that I have" (qtd. in Johnson 1994, 211). This potential did not go unnoticed among federalists and among anglophones. Especially since *distinct society* was undefined in the accord, and since the precise character of Quebec's distinct society was unstated, many saw, in the best case, a lengthy struggle in the courts to define and delimit it and, in the worst case, all kinds of legislative attacks in Quebec against non-francophone civil rights.

In the middle of the public debate two developments sent a chill through Quebec. Just weeks after the accord was penned, Mulroney introduced Bill C-72, which expanded on the 1969 Official Languages Act. The bill promoted bilingualism not just in federal administration but throughout Canadian society, including in education and business. This new federal legislation ran counter to Quebecois' wishes for their distinct society and actually contradicted certain provincial language laws. In addition, in late 1988 the courts struck down Quebec's earlier law prohibiting English on public signs. Quebec's response was Act 178, which legalized the use of English on signs inside businesses but not outside, and only then if the English lettering was smaller than the French.

Like any constitutional amendment, the Meech Lake accord had a limited amount of time for ratification, and ratification had to be unanimous among the provinces. Eight of the ten provinces ratified it within a year, but during the same period two governments, in New Brunswick and Manitoba, changed hands, and their leaders had objections. So it was that in 1990 the amendment died because the two provinces, representing less than 7 percent of Canada's population, refused to support it. Quebecois could claim their latest and perhaps greatest defeat, because they had come so close this time. Understandably, they blamed the anglophones and federalists for their defeat, but there was much more in operation than merely those forces.

To comprehend fully the forces at work in the Meech Lake debate and in Canadian society at large, we must look beyond the anglophone/francophone duality toward the multicultural character of Canada and even more so at the politicization of this multiculturalism. Canada was one of the first, if not the first, state to recognize and adopt multiculturalism as a national fact and a national policy. In a word Canada has many cultural heritages and communities in its midst, like the United States. In Canada, however, unlike the United States, multiculturalism is not the opposite of monoculturalism but of biculturalism. This is the main reason why multiculturalism is more threatening to Quebecois and their nationalism than it is to Canada as a whole.

The fact is that Canada has not been, for a very long time if ever, a simply bicultural society. Although at first Canada (as a "European" colony and state) consisted of and perceived itself as only the "two founding races," that situation and perception could not hold for long. First of all, there are the aboriginal, or "native Canadian," nations. Second, while few if any new French immigrants arrived to settle in Canada after the colonial era, many English and many other nationalities immigrated to the new land. The 1986 census showed that "other" had become a slightly larger category than "French" in terms of ethnic origin of the Canadian population, by a margin of 24.6 percent to 24.4 percent, with English still the plurality at 33.6 percent. Even more important than the statistics on origin self-identification, which may or may not reflect identity matters and certainly do not reflect language ones, are the questions of cultural assimilation and the politicization of these category differences.

The neat picture of two Canadian "language nations" is complicated in two ways. First of all, there is a substantial number of "allophones" in the population as well. The 1986 census indicated that almost exactly half as many allophones as francophones reside in Canada (12.8 percent versus 25.1 percent) and that even in Quebec they accounted for almost 7 percent. Second, and more critically, because of linguistic assimilation of these immigrants it is problematic to equate language with ethnicity. This is strikingly true for anglophones, who have been a mixed bunch for a very long time; it is also, although more recently, true for francophones. In fact, herein lies one of the most serious controversies in Quebec nationalism and the source of Quebec's demand for control over its own immigration policies.

The fact of the matter is that the language communities have long since ceased to be ethnic communities—or, better yet, that the ethnic communities of today based on language (i.e., Quebecois and anglophone) are a new development in ethnicity and not a mere continuation of more original, primordial identities and groups. This is even more true for the anglophone community than the francophone, for two reasons. For one, the French community was historically less open to assimilation than was the English one, guarding more closely the unity of ethnicity, faith, and language; non-French/non-English immigrants were, however, welcomed and encouraged to learn English. For another, French was, for most of the history of Canada, a less prestigious and less practically (i.e., economically) useful language, so that more immigrants desired to learn English than French. Thus, the anglophone population quickly became multicultural in terms of its ethnic origins, with ethnic English composing an ever smaller portion of the group (estimated in 1991 at only 22 percent of Quebec's anglophones). One could go so far as to say that anglophones have not been conscious in the same manner as francophones of their shared ethnicity but, rather, conceive of their commonality in other terms, at least until recently.

It can be appreciated, then, that *anglophone ethnicity* is something of a malapropism until late in the twentieth century, when a *new* kind or definition of anglophone ethnicity has begun to coalesce in response to, in defense against, Quebecois ethnicity. Observers or proponents of this revived or *invented* anglophone ethnicity, like Philip Resnick, point to this fact: "Almost in reaction to nationalist sentiment in Quebec over the past three decades . . . English Canadian nationalism has begun to emerge" (1991, 14). Of course, this is not to suggest that English Canadians have not been conscious of being something in the past; however, what they were conscious of and how they were conscious is not, in this view, the same today as in the past. English Canadians were conscious of being Canadians—a political identity—and identified with the state and its institutions, in which they saw reflected their Englishness; it was not difficult, despite the presence of the French fact, to imagine themselves as Canada. They were also conscious of being English speakers. Yet, in the face of aggressive Quebecois identity and nationalism, and of the discourse of nationalism and ethnicity as the prevailing idiom of identity, "English Canadians" may think and have been asked to think about who they are:

if "French Canadians" are a distinct society, are not English Canadians also a distinct society? And, if Quebec is the national territory of the former nation, is not the rest of Canada the national territory of the latter?

French Canada has been much slower to recognize its own multiculturalism, mostly because that multiculturalism has been much slower in developing. As late as 1988, Jean-Marc Leger pondered whether the mixing of French and non-French in schools would lead to the "deracinating of young Franco-Quebecois" (qtd. in Levine 1990, 145). Nevertheless, by and large the Quebecois movement has come not only to see the nationality mix in its midst but even to *demand* it, as suggested by its members will to control immigration—not to limit it but to encourage it, within the constraints of their francized society. The assimilation of new immigrants into the anglophone sector, most often outside of Quebec, plus the declining birthrate of "French" francophones caused a perception of real danger to the continuation of Quebecois culture. There is obviously little chance they will attract much immigration from France, but they could seek to attract types who would assimilate into Quebecois culture and embrace and contribute to its French society.

Quebec's language policies and legislation and its Meech Lake demand for greater control over immigration were intended to meet these problems. Language laws like Bill 22 and Bill 101, which limited English-language instruction basically to the children of anglophones, were to a large extent focused not on anglophones but on allophones; non-English-speaking families would be expected and required to study and function in French. Consequently, the percentage of allophone children studying in English in Montreal dropped precipitously after 1970, from over 92 percent to less than 34 percent by the time of Meech Lake, according to the Gendron Commission. But Quebec's language policies went beyond standard schooling to what we might call "immigrant orientation." Even by the late 1960s Centres d'Orientation et de Formation des Immigrants (COFI) were established to orient new arrivals to Quebec society, which meant, as studies of COFI literature have shown, a kind of introduction to and indoctrination into Quebecois nationalism. Analyses of the manuals that the Quebec government prepared for instructors at COFI showed that references to Canada were few while references to Quebec were legion. The materials went so far as to advise teachers to instruct students that they would be becoming citizens of Quebec and that, although pluralistic, "the axis for the integration of new arrivals" of their new society was French language and culture (Johnson 1994, 384). When Canada was mentioned, its official bilingualism was overlooked, and a politicized view of its history and duality was presented, in which the English were "Anglo-Saxon, Protestant . . . a minority dominant politically and economically, with the will to assimilate and reduce [French Canadians] to minority status through immigration" (386).

By 1981 Quebecois multiculturalism had evolved to the point that the PQ could present a paper called *Autant de facons d'etre Quebecois* (translated as "So Many Ways to Be a Quebecois"), paying respect to the presence and even the value of other cultural communities in Quebec. The paper refers to Quebec as a nation of "converging cultures . . . from all over the world [in a] society which seeks to respect the cultural traditions of every group while affirming Quebec's essential nature as a francophone society" (qtd. in Handler 1998, 179). Such a formulation shows the truly convoluted character of modern ethnonationalism, which aims to preserve the idea of the nation, ideally a homogeneous thing, even if that nation is an explicitly heterogeneous one.

At the federal level multiculturalism is not merely a demographic fact but an element of consciousness and policy. The first important formal recognition of its multiculturalism was, ironically, in the Royal Commission on Bilingualism and Biculturalism; intended to investigate the status of the two nations, the commission was compelled to acknowledge the others. It even published a second volume to its report entitled *The Contribution of the Other Ethnic Groups.* The patriated Constitution of 1982 was, among other things, a work of just such a multicultural vision, enshrining not only the bilingual and bicultural quality of Canada but also explicitly acknowledging other dimensions of the society and polity including aboriginals and women. McRoberts suggests that this formalization of cultural/communal rights ushered in an era of "minoritarian politics." By making multiculturalism not only an official but a constitutional project, subsequent constitutional issues and debates, like the Meech Lake one, have become opportunities for "'symbolic positioning' in which groups representing various ethnic and sociological categories all jockey for a privileged place in the constitutional standings" (Woehrling 1989, 183).

Consequentially, it is this fact, rather than anglophone resistance, that was a major factor in the death of Meech Lake and the reactivation of Quebecois nationalism and separatism. In particular, aboriginal and women's groups were adamantly and actively opposed to the new agreement, not just because of what it included in regard to Quebec but because of what it left out in regard to them or of its potential repercussions for them. Aboriginal leaders argued, with some justice, against the "two nations" philosophy of Meech Lake, stressing that they were also a distinct society at least as deserving of that status as Quebec. They observed that similar demands by their groups had been rejected only recently and even that the concept of distinct society was one derived from the aboriginal rights movement. Finally, they contended that the accord, with its special concessions to Quebecois as a group, implied the exemption of other groups like their own from such protections and favors. Some aboriginal groups directly affected by Quebec's persistent separatist ambitions, like the Cree, maintained that they would not accept their lands becoming part of an independent Quebec; in such an event they would either secede and rejoin Canada or secede and declare their own sovereign state. And outside Quebec, where constitutional politics was really made or broken, aboriginals organized to block the ratification of the agreement, especially in Manitoba, where the activities of the Ojibwa chief Elijah Harper were instrumental in getting that province to reject it.

Women's groups had their own objections to the Meech Lake accord. One similar concern was that women were not specifically mentioned, suggesting to them that by omission they too were excluded from the new rights being extended; another was that women (like nearly everyone else) had been excluded from the process by which the Meech Lake agreements were arrived at. Beyond that, however, was the fear that the privileges of Quebec in regard to language legislation might negatively impact the rights and conditions of women, especially that language interests would take precedence over gender interests and that Quebec would be empowered to pass legislation that, intentionally or not, would disadvantage women or contradict women's rights laws. Having striven so hard to get gender rights recognized in the 1982 constitution, many saw the new amendment as a retreat from or even an assault upon those earlier gains. Interestingly, the reaction of Quebecois women's groups like the Federation des Femmes du Quebec illustrated just how complex and multifaceted identity and its claims can be: this group came out in support of the distinct society section of the agreement and said to its gender comrades across the linguist divide that "we strongly hope that our sisters will not see threats where we feel they do not exist. In answer to the question: Does the concept of a distinct society threaten Quebec's women? the *Federation des femmes du Quebec* answers: No" (qtd. in Behiels 1989, 296). It is of little real consequence that the Meech Lake amendments were not meant to, and did not in their language or spirit, contradict or undermine the guarantees already extended to various groups other than Quebecois; in the competitive politics of culture and ethnicity any act that did not explicitly include and repeat earlier protections was somehow felt to neglect or even dismantle them.

With the defeat of Meech Lake, Quebecois could now feel neglected and defeated, humiliated once again, which would predictably reenergize nationalism and separatism. It is important, however, to see the state of ethnicity and ethnic conflict in the Quebec and Canada of the 1990s not entirely as a clash of two ethnic groups but also of two philosophies and politics of ethnicity or of two visions of the good society. In other words, it is debatable whether today most anglophones or Canadians have any serious objections to the notion of Canada as bilingual and bicultural; few in Canada believe anymore in a monocultural society, either as a fact or as a goal and a good. Thus, it is not really Quebecois–versus–*les anglais* that defines the debate and the tension anymore, but, instead, it is biculturalism-versus-multiculturalism. The Quebecois movement sees multiculturalism as a threat to *its* rights and status as *the* other in Canadian society. Multiculturalism, they fear, dumps them along with every other cultural or interest group into a cultural politics in which all cats are gray, in which all groups' rights are equal and equally important-or equally unimportant. In this formulation Quebec may be distinct, but it is not special, because everybody is distinct.

This multicultural gloaming is perfectly antithetical to what the Quebecois have aspired to. Some perceive it as a deviation from the true course of Quebecois nationalism, some as a virtual plot to undermine or trivialize that nationalism: Claude Corbo of the University of Quebec at Montreal echoes the latter when he says that "Canadian multiculturalism is apt to worsen the 'minorization' or trivializing of the Quebec identity, which becomes just one particularism among others" (qtd. in Johnson 1994, 389). Rather than being an orchestrated plot against Quebecois nationalism, Quebecois and other nationalists should see in this development the logical outcome of the culturalization of politics or the politicization of culture. Once the notion that culture is relevant to politics, or that politics is the appropriate arena for culture, is accepted, is *instituted,* all cultures are welcome in the arena. Like a millstone that grinds all grain to the same size, the politicization of culture, which almost necessarily takes the form of multiculturalism, makes it impossible to resist any claim on the basis of culture and simultaneously to privilege any claim on the basis of culture.

Even if it were true in some past era that Canada was a nation of two majorities and that the state of Canada was a compact between the two nations, it is today untrue demographically and indefensible philosophically. This, perhaps, is the true cautionary message of multiculturalism and the culturalization of society and politics.

Conclusion: "Oh, Canada"?

In mid-1992 the negotiators went to the table again to try to work out a deal to replace the failed Meech Lake accord; this time not only was Quebec included, but so were four aboriginal organizations. Quebec was again seeking at least an asymmetrical federation premised on the Quebecois nation's distinct status and the provincial government's distinct role in securing the nation's interests and continued existence, which, in the negotiations and draft proposals presented by Bourassa, often sounded like a first step toward sovereignty. Quebec got less than it asked for but more than it had in the agreement, which was ratified by the representatives late in the summer of 1992 at Charlottetown, the site of the original BNA constitutional act back in 1867. A Senate was proposed to provide the missing legislative branch to Canadian government (the so-called Triple-E Senate, which was to be elected, effective, and equal in terms of the provinces), one that offered Quebec eighteen fewer legislative seats than it already held; in exchange, the province got eighteen more seats in the House of Commons and a guarantee of 25 percent of the seats in the future regardless of proportional population changes. In terms of division of powers between levels of government, Quebec got Ottawa to withdraw from some domains and to agree to act with the consent of the province in other domains.

The cultural and multicultural implications of the Charlottetown accord were more problematic, as were the uses to which the ensuing public discussion were put. The compact expressed a governmental "commitment" in the English version but only an "attachement" in the French version to the protection of rights of official language minorities, that is, anglophones in Quebec and francophones everywhere else. For other types of minorities no explicit governmental commitment was made, although it was said that Canadians were so committed; women and ethnic groups could thus raise the same objections they had raised against Meech Lake. At the same time, the aboriginal participants in the process won a major concession in the form of the recognition of aboriginal self-government, although this was largely undefined as well as limited. Meanwhile, as the agreements were put to a public referendum, both sides used the opportunity to test public attitudes toward Quebec sovereignty, attempting to portray the plebiscite as a referendum not on constitutional reform but on sovereignty, which it was not. This tactic appears to have worked most effectively on the majority Canadians, who favored the agreement by over 60 percent in September but who ended up voting it down on October 26. Just over 50 percent of Quebecois eventually voted no, while over 90 percent of anglophone Quebecers did the same. In the political wrangling leaders on all fronts lost credibility: Mulroney's constitutional efforts were repudiated, Bourassa was seen as abdicating the strong pro-Quebec position, and even aboriginal leaders watched as 60 percent of reservation aboriginals voted against the accord.

Cultural conflict and Quebecois nationalism and separatism were not dead, however. In 1995 Quebecers were asked once again to go to the polls to decide a sovereignty referendum, which was narrowly defeated (50.6 percent to 49.4 percent, with a margin of only fifty-four thousand votes). Thus, given a number of opportunities to give voice, directly (as in the 1980 and 1995 referenda) and indirectly (as in the 1992 Charlottetown referendum), to its national will, a majority of regular Quebecois has rejected—though by an ever-declining number—the final national step and claim their sovereignty. Despite decades of political mobilization and confrontation, the inflammatory rhetoric of "national humiliation," and even the terrorism of groups like the FLQ, the nation refuses to answer the call of its nationalistic leaders and claim its national destiny. Maybe the nation has failed to wake up to its true identity and will. Or maybe the nation is not nearly as monolithic as those leaders suggest; maybe its identity and will are not what those leaders believe and claim, more tied up with that of Canada and its bilingual and bicultural, even multicultural, society. Or maybe the nation that the leaders invoke is a "fiction," a goal, a hope, an invention—one that has not discovered or developed the will and consciousness of Quebecois any more firmly than the Canadian one has but which still actively competes with it. Yet the closeness of the latest referendum suggests that the invention may be nearing completion.

In this chapter we have seen how a history and myth of Canada (a history of two European groups sharing a state after the military defeat of one of them and a myth that this history is nothing more than this military defeat and a subsequent string of national humiliations), a traditional, agrarian, and religious society (rural, Catholic francophones), a set of processes and changes (modernization, urbanization, industrialization), a movement and ideology of nationality and of cultural identity, and a fortuitous circumstance of geography or demographics (nearly all French Canadians residing in the territory of Quebec) have conjoined to produce what we encounter in the twentieth century as Quebecois nationalism and separatism. This nationalism and separatism, while having its roots in history and tradition, is not a mere continuation of that history and tradition but, instead, an outcome of many modern and modernizing forces that have altered its face seriously and permanently.

Not only is the conflict as we find it today not primordial or inevitable, but it is also not the single axis of conflict or of identity in Canada, not the single way to view the faults and fissures of Canadian society. Quebec is not the only distinct society in Canada, not even from a provincial standpoint; many of the other provinces can or do claim a kind of distinctness. In the final analysis, however, it is not the amount of distinctness or nondistinctness that makes or will make or fails to make or will fail to make Quebec a nation; as Trudeau astutely observed, "more than language and culture, more than history and geography, even more than force and power, the foundation of the nation is will. . . . Nationhood [is] little more than a state of mind" (1968, 187). In other words, the objective conditions of Quebecois culture, history, economy, or what have you do not alone make it a nation—nor deny it nationhood. Quebec's history has contained a series of defeats, surely enough, but also a series of triumphs; remembering one over the other is an act of choice and will.

Finally, while there has been an undeniable history of inequality and exclusion within the province, Quebec francophones today are "objectively" in a much better economic and political position than they have ever been. Quebec's own Gendron Commission, charged with studying the status of French and the francophone people, found that French is in no danger of dying in the province and that the people are faring better than expected. The commission reported, for instance, that francophones spend most of their worktime functioning in French, more than nineteen out of every twenty days in Montreal. Other statistics indicate that the economic gap between francophones and anglophones has closed considerably as well. The wage gap, reported at 35 percent in 1961, was reduced to 16 percent by 1980; the number of employees working for francophone-run businesses grew to almost two-thirds and the number of francophones in management to over half by the late 1980s. Even at the federal level francophones were slightly *over*represented among federal employees, composing almost 27 percent of the workers while just 25 percent of the population (Dion 1992, 94–98).

The question, then, is what Quebecois will choose to remember and to use as they continue to grow and evolve. What will be their national will and consciousness? Objective historical or present social conditions alone cannot prophesy. Primordial appeals certainly won't help. Only time and circumstances will tell.

Bibliography

Adamson, David. 1965. *The Kurdish War.* New York: Praeger.

Alba, Richard. 1990. *Ethnic Identity: The Transformation of White America.* New Haven: Yale University Press.

Ali, Rabia, and Lawrence Lifschultz, eds. 1993. *Why Bosnia? Writings on the Balkan War.* Stony Creek, CT: Pamphleteer's Press.

Alter, Peter. 1994. "Nationalism: An Overview." In *Nationalism and Ethnic Conflict,* ed. Charles Cozic, 18–25. San Diego: Greenhaven Press.

Anderson, Benedict. 1983. *Imagined Communities: Reflections of the Origin and Spread of Nationalism.* London: Verso.

Arasaratnam, Sinnapah. 1987. "Sinhala-Tamil Relations in Modern Sri Lanka (Ceylon)." In *Ethnic Conflict: International Perspectives,* ed. Jerry Boucher, Dan Landis, and Karen Arnold Clark, 33–53. Newbury Park, CA: Sage.

———. 1964. *Ceylon.* Englewood Cliffs, NJ: Prentice-Hall.

Arfa, Hassan. 1966. *The Kurds: An Historical and Political Study.* London: Oxford University Press.

Aronson, Dan. 1976. "Ethnicity as a Cultural System: An Introductory Essay." In *Ethnicity in the Americas,* ed. Frances Henry, 9–19. The Hague: Mouton.

Banac, Ivo. 1984. *The National Question in Yugoslavia: Origins, History, Politics.* Ithaca: Cornell University Press.

Barth, Fredrik. 1953. *Principles of Social Organization in Southern Kurdistan.* Oslo: Brodrene Jorgensen.

———, ed. 1969. *Ethnic Groups and Boundaries.* Boston: Little, Brown.

Behiels, Michael D., ed. 1989. *The Meech Lake Primer: Conflicting Views of the 1987 Constitutional Accord.* Ottawa: University of Ottawa Press.

Bell, Daniel. 1975. "Ethnicity and Social Change." In *Ethnicity: Theory and Experience,* ed. Nathan Glazer and Daniel Patrick Moynihan, 141–74. Cambridge: Harvard University Press.

Bell, David V. J., and Lorne Tepperman. 1992. *The Roots of Disunity: A Study of Canadian Political Culture.* Toronto: Oxford University Press.

Berreman, Gerald. 1972. "'Bring It All Back Home': Malaise in Anthropology." In *Reinventing Anthropology,* ed. Dell Hymes, 83–98. New York: Random House.

Bicanic, Rudolf. 1981. *How the People Live: Life in the Passive Regions (Peasant*

Life in Southwestern Croatia, Bosnia, and Hercegovina; Yugoslavia in 1935). Trans. Stephen Clissold. Amherst: University of Massachusetts Press.

Boas, Franz. 1928. *Anthropology and Modern Life.* New York: Norton.

Bourassa, Henri. 1919. *La langue, gardienne de la foi.* Montreal: Action Française.

Bourdieu, Pierre. 1977. *Outline of a Theory of Practice.* Cambridge: Cambridge University Press.

Brass, Paul. 1985. *Ethnic Groups and the State.* Totowa, NJ: Barnes and Noble Books.

Bulloch, John, and Harvey Morris. 1992. *No Friends but the Mountains: The Tragic History of the Kurds.* Oxford: Oxford University Press.

Burgess, M. Elaine. 1978. "The Resurgence of Ethnicity: Myth or Reality?" *Ethnic and Racial Studies* 1:265–85.

Chaliand, Gerard. 1994. *The Kurdish Tragedy.* Trans. Philip Black. London: Zed Books Ltd.

———, ed. 1993. *A People without a Country: The Kurds and Kurdistan.* New York: Olive Branch Books.

Chambre, Henri. 1963. *From Karl Marx to Mao Tse-tung: A Systematic Survey of Marxism-Leninism.* Trans. Robert Olsen. New York: P. J. Kennedy and Sons.

Cigar, Norman. 1995. *Genocide in Bosnia: The Policy of "Ethnic Cleansing."* College Station: Texas A&M University Press.

Clifford, James, and George Marcus, eds. 1986. *Writing Culture: The Poetics and Politics of Ethnography.* Berkeley: University of California Press.

Clift, Dominique. 1982. *Quebec Nationalism in Crisis.* Kingston and Montreal: McGill-Queen's University Press.

Cohen, Abner. 1969. *Customs and Politics in Urban Africa: A Study of Migrants in Yoruba Towns.* Berkeley: University of California Press.

Cohen, Lenard. 1993. *Broken Bonds: The Disintegration of Yugoslavia.* Boulder: Westview Press.

Connor, Walker. 1994. *Ethnonationalism: The Quest for Understanding.* Princeton: Princeton University Press.

Crapanzano, Vincent. 1992. *Hermes' Dilemma and Hamlet's Desire: On the Epistemology of Interpretation.* Cambridge: Harvard University Press.

Daniel, E. Valentine. 1996. *Charred Lullabies: Chapters in an Anthropography of Violence.* Princeton: Princeton University Press.

Denitch, Bogdan. 1994. *Ethnic Nationalism: The Tragic Death of Yugoslavia.* Minneapolis: University of Minnesota Press.

Destexhe, Alain. 1995. *Rwanda and Genocide in the Twentieth Century.* Trans. Alison Marschner. New York: New York University Press.

Deutsch, Karl. 1969. *Nationalism and Its Alternatives.* New York: Alfred A. Knopf.

Deutsch, Karl, and William Foltz, eds. 1963. *Nation-Building.* New York: Atherton Press.

DeVos, George. 1975. "Ethnic Pluralism: Conflict and Accommodation." In *Ethnic Identity: Cultural Continuities and Change,* ed. George DeVos and Lola Romanucci-Ross, 5–41. Palo Alto: Mayfield.

Dharmadasa, K. N. O. 1992. *Language, Religion, and Ethnic Assertiveness: The*

Growth of Sinhalese Nationalism in Sri Lanka. Ann Arbor: University of Michigan Press.

Diamond, Stanley. 1972. "Anthropology in Question." In *Reinventing Anthropology,* ed. Dell Hymes, 401–29. New York: Random House.

Dion, Stephane. 1992. "Explaining Quebec Nationalism." In *The Collapse of Canada?* ed. R. Kent Weaver, 77–122. Washington: Brookings Institution.

Djilas, Aleksa. 1991. *The Contested Country: Yugoslav Unity and Communist Revolution, 1919–1953.* Cambridge: Harvard University Press.

Donia, Robert, and John Fine. 1994. *Bosnia and Hercegovina: A Tradition Betrayed.* New York: Columbia University Press.

Dragnich, Alex. 1992. *Serbs and Croats: The Struggle in Yugoslavia.* New York: Harcourt Brace Jovanovich.

Dufault, Roseanna Lewis. 1991. *Metaphors of Identity: The Treatment of Childhood in Selected Quebecois Novels.* London: Associated Universities Presses.

Edmonds, C. J. 1957. *Kurds, Turks, and Arabs: Politics, Travel, and Research in North-Eastern Iraq, 1919–1925.* London: Oxford University Press.

Eller, Jack David, and Reed Coughlan. 1993. "The Poverty of Primordialism: The Demystification of Ethnic Attachments." *Ethnic and Racial Studies* 16: 183–202.

Entessar, Nader. 1992. *Kurdish Ethnonationalism.* Boulder: Lynn Rienner.

Ergang, Robert Reinhold. 1931. *Herder and the Foundations of German Nationalism.* New York: Columbia University Press.

Eriksen, Thomas Hylland. 1993. *Ethnicity and Nationalism: Anthropological Perspectives.* London: Pluto Press.

Evans-Pritchard, E. E. 1951. *Social Anthropology.* Glencoe, IL: Free Press.

Farmer, B. H. 1963. *Ceylon: A Divided Nation.* London: Oxford University Press.

Fischer, Michael. 1986. "Ethnicity and the Post-Modern Arts of Memory." In *Writing Culture: The Poetics and Politics of Ethnography,* ed. James Clifford and George Marcus, 194–233. Berkeley: University of California Press.

Fortes, Meyer, and E. E. Evans-Pritchard, eds. 1940. *African Political Systems.* London: Oxford University Press.

Fullerton, Douglas H. 1978. *The Dangerous Delusion: Quebec's Independence Obsession.* Toronto: McClelland and Stewart Ltd.

Furnivall, J. S. 1956. *Colonial Policy and Practice: A Comparative Study of Burma and Netherlands India.* New York: New York University Press.

Geertz, Clifford. 1973. *The Interpretation of Cultures.* New York: Basic Books.

———, ed. 1963. *Old Societies and New States: The Quest for Modernity in Asia and Africa.* New York: Free Press.

Ghassemlou, A. R. 1993. "Kurdistan in Iran." In *A People without a Country: The Kurds and Kurdistan,* ed. Gerard Chaliand, 95–121. New York: Olive Branch Books.

Glazer, Nathan, and Daniel P. Moynihan, eds. 1975. *Ethnicity: Theory and Experience.* Cambridge: Harvard University Press.

Glazer, Nathan, and Daniel P. Moynihan. 1963. *Beyond the Melting Pot: The Negroes, Puerto Ricans, Jews, Italians, and Irish of New York City.* Cambridge: MIT Press and Harvard University Press.

Glenny, Misha. 1994. *The Fall of Yugoslavia: The Third Balkan War*. New York: Penguin Books.

Gluckman, Max. 1956. *Custom and Conflict in Africa*. Oxford: Basil Blackwell.

———. 1940. "The Kingdom of the Zulu in South Africa." In *African Political Systems,* ed. Meyer Fortes and E. E. Evans-Pritchard, 25–55. London: Oxford University Press.

Government of Quebec. 1956. *Report of the Royal Commission of Inquiry on Constitutional Problems (Tremblay Commission)*. Vol. 2. Quebec City: Queen's Printer.

Gravel, Pierre. 1968. *Remera: A Community in Eastern Ruanda*. The Hague: Mouton.

Greeley, Andrew. 1971. *Why Can't They Be like Us? America's White Ethnic Groups*. New York: E. P. Dutton.

Guidieri, Remo, and Francesco Pellizi. 1988. "Introduction: 'Smoking Mirrors'—Modern Polity and Ethnicity." In *Ethnicities and Nations: Processes of Interethnic Relations in Latin America, Southeast Asia, and the Pacific,* ed. Remo Guidieri, Francesco Pellizi, and Stanley Tambiah, 7–38. Austin: University of Texas Press.

Gunawardana, R. A. L. H. 1990. "The People of the Lion: Sinhala Identity and Ideology in History and Historiography." In *Sri Lanka: History and the Roots of Conflict,* ed. Jonathan Spencer, 45–86. London: Routledge.

Gunter, Michael. 1990. *The Kurds in Turkey: A Political Dilemma*. Boulder: Westview Press.

Gurr, Ted Robert, and Barbara Harff.1994. *Ethnic Conflict in World Politics*. Boulder: Westview Press.

Haaland, Gunnar. 1969. "Economic Determinants in Ethnic Processes." In *Ethnic Groups and Boundaries,* ed. Fredrik Barth, 58–73. Boston: Little, Brown.

Handler, Richard. 1988. *Nationalism and the Politics of Culture in Quebec*. Madison: University of Wisconsin Press.

Harrison, Thomas. 1993. "A Question of International Solidarity." In *Why Bosnia? Writings on the Balkan War,* ed. Rabia Ali and Lawrence Lifschultz, 181–90. Stony Creek, CT: Pamphleteer's Press.

Hellman-Rajanayagam, Dagmar. 1990. "The Politics of the Tamil Past." In *Sri Lanka: History and the Roots of Conflict,* ed. Jonathan Spencer, 107–22. London: Routledge.

Hobsbawm, Eric, and Terence Ranger, eds. 1983. *The Invention of Tradition*. Cambridge: Cambridge University Press.

Horowitz, Donald. 1985. *Ethnic Groups in Conflict*. Berkeley: University of California Press.

Hymes, Dell, ed. 1972. *Reinventing Anthropology*. New York: Random House.

Izady, Mehrdad. 1992. *The Kurds: A Concise Handbook*. Washington, DC: Taylor and Francis.

Jelavich, Charles. 1990. *South Slav Nationalisms—Textbooks and Yugoslav Union before 1914*. Columbus: Ohio State University Press.

Johnson, William. 1994. *A Canadian Myth: Quebec, Between Canada and the Illusion of Utopia*. Montreal: R. Davies.

Kapferer, Bruce. 1988. *Legends of People, Myths of State: Violence, Intolerance, and Political Culture in Sri Lanka and Australia.* Washington, DC: Smithsonian Institution Press.

Kasfir, Nelson. 1979. "Explaining Ethnic Political Participation." *World Politics* 31:365–88.

Kemper, Steven. 1991. *The Presence of the Past: Chronicles, Politics, and Culture in Sinhala Life.* Ithaca: Cornell University Press.

Kendal. 1993a. "The Kurds under the Ottoman Empire." In *A People without a Country: The Kurds and Kurdistan,* ed. Gerard Chaliand, 11–37. New York: Olive Branch Books.

———. 1993b. "Kurdistan in Turkey." In *A People without a Country: The Kurds and Kurdistan,* ed. Gerard Chaliand, 38–94. New York: Olive Branch Books.

Kreyenbroek, Philip. 1992. "On the Kurdish Language." In *The Kurds: A Contemporary Overview,* ed. Philip Kreyenbroek and Stefan Sperl, 68–93. London: Routledge.

Kuper, Adam. 1988. *The Invention of Primitive Society: Transformations of an Illusion.* London: Routledge.

Lamont, Lansing. 1994. *Breakup: The Coming End of Canada and the Stakes for America.* New York: Norton.

Leach, Edmund. 1954. *Political Systems of Highland Burma.* Boston: Beacon Press.

Lemarchand, René. 1994. *Burundi: Ethnocide as Discourse and Practice.* Cambridge: Woodrow Wilson Center Press and Cambridge University Press.

———. 1970. *Rwanda and Burundi.* New York: Praeger.

Lenihan, Donald, Gordon Robertson, and Roger Tasse. 1994. *Canada: Reclaiming the Middle Ground.* Montreal: Institute for Research on Public Policy.

Lenin, V. I. 1939. *Imperialism: The Highest Stage of Capitalism.* New York: International Publishers.

———. 1932. *The Collected Works of V. I. Lenin.* Vol. 21, bk. 2. Ed. Alexander Trachtenberg; trans. Moissaya Olgin. New York: International Publishers.

Levesque, René. 1968. *An Option for Quebec.* London: McClelland and Stewart Ltd.

Levine, Marc V. 1990. *The Reconquest of Montreal: Language Policy and Social Change in a Bilingual City.* Philadelphia: Temple University Press.

Linden, Ian. 1977. *Church and Revolution in Rwanda.* New York: Manchester University Press.

Little, David. 1994. *Sri Lanka: The Invention of Enmity.* Washington, DC: US Institute of Peace Press.

Lockwood, William. 1975. *European Moslems: Economics and Ethnicity in Western Bosnia.* New York: Academic Press.

Ludowyk, E. F. C. 1966. *The Modern History of Ceylon.* New York: Praeger.

Malcolm, Noel. 1994. *Bosnia: A Short History.* New York: New York University Press.

Malinowski, Bronislaw. 1961. *The Dynamics of Culture Change: An Inquiry into Race Relations in Africa.* New Haven: Yale University Press.

Malkki, Liisa. 1995. *Purity and Exile: Violence, Memory, and National Cosmology among Hutu Refugees in Tanzania.* Chicago: University of Chicago Press.

Maquet, Jacques. 1961. *The Premise of Inequality in Rwanda: A Study of Political Relations in a Central African Kingdom.* London: Oxford University Press.

Marriott, McKim. 1963. "Cultural Policy in the New States." In *Old Societies and New States: The Quest for Modernity in Asia and Africa,* ed. Clifford Geertz, 27–56. New York: Free Press.

McDowall, David. 1996. *A Modern History of the Kurds.* London: I. B. Tauris.

———. 1992a. "The Kurdish Question: A Historical Review." In *The Kurds: A Contemporary Overview,* ed. Philip Kreyenbroek and Stefan Sperl, 10–32. London: Routledge.

———. 1992b. *The Kurds: A Nation Denied.* London: Minority Rights Publications.

McRoberts, Kenneth, ed. 1995. *Beyond Quebec: Taking Stock of Canada.* Montreal: McGill-Queen's University Press.

Melady, Thomas. 1974. *Burundi: The Tragic Years.* Maryknoll, NY: Orbis Books.

Minogue, Kenneth. 1985. "Nationalism." In *The Social Science Encyclopedia,* ed. Adam Kuper and Jessica Kuper, 551–52. London: Routledge and Kegan Paul.

Moynihan, Daniel Patrick. 1993. *Pandaemonium: Ethnicity in International Politics.* Oxford: Oxford University Press.

Nader, Laura. 1972. "Up the Anthropologist: Perspectives from Studying Up." In *Reinventing Anthropology,* ed. Dell Hymes, 284–309. New York: Random House.

Nagel, Joane. 1993. "Constructing Ethnicity: Creating and Recreating Ethnic Identity and Culture." In *Majority and Minority: The Dynamics of Race and Ethnicity in American Life,* ed. Norman Yetman. Boston: Allyn and Bacon.

Nagel, Joane, and Susan Olzak, eds. 1986. *Competitive Ethnic Relations.* San Diego: Academic Press.

Nash, Manning. 1989. *The Cauldron of Ethnicity in the Modern World.* Chicago: University of Chicago Press.

Newbury, Catharine. 1988. *The Cohesion of Oppression: Clientship and Ethnicity in Rwanda, 1860–1890.* New York: Columbia University Press.

Nicol, Eric, and Peter Whalley. 1966. *One Hundred Years of What?* Toronto: Ryerson Press.

Olson, Robert. 1989. *The Emergence of Kurdish Nationalism and the Sheihk Said Rebellion, 1880–1925.* Austin: University of Texas Press.

Olzak, Susan. 1983. "Contemporary Ethnic Mobilization." *Annual Review of Sociology* 9:355–74.

Patterson, Orlando. 1975. "Context and Choice in Ethnic Allegiance: A Theoretical Framework and Caribbean Case Study." In *Ethnicity: Theory and Experience,* ed. Nathan Glazer and Daniel Patrick Moynihan, 305–49. Cambridge: Harvard University Press.

Pavkovic, Aleksandar. 1991. *The Fragmentation of Yugoslavia: Nationalism in a Multinational State.* New York: St. Martin's Press.

Pellizi, Francesco. 1988. "To Seek Refuge: Nation and Ethnicity in Exile." In *Eth-*

nicities and Nations: Processes of Interethnic Relations in Latin America, Southeast Asia, and the Pacific, ed. Remo Guidieri, Francesco Pellizi, and Stanley Tambiah, 154–71. Austin: University of Texas Press.

Pfaffenberger, Bryan. 1990. "Introduction: The Sri Lankan Tamils." In *The Sri Lankan Tamils: Ethnicity and Identity,* ed. Chelvadurai Manogaran and Bryan Pfaffenberger, 1–27. Boulder: Westview Press.

Ponnanbalam, Satchi. 1983. *Sri Lanka: National Conflict and the Tamil Liberation Struggle.* London: Zed Books Ltd.

Prunier, Gerard. 1995. *The Rwandan Crisis: History of a Genocide.* New York: Columbia University Press.

Quinn, Herbert F. 1979. *The Union Nationale: Quebec Nationalist from Duplessis to Levesque.* Toronto: University of Toronto Press.

Reiff, David. 1995. "The Slaughter of Bosnia." *Utne Reader* 71:69–73.

Resnick, Philip. 1991. *Toward a Canada-Quebec Union.* Montreal: McGill-Queen's University Press.

———. 1990. *Letters to a Quebecois Friend.* Montreal: McGill-Queen's University Press.

Ress, David. 1988. *The Burundi Ethnic Massacres, 1988.* San Francisco: Mellon Research University Press.

Roberts, Michael. 1982. *Caste Conflict and Elite Formation: The Rise of a Karava Elite in Sri Lanka, 1500–1931.* London: Cambridge University Press.

Roosens, Eugeen. 1989. *Creating Ethnicity: The Process of Ethnogenesis.* Newbury Park, CA: Sage.

Rose, Deborah Bird. 1992. *Dingo Makes Us Human: Life and Land in an Australian Aboriginal Culture.* Cambridge: Cambridge University Press.

Safrastian, Arshak. 1948. *Kurds and Kurdistan.* London: Harvill Press.

Samaranayake, Gamini. 1987. "The Changing Attitude towards the Tamil Problem within the Janatha Vimukthi Peramuna." In *Facets of Ethnicity in Sri Lanka,* ed. Charles Abeysekera and Newton Gunasinghe, 272–97. Colombo: Social Scientists Association.

Schapera, I. 1940. "The Political Organization of the Ngwato of Bechuanaland Protectorate." In *African Political Systems,* ed. Meyer Fortes and E. E. Evans-Pritchard, 56–82. London: Oxford University Press.

Schermerhorn, R.A. 1970. *Comparative Ethnic Relations.* New York: Random House.

Schmitt, Bernadotte. 1937. *The Annexation of Bosnia, 1908–1909.* London: Cambridge University Press.

Scott, Frank, and Michael Oliver, ed. 1964. *Quebec States Her Case.* Toronto: Macmillan Company of Canada.

Scott, George, Jr. 1990. "A Resynthesis of the Primordial and Circumstantial Approaches to Ethnic Group Solidarity: Towards an Explanatory Model." *Ethnic and Racial Studies* 13:148–71.

Segal, Aaron. 1964. *Massacre in Rwanda.* London: Fabian Society.

Seligman, Charles. 1930. *The Races of Africa.* London: Thornton Butterworth.

Simeon, Richard, and Ian Robinson. 1990. *State, Society, and the Development of Canadian Federalism.* Toronto: University of Toronto Press.

Smith, Anthony. 1991. *National Identity.* Reno: University of Nevada Press.

———. 1984. "Ethnic Myths and Ethnic Revivals." *European Journal of Sociology* 25:283–305.

Smooha, Sammy. 1985. "Ethnic Groups." In *The Social Science Encyclopedia,* ed. Adam Kuper and Jessica Kuper, 267–69. London: Routledge and Kegan Paul.

Sowell, Thomas. 1994. *Race and Culture: A World View.* New York: Basic Books.

Spencer, Jonathan. 1990. "Introduction: The Power of the Past." In *Sri Lanka: History and the Roots of Conflict,* ed. Jonathan Spencer, 1–16. London: Routledge.

Stack, John, Jr. 1986. *The Primordial Challenge: Ethnicity in the Contemporary World.* Westport, CT: Greenwood Press.

Tambiah, Stanley J. 1986. *Sri Lanka: Ethnic Fratricide and the Dismantling of Democracy.* Chicago: University of Chicago Press.

———. 1992. *Buddhism Betrayed? Religion, Politics, and Violence in Sri Lanka.* Chicago: University of Chicago Press.

Tennekoon, Serena. 1987. "Symbolic Refractions of the Ethnic Crisis: The Divaina Debates on Sinhala Identity." In *Facets of Ethnicity in Sri Lanka,* ed. Charles Abeysekera and Newton Gunasinghe, 1–59. Colombo: Social Scientists Association.

Thompson, Mark. 1993. "The Final Solution of Bosnia-Hercegovina." In *Why Bosnia? Writings on the Balkan War,* ed. Rabia Ali and Lawrence Lifschultz, 165–80. Stony Creek, CT: Pamphleteer's Press.

———. 1992. *A Paper House: The Ending of Yugoslavia.* New York: Pantheon Books.

Thomson, H. E. 1897. *The Outgoing Turk: Impression of a Journey through the Western Balkans.* London: Heinemann.

Trofimenkoff, Susan Mann. 1975. *Action Française: French Canadian Nationalism in the Twenties.* Toronto: University of Toronto Press.

Trudeau, Pierre Elliott. 1968. *Federalism and the French Canadians.* New York: St. Martin's Press.

Turnbull, Colin. 1983. *The Mbuti Pygmies: Change and Adaptation.* New York: Holt, Rinehart, and Winston.

Vallières, Pierre. 1971. *White Niggers of America: The Precocious Autobiography of a Quebec "Terrorist."* Trans. Joan Pinkham. New York and London: Monthly Review Press.

Van Bruinessen, Martin. 1992a. *Agha, Sheikh, and State: The Social and Political Structures of Kurdistan.* London: Zed Books Ltd.

———. 1992b. "Kurdish Society, Ethnicity, Nationalism, and Refugee Problems." In *The Kurds: A Contemporary Overview,* ed. Philip Kreyenbroek and Stefan Sperl, 33–67. London: Routledge.

Van den Berghe, Pierre. 1987. *The Ethnic Phenomenon.* New York: Praeger.

———. 1978. "Race and Ethnicity: A Sociobiological Perspective." *Ethnic and Racial Studies* 1:401–11.

Vanly, Ismet Sheriff. 1993. "Kurdistan in Iraq." In *A People without a Country:*

The Kurds and Kurdistan, ed. Gerard Chaliand, 139–93. New York: Olive Branch Books.

Vulliamy, Ed. 1994. *Seasons in Hell: Understanding Bosnia's War.* New York: Simon and Schuster.

Wagner, Roy. 1975. *The Invention of Culture.* Englewood Cliffs, NJ: Prentice-Hall.

Watson, Catharine. 1991. *Exile from Rwanda: Background to an Invasion.* Washington, DC: American Council for Nationalities Service.

Weaver, R. Kent, ed. 1992. *The Collapse of Canada?* Washington, DC: Brookings Institution.

Weber, Max M. 1968. *Economy and Society.* Vol. 1. Ed. Guenther Roth and Claus Wittich. New York: Bedminster Press.

Webster, John. 1966. *The Political Development of Rwanda and Burundi.* Syracuse: Syracuse University Press.

Weinstein, Warren, and Robert Schrire. 1976. *Political Conflict and Ethnic Strategies: A Case Study of Burundi.* Syracuse: Maxwell School of Citizenship and Public Affairs.

Willis, William S., Jr. 1972. "Skeletons in the Anthropological Closet." In *Reinventing Anthropology,* ed. Dell Hymes, 121–53. New York: Random House.

Wilson, A. Jeyaratnam. 1974. *Politics in Sri Lanka, 1947–1973.* New York: St. Martin's Press.

Woehrling, Jose. 1989. "A Critique of the Distinct Society Clause's Critics." In *The Meech Lake Primer: Conflicting Views of the 1987 Constitutional Accord,* ed. Michael D. Behiels, 171–207. Ottawa: University of Ottawa Press.

Woodward, Susan. 1995. *Balkan Tragedy: Chaos and Dissolution after the Cold War.* Washington, DC: Brookings Institution.

Woost, Michael. 1990. "Rural Awakenings: Grassroots Development and the Cultivation of a National Past in Rural Sri Lanka." In *Sri Lanka: History and the Roots of Conflict,* ed. Jonathan Spencer, 164–83. London: Routledge.

Wriggins, William Howard. 1960. *Ceylon: Dilemmas of a New Nation.* Princeton: Princeton University Press.

Wright, Robin. 1994. "Ethnic Conflict: An Overview." In *Nationalism and Ethnic Conflict,* ed. Charles Cozic, 157–62. San Diego: Greenhaven Press.

Yinger, Milton. 1994. *Ethnicity: Source of Strength? Source of Conflict?* Albany: State University of New York Press.

Index